NATURAL

NATURAL LAW THEORY

Contemporary Essays

EDITED BY

ROBERT P. GEORGE

CLARENDON PRESS · OXFORD

Oxford University Press, Walton Street, Oxford OX2 6DP

Oxford New York

Athens Auckland Bangkok Bogota Bombay
Buenos Aires Calcutta Cape Town Dar es Salaam
Delhi Florence Hong Kong Istanbul Karachi
Kuala Lumpur Madras Madrid Melbourne
Mexico City Nairobi Paris Singapore
Taipei Tokyo Toronto

and associated companies in
Berlin Ibadan

Oxford is a trade mark of Oxford University Press

Published in the United States by
Oxford University Press Inc., New York

First published 1992
First issued in paperback 1994
Reprinted in paperback 1995, 1996

British Library Cataloguing in Publication Data
Data available

Library of Congress Cataloging in Publication Data
Natural law theory: contemporary essays / edited by Robert P. George.
Includes index.
1. Natural law. I. George, Robert P.
K428.N375 1992 340'.112—dc20 91-28732
ISBN 0-19-824857-1
ISBN 0-19-823552-6 (Pbk.)

Printed in Great Britain
on acid-free paper by
Bookcraft (Bath) Ltd, Midsomer Norton, Avon

FOREWORD

Not long ago the editor of a collection of essays on natural law theory might have introduced the volume with a lugubrious disquisition on the failure of scholars in secular academic institutions to grasp the contemporary relevance of the idea of natural law. In view of the broad revival of interest in natural law theory among mainstream legal, political, and moral philosophers, however, the editor of the current volume is hardly in a position to portray himself as 'a voice crying in the wilderness'. As much as the role appeals to him, he shall let the reader be spared.

One finds a remarkable assortment of natural law theories on offer in today's market-place of ideas. There are 'liberal' and 'conservative' as well as 'procedural' and 'substantive' theories of natural law. Some theories fit comfortably into the tradition of Aristotle and Aquinas, others are related to that tradition only remotely, if at all. Some natural law theorists propose to identify basic principles of practical reasoning and morality and to derive from these principles norms to guide the decisions of legislators and, in some cases, judges. Others seek to guide legal interpretation, reasoning, and adjudication on the basis of a putatively necessary connection between law (or legality) and morality.

The essays presented herein will convey an idea of the diversity of contemporary natural law theories. In an essay entitled 'Natural Law and Rights', Lloyd Weinreb argues that rights have a special significance in legal and political theory in view of the central problematic of natural law that he identified in *Natural Law and Justice* (1987). The reader will discover, however, that Weinreb's conception of natural law has little in common with John Finnis's understanding of natural law, as presented, for example, in 'Natural Law and Legal Reasoning' or Michael Moore's understanding, as set forth in 'Law as a Functional Kind'. Critics who reject 'natural law' in Weinreb's sense may accept the idea in Finnis's or Moore's sense—and vice versa.

At the same time, the implications for legal reasoning and judicial practice of Finnis's account of natural law are considerably more modest than the parallel implications of Moore's account. Neil MacCormick, whose contribution to the volume is a critical study of Finnis's *Natural Law and Natural Rights* (1980), observes that Finnis's legal theory includes an understanding of the essential connectedness of law and morality that positivists may usefully incorporate into their account of law without compromising their contention that 'the mere existence of law is no guarantee of its moral merits'. Positivists such as MacCormick cannot afford to adopt so irenical a stance toward Moore's natural law theory. According to Moore's account of the connection between law and morality, natural law theory and legal positivism are direct competitors: if Moore is correct, then legal positivism is fundamentally misguided—and vice versa.

The volume also presents essays by leading critics of contemporary natural law theories. Jeremy Waldron, in 'The Irrelevance of Moral Objectivity', criticizes Moore's claim that moral reasoning should play a role in, and sometimes control, the interpretation and application of laws by judges. Waldron argues that even those judges who believe in objective moral truths have compelling reasons to respect legal positivism's sharp distinction between law and morality in resolving the cases that come before them. Indeed, according to Waldron, even if morality *is* objective it is none the less irrelevant to judging: '[i]n the end it is moral disagreement, not moral subjectivity, that gives rise to our worries about judicial moralizing.'

In 'Natural Law and Virtue: Theories at Cross Purposes', Russell Hittinger criticizes contemporary natural law theories, as well as contemporary theories of virtue, for aspiring to the characteristically modern ideal of metaphysical austerity. So long as natural law and virtue theorists maintain this aspiration, Hittinger argues, they will remain unable to supply satisfactory answers to the questions of personal and political morality they seek to resolve. Jeffrey Stout, in 'Truth, Natural Law, and Ethical Theory', articulates a similar view of the inadequacies of contemporary natural law theories. Unlike Hittinger, however, Stout argues that metaphysical austerity is an ideal worth preserving. He maintains that social and political theorists therefore need to look elsewhere than to natural law theory for satisfactory approaches to modern problems.

There are, however, defenders of natural law theory. Joseph

Boyle, in 'Natural Law and the Ethics of Traditions', and Robert George, in 'Natural Law and Human Nature', defend a particular natural law theory—one that Hittinger and others have accused of misguidedly embracing modernist metaphysical austerity—against some of its critics and competitors. Boyle engages Alasdair MacIntyre's claim that an adequate ethical theory cannot be 'tradition-independent'. By attending to the nuances of moral epistemology, Boyle proposes to show how moral knowledge is tradition-dependent in some respects yet tradition-independent in others. George defends the natural law theory advanced by Finnis, Boyle, Germain Grisez, and others against the charge made by proponents of alternative accounts of natural law (e.g. Weinreb and Hittinger) that it is a theory of 'natural law without nature'. George maintains that the theory's denial that practical knowledge (including knowledge of moral norms) can be inferred from methodologically antecedent knowledge of human nature does not entail the proposition that moral norms are unrooted in human nature.

In an essay entitled 'That "Nature Has Placed in Our Ears A Power of Judging": Some Reflections on the "Naturalism" of Cicero', Hadley Arkes considers the relevance of Ciceronian ideas about natural law and human flourishing to modern problems of justice and rights. Arkes rejects contemporary versions of 'naturalism' that treat human goods as principles of right action that are somehow independent of moral principles that distinguish just from unjust purposes, morally upright from morally wicked ends. He commends Cicero's naturalism for its acknowledgment that human flourishing or well-being cannot be detached from 'terms of principle' according to which justice may be distinguished from injustice, right from wrong.

Natural law theorists going back to Cicero, and indeed to Aristotle, have praised the ideal of the rule of law. Critics, however, remain sceptical: is the rule of law really desirable? Is it even possible? Does the rule of law depend upon the plausibility of legal formalism? Can a defensible version of legal formalism be devised? In 'Formalism and the Rule of Law', Joseph Raz criticizes recent efforts by Ernest Weinrib to rehabilitate the maligned notion of legal formalism in the service of the rule of law. Raz's essay is followed by a contribution by Weinrib himself entitled 'Why Legal Formalism'. Here Weinrib develops the defence of formalism that he elaborated in the articles that Raz criticizes and offers a rebuttal of Raz's critique. The reader will, I trust, find that the exchange illuminates a crucial issue in contemporary legal and political philosophy.

Little else need be said by way of introduction. Is natural law theory worthy of the renewed consideration it is receiving? Or have critics shown that contemporary natural law theories may safely be set aside? Let the reader consider these essays and decide.

R.P.G.
Princeton
1991

ACKNOWLEDGEMENTS

The editor gratefully acknowledges the advice and assistance of Cindy S. George, Steven Lichtman, Mitchell S. Muncy, Walter F. Murphy, and William C. Porth.

CONTENTS

IV. LEGAL FORMALISM AND LEGAL RATIONALITY

LIST OF CONTRIBUTORS

HADLEY ARKES is Edward Ney Professor of Jurisprudence and American Institutions at Amherst College.

JOSEPH BOYLE is Professor of Philosophy at St Michael's College, University of Toronto.

JOHN FINNIS is Professor of Law and Legal Philosophy at Oxford University.

ROBERT P. GEORGE is Assistant Professor of Politics at Princeton University.

RUSSELL HITTINGER is Associate Professor of Philosophy at The Catholic University of America.

NEIL MACCORMICK is Regius Professor of Public Law and the Law of Nature and Nations at the University of Edinburgh.

MICHAEL S. MOORE is Leon Meltzer Professor of Law at the University of Pennsylvania.

JOSEPH RAZ is Professor of Philosophy of Law at Oxford University.

JEFFREY STOUT is Mellon Professor of the Humanities and Professor of Religion at Princeton University.

JEREMY WALDRON is Professor of Law at the University of California, Berkeley.

LLOYD L. WEINREB is Professor of Law at Harvard University.

ERNEST J. WEINRIB is Professor of Law and Special Lecturer in Classics at the University of Toronto.

PART I
NATURAL LAW, PRACTICAL REASONING, AND MORALITY

1

Natural Law and the Ethics of Traditions

JOSEPH BOYLE

A major theme in contemporary discussions of moral philosophy is dissatisfaction with the condition of ethical theory. Ethical theory can be characterized as the effort to develop general criteria for distinguishing correct from incorrect moral judgements, within an overall account of moral life and experience. Currently, the chief representatives of ethical theory are utilitarianism, Kantianism, and various forms of contractualism. These theories are found wanting both because they are believed to be excessively abstract and rationalistic, and because they are held incapable of providing a plausible account of the rich diversity of moral life. The objections to these theories are generalized so as to apply to ethical theory as such. Thus, ethical theory must be replaced and several alternatives to ethical theory have been ventured.[1]

The best known of these alternatives might be called 'virtues ethics'. Virtues ethics seeks to provide an account of moral life and judgement without reliance upon general moral principles like the principle of utility or the categorical imperative. Instead, the valued character traits designated as virtues provide the foundations for moral judgement and life. Since the character traits valued as virtues vary across communities of people, the universalism of ethical theory is avoided without an apparent implication of relativistic subjectivism. Moral life is rooted in the concrete practices and traditions of communities, but is not beyond criticism. Critical reflection within a moral tradition is possible since the deeper resources of the tradition can be called into play because of conflicts which arise in the tradition, because of new problems which arise because of various cultural developments, and because of moral challenges which emerge from the competition between moral traditions. Thus, moral theorizing has a role in moral life: elaborating and developing the resources of moral traditions in the face of internal and external challenges.[2]

This development in moral philosophy has obvious connections with natural law theorizing. For much of what is now
regarded as natural law thinking plainly has developed within a
moral tradition, that of Christianity and, more specifically, medieval and post-Reformation Catholicism. Furthermore, most natural law theorists are self-consciously members of a continuous
tradition of moral enquiry which reaches from contemporary
neo-scholastic writers back to Aquinas, and which takes Aquinas'
moral writings as a classical source. Finally, this tradition of
moral enquiry puts strong emphasis on the role of virtue in moral
life, and relies heavily on the moral analyses of Aristotle, who can
plausibly be regarded as the ancestor of contemporary virtues
ethics.

But these connections are not unambiguous. For natural law
theory has many of the features of the kind of ethical theory
which virtues ethics is meant to replace. A simple reflection on
the meaning of 'natural law' makes this plain. This expression
has commonly been understood by natural law theorists (and by
many of their theoretical opponents as well) as referring to a set
of universal prescriptions whose prescriptive force is a function
of the rationality which all human beings share in virtue of their
common humanity. The basic principles and norms of the natural
law, as *natural*, are addressed to all human beings, and they are
held to be accessible to all who are capable of forming the
concepts which comprise them. Furthermore, the foundations of
moral life and judgement are in the moral *law*, and moral laws are
propositional realities, 'dictates of reason', not character traits,
practices, or cultural creations. These fundamental prescriptions
of the natural law are held to have sense and reference, and
indeed to be truths of a kind. The most basic referents of natural
law prescriptions are the goods which perfect human nature. The
reference to goods in these prescriptions does not, however,
presuppose the rich experience of goods which comes through
long experience and virtuous living within a decent community.
Rather it presupposes only the awareness of goods necessary for
the most preliminary interest in them, and this is the common
condition of all who are capable of rational action and volition.

This ambiguous relationship between natural law theorizing
and virtues ethics and allied views about the tradition-dependent
character of ethical thinking provides the subject-matter of this

chapter. More specifically, I will seek to determine in what ways natural law and natural law theorizing are tradition-dependent, and whether key natural law claims are compatible with recognition of these sorts of tradition dependence. Finally, I will consider several objections to natural law thinking which this analysis raises, and begin to address them.

1. NATURAL LAW THEORIZING AS TRADITION-DEPENDENT ENQUIRY

The concept of a moral tradition is at the very least complex; indeed there is some reason to think that there is not a single concept here, but several related concepts. I will distinguish three ways in which an enquiry can be tradition-dependent, and then for each of them in turn consider whether natural law theory is tradition-dependent, and then in turn whether the results of this consideration are compatible with key natural law claims.

All intellectual efforts, including their results in such things as theories, propositions, or arguments, appear to depend in a variety of ways upon cultural contingencies and particularities. The dependence of theorizing upon language is perhaps the clearest of these. For the languages within which people theorize are clearly cultural products which shape theorizing in several ways. Language provides the set of concepts available for use in theory and the modes of expression which make possible the creative use of these concepts. Perhaps more importantly, intellectual achievements of any kind respond to particular questions posed by people in definite cultural circumstances. Even the scholar whose interests are far removed from immediate cultural concerns must make use of the current state of knowledge and must deal with the ideas and controversies within his or her area of enquiry. Again, this whole body of knowledge and opinion is not handed down from heaven but part of a cultural patrimony which could be quite different from what it is.

It may be stretching the meaning of 'tradition' to regard as parts of a tradition these elements of contingency and particularity within which all enquiry seems to take place. For these things affect the work of all who engage in enquiry, including those who ignore the dependence of their thinking on established language and on the prior work of others, and even those who repudiate such dependence. Still, however this contingency and particularity of intellectual work is to be properly named, it is real, and it is related to the cultural inheritance and social context of the theorist. Thus, it is not improper to regard it as a matter of tradition, although for most thinkers there is no single tradition which forms the context of their work, but rather a variety of disparate social influences which may or may not constitute a coherent tradition of life, culture, or enquiry.

Of course, those who develop ideas about morality or anything else can be critical about the cultural contingencies and particularities which shape their theorizing. But the effort to be critical, even the successful effort, is not the same thing as having a disembodied viewpoint which is that of humans as such, much less that of an objective, outside observer of the world.

In this sense, the work of natural law theorists is obviously tradition-dependent (though it would be a mistake to suppose that there is any single set of cultural contingencies within which natural law theorists as diverse as Aquinas, his sixteenth-century interpreters, and his twentieth-century followers operate).

More importantly, this is a kind of tradition dependence which natural law theory need not deny. Natural law theorists have surely not developed an account of this kind of tradition dependence, but, equally surely, they have not denied it. So, if natural law theory cannot account for its being dependent on various cultural contingencies and particularities, that must be because of implications of some of its key assertions which its proponents have not drawn.

Perhaps the universality of some natural law prescriptions, and the claim that the knowledge of these prescriptions is accessible to all human beings, have implications incompatible with this kind of dependence of enquiry upon cultural contingencies. But it is not clear why. Surely, a universal prescription cannot be impugned just because it is formulated in a particular language by an individual moralist; a *reason* why the prescription is mistaken is plainly necessary. The natural law claim that its most basic prescriptions are accessible to all (more precisely, to all capable of understanding their terms) may seem more difficult to accommodate within a view in which the cultural contingency and particularity of enquiry is acknowledged. However, strong and controversial claims about language, theory, and propositions would have to be accepted if the universality of access to moral principles is to be inconsistent with the contingency of enquiry and language. For why should it be impossible that the same proposition or prescription can be expressed in different languages or arrived at by enquiries with very different starting-points and presuppositions? Or why should it be impossible that two distinct propositions or prescriptions should make reference to the same moral reality, or to realities which are integrally related and more or less well expressed in the distinct propositions or prescriptions? In a word, the apparently undeniable dependence of all enquiry on language and on other cultural features is consistent with what natural law theorists are required by their own views to believe about their own theorizing.

There is a second and much stronger sense in which an enquiry can be tradition-dependent, namely, the sense of tradition dependence which applies to those engaged in an enquiry and who recognize themselves to be developing a body of thought which prior thinkers have originated and developed but left incomplete, at least as far as its application to the problems and challenges, both internal and external, which the theory must deal with at any given time.

In this sense too, it seems obvious that natural law theorizing is tradition-dependent. In fact, the practice of natural law theorists provides a paradigm of moral enquiry that is self-consciously the development of a tradition. Contemporary natural law theorists understand themselves as elaborating and applying ideas rooted in Aquinas and developed by the later scholastics. But many of them do not understand their work as simply restating a moral system whose essential construction and application is complete. Rather, they see their work as providing application of ideas developed in the tradition to actions which the earlier tradition did not have to deal with, and as developing the tradition to meet challenges from other ethical approaches. A survey of the writing of natural law theorists in recent decades would reveal that, both concerning the issues of moral theory and meta-ethics, and concerning more specific moral issues such as nuclear deterrence, abortion, sex and family issues, and the redistribution of wealth, these moralists are developing accounts which, though self-consciously rooted in the tradition of moral thinking which takes

Aquinas as its classical source, are responsive to new practical questions and new theoretical challenges.

This self-consciousness has not led natural law theorists to undertake explicit self-referential analyses of their theorizing as a tradition-dependent activity. Analysis of this kind might, however, prove quite valuable for the successful development of natural law. For the tradition provides a rich and nuanced body of moral reasoning, both about casuistical matters and about ethical theory, which might be better used if natural law theorists were more explicit about the dependence of their work on the earlier tradition.

Such reflection might also provide a useful reminder of a distinction important for successfully carrying out tradition-based moral enquiry. The distinction is between the internal questions of how to bring the resources of the tradition to bear on new problems and the external challenges provided by other ethical theories and alternatives to ethical theory. It is one thing to try to determine the natural law tradition's answers to questions about new biomedical technology, for example, and quite another to respond to the challenges provided by, say, consequentialism. The expectation that a reasonable development of the tradition's position on a problem such as *in vitro* fertilization must be plausible to everybody, including consequentialists, will make impossible the development of the tradition's answer to that question. For that question requires an internal development of the tradition's resources, a development which will hardly be plausible to those who reject basic principles from which the tradition proceeds. The failure to develop the internal resources of the tradition is in turn likely to block the development of the resources necessary for responding to external challenges. For in the dialectic between opposing moral views, each view must show its capacity to provide its own reasoned answers to the difficult issues of the day. That is not the whole of this dialectic, but surely a necessary part of it.

One might wonder, however, whether this kind of reflection, even though very useful for the conduct of natural law theorizing, is not, at some level, inconsistent with natural law claims. For, as in the case of the first type of tradition dependence considered, there is at least a worry that the universality of natural law prescriptions and the claims to universal accessibility to these prescriptions are incompatible with a serious recognition of natural law theorizing as continuing a moral tradition.

In fact, however, as in the case of the first kind of tradition dependence, there is no inconsistency here. Recognition that normative claims are based upon analyses developed from within a particular tradition of enquiry does not provide a reason for thinking that these claims are not critically vindicated, whether or not these claims are universal. This recognition might well have another, quite different effect. For awareness that one works within a moral tradition can provide a motive for critical reflection to remove biases generated by the tradition's outlook, as well as a ground for confidence that the tradition as a whole has considered far more of the possible objections than any individual theorist could investigate.

Perhaps it might be easier to justify the normative conclusions of moral reflection if those normative conclusions were not universal, but limited to the members of communities with which the moral theorist has some acquaintance. But there is no inconsistency in holding that the formulation of moral norms emerges within a tradition of enquiry and that these norms apply to everybody. Similarly, there is no inconsistency in thinking that some of these universal norms can be, and even are actually, known by everybody. This tenet of natural law is surely not an obvious fact about morality; indeed, it appears to many people to be false. But suppose it were more widely accepted than it is. That possibility would surely be in no logical tension with the recognition that natural law theorizing is the development of a moral tradition.

2. NATURAL LAW AND THE LIVED VALUES OF COMMUNITIES

A third and still stronger sense of tradition dependence is that according to which ethical enquiry, including its results in moral claims, must be rooted in the lived ethical experience of people who share a common way of life. Clearly people who share a common view of human life and its goods and live them out within a community which embodies these shared values constitute a moral tradition—not simply or primarily a tradition of enquiry, nor simply a group who willy-nilly share a language and other cultural assumptions, but a group of people who have a common commitment to values which are actually embodied in their institutions and culture.

There are paradigm cases of such communities in modern society, especially those relatively marginalized groups who make a significant effort to maintain their values and identity within the larger society. But other groups may, more or less, have some of the characteristics of moral communities whose values can provide the basis for traditions of moral thought. Perhaps some religious groups which, though not sociologically isolated from the mainstream of society, maintain a strong sense of group solidarity and identity are examples of such communities, and perhaps also entire polities in earlier times, or some national and racial groups in the world today. But there seem to be limits to the identifiable groups of people who can constitute a moral community in this sense: surely the citizens of a modern, pluralistic nation such as the United States or Canada do not form a moral community, even though they share some common values. There is simply too much diversity on important issues, in spite of the levelling of values by the working of modern communications and economics. Similarly, it is most implausible to think that such people form a moral community with citizens of those polities a hundred years ago.

The continuing effort of natural law theorizing does not seem to be rooted in this kind of a moral community. It is true that natural law theorists often have religious motivations for their work and that many of them are Catholics. So, as a practical motivational matter, some of the values of Catholicism, as a way of life actually lived out and experienced by Catholics, have in fact entered into at least the motivation of the work of natural law theorists. Furthermore, many of the questions to which natural law theorists have given their attention have arisen because of problems and questions which emerge in the effort to live out Catholic values in their cultural circumstances.

But these considerations do not show that natural law is tradition-dependent in this strong sense. For motivations of a traditional sort and questions raised by traditional concerns can arise for people who do not share a set of common, lived values, at least not in any very significant degree. The tradition of natural law enquiry stretches over more than five hundred years and has been carried out by people in very different cultural circumstances within communities which certainly seem distinct. In short, it seems that whatever unifies those who think about moral questions within the natural law tradition it is not a community of shared, lived values.

This state of affairs is not surprising on natural law grounds. For the natural law account of moral life and thinking includes a set of views according to which much of moral thought is not essentially dependent upon the lived values of a moral community. To make this clear, it is necessary to distinguish various components within moral thinking according to the natural law account.

The first of these components is the view that there are moral principles which all mature human beings can know, the naturally known principles which are written on the human heart. According to natural law theory, these principles, the foundational prescriptions of the natural law, are accessible to all, providing the most fundamental grounds for the self-condemnation of those who would repent their immorality, and the basis for people's criticizing the distortions of the lived values of their culture. In fact, it understates the matter to say that these principles are *knowable* by all. Aquinas seems to hold that they are actually known by all, or at least by all who have the concepts prerequisite for human action.[3] Clearly, the claim of natural law theory is that these principles are known or at least knowable by anyone, independently of whether one is part of a vital moral community.

Another component of natural law is the view that some specific moral norms follow from these principles in such a way that it is easy for people to see their truth, even though it is possible, because of cultural distortion or personal immorality, that people be ignorant of them. Some general norms, like the precepts of the Decalogue, follow from the basic principles of natural law by a short, deductive process in which the conceptual analysis which allows for the linking of terms like stealing and adultery to the basic moral predicates is straightforward, for example, that killing someone is harming them. As Aquinas puts it, the precepts of the Decalogue follow from the most basic moral principles *statim, modica consideratione* ('immediately, with little thought').[4] Here again membership in a community of shared values does not seem necessary for the relevant knowledge. Those who are not part of a community of shared values shaped by the Decalogue can surely do the relevant deduction and analysis. Indeed, it would seem that members of communities where the values underlying one or another of the precepts of the Decalogue are overlooked or even rejected, for example the Germani, who were reported by Caesar as ignorant of the pro- hibition against brigandage,[5] would not appear to be incapable of this kind of thinking, even though, given their cultural distor- tions, they might be ill-disposed to engage in it. So, here again one does not need to be a member of a community of shared values to have knowledge of natural law norms.

Another component of natural law is its conception of how moral principles and norms are to be applied to the more complex circumstances of difficult cases. This also is held to be a matter of analysis and reasoning, but at a degree of complexity which renders the results beyond the reach of most people, and avail- able only to those who are wise in moral matters.[6]

Even this casuistical development of the natural law does not, at least not essentially and in all cases, require that those who would apply the principles of the natural law correctly should be part of a community of shared values. The work of casuistry is hardly intelligible (as honest intellectual work, as distinct from its perversion in intellectually elaborate rationalization) except for those who care deeply about what is morally good. But the work itself is largely analytical; as such the tradition it presup- poses is the tradition of intellectual enquiry, not a community of shared values.

Of course, one who is not a member of such a community is likely to have difficulty in understanding the human significance of the actions of members of that community. To the extent that this significance is alien, great intellectual sympathy is needed, and the possibility of mistakes, always a problem in applying moral principles to difficult cases, is very real. But so is the opportunity for correcting it, as is the possibility of correcting community members' self-understanding of the meaning of their actions. For example, natural law theorists examining the morality of the West's nuclear deterrent need to understand correctly the complex social act which constitutes the deterrent.[7] Natural law theorists who are citizens of the nations using the deterrent are not alien observers of it, as an anthropologist from another culture or planet might be (although it is by no means clear that being a member of a Western polity is necessarily an advantage in understanding this act). But equally, such theorists need not be members of a community of shared values which either endorses or rejects the deterrent. Indeed, with respect to this matter as with many others, there is deep disagreement within the Western polities and within the smaller moral communities which comprise them. If the analysis of the action of deterrence by one or another natural law theorist is mistaken (and some surely are since they are contradictory) that needs to be established by looking at the facts and their analysis.

There is another important component of the natural law view of moral thought. For on the natural law account there are many important moral judgements within a person's life which cannot be known on the basis of analysis and deduction alone,[8] and there are very many situations in life in which the morally correct course of action cannot readily and confidently be discerned unless one's capacity for moral judgement is highly developed and perfected. Thus, in many of the choices which comprise a person's life, what Aquinas called *prudentia* is necessary if competent moral judgements are readily to be made. *Prudentia* is Aquinas' rendering of Aristotle's notion of *phronesis*, which is usually translated as 'practical wisdom'. Following Aristotle, Aquinas regards practical wisdom as an intellectual virtue, as a disposition of practical intelligence to do its proper work well. That work is to make concrete moral judgements.[9]

The developed capacity to make moral judgements readily and correctly has several conditions. One is an awareness of the universal principles of the natural law, which are known to all through a natural disposition which Aquinas calls *synderesis*.[10] The other is a basis for rationally evaluating the particularities of the concrete possibilities for action which one faces. This evaluation is necessary because these alternatives not only have a rational connection to the goods which form the basis of the natural law but also, as particulars, have a distinct emotional appeal which may or may not be in accord with the demands of rational action. Thus, a person must be able to evaluate and control his or her emotional responses to the particularities of the alternatives available if his or her actions are to be completely in line with what is good. This evaluation and control presupposes that one possess the relevant moral virtues, namely, the character traits through which emotional responses are integrated into a morally upright personality. Thus, as Aquinas argues, practical wisdom is needed if one is to be fully rational in acting and this virtue is impossible without the moral virtues.[11] So, a person's capacity to make sound moral judgements over the whole set of choices which arise in life will not be satisfactorily developed unless the person has acquired practical wisdom and the moral virtues.

Thus, according to the natural law account, the moral virtues have an irreducible role in moral knowledge. As dispositions of character necessary for the developed capacity to make moral judgements correctly and easily they are necessary for mature, competent moral decision-making. But it is clear that the moral virtues do not constitute a source of moral knowledge independent of the knowledge of the universal principles of the natural law.[12] It is true that the possession of the virtues adds to these principles what reasoning alone from them cannot provide, that is, an ability to appreciate the moral significance of the emotional appeal of the particularities of possible actions. But these character traits would not be moral virtues unless they were shaped by the principles of the natural law.[13]

Thus, although the virtues are an essential part of moral life according to natural law theory, their cognitive function is strictly limited and subordinated to the natural law. According to Aquinas, the virtues are principles of good living, but they are intrinsic principles, dispositions which give shape to moral life.[14] In this way they are contrasted to the exterior principles of good living, the ultimate of which is God. God leads people to live well in several ways, one of which is by instructing them. He does this by way of law, and natural law is a part of this instruction.[15]

The importance of the virtues within the natural law account of moral life does not immediately settle the extent to which, on natural law grounds, virtuous living presupposes a community of shared values. For on this account of the virtues they are not simply the character traits which are prized within a community but depend, at least partially, upon general moral convictions.

Surely, natural law theory can admit that decent institutions and social practices, adequate mechanisms for moral education, and good role models are very helpful for the development of the virtues. Likewise natural law theory recognizes that virtuous living involves coming to terms with the particular institutions, practices, and possibilities for good action which one's culture provides. Moreover, natural law theory recognizes that these institutions and practices are not uniquely determined by moral considerations, even when they are morally legitimate. Like good positive law, these realities are shaped by reasonable decision and convention.[16]

Still, natural law theory seems to allow for the possibility of virtuous living within communities that are less than morally perfect and even within those that are in various ways positively bad. For access to human goods and other basic moral considerations cannot, on natural law grounds, be simply a matter of experiencing them in so far as they are lived within a particular community and embodied in the character traits of a community's members. There is an awareness of and an interest in these goods which are prior to and principles of their realization in human action. And this awareness and interest is held to be natural to human beings.[17]

In short, with respect to the third and strongest sense of tradition dependence, natural law theory is committed to the significant tradition *independence* of moral knowledge. An important part of the moral knowledge which people need to have in order to live morally does depend on possessing moral virtue, but possessing virtues is not, on natural law grounds, as dependent on the lived values of a community as many think it must be.

This conclusion allows us to frame with some precision the issue between natural law theory and the ethics of traditions: is it more reasonable to think that moral judgement depends essentially upon a set of values which are lived out and made actual within the life of a community, or to think that such actual but localized values are not necessary for moral judgement?

The natural law view of this matter is based on the conviction that moral norms are found among the principles of practical reasoning, and that these principles are goods which all humans know and are interested in. It seems to me that the most interesting versions of the ethics of traditions do not deny that morality is a matter of practical reason. These views are not subjectivist, and ground the limited objectivity of morality on practical reason.

Thus, according to these views, moral norms are intelligible; they make sense and provide reasons for action and rational motives for acting morally. In this respect, this account of morality shares a rationalist assumption of natural law and many other ethical theories and rejects various forms of non-cognitivism and voluntarism.[18]

What distinguishes such views from natural law theory and other universalist forms of ethical theory is that they conceive practical reason as based on and limited by the values lived within a community. The grounds for moral judgement, therefore, are not accessible to those who do not share the life of a community. In a community of shared values the operative values are actual; they are not abstract or ideal values but actual interests which motivate people and become embodied in the lives of its virtuous members and in the community's institutions. So, such views provide an alternative to the universalism of natural law theory by holding that the actuality of a set of values is a necessary condition for moral knowledge. Moral norms on this account will apply only to those for whom those values are actual. Such norms will be intelligible not to humans as such, but only to those for whom the relevant values are actual—that is, only those who share in the life of a community within which those values are actually lived out and experienced.

Is it reasonable to think that the actuality of a set of values is a necessary condition for moral knowledge? I think not. My basic reason is that the actual lived values of a given society are frequently more or less distorted and perverse. Serious moral reflection must surely include the critical scrutiny of institutions and of the character traits taken in any society as virtues. There is no society which is beyond at least the possibility of moral criticism, and its actual lived values do not, just as such, provide a basis for this criticism.

The lived values of a community may not form a coherent whole. When they do not, some may be forced to give way. On what basis? Surely, it cannot be simply on the basis of which values are more actual, which are more deeply embedded in the lives and institutions of the society. Judgements about the values themselves and not simply their actuality are surely required. Further, serious moral reflection is not limited to the effort to make a given set of values coherent. Surely, people are capable of thinking: this is how we live; these are our values; but is this really the way we should live? Are these values concretized in these institutions and character traits the values to which we should be giving our allegiance?

I see no reason to suppose that the grounds for this kind of moral criticism must be limited to values actually lived within the community. Such grounds must, of course, be things which members of a community can understand. So it is not surprising that these grounds will be (or be expressed in terms of) traditional values which have some status within the community. But it is question-begging to assume that these values must be actually lived within the community if they are to be intelligible to its members.

Alan Donagan's critique of Hegel's conception of *Sittlichkeit* is instructive here. Donagan makes use of the case of Franz Jäggerstätter. Donagan notes that the just war doctrine of Catholic moral theology had degenerated in Germany during the Second World War. The terms of this doctrine were clear enough within the tradition of Catholic theology but they had been rendered a dead letter by the presumption of the community in favour of the claims of the government. Jäggerstätter saw the obvious and would not accept military service. He was hanged. But the local religious authorities assured him that he was wrong; that his duty was to accept military service. And they maintained this judgement even after the war.

Donagan observes:

Is it possible to find in this anything but the depravation of the *Sittlichkeit* of an ethical community whose members had lost the habit of moral self-criticism? . . .

Hegel disparaged the point of view of morality on the ground that being abstractly rational, it could find content for its judgements only in the mores of some actual community. The case of Jäggerstätter reveals an opposite process. The moral theory of Catholic Christianity furnished specific precepts on the subject of legitimate war service, which applied to the case in question on the basis of stated facts which were not questioned. But, by recourse to the mores of their actual community, Jäggerstätter's spiritual advisers were able to evaporate the precepts whose applicability to his case they could not dispute. For, according to those mores, apart from such fanciful possibilities as a war with the declared intention of destroying the Church as an institution, no individual citizen was deemed capable of assuring himself that any war his country proposed to wage was unjust. Here, what is exposed as empty, as lacking specific content, as allowing any filler whatsoever, is not *Moralität*, but *Sittlichkeit*.[19]

Donagan is not denying that Jäggerstätter's advisers were part of an intellectual tradition which had the resources for correcting their mistake. His point is that this intellectual tradition had ceased to be an effective part of the lived mores of their community. Deprived of the judgements of the intellectual tradition, moral criticism became impossible. Thus, if the only resources available are those lived mores, then it is hard to disagree with Donagan that serious moral criticism becomes impossible.

Of course, Donagan's argument does not establish his version of Kantianism, nor does it establish natural law claims that basic moral norms and principles apply to all humans. It shows only that something more than the lived mores of a community is necessary for moral life. Still, the argument does suggest that if one assumes that moral judgements are intelligibly grounded, then the basis for moral norms is not easily found in anything less than considerations which apply to all human beings. And that is what the natural law tradition holds.

In short, it is by no means clear that all the theoretical advantages are on the side of those who hold that moral judgement presupposes a community of shared values.

3. NATURAL LAW AND MORAL DIVERSITY

The elaboration in the previous sections of natural law theory's capacity to accommodate the various ways in which it is and is not tradition-dependent raises an obvious objection to natural law. For central to the natural law account of its tradition dependence and independence is the claim that the basic principles of the natural law are universally accessible, and, apparently, universally known. This account seems inadequate to account for the extent and depth of the moral diversity which is known to exist, and to imply that people know things which they evidently do not know.

To make these objections specific, it is necessary to consider how natural law theory seeks to account for moral diversity and disagreement. This account includes at least three elements, all of which have emerged in the preceding section. First, natural law theory recognizes that people can be ignorant even of very basic moral truths because of mistakes in reasoning. Even the precepts of the Decalogue are conclusions from the most basic moral principles, and, it would seem, where there is reasoning, there can be mistakes, even when the reasoning is very simple. This fact is surely part of the reason why, according to Aquinas, the Old Law contains moral precepts. It is not, he maintains, because humans could not know the precepts of the Decalogue without the promulgation of the Law of Moses, but rather it is because the implications of moral principles can be obscured by sinful customs, even at this very basic level.[20] Aquinas emphasizes the role of sin and corrupt mores in accounting for these mistakes, but it is not clear why some such mistakes could not be completely innocent.

Second, natural law theory accepts the difficulty of dealing with hard cases—the many situations in life in which the application of moral principles is not clear and straightforward, but complex and difficult. Casuistry is not easy, nor could it be carried out by a well-programmed computer. For the actions which need analysis are often very difficult, especially when they are group actions carried out in complex institutional settings, or are new kinds of actions made possible by modern technology. Moral agreement at this level, even among those who share a tradition of moral enquiry or a common set of values, is a considerable achievement. The continued existence of moral disagreement about hard cases is not a fact which natural law theorists should find surprising.

Third, there is a good deal of real variation in people's actual responsibilities due to different vocations and opportunities, and due to the possibilities for action created and blocked by differences in cultural and social context. So there will necessarily be considerable diversity among people and across communities concerning what people's actual responsibilities are. The natural law account of property and the ethics of stealing exemplifies this. Stealing is always wrong, but what makes something the legitimate property of some person or group is variable, depending not only upon general principles concerning the just use of the things of the world but upon a variety of social factors and conventions. Thus, differences in property arrangements, both within the world at a given time or over different times, need not express moral disagreements or mistakes on the part of some. The different property arrangements might be equally justified by the relevant principles of justice (or more likely, equally unjustified) in light of these principles.[21]

So, natural law theory justifies a considerable amount of legitimate moral diversity, and recognizes that moral disagreement about hard cases is a fact of life. Thus, it provides grounds for lowering our expectations about what should be anticipated by way of moral agreement. Furthermore, natural law theory has an account of moral ignorance and mistakes which can explain a good bit of cultural variability in morals without surrendering its claims about the universality of accessibility of those norms and the universality of the awareness of basic principles.

Thus, Alasdair MacIntyre is correct in emphasizing that Aquinas is not committed to extensive claims about what all people know in moral matters. Unlike most intuitionist moral theorists, Aquinas does allow that 'there are absolute and unconditional prohibitions which a whole culture may infringe without recognizing that it is so doing'.[22] But Aquinas, and much of the natural law tradition following him, do hold that there is some moral knowledge which all people capable of deliberation and human action have: knowledge of the most basic principles of the natural law. Even this limited claim may seem to be implausible, and, indeed, false. This, I believe, is the specific formulation of the objection that natural law theory is incompatible with moral diversity. It is a serious difficulty for natural law theory.

The difficulty arises as follows. Aquinas and other natural law theorists hold there are self-evident principles of practical reason and the natural law which everybody capable of deliberation and human action actually knows. The best known of these are that good is to be done and pursued, that certain ends of human action such as life, knowledge, and friendship are goods to be pursued, that we should act in accord with reason, that we should not harm people, and perhaps that we should love God above all and our neighbour as ourselves. However, many people who are capable of deliberating and acting do not seem to know these things, and indeed, appear never to have formulated these prescriptions. More troubling still, many moral theorists do not accept these prescriptions and some think that contrary principles, such as the principle of utility, are the basis for all moral thinking.

One tempting way out of this difficulty is to argue that these claims about the universality of knowledge of the principles of the natural law are simply a mistake which can be excised from natural law thinking without substantial loss. I think, however, that they cannot be excised without extensive revision of the entire natural law enterprise.

If people lacked knowledge of the principles of the natural law, the entire character of moral theory would have to be quite different from what Aquinas and other natural law theorists have supposed. For, as Aquinas' discussion of the relationship between general moral principles and practical wisdom makes clear, natural law theorizing supposes that people's everyday moral reasoning is continuous with general moral norms and principles. Natural law, as already noted, is the name for these general norms and principles. Natural law theorizing is the attempt to formulate those principles in an analytical and systematic way and to make clear how they bear upon everyday moral judgements. Thus, natural law theorizing makes reference to common moral experience, not to theoretical constructs which seek to organize moral experience without being part of it. On this conception moral theory is quite different in structure and purpose from scientific theory, and analogous in structure and purpose to logic. Moral theory seeks to elaborate and put in a systematic and critically reflective form the thinking we all do about moral questions. So it should not be surprising that natural law includes claims about what people actually know about moral principles. Indeed, lacking such claims, the transparency of moral reasoning which such an approach presupposes would not seem possible. For then people would not have within their own conscious experience the wherewithal to criticize their own moral judgements.

This capacity to criticize one's own moral beliefs and reasoning appears to be central to the natural law conception of human dignity. Morality deals with that aspect of human life in which humans most properly function as God's image: that part of life in which people are creative, acting according to their own deliberation and will.[23] Moral standards provide rational guidance for this creative activity; they are fundamentally a

participation by rational creatures in God's providential ordering of the created world.[24] Thus, natural law is an essential aspect
of human dignity: it directs humans in so far as they are made in
God's image and does so by participating in his providence.

But one who is incapable of criticizing his or her moral beliefs
and reasoning cannot participate in God's providence as a rational
creature. Whether or not such a person's belief or reasoning is
correct is not something he or she is in a position to know. So, if
the person's belief conforms to God's providence that is a matter
of happy circumstances and not his or her knowledge; and that
kind of conformity to providence is hardly rational participation
in it. But if criticism of the needed kind is possible, there must be
principles which ground it, and if they are not known in some
way they can hardly prevent moral thought and belief from
being related to providence merely as a matter of luck.

In other words, it seems that knowledge of moral principles is
a necessary condition for the kind of moral self-criticism and
repentance which natural law theory regards as real and as
important for the conception of human dignity. If these principles
are not actually known, then there must be some way they come
to be known. But all such ways are inevitably a matter of luck:
perhaps one grasps a concept which one did not previously
understand, or happens to see an inference one did not see
before (hardly a possible scenario if these are genuine principles).
But one thing which is not possible here is that they come to be
known by a responsible procedure of enquiry: as responsible
action that would be governed by moral principles, and these
might or might not be the correct ones. So, the most we could
hope for on behalf of one who does not know the basic principles
is that he or she would be lucky enough to discover them. But
until he or she did so, it is hard to see how he or she could be, as it
were, in the moral ballpark. Landing in the moral ballpark by the
luck of an insight for which one is not responsible is hardly what
we mean by acknowledging our immorality or by conversion
and repentance. Thus, if the natural law conviction that people
mature enough to choose and act are in the moral ballpark is true,
then they must have some *actual* grasp on moral principles.

In a word, those who engage in human action can be mistaken
about many of their moral judgements, and in many cases
innocently. But such people are morally responsible for their

lives. And no one could be morally responsible if he or she were altogether ignorant of even the most basic moral principles.

There is another, distinct reason for thinking that the claims about the universal knowledge of the principles of the natural law are not incidental to Aquinas' views or to those of the later tradition, and that is the use Aquinas makes of the notion of self-evidence in regard to moral principles. Aquinas characterizes the basic principles of the natural law (but *only* the principles, not even very immediate implications such as the specific norms of the Decalogue) as self-evident and as naturally known. The latter expression appears to be synonymous with the former.[25]

Aquinas' conception of self-evidence, which by his own account is Aristotelian, is not primarily a thesis about the cognitive response of knowers but about the character of certain propositions. According to this conception, certain propositions are 'known through themselves'. And what defines a proposition as *per se nota* is that it is a necessary truth in which the connection between the terms is immediate, unmediated by the middle term of a demonstrative syllogism.[26] So, on Aquinas' account there is no absurdity in saying that a proposition is self-evident, that is, known through itself, and that some people do not see that it is self-evident. For it is possible that they do not understand its terms, or do not understand them sufficiently to see the immediate and necessary connection between subject and predicate. Aquinas' standard example of such a proposition is that angels are not in a place. This proposition is self-evident, but will be known to be such only to those wise enough to have the concept of an angel as an immaterial being.

So, saying that a proposition is self-evident does not involve the claim that all who consider it will immediately assent to it, much less see that it is self-evident. Nor does saying this involve the claim that no further discussion of the proposition is possible. The appeal to self-evident truths is not a piece of dogmatism which arbitrarily stops philosophical enquiry and debate. It is true that self-evident truths are basic and cannot be demonstrated, that is, they cannot be deduced from more basic truths. The self-evident truths concerning any subject-matter are held to be the most basic truths available for reasoning about it. So they are held to be undemonstrable; if they were demonstrable, then their terms would be connected by way of a middle term and they would not be self-evident, nor would they be basic. But this does not imply that nothing can be said on their behalf. They can be defended dialectically: the broader context in which these propositions operate can be delineated, as well as their capacity to cover the subject-matter of which they are the principles, and alternative principles can be shown to be incoherent, incapable of covering the subject-matter, and so on. In fact, natural law theorists engage in considerable dialectical reasoning to vindicate their overall moral outlook and the particular principles which they think govern moral enquiry.[27]

However, the self-evident propositions in question, basic moral principles and principles of practical reason, are not based on the relationships between complex ideas that many people are likely not to grasp—such as Aquinas' example of the proposition that angels are not in a place. Rather these self-evident truths are based on the most elementary ideas which everyone capable of human action must have—ideas related to the concept of the good and to the ends of human action which provide the content for the human good. So it seems that Aquinas is committed to holding that everybody does understand the terms of these propositions sufficiently to grasp their immediate and self-evident connection. These propositions are not only self-evident in themselves, they are self-evident to all.[28]

If these considerations are as compelling as I think they are, then the tempting solution of simply excising the claims about the universal knowledge of moral principles from the natural law account is not a real possibility. These claims must somehow be made plausible.

A start can be made by considering the principle of non-contradiction, which Aquinas regards as the most elementary of the self-evident propositions. In Book Gamma of the *Metaphysics* Aristotle showed that anyone who tried to deny this principle was afflicted with a particularly noxious form of self-refutation: the principle could not be denied without its being assumed in the very denial. One important thing which this discussion reveals is that even the most basic self-evident principle can be denied, even if only verbally. Surely it is possible and even likely that one who denies this principle believes he does not know it to be true, at least not until he is confronted by Aristotle's refutation. But equally surely, such a person knows the principle sufficiently to make use of it in affirming that it is not true. The principle remains implicit in his act of affirming or denying, but it is present within his cognitive activity, although not formulated as a proposition.

The possibility raised by the status of the principle of non-contradiction in the thinking of those who explicitly deny it, as well as in the thinking of those who never formulate it propositionally, can be extended to the principles of practical reason, including specifically moral principles. This extension is especially plausible with respect to what Aquinas calls the first principle of practical reason: that good is to be done and pursued and evil is to be avoided. For this principle, like the principle of non-contradiction, does not normally function as a premiss in practical reasoning.[29]

The general point to be drawn here is that Aquinas is not committed by his view that the basic principles of the natural law are self-evident to all to holding that everyone has articulated these principles propositionally, or that everything people say and believe about moral questions, including moral principles, is consistent with them.

Thus, part of the natural law response to the charge that it requires people to have knowledge that they evidently do not have is that the knowledge of basic moral principles possessed by everyone need not be articulate, philosophically elaborated knowledge. Principles can be present and operative within knowledge without being explicitly formulated. Basic moral principles can therefore be operative within a person's moral thinking, as the grounds of norms he or she regards as true, even if they are not explicitly articulated, and they can be teased away from these norms sufficiently to allow for serious moral criticism. Those who deny their philosophical elaboration may do so because they do not understand that elaboration or its context. It is also possible that the denials of the elaborations of these principles are merely verbal, and possible also that they are based on an unwillingness of people to accept some implications of the philosophical formulations.

Similar things can be said about people who explicitly endorse contrary moral principles. Those who accept a consequentialist moral principle, for example, must, on the natural law account, be holding a view which contradicts something which at some

level they know. But people are notoriously capable of contradict-
ing themselves, particularly when the contradictory propositions
are not formulated together and compared.

Still, the natural law theorist must account for how the consequentialist can hold views that are logically incompatible with
what is self-evident and naturally known to the consequentialist
himself. I believe that the natural law theorist can develop such
an account. Part of it is that the consequentialist does have hold
of something that is part of the foundation of morality: the
dependence of moral judgement on considerations about the
good. But he adds to it considerations which are not really self-
evident but may easily appear to be so—for example, the assumption that the good can be maximized in the way he supposes, that
such maximization is both determinable and relevant to decision-
making, or that the task of morality is to discover ways of
realizing the best states of affairs. None of these beliefs is self-
evident, but each is sufficiently plausible to be mistakenly judged
to be such.

So, the natural law account can provide an explanation of how
the advocates of theories with alternative principles can be
mistaken about so basic and obvious a matter. The needed
explanation, of course, will be a matter of detailed argumentation,
and will vary depending on specific challenges to specific natural
law claims. But it is a task necessary for natural law theorists if
their claims about everyone's knowledge of moral principles are
to be squared with experience.

The argumentation needed to complete this task largely remains
to be done. In fact, with the exception of Aquinas' efforts to
exhibit the self-evidence of the first principle of practical reason,
there has been little work within the tradition to show that the
principles which Aquinas claims are self-evident are in fact
reasonably thought to be so.

Of course, there are deep semantic and epistemological objections to the entire conception of self-evidence which Aquinas
takes over from Aristotle, and to the foundationalist understanding of human knowledge of which this conception is a part.
Natural law theorists and others who think there is abiding
philosophical merit in Aquinas' work need to address these
problems more adequately than they have. Perhaps the central
claims of natural law theory about moral principles and their

universal accessibility can be formulated independently of this epistemological framework.

But the underlying foundationalist theory of knowledge, whatever its merits in epistemology generally, has considerable power in the area of moral knowledge. For moral judgements appear to be justified by reasoning, and reasoning from more general moral considerations. Thus, moral judgements will be correct only if these more general moral considerations are correct. How can these general moral considerations be known to be correct? There are surely alternatives to thinking that they are basic truths (truths, that is, of a special, normative kind). One could maintain that they are necessary but not basic, although it is difficult to understand how we could come to know they are necessary truths. And one might provide a coherentist account of their special status as the basis of moral thinking. But what would be the elements whose coherence would constitute grounds for thinking certain principles basic? Reflective equilibrium between principles and moral judgements appears to deny the dependence of the latter on the former. Coherence between moral principles themselves appears to suppose that there are enough elements to relate so that a plausible, and non-question-begging picture will emerge. The implications of both these forms of coherentism are troubling, and indeed incompatible with the way people actually think about moral questions. The more natural way to think of these matters is that suggested by natural law's (and perhaps ethical theory's) foundationalism: there are moral principles which are known to be in the appropriate way true.

In *Whose Justice? Which Rationality?*, Alasdair MacIntyre emphasizes the difficulty and complexity of the dialectic needed to justify a tradition's basic principles and the theory of which they are the basic elements. Given the conceptual diversity of the contending theories and the depth of their disagreements about virtually every aspect of moral life, that dialectic is not likely to be a short decisive argument like Aristotle's defence of the principle of non-contradiction. The history of ethical theory and the logic of the issues suggests there is little prospect for developing anything like self-refutation arguments against ethical theories one thinks mistaken.

Whatever one thinks of MacIntyre's more radical claims about conceptual incommensurability and the impossibility of achieving neutral standards for evaluating competing moral theories, the competing ethical theories are complex philosophical elaborations whose architects have different problematics, diverse starting-points, methods, and criteria for success. All the major philosophical approaches to morality are the work of philosophers of considerable ability, and of traditions of thought stretching over generations. Thus, they have covered the data and met the obvious objections. Given the complexity of the subject-matter and the philosophical character of the enquiry, it is not surprising that the dialectic will be complicated enough to make it unlikely that there will be clear winners or a meeting of minds.

There does not therefore seem to be any procedure for resolving the disagreements among competing ethical theories—none at least which are likely to lead to agreement in anything like the short run. But natural law claims about the self-evidence of basic moral principles are not falsified by this fact. MacIntyre's argument is surely compatible with a coherentist conception of moral theory and moral principles, but it does not imply such a view. The open-ended character of philosophical debate does not imply that at least some of the claims of parties to that debate cannot be rationally vindicated.

So, to sum up this section: natural law theory can account for the diversity of moral opinions, including such disagreements as exist concerning basic moral principles. In the nature of the case, any such account will be incomplete. For there are always likely to be new alternative positions, new developments of rival positions, and analytical developments of one's own position. Still, this fact does not suggest that the natural law theorist is out of line in making universal claims about moral principles and about people's knowledge of them.

NOTES

1. Two influential books which argue along these lines are Bernard Williams, *Ethics and the Limits of Philosophy* (Cambridge, Mass.:

Harvard University Press, 1983), and Alasdair MacIntyre, *After Virtue*, 2nd edn. (Notre Dame, Ind.: University of Notre Dame Press, 1984).

2. See *After Virtue*, chs. 14–17, and Alasdair MacIntyre, *Whose Justice? Which Rationality?* (Notre Dame, Ind.: University of Notre Dame Press, 1988).

3. See Thomas Aquinas, *Summa Theologiae*, Ia IIae q. 94, a. 4. This claim of Aquinas' appears frequently throughout this work.

4. *S.Th.* Ia IIae, q. 100, aa. 1–2.

5. *S.Th.* Ia IIae, q. 94, a. 4.

6. *S.Th.* Ia IIae, q. 100, aa. 1–2.

7. For an analysis of this social act by philosophers in the natural law tradition, see John Finnis, Joseph Boyle, and Germain Grisez, *Nuclear Deterrence, Morality and Realism* (Oxford: Oxford University Press, 1987), ch. 5.

8. For a development of this claim, see my 'Practical Reasoning and Moral Judgment', in *Proceedings of the American Catholic Philosophical Association*, 58 (1984), 37–49.

9. See *S.Th.* Ia IIae, q. 57, a. 4.

10. See *S.Th.* I, q. 79, a. 12.

11. *S.Th.* Ia IIae, q. 58, a. 5.

12. See *S.Th.* Ia IIae, q. 58, a. 4.

13. For a development of the argument in this paragraph, see Germain Grisez, Joseph Boyle, and John Finnis, 'Practical Principles, Moral Truth, and Ultimate Ends', *The American Journal of Jurisprudence*, 32 (1987), 129–31.

14. *S.Th.* Ia IIae, q. 50, Introduction.

15. *S.Th.* Ia IIae, q. 90, Introduction.

16. For a discussion of the way in which, according to Aquinas, the moral law is specified by reasonable choice, see John Finnis, *Natural Law and Natural Rights* (Oxford: Clarendon Press, 1980), 281–90.

17. See *S.Th.* Ia IIae, q. 94, a. 2; see also Grisez, Boyle, and Finnis, 'Practical Principles', 102–6.

18. The position developed by MacIntyre in *After Virtue*, chs. 14–16, seems to be an example of the view I am articulating here.

19. Alan Donagan, *The Theory of Morality* (Chicago: The University of Chicago Press, 1977), 16–17.

20. See *S.Th.* Ia IIae, q. 99, a. 1, ad 2; see also *S.Th.* Ia IIae, q. 94, a. 4.

21. For a brief explanation of the natural law account of property see my 'Natural Law, Ownership and the World's Natural Resources', *The Journal of Value Inquiry*, 23 (1988), 191–207.

22. MacIntyre, *Whose Justice?*, 321.

23. *S.Th.* Ia IIae, Prologue.

24. *S.Th.* Ia IIae, q. 91, a. 2.

25. The classical source for these assertions is *S.Th.* Ia IIae, q. 94, a. 2. These and similar assertions are found throughout this work, particularly in the parts to which I have been referring.

26. For a useful short account of Aquinas' idea of self-evidence, see Germain Grisez, 'The First Principle of Practical Reason: A Commentary on the *Summa Theologiae*, 1-2, Question 94, Article 2', *The Natural Law Forum*, 10 (1965), 172–5.

27. See e.g. Grisez, Boyle, and Finnis, 'Practical Principles', 111–13, for a description of a strategy for dialectically defending natural law claims that certain ends of human action are fundamental goods.

28. *S.Th.* Ia IIae, q. 94, a. 2.

29. For an account of the way the first principle of practical reason functions, see Grisez, Boyle, and Finnis, 'Practical Principles', 119–20; for interpretation of Aquinas on this, see Grisez, 'The First Principle of Practical Reason'.

2

Natural Law and Human Nature

ROBERT P. GEORGE

I

The natural law theory originally proposed by Germain Grisez, and developed and defended over the past twenty-five years by Grisez, John Finnis, Joseph Boyle, William May, and Patrick Lee, among others, has been sternly criticized by many philosophers who are sympathetic to the idea of natural law.

Some of these critics suggest that Grisez's view of the relationship between morality and nature disqualifies his theory as a theory of natural law. Russell Hittinger, for example, asserts that the idea of natural law 'obviously requires a commitment to law as in some sense "natural," and nature as in some way normative'.[1] As Hittinger understands Grisez's theory, it suffers from a 'failure to interrelate systematically practical reason with a philosophy of nature'.[2] In other words, it fails to do the very thing that makes a theory of practical reasoning and morality a *natural law* theory.

Lloyd Weinreb advances a similar criticism. He maintains that Grisez's approach substitutes a 'deontological' understanding of natural law for the original 'ontological' understanding. According to Weinreb, modern 'deontological' natural law theories such as Grisez's differ from the 'ontological' theories of classical and medieval natural law theorists in so far as the deontological theories dispense with the idea of a 'normative natural order'.[3] They are theories of 'natural law without nature'.[4] Theories of this sort purport to identify principles of natural law without deriving them from nature. Defenders of such theories, in effect, excuse themselves from providing metaphysical or ontological grounds for the moral propositions they assert. In Weinreb's judgement, they pay a heavy price for refusing to argue from metaphysical or ontological premisses: they are forced to rely— as Weinreb supposes Grisez, Finnis, and their collaborators rely—on implausible claims that certain propositions in normative ethics and political theory are self-evidently true.[5]

Yet another critic, Henry Veatch, faults Grisez and his collaborators for erecting a 'wall of separation . . . between practical reason and theoretical reason, between ethics and metaphysics, between nature and morals, between "is" and "ought" '.[6] As Veatch interprets their writings, Grisez and Finnis, for example, maintain the 'absolute independence of ethics as over against metaphysics, or of morals with respect to a knowledge of nature',[7] so that 'principles of morals and ethics are not thought [of] as being in any sense principles of being or nature at all'.[8] Thus Veatch suggests that the theory of morality they propose, whatever its merits, is not a *natural law* theory.

Veatch's suggestion, however, is less extreme than the claim levelled against Grisez and Finnis by Ralph McInerny. According to McInerny, Grisez and Finnis hold a 'Humean' view of practical reasoning 'which regards knowledge of the world to be irrelevant to [practical reason]'.[9] Obviously, any theory of practical reasoning that merits identification with the practical philosophy of David Hume cannot plausibly be counted as a natural law theory.

When these critics talk about the need to ground morality in 'nature', they mean to refer principally to *human* nature and the place of *man* in nature. In their view, a sound natural law ethics derives moral norms from methodologically antecedent knowledge of the nature of man and man's place in nature.

According to this approach, metaphysics—in particular that branch of metaphysics that studies man—precedes ethics. Metaphysical anthropology reveals the facts about human nature; ethics then prescribes or prohibits possible acts (or classes of acts) on the basis of their conformity, or lack of conformity, to these facts.

Grisez and his collaborators reject this approach on a number of grounds. Most importantly, they maintain that it involves 'the naturalistic fallacy' of purporting to infer moral norms from facts about human nature. Logically, a valid conclusion cannot introduce something that is not in the premises. Grisez and his followers insist, therefore, that moral conclusions inasmuch as they state reasons for action can be derived only from premises that include still more fundamental reasons for action. They cannot be derived from premises (e.g. facts about human nature) that do not include reasons for action. According to Grisez and others, natural law theory need not—and a credible natural law theory cannot—rely on this logically 'illicit inference from facts to norms'.[10]

Of course, Grisez's 'neo-scholastic' critics contend that the naturalistic 'fallacy' is no fallacy; for the facts about human nature from which they seek to infer norms of morality are, they say, laden with moral value. Veatch, for example, defends the neo-scholastic approach on the grounds that 'the very "is" of human nature has . . . an "ought" built into it'.[11] Thus, one discovers what one ought to do by understanding the facts about human nature.

My aim in this brief essay is to show (1) that contrary to what their critics claim the natural law theory advanced by Grisez and his collaborators does not entail the proposition that basic human goods or moral norms have no connection to, or grounding in, human nature, and (2) that Grisez and his followers are correct in maintaining that our knowledge of basic human goods and moral norms need not, and logically cannot, be deduced, inferred, or (in any sense that a logician would recognize) derived from facts about human nature.

II

It would be tedious, but not difficult, to show that neither Grisez nor any of his principal followers has ever denied that basic human goods and moral norms have a grounding in human nature. Nor have they ever alleged that theoretical knowledge (McInerny's 'knowledge of the world') is irrelevant to practical reasoning and morality. Critics who assert the contrary should reread the texts carefully. Indeed, Grisez and his followers affirm that basic goods and moral norms *are* what they are because human nature *is* what it is. Finnis, for example, in the very section of *Natural Law and Natural Rights* to which Veatch points in making the allegations I have quoted (a section entitled 'The Illicit Inference from Facts to Norms') *endorses* the proposition that 'were man's nature different, so would be his duties'.[12] More recently, Grisez, Boyle, and Finnis have set forth in some detail their account of how theoretical knowledge contributes to our understanding of basic human goods and moral norms.[13]

The real issue, then, is not whether Grisez and his followers deny that morality is grounded in (human) nature; the simple, demonstrable truth is that they do not. The real issue is whether their claim that basic human goods and moral norms are not inferred from prior knowledge of human nature somehow entails the proposition that morality is not grounded in nature.

III

If Grisez and his followers are correct to hold that the most basic reasons for action are not derived from facts about human nature, how are these reasons known? They are known in non-inferential acts of understanding in which we grasp possible ends or purposes as worth while for their own sakes. The most basic reasons for action are those reasons whose intelligibility does not depend on deeper or still more fundamental reasons. As *basic* reasons, they cannot be derived; for there is nothing more fundamental that could serve as a premiss for a logical derivation. Therefore, they must be self-evident.

Only intrinsic goods, i.e. things that are intelligibly desirable for their own sakes, can be basic reasons for action. Instrumental goods are reasons for action; they are not, however, basic reasons. They are reasons whose intelligibility depends on deeper or more fundamental reasons (and ultimately on basic reasons). Therefore, they are *derived* and are not self-evident.

If Grisez and his followers are correct in supposing that the most basic reasons for action are not inferred from propositions about human nature but are instead self-evident, does that mean that these reasons (and the moral norms whose derivation they make possible) are detached from human nature?

The answer is no. Here is why: only that which is understood to be worth while can provide a reason for action. Only that which is humanly fulfilling can be understood to be worth while. Intrinsic goods are basic reasons for action precisely because they are (intrinsic) aspects of human well-being and fulfilment. They perfect human beings, i.e. beings with a human nature. As human perfections, 'basic goods' belong to human beings as parts of their nature.[14]

Finnis has usefully explicated the relationship between morality and nature by distinguishing an 'epistemological' from an
'ontological' mode of analysis. He begins the analysis in the
'epistemological' mode:

Propositions about primary human goods are not derived from propositions about human nature or from any other propositions of speculative
reason; as Aquinas says with maximum clarity, and never wavers from
saying, they are *per se nota* and *indemonstrabilia*. [*Citations omitted*.] For
we come to know human nature by knowing its potentialities, and these
we know by knowing their actuations, which in turn we know by
knowing their objects—and the objects . . . are precisely the primary
human goods. (So, if anything, an adequately full knowledge of human
nature is derived from our practical and underived (*per se notum*)
knowledge of the human goods . . .)
    But . . . if we shift from the epistemological to the ontological mode,
the same methodological principle, in its application to human beings,
presupposes and thus entails that the goodness of all human goods (and
thus the appropriateness, the *convenientia*, of all responsibilities) is
derived from (i.e., depends upon) the nature which, by their goodness,
those goods perfect. For those goods—which as ends are the *rationes* of
practical norms or 'oughts'—would not perfect that nature were it other
than it is.[15]

Neo-scholastic critics of the position Finnis defends have
ignored the distinction between ontology and epistemology to
which he appeals. They seem to have assumed, gratuitously, that
anyone who maintains that our knowledge of human goods is
not derived from our prior knowledge of human nature must
hold that human goods are not grounded in nature. This assumption, however, is unsound. There is not the slightest inconsistency
in holding both that (1) our knowledge of the intrinsic value of
certain ends or purposes is acquired in non-inferential acts of
understanding wherein we grasp self-evident truths, and (2)
those ends or purposes are intrinsically valuable (and thus can be
grasped as self-evidently worth while) because they are intrinsically perfective of human beings, i.e., beings with a human
nature.
    In short: the proposition that our knowledge of basic human
goods and moral norms is not derived from prior knowledge of
human nature does not entail the proposition that morality has
no grounding in human nature. Our knowledge of the most

fundamental principles of human well-being and fulfilment may be underived— because these principles are self-evident practical truths—yet remain knowledge of human well-being and fulfilment.

IV

Still, would not our claims to moral knowledge be somehow more secure if they could rest on solid facts about human nature rather than on putatively self-evident propositions?

Perhaps the single most commonly misunderstood feature of Grisez's natural law theory is its appeal to self-evidence. Sometimes Grisez and his collaborators are interpreted as claiming that truths about disputed issues in normative ethics and political theory (such as whether abortion is immoral or whether it ought to be made illegal) are self-evident. No proponent of the theory, to my knowledge, has claimed that the truth about any issue in normative ethics or political theory is self-evident.

Lloyd Weinreb's critique of Grisez's theory miscarries on this very point. It is obvious that truths about issues in normative ethics and political theory are not self-evident. If, as Weinreb supposes, Grisez, Finnis, and the rest were reduced to claiming that their positions on matters of this sort were self-evidently true, then there would be something deeply wrong with their approach. Weinreb, however, is simply mistaken in supposing that Finnis, for example, maintains that his position on abortion is self-evidently true.[16]

According to Grisez, Finnis, and their collaborators, only the most basic reasons for action are self-evident. These reasons provide only the most basic premises for moral arguments. Indeed, moral questions arise because of the diversity of basic reasons for action. One may have a basic reason to do X, but at the same time a basic reason not to do X because one also has a basic reason to do or preserve Y, and the doing or preserving of Y is incompatible here and now with X. What is one to do? Which, if either, course of action is not merely rational but fully reasonable? Are both courses of action fully reasonable?

One cannot decide simply by knowing that X and Y are basic reasons for action. One requires some knowledge of *moral norms* that guide one's morally significant choosing, i.e. one's choices between *rationally* appealing but incompatible alternatives. The most basic reasons for action are not themselves moral norms, though they are the principles which taken together provide the first and most general moral principle and remain principles relevant to all moral reasoning.

Still someone might object: is there not something unsatisfying about appeals to self-evidence even at the level of the most basic premisses of moral arguments? After all, people can simply refuse to accept a claim that something is self-evident. That is true. It is also true, however, that people can refuse to accept any claim. Basic reasons for action are simply ends (goods) whose intelligible point can be grasped without the benefit of a deduction or inference by anyone who knows what the terms referring to them signify. Such reasons can frequently be defended by indirect (dialectical) arguments that bring other knowledge to bear to highlight the rational unacceptability of denying them.[17] At the same time, because they cannot be argued for directly (for there are no premisses from which to derive them)[18] anyone who does affirm them must acknowledge their self-evidence.

It seems to me that Grisez's appeals to self-evidence, when properly understood, do not fail to provide a solid foundation for moral reasoning. In any event, they provide no less solid a foundation than appeals to the facts of human nature. Someone who fails to see the point of pursuing knowledge just for its own sake is unlikely to be impressed by arguments meant to establish that truth-seeking is natural to human beings. Or, again, someone who finds it baffling that anyone would pursue a friendship just for friendship's sake is unlikely to understand the value of friendship any better by being informed (or even persuaded) that man is by nature a social being.

Moreover, someone who does not grasp the intelligible point of pursuing knowledge or friendships just for their own sake lacks a rational warrant for judging these goods to be reasons for action. To derive reasons for action from more fundamental premisses, more fundamental reasons for action must be in those premisses. Propositions like 'truth-seeking is natural to human beings' or 'man is a social being' do not state reasons for action. Grisez and his followers are correct, then, to conclude that propositions like these logically cannot serve as premisses for moral conclusions.

In the end, even Henry Veatch admits as much. 'I concede', he says in a published debate with Finnis, 'that there can be no *deduction* of ethics from metaphysics, and no *inference* of "propositions about man's duties and obligations" simply from "propositions about his nature".'[19] 'Yet,' Veatch asks, 'is not the soundness of such contentions due to one's taking the terms "deduction" and "inference" in a somewhat straitened and overly technical sense?'

I think that the answer to Veatch's enquiry is 'no'. The distinction between what 'is the case' (about human nature or anything else in the natural order) and what 'ought to be' is logically significant.[20] Muddle is the best we can hope for if we ignore this distinction or sweep it under the rug. A pretty good example is Veatch's own claim that 'the very "is" of human nature has an "ought" built into it'. That claim is not flatly wrong; it is just muddled. Knowledge, friendship, and the other basic reasons for action are aspects of human well-being and fulfilment. In that sense, human nature has an 'ought' built into it. As Veatch concedes, however, we cannot deduce or infer the 'ought' from the 'is' of human nature. We cannot deduce or infer reasons for action from premises that do not include reasons for action. We cannot deduce or infer *basic* reasons for action from anything. Our knowledge of basic reasons is underived and non-inferential.

In no sense, however, do we simply 'make up' basic reasons for action or manufacture our knowledge of them out of our own subjectivity. Their directiveness and their truth are not mere 'structures of the mind'. According to some of Grisez's neo-scholastic critics, to hold that our knowledge of basic reasons for action is underived is to hold that the truth of practical judgements consists in their 'conformity to practical reason's own inner requirements, i.e., to itself or its directive structure'.[21] But this claim is unwarranted. Although practical judgements are not inferred from prior theoretical knowledge, they do not refer to the 'structures of practical reason' itself; indeed, as Grisez has pointed out, it is scarcely possible to see what such phrases mean.[22] Rather, 'the truth of practical knowledge with respect to its first principles is their adequation to possible human fulfillment considered precisely insofar as that fulfillment can be realized through human action'.[23] To say that possible fufilment thus considered may be understood (or, when things miscarry, misunderstood) by the enquiring intellect is not to reduce the truth of propositions that refer to such fulfilment to conformity with any 'inner structures' of the mind that grasps those propositions and, thus, knows that truth. To hold that basic reasons for action are underived is not, then, to lapse into some form of subjectivism.

At the same time, there are aspects of human nature that are relevant to practical thinking and can indeed be known prior to practical reasoning, for example, ranges of empirical possibility and environmental constraint. Human nature, however, is not a closed nature. It could be known in its fullness only by grasping all the ways that human persons may be fulfilled through their understanding of basic reasons for action and their reasonable and creative choices. Such choices are choices of purposes which will instantiate and realize the human goods that are the basic reasons for action; and it is characteristic of those reasons, those goods, and thus of human nature that many of those possible intelligent purposes remain as yet unenvisaged. A complete theoretical account of *human* nature (unlike accounts of closed natures) would depend, therefore, on data provided by practical enquiry, reflection, and judgement. Those who claim that theoretical knowledge of human nature is methodologically prior to basic practical knowledge have things, in this respect, exactly backwards.

NOTES

© Robert P. George 1992.

1. Russell Hittinger, *A Critique of the New Natural Law Theory* (Notre Dame, Ind.: University of Notre Dame Press, 1987), 8.
2. Ibid.
3. In *Natural Law and Justice* (Cambridge, Mass.: Harvard University Press, 1987), 108–16, Weinreb criticizes Grisez's theory as it appears in John Finnis's *Natural Law and Natural Rights* (Oxford: Clarendon Press, 1980). He cites the theory as an example of contemporary 'deontological' theories of natural law. He judges all such theories to be seriously defective. In their place, he would 'restore[ ] the original

understanding of natural law as a theory about the nature of being, the human condition in particular' (p. 7).

4. The phrase here quoted is the title of ch. 4 of Weinreb's *Natural Law and Justice*. In that chapter, he considers a number of contemporary writers whose theories he classifies as 'deontological natural law theories'. In addition to Finnis, he criticizes Lon Fuller, David Richards, and Ronald Dworkin for proposing theories of 'natural law without nature'.

5. For the suggestion that Finnis, for example, maintains that certain conclusions in normative ethics and political theory are self-evidently true, see Weinreb, *Natural Law and Justice*, 112–13. For the specific suggestion that Finnis maintains that his position on the morality of abortion is a self-evident truth, see ibid. 296 n. 32.

6. Henry Veatch, 'Natural Law and the "Is"–"Ought" Question', *Catholic Lawyer*, 26 (1981), 265.

7. Ibid. 256.

8. Ibid.

9. Ralph McInerny, *Ethica Thomistica* (Washington, DC: The Catholic University of America Press, 1982), 54–5.

10. Finnis, *Natural Law*, 33.

11. Veatch, 'Natural Law', 258.

12. Finnis, *Natural Law*, 34.

13. Germain Grisez, Joseph Boyle, and John Finnis, 'Practical Principles, Moral Truth, and Ultimate Ends', *American Journal of Jurisprudence*, 32 (1987), 99–151, at 108–9.

14. Cf. ibid. 127.

15. J.M. Finnis, 'Natural Inclinations and Natural Rights: Deriving "Ought" from "Is" According to Aquinas', in L.J. Elders and K. Hedwig, eds., 'Lex et Libertas', *Studi Tomistici*, 30 (Vatican City: Pontificia Accademia di S. Tommaso, 1987), 45–7.

16. On the basis of a misunderstanding of which sorts of propositions Finnis claims to be self-evident, Weinreb charges that Finnis 'has confused self-evidence with personal conviction', *Natural Law and Justice*, 113. I have criticized Weinreb's attribution to Finnis of the view that certain conclusions in normative ethics and political theory are self-evident in 'Recent Criticism of Natural Law Theory', *University of Chicago Law Review*, 55 (1988), 1371–429, at 1386–9.

17. On dialectical arguments in defence of self-evident practical truths see Grisez, Boyle and Finnis, 'Practical Principles', 111–13. See also George, 'Recent Criticism of Natural Law Theory', 1410–14.

18. There are, however, data (experienced inclinations and a knowledge of empirical patterns that underlie possibilities of action and accomplishment).

19. Veatch, 'Natural Law', 254.
20. Ralph McInerny asserts that '[t]he concern not to infer value from fact, Ought from Is, may be a symptom of fastidiousness', *Ethica Thomistica*, 55. Whether or not one credits Professor McInerny's psychological speculation, it remains logically invalid to move from premises that do not include reasons for action to conclusions that state reasons for action. To conclude to specific moral norms, for example, one's premises must include reasons for action that are more fundamental than those norms. This is not to say, as McInerny imagines Grisez and Finnis to say, that 'knowledge of the world is irrelevant to [practical reason]'. Grisez and Finnis do not argue that such theoretical knowledge is irrelevant to practical enquiry and moral judgement. Their claim is merely that basic practical principles and the specific moral norms derived from them cannot be deduced, inferred, or, in any strict sense, derived from purely theoretical premises. They hold, with Aquinas, that practical reasoning, like theoretical reasoning, has its own underived (i.e. *per se nota* and *indemonstrabilia*) first principles. (See *Summa Theologiae*, Ia IIae, q. 94, a. 2.) These principles are indispensable premises in reasoning that concludes validly to propositions about specific moral norms. Other premises include 'theoretical' propositions about e.g. the structure of human action as intentional behaviour, the causality of means, etc.
21. Brian V. Johnstone, 'The Structures of Practical Reason: Traditional Theories and Contemporary Questions', *Thomist*, 50 (1986), 417–46, at 432.
22. Germain Grisez, 'The Structures of Practical Reason: Some Comments and Clarifications', *Thomist*, 52 (1988), 269–91, at 277. See also Grisez, Boyle, and Finnis, 'Practical Principles', 125 and 115–20 (on practical truth).
23. See Grisez, 'The Structures of Practical Reason', 278, n. 8.

3

Natural Law and Virtue: Theories at Cross Purposes

RUSSELL HITTINGER

I

This essay will explain how the subjects of virtue and natural law have become quite different foci for theories about human conduct, not only placing different requirements on the theorist, but requirements which seem to be at cross purposes. Natural law can be reserved for an important, but narrow problem: the articulation of some basic human goods or needs that any system of positive law must respect, promote, or in any case protect. Natural law theory, on this assignment, would disclose the overlap of law and morality requisite for legislation and for the public and legal vindication of individual rights. The term 'nature' can carry the relatively weak meaning of what is not a mere artefact of our practical reasoning. The goods of life, or freedom of speech, are not generally regarded as values simply by dint of subjective preference or the idiosyncracies of private life plans. In this sense, they could be treated as publicly recognizable 'natural' values which guide legal judgements. Hence, in American constitutional law principles of natural justice are summoned to highlight moral requirements of the legal and political order, to defend individual rights against the utilitarian interests of a political majority, or to guide the adjudication of hard cases which fall into textual gaps or open-ended clauses of the Constitution.

On the other hand, it might be argued that this legal-political paradigm of natural law theory is not a very suitable tool for addressing matters of virtue and character. Virtues are not necessary conditions for agency in the sense of having the material wherewithal for life, being treated with equality under the law, or possessing certain personal liberties to speech, property, and privacy. Virtues are not justiciable things or principles in that respect. Principles like freedom of speech, property, or due process of law—to mention a few which routinely crop up in American law as natural principles of justice—can be defined without making further claims either about the differential capacities and excellences of persons, or about the ends and completions which rights can serve. If we take our bearings from Aristotle on the subject of virtue, then it is not correct to describe virtues as natural capacities subsisting in the individual simply by dint of being human. Furthermore, virtues are not adequately defined in terms of untutored human inclinations or needs, but are seen in the perfection of actions towards ends. As Aristotle said: 'virtues arise in us neither by nature nor against nature, but we are by nature able to acquire them, and reach our complete perfection through habit.'[1] Whatever it might mean to articulate a natural context or norm for virtue, it would have to be somewhat different from what is ordinarily in the interest of natural law theory, which is to explicate minimal public standards according to a minimal notion of what is naturally required for a legal account of civil transactions.

Theorizing about natural law and virtue, therefore, can be sharply distinguished for three reasons. First, for the reason of the demise of the older teleological view of nature that permitted theorists like Aquinas to interrelate the analogous meanings of law and nature around the theme of natural inclinations. These inclinations, on Aquinas' view, are the soil for both virtues and the first precepts of the natural law.[2] The reason of law as well as the cultivation of the habits take their bearing from a pre-given teleological order. 'Nature' designates not only the quiddities of things—the formal cause that which makes a thing what it is—but more importantly the finality governing completions. Right reason, on the traditional teleological view of natural law, cannot mean simply judgement in accord with natural values, but judgement in accord with what completes these values. While the older teleological theories permitted natural law analysis to play both roles—to explicate the goods embedded in human actions as well as their completions–the modern rejection of teleological thinking guarantees that a natural law doctrine of *recta ratio* must restrict itself to discourse about natural goods or values. It will prove very difficult to include the virtues in this discourse.

Second, the issues of law as a political and legal problem and the internal qualities of virtue and character are, in any case, distinguishable. Even on Aquinas' terms, giving theoretical accounts of law and virtue are different, and what should count as an adequate discussion of one is not the same as what might count as an adequate discussion of the other.[3] Third, modern institutions place special constraints upon theorizing about 'nature' and 'law'. Theories have institutional functions. In the context of American constitutional law, theoretical formulations of natural principles of justice are cut and trimmed to win legal arguments. One claims no more about the overlap between morality and law than what is needed to get the job done.[4] This is not only true of a legal culture that has a written constitution, but it is especially true of a legal culture that must tolerate an enormous range of moral and religious pluralism—pluralism that constrains what can be publicly assumed about virtue and perfection.

The sharp distinction between natural law theory and virtue theory has emerged, therefore, for a variety of reasons: some are philosophical, others involve historical contingencies and exigencies of institutions. In the contemporary literature, the distinction is not altogether a happy one. Virtue theorists are ready to surrender the natural law framework to the legal-political problematic, and then claim that such a focus distorts moral analysis. This move is not only true of such virtue ethicists as Edmund Pincoffs and Stanley Hauerwas, and in a qualified way of Alasdair MacIntyre and Bernard Williams,[5] but also of some who lay a more direct claim to the older Thomistic system. Vernon Bourke, a well-known historian of medieval theories of practical reason, has recently insisted that the term 'natural law' be summarily jettisoned as a tag for Aquinas' work. Whatever Aquinas meant by the law of nature, Bourke argues, it is certainly not the same as what the term has come to mean in modern thought, and therefore it ought to be replaced with the term 'ethics of right reason'.[6] This promises to restore the emphasis upon virtue, which is where it always was in Aquinas' moral theory.

Contemporary natural law theorists are extremely wary of virtue discourse, for the obvious reason that it requires an ancillary discussion of the human good which is not only inconvenient, but an impediment to the kind of reasoning that defends rights in a liberal polity. One can imagine the reception that is apt to be given the claim that *iura* are derivative of more primary moral phenomena such as the cardinal virtues, and that any analysis of the moral rightness or wrongness of human acts is left under-determined until they are assessed in terms of virtue. This would not only commit moral theory to a level of variability beyond the competence of public law, but would also require the law to directly regard the moral differences among citizens. Everyone is not equally excellent in respect to virtue. Hence, natural law theorists jealously guard the universal public standards of natural justice against what looks to be private, if not religious, standards of moral qualities.

In order to see how the theories of natural law and of virtue operate in contemporary literature at cross purposes, we will look at two discussions. The first is Alan Gewirth's criticism of Alasdair MacIntyre's *After Virtue*. Gewirth wants to show that virtue discourse is a totally inadequate substitute for moral rules governing individual rights. Although he makes some telling points about the inappropriateness of making the virtues a first-order discourse in public institutions, Gewirth, we shall argue, over-claims what can be secured by natural rights theories. The over-claim not only concerns the content and the extent of the natural law principles—principles, he says, which are denied only upon pain of self-contradiction—but also Gewirth's assimilation of the virtues to rights. The second discussion has to do with Edmund Pincoffs's case for the recovery of virtues as an alternative to the ethic of minimal public standards. Pincoffs makes some interesting points about why an ethic of minimal standards distorts the everyday focus of moral concerns, which, he says, has more to do with personal character and virtue than precepts about rights. Yet despite his insistent and sharply drawn contrast between rules and virtues, he finally recommends that we ought to see that some virtues are needed regardless of what other goals and ideals we have for life. In doing so, Pincoffs adopts a position that is not unlike Gewirth's. We will point out that neither Gewirth nor Pincoffs is satisfied with pointing out the difference between rules and virtues.

Gewirth and Pincoffs represent polar extremes of this problem. Few contemporary theorists laying claim to natural law would agree with Gewirth's stringently apodictic standards. Further-more, few if any virtue ethicists would go so far as to defend tables of virtues without any natural or objective hierarchy. Granted that these are extremes of the discussion, they are useful for indicating where natural law and virtue theories decisively depart in the absence of an intermediate level of discussion. This essay makes no effort to reconcile the two perspectives. Rather our goal is to uncover their cross purposes, and to indicate the absence of an intermediate level of discussion. At the end, we will have a few words to say about the intermediate level.

II

In *After Virtue*, MacIntyre treats virtue in terms of practices rather than the conventional scholastic method of looking at potency-act continua rooted in human nature. He sets aside Aristotle's 'metaphysical biology'.[7] It is set aside in the sense, first, that he takes no philosophical stand one way or the other on the Aristotelian philosophy of nature, and second, he does not use potency-act to explicate the subject of virtues. MacIntyre defines virtue as follows: 'A virtue is an acquired human quality the possession and exercise of which tends to enable us to achieve those goods which are internal to practices and the lack of which effectively prevents us from achieving any such goods.'[8] Practices, he argues, never have 'fixed goals for all time'.[9] Painting, for example, is a practice transmuted by the activity. The goals undertaken in the activity are subject to historical development and emergent standards of achievement. The historicity of prac-tices is also shaped, for good or ill, by technical skills and institutional settings.

MacIntyre juggles four terms: virtues, practices, skills, and institutions. Institutions, however, can corrupt and desiccate goods internal to practices; technical skills can flatten out a community's sense of the development of a practice by shifting attention to external *factibilia*.[10] More important, virtues can only be partially defined in terms of practices. Torture and sado-masochism, he notes, might qualify as practices, but not moral virtues.[11] There are practices which might be productive of goods in some cases (he mentions techniques for survival in the wilderness, with the attendant internal quality of ruthlessness), as well as good practices productive of evil (the artist who neglects his family). Both are to be distinguished from moral virtue. Therefore, MacIntyre insists that the first stage of analysis— the definition of virtues in terms of practices—must be supplemented by two additional considerations.[12]

In the first place, he argues that for an activity to be adjudged virtuous, it must also satisfy the conception of a 'telos which transcends the limited goods of practices by constituting the good of a whole human life'. So long as the excellences internal to practices are taken piecemeal, an account of the virtues will be vulnerable to a 'subversive arbitrariness'. Again, the internal quality of ruthlessness might be developed as a good necessary to the practice of taming the wilderness, but an agent who is formed exclusively around this practice is liable to strike us as a grotesque example of human development. If this is the measure for virtue, then we are perhaps justified in suspecting that moral qualities serve practices, and that practices serve institutional goals, which in turn serve the arbitrary needs of a society— arbitrary, because such needs cannot themselves be assessed by a standard distinct from the social arrangements. Various societies cut and trim human activity for this or that need, producing kamikaze pilots, explorers of the wilderness, or tolerant consumers. MacIntyre understands that should the account of virtues remain only within an account of practices, virtue theory would not only countenance the worst kind of relativism, but it would unravel the distinction between internal and external goods. In the second place, MacIntyre contends that virtues must be 'integrated into the overall patterns of a tradition informed by a quest for *the* good and *the* best'.[13] The verdict about virtue is not just a problem for the individual. It requires a tradition that has accumulated some experience about goods internal to practices.

For MacIntyre, then, a quality is to be counted a virtue only if it passes muster at all three stages. Therefore, although it was important for him to avoid a descriptive and normative anthropology in order to get the discussion of virtue under way, the second and third stages are crucial if he hopes to keep virtue ethics from being reduced to ethnography. These latter stages (or criteria) involve a teleological standard for judging goods internal to practices. The teleological standard is quite explicit in the second stage, and is implicit to the notion of a tradition of enquiry. The issue of natural law arises at this precise point. Of all the ways that human potential can be actualized and formed in practices, the question is which ways ought it to be formed. Which sorts of human dispositions and activities—and correlatively, institutions and skills—befit human nature? MacIntyre would answer, those which befit the telos or quest, and which are consonant with the *traditio* of those making such an enquiry. So long as one moves to a particular tradition, an answer to the question is not left completely indeterminate; for we could give a descriptive account of, say, the Augustinian tradition, but by the same token, we can do so for the Japanese warrior ethic. How do we break out of the loop of historical descriptions? Or, to put it in another way, how do we retain the specificity of the first and third stages (concrete practices, and a determinate tradition) while at the same time defending a normative account of what is included at the second stage (the telos of a whole life)? This problem opens MacIntyre to criticism.

Alan Gewirth, for example, has criticized MacIntyre's virtue theory chiefly on the point that it leaves indeterminate what is central to, or in any case what is first problem of, moral theory: namely, resolving whether types of actions satisfy or violate a specifically moral rule. Gewirth writes: 'When the criterion for a quality's being a virtue does not include the requirement that the virtue reflect or conform to moral rules, there is no assurance that the alleged virtue will be morally right or wrong.'[14] Moral virtue on MacIntyre's account, he contends, leaves the content indeterminate, and thus provides for mutually opposed moral outcomes.

Gewirth argues that none of MacIntyre's three stages sufficiently nail down whether an action or quality of an action is morally virtuous.[15] Granting, at the first stage, that a practice like torture realizes some real or apparent internal good, Gewirth asks for the grounds of the judgement that it is not morally virtuous. Since the ground cannot be practices, MacIntyre must move to the second stage. Yet the *telos* or quest, Gewirth charges, can include any number of pictures of a unified end. What is the precise 'good' that anchors the quest such that we can judge whether Hitler and Stalin, for example, should qualify as authentic questers? To redescribe the quest in terms of a virtue—like constancy or singleness of purpose—will not do, for all sorts of characters in the historical gallery of rogues would easily satisfy this description. The move from practices to quests still fails to establish any morally normative principles. Moving, then, to the third stage, Gewirth argues that the notion of a tradition is the culminating stage of MacIntyre's scheme, but that there is no sure standard for adjudging whether the resources of a tradition lead to a genuine knowledge of the relevant goods.[16]

The lack of standards for making a moral judgement about the communal suppositions, according to Gewirth, is unacceptable. He asks:

But which community? Aristotle's perfect community required the enslavement of farmers and mechanics; the Nazi community required the murder of Jews and others; the contemporary Afrikaner community requires the subjugation, economic and personal as well as political, of millions of blacks. For all his endorsement of a morality of laws, MacIntyre's specification of their 'point and purpose,' together with his unclear evaluation of moral universalism, leaves available such violations of basic rights, and hence a *drastic moral indeterminacy*.[17]

Of course, MacIntyre expressly denies that exploitation and ruthlessness could ever count as moral virtue. In fairness to McIntyre, *After Virtue* can hardly be read as a treatise on the substantive principles of morality; rather, it concerns historical and cultural contexts of arguments about such principles. Be that as it may, Gewirth contends that the 'conceptual resources [MacIntyre] deploys in making the virtues central to moral philosophy are inadequate substitutes for the more traditional view that derives the content of the virtues from moral rules about rights and duties'.[18]

Gewirth's notion of the 'traditional view' represents a misleading half-truth. True enough, there are traditions of natural law theory which take categorical moral rules as their central focus. As will be pointed out shortly, Gewirth is eager to identify himself with that tradition—albeit on his own terms, which are more deontological than Aristotelian.[19] It is also true that a natural law of rights, to be publicly avowed and deployed in the political and legal arena, can be regarded as the central concern of some modern legal cultures. There is any number of political and legal theorists who contend that the American Constitution, including the Bill of Rights, would leave the moral dimension of political power intolerably indeterminate were it not for the traditional belief in a natural law of rights. On this view, certain principles and goods must be nailed down as the invariable moral elements of a public *ordo juris*. Laurence Tribe, D.A.J. Richards, and Ronald Dworkin, among others, speak in this way.[20] Indeed, in the context of American law, nearly any position that postures as the antipode to legal positivism and unmitigated utilitarianism is accredited as 'natural law'.[21] In this sense, there is a tradition of pressing natural law theory into the service of determining moral principles as public rules. And virtue theory would seem to be an unacceptable substitute for that tradition.

Gewirth identifies himself with the natural law tradition, but not without criticizing it, and refitting it to his own purposes. In particular, he criticizes the scholastic tradition, which also tolerates, he claims, moral indeterminacy with respect to the sources and formulations of natural law precepts. His criticisms of this tradition are similar to his charges against MacIntyre's virtue ethics: first, human nature is too varied to provide a determinate set of precepts,[22] and the specific natural law precepts which Aquinas posits allow for considerable indeterminacy;[23] second, scholastic theorists simply build into their starting-points all of the content which they then claim to unpack;[24] third, the shift to a telic standard of what is excellent or best in human action rests upon ideals which are too varied and contentious, and which easily lead to the toleration of inegalitarian social structures;[25] and finally that scholastic natural law principles 'have not been shown to be *inherently* rational, such that to reject them is to incur self-contradiction'.[26] The Aristotelian–Thomist natural law theory, he concludes, 'allows a dangerous degree of indeterminacy'. True enough, Aquinas and scholastic natural law theorists regarded experience with the inclinations as starting-points rather than a full-blown moral code. Like any blueprint, the natural law leaves considerable room for the rational direction of conduct according to circumstances and the various stations of life. Natural law, for Aquinas, is not a substitute for practical reason. One who looks to Aquinas for a natural law of apodictically generated rules, arrived at even while prescinding from experience and custom, will be disappointed.

For his part, Gewirth insists that his position is a natural law account, shorn of the impediments and questionable starting-points of the scholastic tradition. He points out that his position has three natural-law-like characteristics: it has 'ontological groundedness', 'universal validity', and is 'based on reason in the most stringent sense, because it can be denied or violated only on pain of self-contradiction'.[27] According to these criteria, law can be counted as 'natural' not because it is inferred from a full picture of human nature, but because certain goods are necessities of any purposive development of human action. Gewirth frankly admits that his position is based upon a minimal requirement of rationality, 'of which all agents are capable'.[28] To eliminate the dangerous indeterminacy in various ethical traditions, one naturally has to start by assuming very little. What is the minimum, which cannot be denied except on pain of self-contradiction? For Gewirth, every agent logically must claim rights to 'freedom and well-being' because they are necessary to the generic features of purposive action.[29] These cannot be evaded by any prospective agent 'regardless of his variable inclinations, ideals, or beliefs'.[30] In claiming what is required as the necessary conditions of purposive action, the agent must go on to accept and respect the same needs in other agents. Gewirth calls this the Principle of Generic Consistency, which is the supreme moral principle. The position, in its essentials, is based upon the notion that an agent can discover what is necessary to any prospective action on his part, and thus can rationally lock both himself and others into a moral law regulating any and all claims about purposive actions. The agent's other 'inclinations, ideals, or beliefs' may be important, but they must be disciplined by the minimal standards of rationality fit for the public domain.

What is to be gained by finding moral principles in the necessary and generic features of purposive action? Gewirth contends that it solves the problem of moral indeterminacy. It locates the ground for 'justified demands for or claims to certain kinds of *guaranteed* conduct', and hence furnishes a method of debate-stopping.[31] We need not enquire into the sufficient conditions of human well-being, or into the 'variable' conditions of the agent, in order to reach categorical norms for conduct. Gewirth's method secures a way of talking rationally about conduct among those who might disagree on many other substantive issues of morality. Without a moral principle grounded in the most generic features of purposive action, these agents are liable to deny one another moral status, or to subordinate an individual's participation in basic goods to utilitarian considerations. Gewirth writes: 'The ultimate purpose of the rights is to secure for each person a certain fundamental moral status: that of having rational auto- nomy and dignity in the sense of being a self-controlling, self- developing agent who can relate to other persons on a basis of mutual respect and cooperation, in contrast to being a dependent, passive recipient of the agency of others.'[32] Natural law discourse is geared to 'guarantee', 'secure', and 'protect' rights.

The problem with virtue ethics is clear if one takes Gewirth's perspective. Virtue ethics focuses upon goods—individual and communal—but goods are more general than rights, and there- fore virtue ethics fails to reach a principle that delimits the *moral* field. Gewirth insists that all moral concepts are derivative from human rights, and all moral duties are for the sake of rights. 'Moral virtues', he adds, 'are dispositions to action, and hence presuppose the necessary conditions to action which are the objects of human rights; moreover, the justified contents of the virtues must involve at least the nonviolation of human rights, and the most important moral virtues are dispositions to act for the promotion of human rights.'[33] Gewirth surely overreaches himself in this conclusion. It is one thing to say that certain political and legal cultures need to render the moral basis of rules highly determinate; it is quite another thing to propose that these determinations are adequate for describing, much less for recommending, the virtues. Indeed, a salient mark of liberal legal cultures is the commitment to leave such conceptions of the good to the private sphere. To stipulate, on the basis of public rules grounded in natural needs, which personal qualities are virtuous is not just a matter of venturing into a subject without adequate conceptual resources, but to intrude upon a private sphere that the natural law of individual rights is expressly geared to protect.

Gewirth's theory is a statement of what I have called in another essay 'minimalist natural law'.[34] It conceives of natural principles of justice in terms of the minimal conditions of agency quite apart from religious or philosophical conceptions of a unified end for human action (MacIntyre's second stage), and apart from member- ship in a tradition of discourse which teaches one how to think about human actions (the third stage). Regardless of what one thinks of the theory, its purpose is not completely unreasonable. The theory serves moral problem-solving among individuals in a liberal, pluralistic society. However, for reasons which I shall now outline, I do not believe that it is as reasonable as the claims made for it, and in any case I do not believe it meets the chief arguments advanced by the virtue theorists.

First, how can we be assured that this drastic reduction of moral discourse to apodictically grounded principles of merely generic action is not itself a tool of a certain kind of society which requires humans to serve its peculiar institutions? Gewirth presses this issue insistently against MacIntyre's theory of virtue, and the question can be turned around. Gewirth no doubt would say that the rights located in the generic features of action guarantee that individuals are minimally protected against distortive institutions and policies. This answer, however, presupposes that the inclusion of this rather than that bevy of generic goods is not dictated by the needs and exigencies of the institutions—namely, modern pluralistic institutions which require that conceptions of the full good of humans be put out of play. Not all human legal and moral cultures have made such an assumption about what it means to treat persons with moral respect. As Joseph Raz has pointed out, the notion that 'respect' for human beings minimally requires treating them in accordance with sound moral principles means only that one would be showing disrespect to another 'if one ignored moral considerations'.[35] But whose sound moral considerations? The liberal theory of rights, which sets aside standards of perfection in favour of primitive and generic goods, is one way, but not the only way, to bring moral considerations to bear, and hence to respect persons.

There is no apodictic ground, but rather only historical and social ones, for beginning with Gewirth's minimal goods. If Gewirth argues that the rights protecting these goods provide a lever for criticizing social institutions, he is correct; but what he has not apodictically proven is that this particular collection of goods is not reached by an antecedent accommodation to the exigencies of discourse and debate within such institutions. In making this criticism of Gewirth, we need not question whether his list of basic goods are objective, or 'natural'. Indeed, we can agree, for the sake of argument, that there are basic goods which are pervasive in human action, and which constitute some ground for judgements about justice. Our criticism is directed to the claim that goods arrived at by this method are exclusively

entitled to count as the foundational, public standards for morality. There may be other goods and principles which are also
important, but which cannot be yielded simply on the basis of
self-referential logics. Is there an apodictic ground for beginning
in this fashion, and, in effect, binding ourselves orally only to
what we cannot deny upon pain of self-contradiction? Gewirth
does not relieve the suspicion that the principle of inclusion and
exclusion—what ought to count as 'rational' and 'natural'—is
determined by the needs of particular institutions, and that
while some institutions are dependent upon minimal standards
of rationality, this dependence can hardly be universalized.

Second, we can agree perhaps that freedom and well-being are
generic necessities, but this says little about these goods. What is
self-evident, or at least very evident, is not necessarily what is
most important. It is an old saw, but a good one, to point out that
agents give up their lives, or in any case are willing to allow their
physical well-being to be severely diminished, for the sake of so-
called higher goods. Goods which are most vivid and pressing
are not necessarily the most desirable. In any case, propositions
about basic goods have nothing immediately to do with morality
until principles of ordering are supplied. To say that life and
freedom are basic goods is to make an unremarkable and, on the
whole, morally uncontroversial claim. Moral questions arise
once the goods are put in relation, according to concrete issues of
means and ends, contexts, and judgements concerning how they
are to be balanced when they conflict. Consensus about basic or
necessary goods is not the same thing as consensus about morality.
The problem of proceeding from consensus about goods is nicely
expressed by Clifford Geertz, who remarked that the norm of
consensus 'leaves law the most powerful where the least needed,
a sprinkler system that turns off when the fire gets too hot'.[36]
Even if we agree that Gewirth's method achieves determinacy
about what we ought to agree to in the way of some necessary
goods—as something more than merely provincial understandings of what agents must want or need—it is still less than clear
whether it achieves it with regard to morality. That one wants to
live and be free, and must remain consistent in recommending
the values to others, bespeaks nothing particular about *how* to
live and be free.

Third, the appeal to rules for debate-stopping would seem to confirm, rather than answer, the charge of virtue ethicists like Pincoffs (to be treated shortly) that such theories confuse legal and moral indices for behaviour. It would be absurd, for example, to reduce judgements about the excellence of performances, say in baseball, to the precepts found in the official rule book. A rule-abiding performance tells one very little about the excellence of the act. Certainly, no one would say that the virtues and dispositions governing baseball performances are meant to serve the claims players can make with regard to the rule book. What Gewirth fails to justify is the drastic reduction of morality to the determination of rules, which themselves are severed from considerations of wider ends, moral dispositions, and the office of practical reason which must make judgements about the manner and mode of actions in variable settings. Gewirth's moves make sense in the context of a certain kind of institution—a pluralistic society that needs above all else to reach guaranteed standards of rule-abidingness—but it is not at all obvious that this is the only, the best, or the apodictically necessary ground for moral judgements as such.

If Gewirth were to limit his main point to the observation that MacIntyre's levels of analysis are inappropriate, or in any case, inefficient, with regard to the structure of modern political and legal institutions, his point would be better taken. After all, it is not implausible that a natural value like freedom of speech can be isolated as a basic good, and find protection in positive law, without having to sift the virtue of speech through MacIntyre's three levels of analysis. How many goods can be isolated in Gewirth's fashion is another issue. Freedom of speech is one that theorists as diverse as Jürgen Habermas and Lon Fuller have emphasized,[37] and it has been given an especially prominent place in American constitutional law.[38]

Limiting Gewirth's argument to this relatively narrow area, we can agree that natural law theory can be (in modern legal institutions) an effort to isolate the minimal moral standards that can be articulated even while prescinding from full-scaled elaborations of which moral qualities (virtues) best befit the development of human agents. If we stipulate that this is the way we should use the term natural law, then we must recognize what natural law theory leaves, and must leave, indeterminate. First, natural law theory, on this definition, cannot account for the emergence or even the desirability of those institutions which make such a theory necessary. Presumably, that account would be drawn from a richer kind of political theory that treats precisely those kinds of historical and sociological variabilities that Gewirth wishes to exclude from a theory of generic goods. Second, the natural law or natural rights theory of generic goods cannot, of itself, account for the detailed patterns of practical reasoning that mediate the generic goods (as first principles) and concrete issues, legal contests, etc. Third, a natural law theory that focuses upon generic goods should be regarded as an all-purpose account of the moral life. To say what kinds of actions are absolutely required if we are to treat each other justly in the civil sphere does not determine how any of us will, in a positive sense, use our freedom beyond those negative requirements.

The characteristically modern, debate-stopping paradigm of natural law includes, as Gewirth correctly notes, three components which all natural law theories include in one way or another: ontological groundedness, claims to universality, and reason. Yet this kind of natural law theory is exceedingly limited, designed as it is to play a very specific function in modern political and legal institutions. Its role is to support elementary claims to moral personhood, and thereupon to constrain in advance certain actions of individuals and communities in terms of rights claims. Again, as Joseph Raz has said, the interest of liberal theorists in the rather abstract right of personhood delivers little of a concrete nature about morality. Usually, it is invoked 'not as a claim for any specific benefit, but as an assertion of status'. 'To say, "I have a right to have my interest taken into account" is like saying "I too am a person".'[39] This is not an unimportant issue, and if one takes the problems endemic to modern liberal societies as the definitive context for moral reflection, it is probably the most important issue.[40] However, the most cursory study of comparative law and morality would indicate that it is not the only paradigm. Not every society, after all, relies upon apodictic arguments to settle the issue of personhood, and a society that does so is apt to be regarded as having become desperately indeterminate in its moral compass.

III

Edmund Pincoffs has contended that 'standard' moral theories—
such as utilitarian, deontological, and contract theories[41]—
'restrict and warp moral reflection by their insistence that moral
considerations are related in some hierarchical order'.[42] They are
one-principle systems which reduce the range of moral considerations to the primary analogate of contract law.[43] The moral
theorist is given the task of reducing ethics to a 'code of minimal
standards of behavior, standards that cannot be ignored without
social disaster'.[44] Hence, a standard theory is a tool that can be
passed from hand to hand, and applied from city to city, for the
purpose of arbitrating quandries and conflicts which arise in the
public sphere. We can imagine the natural law theorist, on
Pincoffs's description, as a cosmopolitan ethicist whose theoretical apparatus is designed to serve the same art as the deontologist, utilitarian, or contract theorist.

Pincoffs admits the 'defensible idea that some moral rules are
socially essential'.[45] 'Indeed, it would be hard to imagine a world
in which we should not make it a principle not to do to others
what we would not want them to do to us.' But it would also be
hard, he says, to 'imagine a world in which the quality of justice
was without relevance'.[46] In the first place, the kinds of quandries
and problems an agent permits himself to deliberate about are
shaped to a considerable extent by the character of the agent.
This is not to say that there are not common necessities and
issues of justice; it is only to say that the various subject-matters
of morality are not merely disclosed through doctrinal analysis,
but also through character. Cruelty to another, Pincoffs notes, is
not just a doctrinal mistake but a flaw in character.[47] In the
second place, all agents are not equally situated, especially with
respect to their moral development. While this does not contradict
the principle of equality, it does say something about the self that
confronts problems with a moral theory in hand. We expect
children to be in a process of moral development before they are
practitioners of any standard theory, and certainly before they
become theorists who iron out public quandries.[48] In the third
place, common or garden variety moral judgements which agents
must continually make more often have to do with 'choice made
of persons' than with the public administration of rules. Whether

or not to enter into a relationship, how deeply it ought to be joined, and expectations about how it ought to persist, require the agent to assess the dispositions and character of other persons.

Pincoffs points out that we have 'a very rich language for the assessments of persons, actions, policies, and practices—a language that is mostly relegated by contemporary theories to the region of "virtue and vice", a region that is then set aside, never to be returned to'.[49] This language consists of what Bernard Williams has called the 'thick concepts' referring to the moral qualities of persons and relationships.[50] For his part, Pincoffs mentions over two hundred different qualities which are commonly predicated of persons, ranging from such qualities as 'tender' and 'honest' to 'waspish' and 'whimsical'.[51] Virtue ethicists make a good point when they insist that the field of moral issues and assessments goes well beyond the favoured turf of what Pincoffs calls 'standard theories', and what we have depicted earlier as a standard form of natural law reasoning. Gewirth's understanding of apodictically grounded precepts of morality is certainly not a very suitable way to articulate or make sense of the myriad of moral judgements we make of ourselves and other persons.

Where does this leave virtue ethics? One could propose that we have to live with a two-track scheme: a moral vocabulary for the administration of the public order, and moral vocabularies which articulate matters of virtue and character. The problem is that neither Gewirth nor Pincoffs is satisfied with such an arrangement. Gewirth, as we saw, wishes to determine the moral virtues on the basis of rights and duties. Pincoffs, for his part, argues that giving virtues equality of place along with moral rules does not mean that theorists like Gewirth merely have to recognize that there are other ways of addressing moral issues than in the language of duties and rights. Matters of virtue and character, he insists, are not luxuries, or issues of supererogation, to be assigned to moral reflection after the scheme of rules is resolved.[52] Whatever distinctions we need to make between rules and virtues, such distinctions cannot displace virtue from the centre of the picture—including our public business of policies. If we pause to consider what and how we actually debate moral issues in the public domain, Pincoffs is correct to resist the idea that the field of morality can be divided into the public part concerning rules and the private part concerning virtue.

Take, for example, the question of how (American) public schools are to convey the ideals of equality and equal respect for persons. These are clearly issues which would all under a natural law type account of constitutional rights to equal protection and due process, as well as administrative regulations prohibiting discrimination on the basis of gender. These Golden Rules being adequately conveyed in the school, should we leave untouched the standards which bespeak judgements about virtue and character—judgements which align qualities like 'tender' and 'vivacious' (to borrow from Pincoffs's master list of qualities) with feminine character, and 'courageous' and 'disciplined' with the male? Without doubt, this would incite disputes which transcend an exclusive focus upon either rules or virtues. For the dispute would concern their interrelation.

We have at least three options. One option is to leave the two areas as loosely related as possible: Rules for the public, perfectionist standards for the private, and some thinly described virtues like toleration for their overlap. Although this might appear, at first glance, to be the solution appropriate to a liberal democracy, it is not apt to win the allegiance of people caught up in such debates. To allow the purported vice of 'sexism' to be reserved exclusively for the private sphere, tamed only by the virtue of tolerance in the public, would subvert the very purpose of minimal public standards. Having the right ideas about rules and the qualities of character require, at least in this area, a more substantial appreciation of how rules and virtues condition one another.

Another option is Gewirth's method of unpacking the virtues from an antecedent table of principles which secure rights. '[M]oral virtues are dispositions to act for the promotion of human rights.' These indeed can suggest *some* virtues, but whether or not traditional or progressive notions of social roles and personal qualities best suit certain abstract notions of equality is a question that can hardly be resolved on the basis of a method that purports to generate apodictically grounded rights claims. If we believe, for example, that uncoerced speech is a basic value of the sort that cannot be gainsaid except on the pain of self-contradiction, it still does not follow that certain qualities of character are so commanded and commended. Truth-telling may be a norm of speech acts, but truth-telling is not the same thing as honesty. One needs to appeal to other sorts of experience and modes of reflection to move from Gewirth's rules to the subject of virtue.

Finally, we could adopt an older natural law type account of human nature that seeks to identify natural human ends, and then keys the discussion of both law and virtue to the achievement of those ends. In the Aristotelian tradition, nature is not exclusively designated by the object of formal causality, but also finality. Nature aims at the best. The older method does not infer either rules or virtues from rights, but rather considers actions in the light of what subserves unified ends. This method presupposes a social and institutional context so unlike our own, not only in what counts as the conditions of warranted assertability about 'nature', but even more importantly in terms of the massive agreements about experience and tradition which frame it, that it will not relieve our disagreements about the interrelation of law and virtue.

Pincoffs rejects the third way of proceeding. He adopts what he terms a 'non-teleological functionalism'.[53] Pincoffs maintains that if we compile a list of virtues and vices we will find that the list is 'lengthy, unordered, and theoretically amorphous'.[54] There is no hierarchy, and no hierarchy is needed. 'I am a functionalist,' he says, 'not a teleologist.' He writes: 'The functionalist perspective is that of the engineer, rather than that of the captain of the ship. Wherever the captain may want to go, the engine and working parts of the ship must operate well if he is to get there. We can say things about the optimum performance of the ship and about what is a necessary condition of optimum performance that presuppose nothing about the courses it is to follow.'[55] Dropping the metaphor, Pincoffs explains that virtues are those qualities which permit a person to work well. We do not need to know 'some supervenient common end' in order to affirm virtues as the conditions which enable their bearer to pursue a good life, whatever that might be.

His position on the relation between rules and virtues in the public domain is not, after all is said and done, very different from Gewirth's. To be sure, Pincoffs rejects any one-to-one matching of rules and virtues, much less an hierarchical order

that interrelates the most important rights with the most important virtues. As we already pointed out, he rightly rejects the
notion that virtues are simply spun out, *more geometrico*, from
rights. Nevertheless, his functionalism requires that, to take his
metaphor of the ship and its crew, we can identify certain rules
and virtues which ought to prevail in a social order regardless of
the specific port of call. Is this a credible idea?

What gives Gewirth's position some force, in contrast to
Pincoffs's functionalism, is that we can imagine how certain
human needs must be met regardless of the particular function of
a social group. Lon Fuller, the dean of American natural lawyers,
once said that we can see that murder is wrong without having to
resolve what the ultimate end of human life consists in.[56] Indeed,
there are generic goods to which we can plausibly tether legal
and moral norms. These do not need to be described in terms of
the conditions of optimal performance. The whole point is that
some natural values can be affirmed without having to supply
reasons about unified ends: life is a generic good of action,
whatever else it might mean to live well. Pincoffs, however, says
that the virtues must be understood in some way other than by a
scheme of minimal public standards. Why is he now describing
the virtues according to generic needs of a social structure?

Pincoffs apparently wishes to correct the ethic of minimal
public standards by arguing that even if we prescind from ends,
we can still see the need for something more than rules. To
extend his metaphor, it is possible perhaps to imagine a crew of
vicious rogues who obey the law, and yet no one who has any
choice in the matter would want to ship out with such a crew. It is
reasonable to want to know something about the personal qualities of the captain and crew. We want a higher-ceilinged minimum than what is provided by rules. This is a good point. But it
does not seem true to say that these virtues and traits of character
can be given any specificity until we know precisely what
Pincoffs claims we do not need to know: namely the particular
ends in view. For example, I can have much lower standards for
what is needed to take the Staten Island ferry to work than if I
were to yacht around the Caribbean on a pleasure cruise. And I
would not be disposed to do either unless I were assured that
there was some plan about where we were going. Gewirth's
understanding of moral rules more easily reaches certain all-

purpose specifics: whether one takes a twenty-minute ferry trip
to work, or a more extended cruise, one can rightly demand not
to be arbitrarily tossed overboard. How much I need to assume
about the disposition of the crew not to throw me overboard is
another matter which might prove in the overall scheme of social
relations more important. But the obvious point is that to elaborate the moral dimension of these expectations about virtue and
character requires much more than Pincoffs's thin functionalism.

IV

We can expect a natural law theory to do three different things,
and we shall conclude by sorting them out, and then ask on what
grounds it makes sense to continue using the rubric 'natural
law'. In the first place, we might conclude that natural law theory
cannot address all areas of conduct, but that it is best suited for
articulating the ground rules of rights claims. In an institutional
setting like American constitutional law, there is always some
point to articulating consensus about natural principles of justice,
and of recalling which goods are necessities which must needs
be respected if there is to be a morally ordered system of liberty.
Gewirth's position, for all its methodological rumbling about
apodicticity, none the less has a readily identifiable function:
from time to time, it is worthwhile to contrast nature and convention in order to pinpoint those moral principles entitled to
govern the juristic and political institutions. In modern institutions, the meaning and function of natural law theory is over-
whelmingly given to the juristic problem. Strong claims are
made about the legal facet, and relatively weak claims are made
about nature. As we have argued, this kind of natural law theory
is not well suited for making all-purpose claims about morality,
or for interrelating public rules and the subject of personal virtue
and moral character.

In the second place, natural law theory might be used, recalling
the Aristotelian tradition, to articulate the natural contexts involved
in the transition from first to second nature. This is less a legal
problem than it is one of moral anthropology and psychology.
Given certain human powers and potentials, which ought to be
developed, and to what ends? Which realizations best suit human
dignity? This way of proceeding differs from the legal model not

just because it eschews minimal public standards as the central point of focus for theorizing about nature, but more especially because it does not so much require a contrast between nature and convention, but rather a contrast within the term 'nature'. Virtues are neither the primitive necessities and givens of nature nor the ends: they are the qualities of persons and actions which disclose both the rough and ready givens (inclinations, needs, or basic goods) and the unified good of the agent. This is, in short, an older teleological conception of nature in the human beings along the lines developed by Aristotle. While this approach distinguishes between nature and convention, the contrast serves not so much the interests of a lawyer as those of the moral psychologist.

In the third place, natural law theory might be used to inter-relate the juristic and the telic, the minimal and the perfectionist, foci. This is not the place to engage the level of detail necessary for examining pre-modern theorists like Aquinas and Hooker, but it is fair to generalize and say that what is particularly distinctive about Aquinas' understanding of natural law is that it was neither exclusively juristic nor just a tag for discussing natural order in human powers. Nature and law are analogous terms in his system, encompassing matters of moral precepts, virtues, ends, custom, human legislation, and not the least, the relation between philosophical and theological conceptions of the good in human actions. The first discussion of the moral law of nature in the *Summa Theologiae* concerns the question of whether angels are naturally required by a moral precept as well as by divine positive law to love God more than themselves—a subject that hardly qualifies for apodictically grounded precepts governing law in the civil state.[57] Enquiries of this sort, which stress the analogous meanings of natural law, are not part of the modern repertoire of natural law theorists. For as we have said, modern theories are not given to articulating a way of life, or to investigating the connections between various levels of moral knowledge. Our institutions not only embody, but require, a style of theorizing much more like Gewirth's, in which a natural law of rights traces out the bare consensus needed for an *ordo juris*.

Our analysis is not an argument for a recovery of an older system that interrelates rules and virtues. If, however, one were to reconsider a system like that of Aquinas, it would be essential to weigh the purpose of a richer natural law vocabulary, and the kinds of institutions presupposed by those who are interested in interrelating rules and virtues. It would be a community that regards human perfection as a central theme of moral enquiry. Any effort, therefore, to enter the breech of the contemporary debates with theoretical tools crafted to serve perfectionist discourse, overlooks the most salient point of the contemporary debate about a natural law of rules and rights and an ethic of virtue: namely, that our political and legal institutions appear to require a two-track language of public rules and private excellences. Without institutions which require us to develop theories which interrelate the various possible meanings of nature and law, rules and virtues, the term 'natural law' is consigned, for better or worse, to something like what Gewirth propounds. On the whole, it is worse, for the reasons outlined in our foregoing discussion. Here, then, I shall summarize.

A natural law of rights claims, designed to protect a few basic goods regardless of our experience and conceptions of ends, personal moral qualities, and even institutional exigencies, perhaps achieves determinacy about moral rules, but at a terrible cost. On the one hand, it is bound to distort the other areas of moral concern, including issues of virtue and character. Gewirth, we saw, could not restrain himself from applying the natural law rules to the virtues, and understandably so—for rules apply to actions, and actions involve a wide array of ends as well as multiple levels of what it means to be an agent. In other words, natural law theory cannot just determine rules, but must also treat the range of actions which can be rendered rule-abiding. It is not realistic to think that a minimalist natural law theory can be constrained in principle to its minimal point of departure.

On the other hand, a Gewirth-type model of natural law invites virtue ethicists not merely to contrast the moral domain of personal qualities with the moral domain of rules, but to define the interest in virtues as the antipode to rules. Virtue theory, then, is bound to be theory devoted to something less than what is to be accredited natural, universal, and rational in the sense of standards of reasoning appropriate to public institutions. As we saw, Pincoffs, for all his criticism of the reduction of morality to rules, finally describes the virtues in generic terms not unlike Gewirth's. Virtues, after all, should not be mere matters of idiosyncratic preferences, nor qualities which have value only by dint of this or that set of institutional ends. Thus we find Pincoffs recommending generic virtues, which appear to be only a dimmer mirror image of Gewirth's rules.

We can be rightly sceptical about the capacity of modern 'natural law' theories to integrate and explicate the moral interests of those who conceive of the moral life as something more than rights claims. If there exists a law of nature, it presumably exists independent of our theories about it. But our theories about it have so drastically restricted the meaning of 'nature' in human actions to a political epistemology of consensus about basic good or needs, that discourse about the role of the virtues, as completions rather than mere recognitions of needs, will have to find a language other than that of modern natural law theory. In this essay we have conceded that there is some point to the narrow legal and political purposes of modern natural law theories. In a pluralistic society, it does seem convenient to appeal to goods or needs which are not matters of mere individual preference, and which can be described without reference to an end or ends which complete them. None the less, we should be suspicious of natural law theories which accomplish this task at the price of either excluding the virtues or including them in a reductive way.

NOTES

© Russell Hittinger 1992. I should like to thank Stanley Hauerwas and Jeffrey Stout, who read earlier drafts of this chapter. I also thank Victor Preller, with whom I have enjoyed a continuing conversation about the subject of this essay. Finally, a note of gratitude to the Earhart Foundation for their generous assistance during the time the essay was prepared.

1. Aristotle, *Nicomachean Ethics*, 2. 2. 1103^{a}25.
2. For Aquinas' discussion of the natural inclinations as the *seminalia* of the virtues, see *Summa Theologiae*, Ia IIae, q. 27, a. 3, ad 4; q. 63, a. 1. For his analogy between law and virtue—*principia juris communis* and *seminalia virtutum*—see *S.Th.* Ia IIae, q. 51, a. 1. The

discussion of the first precepts of the natural law is at *S.Th.* Ia IIae, q. 94, a. 2.

3. It is not often remarked that Aquinas characterized his own discussion of law as a treatment of the 'extrinsic principles' of human acts; the account of human powers and habits represents the 'intrinsic principles.' *S.Th.* Ia IIae, prologues to qq. 49, 90. In other words, Aquinas warns that we should read the treatment of the intrinsic principles of the *actus humanus* (qq. 6–67), not the treatise on law (qq. 90–114), as the account of morality. Modern interpreters wrongly assume that the two are equivalent, and hence that an understanding of the principles of natural law is the point of departure for Aquinas' moral theory. It is worth noting that at the outset of *S.Th.* Ia IIae, where he takes up the moral life in detail (the *singularia* in contrast to *sermones* about abstract generalities), Aquinas remarks that the entirety of morality can be reduced (*reducta*) to the subject of virtues.

4. International bodies, like the United Nations, make expansive claims about rights, but these rights are not formulated with the concrete expectation that they will prove justiciable in a court. Similarly, the Catholic magisterium routinely makes pronouncements about both natural rights and virtues, but it is not often remarked that canon law leaves little, if any room, for litigation of such natural law or natural rights claims in a rotal court. In the *Codex Juris Canonici* (1983), we find a canon guaranteeing that 'The Christian faithful can legitimately vindicate and defend rights which they enjoy in the Church before a competent ecclesiastical court in accord with the norm of law' (Canon 221). There is no textual authorization, however, for a litigant to bring a natural rights claim before a rotal court. In fact, there is but one canon that betokens anything resembling what American natural lawyers would recognize as appeals beyond the text: 'Ecclesiastical laws are to be understood in accord with the proper meaning of the words considered in their text and context. If the meaning remains doubtful and obscure, a recourse is to be taken to parallel passages, if such exist, to the purpose and circumstances of the law, and to the mind of the legislator' (Canon 17). This mention of parallel places—*ad locos parallelos*—is a slim basis for any appeal to natural law. At best, it would authorize a natural law jurisprudence of the 'gaps'.

5. See Stanley Hauerwas's criticisms of natural law, in *The Peaceable Kingdom* (Notre Dame, Ind.: University of Notre Dame Press, 1981), 11–12, 55–64. Bernard Williams, *Ethics and the Limits of Philosophy* (Cambridge, Mass.: Harvard University Press, 1985), *passim*.

6. '[I]n the case of Thomas Aquinas, the theory of right reason seems to

me to take precedence over the theory of natural law. Instead of classifying St. Thomas's ethics in terms of natural law, we would do better to call it an orthological ethics.' Vernon Bourke, 'Is Thomas Aquinas a Natural Law Ethicist?', *Monist*, 58 (Jan. 1974), 66.

7. Alasdair MacIntyre, *After Virtue*, 2nd edn. (Notre Dame, Ind.: University of Notre Dame Press, 1984), 196–7.

8. Ibid. 191. Emphasis in original.

9. Ibid. 193–4.

10. Ibid.

11. Ibid.

12. In the Postscript to the 2nd edn. of *After Virtue*, 275, MacIntyre points out that critics have misunderstood him to say that the definition of virtue in terms of practices is adequate, and only needs to be enriched by additional considerations.

13. Ibid. 275. Emphasis in original.

14. Alan Gewirth, 'Rights and Virtues', *Review of Metaphysics*, 38: 4 (June 1985), 752.

15. Ibid. 753–7.

16. Ibid. 755–6.

17. Ibid. 758–9. Emphasis added.

18. Ibid. 760.

19. One of the earliest analysts of the appropriation of Kant for the tradition of natural law theory was Max Weber, who noted the new natural law theorists 'substitute' law for nature, and then claim for the moral objectivity a natural status. *Wirtschaft und Gesellschaft*, translated in part as *Max Weber on Law in Economy and Society*, by Max Rheinstein (Cambridge, Mass.: Harvard University Press, 1954), 313. Earlier in this century, Oliver Wendell Holmes, who was irrepressibly hostile to natural law theory, took it for granted that natural law is what Kantians propose. See his essay 'Natural Law', in *Collected Legal Papers* (New York: Harcourt, Brace, and Howe, 1920), 313. For a recent summary of 'deontological' natural law, see Lloyd Weinreb, *Natural Law and Justice* (Cambridge, Mass.: Harvard University Press, 1987), esp. ch. 4, entitled 'Natural Law Without Nature'.

20. Laurence Tribe, *American Constitutional Law*, 2nd edn. (Mineola, NY: Foundation Press, 1988), 1308–10. D.A.J. Richards, *The Moral Criticism of Law* (Encino, Calif.: Dickenson Pub. Co., 1977), 7–38. Ronald Dworkin, 'Natural Law Revisited', *University of Florida Law Review*, 34 (1982), 165.

21. As Lon Fuller remarked, natural law 'is the method men naturally follow when they are not consciously or unconsciously inhibited by a positivistic philosophy' *The Law in Quest of Itself* (Chicago:

Foundation Press, 1940), 103. And see also John Hart Ely's equation of natural law with non-interpretivism in legal theory, in *Democracy and Distrust: A Theory of Judicial Review* (Cambridge, Mass.: Harvard University Press, 1980), 1. In a recent comparative study of English and American legal systems, natural law is the tag for 'substantive' in contrast to 'formalist' emphases in legal systems. P.S. Atiyah and Robert S. Summers, *Form and Substance in Anglo-American Law* (Oxford: Oxford University Press, 1987), 35.

22. Alan Gewirth, 'Law, Action, and Morality', in *The Georgetown Symposium on Ethics: Essays in Honor of Henry Babcock Veatch*, ed. Rocco Porreco (Lanham: University Press of America, 1984), 73.
23. Ibid. 82–3.
24. Ibid. 73.
25. Ibid. 84–5.
26. Ibid. 85.
27. Ibid. 87.
28. Gewirth, 'Rights and Virtues', 748.
29. The argument is worked out in detail in Gewirth's *Reason and Morality* (Chicago: University of Chicago Press, 1978); restated in his critique of MacIntyre, 'Rights and Virtues', 742–8, and then in his critique of conventional natural law theory, 'Law, Action, and Morality', 86–8.
30. Gewirth, 'Rights and Virtues', 742.
31. Ibid. 743. Emphasis added. On this subject of debate-stopping, I am indebted to the work of Gerald Postema, who emphasizes this theme in connection with Bentham. 'Law, on this model (which, in this respect, represents only a refinement of the basic tendency of positivist legal theory), is a political debate stopper, a technique for either preventing disputes from arising or taking public form at all, or for enforcing and executing the results of political debate carried on in other forms (and, in Bentham's theory, debate carried on at a different time, viz. at the establishment of the code). The aim of law, according to the British legal theory, from Coke to Bentham (and beyond to the present) was, in Hume's words, "to cut off all occasion of discord and contention".' Gerald J. Postema, *Bentham and the Common Law Tradition* (Oxford: Oxford University Press, 1986), 463, quoting David Hume, *A Treatise on Human Nature* (1739 edn.), 502.
32. Gewirth, 'Rights and Virtues', 743.
33. Ibid. 743.
34. See Russell Hittinger, 'Varieties of Minimalist Natural Law', *American Journal of Jurisprudence*, 34 (1989). The minimalist theories in American law are treated in some detail in Hittinger, 'Liberalism and the American Natural Law Tradition', *Wake Forest Law Review*, 25 (1990), 429–99.

35. Joseph Raz, *The Morality of Freedom* (Oxford: Clarendon Press, 1986), 157.

36. Clifford Geertz, *Local Knowledge* (New York: Basic Books, 1983), 217.

37. Lon Fuller wrote: 'If I were asked . . . to discern one central indisputable principle of what may be called substantive natural law—Natural Law with capital letters—I would find it in the injunction: Open up, maintain, and preserve the integrity of the channels of communication by which men convey to one another what they perceive, feel, and desire.' *The Morality of Law*, rev. edn. (New Haven, Conn.: Yale University Press, 1969), 186. Clearly, this represents a rather thin notion of what should comprise the indisputable, the capital-lettered, substance of natural law. Fuller's natural law theory affirmed a 'natural law concerned with procedures' rather than a traditional one of 'substantive ends'. It has family resemblances to Jürgen Habermas's understanding of ideal speech conditions. See 'Towards a Theory of Communicative Action', *Inquiry*, 13 (1970), 372.

38. The *locus classicus* in modern American law is Justice Cardozo's argument that freedom of speech is one of the goods in the original Bill of Rights which ought to be incorporated via the Fourteenth Amendment to the states. Speech, he reasoned, is one of the values which can be said to be 'of the very essence of a scheme of ordered liberty'. *Palko* v. *Connecticut*, 302 U.S. 319, 325 (1937).

39. Raz, *The Morality of Freedom*, 190. Raz's general discussion of anti-perfectionism in these liberal theories is worth consulting.

40. D.A.J. Richards, for example, proposes a Gewirthian-like standard of rationality for the principle of respect: 'Moral principles are those that perfectly rational beings, irrespective of historical or personal age, in a hypothetical position of equal liberty and having all knowledge and reasonable belief except that of their own personal identity, would agree to as the ultimate standards of conduct that are applicable at large. Mutual respect is inherent in the idea of moral principles as standards to which all people would consent, defining the ways in which they, as well as others, should be treated in comparable circumstances.' Richards, *The Moral Criticism of Law*, 45.

41. Edmund Pincoffs, *Quandries and Virtues: Against Reductivism in Ethics* (Lawrence, Kan.: University of Kansas Press, 1986), 37.

42. Ibid. 2.

43. Ibid. 127.

44. Ibid. 31.

45. Ibid.

46. Ibid. 18.

47. Ibid. 65.

48. Ibid. 30.

49. Ibid. 42–3.
50. Williams, *Ethics and the Limits of Philosophy*, 155.
51. Pincoffs, *Quandries and Virtues*, 76–7.
52. Ibid. 105.
53. Ibid. 6.
54. Ibid. 44.
55. Ibid. 6.
56. Fuller, *The Morality of Law*, 11. Fuller conducted a protracted debate with H.L.A. Hart on the subject of natural law. Hart, of course, conceded the idea that there is a 'minimum content of natural law', and that it consists of certain generalizations about the human condition—conditions of vulnerability—which can be recognized without proffering 'grandiose' claims about human ends. H.L.A. Hart, *The Concept of Law* (Oxford: Oxford University Press, 1961), 187–93. Their debate over the intrinsic versus extrinsic value of human goods notwithstanding, Fuller and Hart were more in agreement than disagreement over what natural law theory should produce: namely, a short list of basic goods that positive law must bear in mind if the system of justice is to have any point.
57. *S.Th.* I, q. 60, a. 5.

4

Truth, Natural Law, and Ethical Theory

JEFFREY STOUT

Human beings, being less than perfect in knowledge and virtue, construct imperfect moral codes. The beliefs their codes embody, though imposed by the powerful or accepted by the majority, are all too often untrue. We therefore honour women and men who, in the name of moral truth, have risked their lives in disobedience. Unfortunately, much of what they say in their own defence is hard to believe.

Antigone, in the Sophoclean tragedy that bears her name, defended her defiance of the mortal Creon by invoking the 'unwritten and unshakable' laws of the gods. Speaking of the decree that her brother be left unburied, she said: 'It wasn't Zeus, not in the least, who made this proclamation—not to me. Nor did that Justice, dwelling with the gods beneath the earth, ordain such laws for men.'[1] Thomas Jefferson, declaring independence from British tyranny, appealed to the 'laws of nature and of nature's God'. The God in question was Deism's. The laws, which he held to be self-evident, were largely Locke's. Martin Luther King, Jr., writing as a Baptist preacher from a gaol in Birmingham, Alabama, claimed that an 'unjust law is no law at all' and defined an unjust law as 'a human law that is not rooted in eternal and natural law'. His authorities for this doctrine were Augustine and Aquinas, but the content of the moral law he envisioned derived from the personalism he learned while earning his doctorate at the Boston University School of Theology: 'Any law that uplifts human personality is just. Any law that degrades human personality is unjust.'[2]

The theologies of Antigone, Jefferson, and King could hardly be further apart: pagan polytheism, Enlightenment Deism, and trinitarian Christianity. When such people claim that there is a law higher and better than the artificial constructions of human society, they differ drastically over the source and substance of that law. They cannot all be right, and they might all be wrong. Is

there any point in speaking of such a law once the dubious
metaphysical trappings are stripped away? Is the idea of a higher
law worth explicating and preserving? Is it wise to construct an
ethical theory around it, as a long succession of natural law
theorists have done?

Do not expect definitive answers to these questions from this
chapter. Expect something more modest—a collection of doubts
that keep me from becoming a theorist of natural law, doubts that
true believers might wish to contemplate or address. I will begin
by examining a few explications of the concept of a higher law
and assessing their metaphysical costs. I have reservations about
all of them except the least costly, which treats the higher law as
an imaginative projection, but readers need not share these
reservations to share my interest in determining what the costs
are. I will then offer two sets of reasons for suspecting that
natural law theory, as commonly understood, may not be a good
thing to pursue. The first set has to do with the quest for system,
the second with the doctrine of realism as natural lawyers have
typically construed it.

Aquinas' conception of higher law can serve as a point of
comparison. He held that promulgation is essential to law, that
there is (literally) no such thing as a law not promulgated *by*
someone.[3] This implies that a higher law, if there is one, has a
promulgator as its source. That promulgator cannot be merely
human—not if the law in question is higher and better than all
codes promulgated by the likes of us. The promulgator is God,
the law he promulgates eternal.[4] The natural law, which participates in the eternal law, is something that can be known by
human beings naturally.[5] The higher law, in both of these
senses, is implicated in a beautiful but complicated metaphysical
scheme. Assume a biblical divine promulgator, plus various bits
of metaphysics that Aquinas borrowed from Greek and Latin
writers, and you can have the Thomistic higher law; otherwise,
not.

Thomism remains one prominent form of natural law theory.
Other forms of natural law theory influential in the modern
period but still dependent on the idea of a divine lawgiver
include those of John Calvin, Thomas Hooker, John Locke, and
Samuel Pufendorf. Yet it is easy to see why some modern
theorists have found the metaphysical costs of this idea exorbit-

ant. Ours is a context of religious diversity, marked at some times by religious warfare and at others by prudent avoidance of religious controversy. In a setting like this, where rational argument over theological questions has long since broken down, an ethical theory will have limited appeal and utility if it argues from theological premises. How, then, can one make sense of a higher law, if not by defining it in reference to a divine promulgator? In either of two ways: by finding a surrogate for God as promulgator of the higher law or by detaching the concept of law from that of promulgation.

The first way is to grant that promulgation is essential to law and then set out in search of a suitably defined promulgator. The trouble is that the promulgator must possess an authority capable of overriding any particular legal or moral code devised by human beings—otherwise the law it promulgates will not be a higher law in the relevant sense. But it is not immediately clear how any promulgator can possess such authority without being defined theologically, without being divine. Enlightenment philosophers made several attempts to resolve the paradox by raising Reason to the status of quasi-divinity. The most influential of those attempts in our day is Kant's. The higher law, he argued, derives from our own *self*-legislating capacity as rational agents. It is none the less able to override any code that might conflict with it because pure practical reason possesses an authority that no ordinary code, constructed by sensuous human beings, can have. Though ultimately affirmed as divine in the eyes of pure rational faith, this law can be defined for philosophical purposes without help from theological premises.

The result of Kant's work was a marvellous, if rather forced, intellectual achievement, and one whose difficulties are well known. While he was indebted to a heritage of natural law ideas, it would be misleading to describe him as a natural law theorist. Kant departed from natural law tradition by locating the authority of the higher law in an autonomous human capacity, not in an objective natural order. The doctrine of the *ordo quem ratio non facit* goes by the boards. According to Kant, we do not discover the higher law, we give it to ourselves.[6]

Something like the doctrine of the *ordo quem ratio non facit* does survive in modernity, however, and not only in Catholic thought. It is, for example, a major theme in Cambridge Platonism, Deism, and the Scottish Enlightenment.[7] The order of nature, though it may have been created by a divine being, is said to be governed by laws that human beings can discover through rational enquiry unaided by revelation or theological assumptions. In its fully secularized form, this idea involves jettisoning the assumption that promulgation is essential to law. The laws of nature, whether promulgated by someone or not, are to be defined simply as the deep structure of the natural order that reason aims to discover. If they are ultimately to be construed as the outcome of a divinity's creative work, that will have to emerge as the conclusion of an argument. It cannot be assumed in advance.

In early modern Europe the reasons for disconnecting laws of nature from divine decrees had as much to do with natural philosophy as with moral philosophy. The relevant developments in natural philosophy are summarized by Bas C. van Fraassen in a passage worth quoting at length:

The *Drang nach Autonomie* of physics, even as developed by such theological thinkers as Descartes, Newton, and Leibniz, needed an intermediate link between God's decree and nature. Aquinas had needed such a link to explain proximate causation, and found it in the Aristotelian substantial form (individual natures). For the seventeenth century another link was needed, one that could impose a global constraint on the world process [and thus integrate physics and astronomy]. In general terms this link was provided by the idea that nature has its inner necessities, which are not mere facts, but constrain all mere facts into a unified whole. The theological analogy and dying metaphor of law provided the language in which the idea could be couched.

This distinction between laws and mere facts suited philosophical reflection on science especially well, because science had rediscovered the axiomatic ideal of theoretical form. All science was to be developed *more geometrico*, with each proposition about fleeting or replicable circumstances to be deduced as an instance of basic principles.[8]

The new scientific concept of a law of nature was connected with the concepts of axiom and global constraint, necessity and universality. The axiomatic ideal gave laws of nature a life of their own, independent of theology. The same ideal holds out hope for a conception of higher law suited to a secular moral philosophy. I want to construct such a conception, keeping metaphysical assumptions to a minimum, and then to determine what additional assumptions would be needed to make it serve the purposes of a natural law theory of ethics.

First consider some explications of the scientific concept, then some ethical analogues. By the time we reach the nineteenth century, laws of nature have shed the theological shadow they had even one or two centuries earlier. John Stuart Mill's *System of Logic* identified laws of nature with the 'fewest and simplest assumptions, which being granted, the whole existing order of nature would result'.[9] In our century F.P. Ramsey once defined scientific laws as 'consequences of those propositions which we should take as axioms if we knew everything and organized it as simply as possible in a deductive system'.[10] Notice how these definitions avoid the reference to actual divine decree by going counterfactual. The laws of nature are that from which the whole existing order of nature *would* result, if creation proceeded according to the fewest and simplest axioms. The laws of nature are what you *would* know, if you were omniscient and if you organized your empirical knowledge in accordance with the axiomatic ideal.

The most recent descendant of the definitions offered by Mill and Ramsey is the one David Lewis put forward in 1973. I will use it as a paradigmatic account of lawhood because I share the view, recently defended by van Fraassen, that it is the least metaphysical and most promising definition of lawhood currently under discussion in the philosophy of science.[11] It does not take a counterfactual form, and it sets out to resolve some problems left unresolved by Mill and Ramsey. Lewis writes:

Whatever we may or may not ever come to know, there exist (as abstract objects) innumerable true deductive systems: deductively closed, axiomatizable sets of true sentences. Of these true deductive systems, some can be axiomatized more *simply* than others. Also, some of them have more *strength*, or *information content*, than others. The virtues of simplicity and strength tend to conflict. Simplicity without strength can be had from pure logic, strength without simplicity from (the deductive closure of) an almanac. Some deductive systems, of course, are neither simple nor strong. What we value in a deductive system is a properly balanced combination of simplicity and strength—as much of both as truth and our way of balancing will permit.[12]

An ideal deductive system achieves a best possible combination of simplicity and strength—if not the one and only best combination, then one of the combinations tied for first place in the ranking of all such systems. (Mill and Ramsey had not allowed for the possibility that there might not be a uniquely best theory among all the true ones.) The notion of an ideal deductive system allows Lewis to propose this definition: 'a contingent generalization is a *law of nature* if and only if it appears as a theorem (or axiom) in each of the true deductive systems that achieves a best combination of simplicity and strength.'[13]

It is not hard to sketch a conception of lawhood for ethics along the same lines. Grant, for the purposes of argument, that there are moral truths. Assume that all the moral truths can be organized into deductive systems and that these, like Lewis's systems of empirical truths, achieve varying degrees of simplicity and strength. Now we can define *the moral law* as precisely those generalizations appearing as theorems or axioms in each of the best moral systems. *The natural law* would be that part of the moral law we human beings can discover unassisted by divine revelation. Here we seem to have the rudiments of a secularized natural law theory of ethics.

To employ the notions I have just defined, you need not be a theist. If you are a theist, you might wish to add that God is the author of the moral law. You might go on to describe the moral law as promulgated providentially or as an ordinance of divine reason for the common good. But you will still be able to spell out what you mean by the rudimentary concepts of your theory without resorting to theology. Lawhood has been defined not in terms of someone's decree, nor even in terms of what one would decree or know if one were like God, but rather in terms of concepts like truth, deductive system, axiom, strength, and simplicity.

If you did make the theological additions, you would of course be taking the moral law closer to what Aquinas calls the eternal law. Even so, the two notions will not be identical. To see why, consider what is involved when Lewis, in an aside, invites us to imagine a *Concise Encyclopedia of Unified Science*, written according to God's 'standards of truthfulness and our standards of simplicity and strength'.[14] A published version of the moral law would be like Lewis's imaginary *Encyclopedia*. God's standards of truthfulness would prevail in that he, being omniscient, would be in a position to edit out all traces of falsehood. But our standards of simplicity and strength, vague as they are, would also constrain the resulting system. Because these standards tend to conflict, it is likely that our need for reducing complexity to manageable levels will lead to significant sacrifices in strength. In contrast, there seems to be no such concession to human standards in Aquinas' concept of the eternal law.

The Thomistic eternal law satisfies God's standards of truthfulness, but what standards of simplicity and strength does it satisfy? In a word, God's. Aquinas would not presume to know what such standards are, but he does at various points seem to assume that the eternal law is maximally strong. No moral truth falls outside it. It forbids all the sins there could ever be, including those secreted away in the human heart. It encompasses all the moral truths and none of the moral falsehoods. Is the eternal law also maximally simple? Assuming that God is omniscient, there is no need for simplicity in this system. An omniscient being would know every detail of an infinitely long almanac of moral truth. If the eternal law is simpler than that, the simplicity must come without loss of strength. If God prizes simplicity for its own sake, then the eternal law may tentatively be defined in terms of generalizations appearing as axioms or theorems in each of the simplest of the maximally strong deductive systems of moral truth. How simple that might be we have no way of knowing. God only knows, if anybody does.

We have seen that it is possible to define the moral law non-theologically. What do we get if we strip the theology from the Thomistic concept of eternal law? We get something like the tentative definition just given of the eternal law minus the implication that the standards to be satisfied are God's. This should be no problem, provided that the notion of moral truth does not require theological gloss. But the non-theological concept of eternal law remains distinct from the moral law as I have defined it, for the following reason: if a system is the simplest of the strongest systems of its kind, it is not necessarily a system that achieves a best combination of simplicity and strength for systems of that kind.

Suppose a logic professor has given you several deductive systems of moral truths and the assignment of judging some of them ideal in the two senses just distinguished. The method for finding the simplest of the strongest systems is to begin by

isolating the strongest and then to select the simplest of those.
The method for finding a best combination of simplicity and
strength is to begin by isolating systems that are both simple and
strong in high degree and then to select the ones that strike an
ideal balance overall. It is possible but not necessary that the two
methods would yield the same result. Given sufficiently various
systems to pick from, the second method is likely to pick out
systems that are simpler and weaker than the first.

I have now done enough to show how one could go about
eliminating theological connotations from traditional concepts
of higher law, but the value and metaphysical cost of these
secularized versions of the concepts will remain unclear until we
specify their interpretation more fully. I will attend mainly to one
of these concepts, the moral law, on the assumption that it would
be easy to infer conclusions about the other two concepts from
conclusions we reach about this one. How, then, should our
secularized concept of the moral law be interpreted?

It must be admitted at the outset that the moral law is at least as
indeterminate as our standards of strength, simplicity, and balance
are vague.[15] Because those standards are quite vague, the resulting indeterminacy of the moral law may be too great for the
purposes or tastes of some natural lawyers. I do not know how to
reduce it substantially without resorting to drastic metaphysical
remedies, but then I have no theoretical purpose that requires
the moral law to be determinate. Nor am I concerned by the
question of exactly whose standards are being invoked as 'ours'.
If standards of strength, simplicity, and balance (as applied to
moral systems) vary from group to group, I am happy to allow the
meaning of the expression 'moral law' to vary accordingly for
anyone who adopts my definition. The important thing, for my
purposes, is for me to clarify what I mean by it. The standards
relevant to that concern are mine.

My explication refers to systems of moral truths without saying what sort of thing a moral truth is. Lewis's definition of
scientific law refers to axiomatizable sets of true sentences,
presumably sentences of whatever kinds one finds in empirical
science. Sentences in what language? van Fraassen asks. The
question is apt here as well. A system formulated in one language
might be relatively simple as compared with the same system
translated into some other language.[16] It is a familiar fact of life

for translators that a rendering in one language conveys some-what different information (less or more or both) than a render-ing in the language one is translating. This implies that translation can affect a system's strength. And the problem may be even more serious than that, for there are occasions when initial attempts at translating certain sentences go so poorly (when, for example, the loss of information is virtually total) that the trans-lator's work will involve inventing new locutions, thus complic-ating the language in which the translation is cast. It is not clear, therefore, how we could know which systems of truths possess a best combination of strength and simplicity unless we first settle on a language in which the competition among systems will be run. Selection of a language for the competition seems bound to determine (or bias) the result.

Lewis responds to these difficulties by requiring that the competition among empirical systems be run in a 'correct' lan-guage, by which he means a language the basic predicates of which have as their extensions only 'natural classes'. Natural classes are marked by 'real', as opposed to 'arbitrary', distinc-tions.[17] Suddenly, Lewis's account takes a sharp turn into a patch of fog. Thomists will find this talk of natural classes and real distinctions familiar and comforting, for these are two of the metaphysical weapons Thomists have long wielded in the battle with nominalists. A correct moral language, by Thomistic lights, would be one in which the basic ethical expressions correspond to the *real* moral species. Anyone suspicious of such talk is bound to demur. It is clear how to expand on such talk theologic-ally: the real moral species will be the ones given unique meta-physical status by the Creator; all others will be the result of arbitrary human classifications. If, however, you delete the refer-ence to the Creator, it becomes unclear how the line between real and arbitrary is to be drawn. It is still less clear why a secular philosopher would want to make ethics depend on the resolution of such a murky question.

What happens to my explication of the moral law if we do not restrict the competition among moral systems to those couched in a metaphysically designated 'correct' language? It quickly becomes evident that the competition among moral systems will turn on the question of which moral language to employ.[18] When that question remains open instead of being closed off by metaphysical stipulation, it becomes central. To judge a moral system by the standards of properly balanced strength and simplicity is to judge a set of sentences *in a given language*. The conceptual resources of that language will determine the strength and simplicity of which the system in question is capable. The competition is not between sets of language-independent propositions.[19] A crucial aspect of the competition involves the issue of conceptual adequacy or fecundity.

I need to be explicit about what this metaphysically austere interpretation of the moral law entails—namely, that the moral law is an indeterminate ideal projected by an active philosophical imagination. There is nothing wrong with having an active imagination, unless its projections are mistaken for metaphysical findings.

What do you need to imagine to speak of the moral law in my sense? First, you need to imagine the possibility of the various conceptual improvements that could be made in the ways we think and speak about moral matters. Second, you need to imagine the possibility of the various sentences that could appear in the resulting language games. I do not mean that you need to be capable of knowing what all these possibilities consist in. There are too many of them for that—infinitely many, in the case of the sentences. And there is no way of knowing the conceptual improvements we could adopt until somebody invents or discovers them. If we knew what any unactualized improvement consisted in, we could instantaneously make it actual by changing our ways. The point of the present exercise is to imagine the full range of possible improvements not yet actualized, while remaining agnostic about the details.

In addition to performing these acts of imagination, you need to accept the standard apparatus of deductive logic and grant that systems of moral sentences can be more or less simple and possess varying degrees of strength. Finally, and most importantly, you must be prepared, as I am, to apply the concept of truth to moral sentences. If you do all of these things, you can make intelligible use of the expression 'moral law' without entering the disputed domains of metaphysics. The improvements you will be projecting above and beyond the already existing moral codes will remain indefinite. Speaking of the moral law in this sense does not commit you to a view of what those improvements would look like. It merely holds out the idea that improvements are possible. It does not assume (nor does it deny) that all the true moral sentences and the ideal systems containing them already exist in some metaphysical realm of abstracta or possibilia, waiting to be known.

Presumably, like their empirical counterparts, the (projected) ideal moral systems would include some sentences cast in vocabularies yet to be invented. So a metaphysically parsimonious philosopher might well hesitate to say that such sentences and the systems constructed from them, as well as the laws defined in terms of them, already exist.[20] But that need not be seen as a problem for the minimal interpretation of the moral law. The whole point of an ideal, one might say, is to suggest a possibility that contrasts favourably with the actual. You can suggest a possibility without taking a stand on the ontology of possibles or committing yourself to propositions as timeless entities.

What good will my minimalist explications do me? They will allow me to use such phrases as 'the moral law' and 'the natural law' in good conscience. I shall hereafter know what I mean when I echo Sophocles, Jefferson, or King and refer to a law higher and better than the codes of my peers. I will know how to mean what I say about that law without meaning too much.

Why preserve these locutions at all? They have long been a rhetorically effective means of emphasizing that the all-too-human codes we confront in society are always likely to include moral falsehoods and conceptual deficiencies. This fact makes room for conscientious objection to such codes. It underscores the need for social criticism. It assures us that a lonely dissenter or critic, taking a stand against the crowd or the powers that be, might be right.

Admittedly, the same point can be made without the concept of a higher law. What matters most in this context is the underlying concept of truth. If truth were a function of what the powerful dictate or what one's peers accept—or even what we, in our humble epistemic condition, are justified in believing—then we would have less reason to give dissidents a hearing or to entertain the possibility of becoming critics ourselves. But truth cannot be reduced to any of these things. It makes perfect sense to say, for example, that my peers and I are justified in believing a proposition and then to add that the same proposition might not true.

This has been called the cautionary use of 'true'. Reductive analyses of truth tend to neglect or eradicate the concept's cautionary use, the very use that has proven most useful to dissenters and social critics.[21] It is well worth resisting the reductions, thus helping keep the cautionary use of 'true' alive.

On the minimalist reading, the rhetoric of a higher law is little more than an imaginative embellishment of the cautionary use of 'true'. It evokes a picture of what some of our codes would be if they were perfectly true and perfectly systematic. It thereby gives the project of discovering particular imperfections something picturesque to strive for. The picture is less diffuse than the image of an infinitely long list of true moral sentences, and more inspiring than the image of an ideal moral almanac. Since our codes are sometimes expressed systematically in law-like form, the image of a higher law encourages striving for something of the same kind but better.

Better in what respects? Antigone, Jefferson, and King all rejected some feature of their opponents' codes. When they charged Creon, George III, and Bull Conner with acting on the basis of beliefs out of kilter with the higher law, the main point was that those beliefs were false. Sometimes, however, debates arise within the sphere of non-philosophical moral deliberation about how to strike a better balance between simplicity and strength—as when Pharisees, canon lawyers, or casuists have constructed a legalistic code around countless fine distinctions and someone like Jesus, St Francis, or Pascal argues for radical simplification. While overcomplicated codes may arise from honest efforts to engross truth and avoid falsehood, they arouse suspicion not only for making 'false' distinctions but for draining the spirit from life and fostering bad habits of rationalization. Oversimple codes have their share of notable critics too. Reinhold Niebuhr told the pacifists that love is not all you need. Edmund Burke denounced the Jacobins for reducing a rich moral inheritance to a few simple principles of liberty and equality.

Burke's occasional references to a higher law have caused puzzles for his interpreters. How could the same thinker consistently accuse Warren Hastings of violating 'the eternal laws of justice to which we are all subject' while also excoriating natural law theory as a threat to civilization?[22] Some of Burke's interpreters attack him as an inconsistent theorist, others try to defend him by explaining away either the references to a higher law or the abhorrence of theory.[23] The debate is misplaced. It is possible to use the rhetoric of a higher law selectively, in *ad hoc* criticism of an existing code, without putting the notion to work in an ethical or political theory.

Moral thinking, for Burke, is an essentially practical affair, properly guided by experience, detailed knowledge of an evolving way of life, and practical wisdom, not by an ethical theory. The project of theory, of trying to approximate the form and content of the higher law by constructing a deductive system of moral truth, is in Burke's eyes intrinsically biased toward simplicity. It is therefore likely to distort and diminish the complicated moral traditions we use to make sense of ourselves and each other in day-to-day life. Wedded to power, the project of theory can only do violence to such traditions and to the people who depend on them (namely, all of us). As a theist (of sorts), Burke believes that there is a higher law, and he does not hesitate to refer to it when highly certain of a particular moral judgement, especially when criticizing the behaviour of corrupt English imperialists in Ireland and India. He would not presume, however, to capture that law in a theory. The project of theory, according to Burke, is idle when not destructive. It leads not to greater wisdom but into the endless disputes of metaphysical speculation—which he calls, in a characteristically Miltonian allusion, 'the great Serbonian bog . . . where armies whole have sunk'.[24]

There are many natural law theories, some less objectionable than others. But if a natural law *theory* does anything, it surely seeks to make some concept of a higher law central to a *theoretical* project. Whether such a project ought to be undertaken is distinct from the issue of whether the relevant concepts have an intelligible use. Burke used a concept of higher law. He believed that such a law exists and that its author is divine. Yet he wanted no part of the associated ethical theories. The example of Burke shows that you can believe in something, and be willing to use the concepts that refer to it when the time seems right, without holding that theorizing about its structure and content is an essential or desirable activity.

Something resembling Burkean resistance to theory has recently been revived, though not under Burke's name or in association with his politics, by moral philosophers like Bernard Williams and Annette Baier. In the remainder of this chapter, I want to determine what sort of opposition to natural law theory this form of Burkean resistance entails. The question at issue is essentially this: how is it possible to oppose natural law theory without joining it in the Serbonian bog? How can one resist natural law theory on Burkean pragmatic grounds without committing one-self, even if only implicitly, to a competing ethical theory?

Williams defines an ethical theory as 'a theoretical account of what ethical thought and practice are, which account either implies a general test for the correctness of basic ethical beliefs and principles or else implies that there cannot be such a test'.[25] Natural law theories are paradigmatic instances of positive ethical theories in Williams's sense, for they typically propose some set of basic principles (derived from reflection on the nature of the cosmos, of humankind, or of rational agency) as definitive of the moral law. Then they propose a method for applying those principles to cases. One way of opposing such theories is to expose weaknesses in their constructive arguments, conclude from this that there are no rational tests in ethics, and then explain away the apparent evidence to the contrary. Williams argues that there is 'good reason to call that an ethical theory too, a negative one'.[26] His purpose in using the phrase 'ethical theory' in this way 'is to bring out the similarity of positive and negative theories in the claims they implicitly make for philo-sophy'.[27] Williams wants to oppose theories of both sorts.

Williams does, of course, hold reflective views about ethics. He is not denying the desirability of reflection. Neither is he denying that there are sometimes reflective tests for the accept-ability of certain moral beliefs and principles. We do think in ethics, he says, 'in all sorts of ways'. His point is that such tests as there are tend to vary with one's circumstances and that the all-or-nothing game of the theorists is therefore played at the wrong level of generality and ambition. This is the level at which natural law theories typically operate. One need not be committed to a negative ethical theory like moral scepticism, nihilism, or relat-ivism to deem this a bad thing. Even granting that there is a moral law in some significant sense, is it wise to ask philosophers to devise systems that approximate its simplicity and deductive structure? What good and what harm will the resulting approximations lead to? These are questions natural law theorists need to confront.

Williams argues at length against various positive ethical theories. It is not surprising that some of his arguments parallel the arguments negative ethical theorists have directed at the same targets. His most interesting arguments, however, are more nearly Burkean in their view of the potential harm a positive ethical theory can do. The theorist's bias, on this view, is toward the highly general, the systematic, and the simple:

Theory looks characteristically for considerations that are very general . . . because it is trying to systematize and because it wants to represent as many reasons as possible as applications of other reasons. But critical reflection should seek for as much shared understanding as it can find on any issue, and use any ethical material that, in the context of the reflective discussion, makes some sense and commands some loyalty. . . . Theory typically uses the assumption that we probably have too many ethical ideas, some of which may well turn out to be mere prejudices. Our major problem now is actually that we have not too many but too few, and we need to cherish as many as we can.[28]

When Baier says that she wants 'to attack the whole idea of a moral "theory" which systematizes and extends a body of moral judgements', I take her to mean by such a theory 'something which is more philosophical and less committed than moral deliberation, and which is not simply an account of our customs and styles of justification, criticism, protest, revolt, conversion, and resolution . . . '.[29] If that is what she means, then she is not necessarily opposing all attempts to achieve reflective equilibrium between general beliefs and specific judgements in a particular area of moral concern, for some such attempts belong to ordinary moral deliberation. Her point is simply that ethical theorists consider it a professional obligation to impose law-like system on the codes they encounter and that this is not necessarily a good thing.

Most moral education gets along without benefit of 'explicit verbal codes of general rules', and the codes actually in use around us rarely exhibit the systemic structure of a moral theory.

Now if philosophers choose to see implicit rules wherever there is a tradition and a teachable practice, and implicit systems or theories wherever there are general rules, that is their hang-up (and one that a reading of the *Brown Book* might cure). It is a mere Kantian dogma that behind every moral intuition lies a universal rule, behind every set of rules a single stateable principle or systems of principles.[30]

I would add that the mere dogma is not merely Kantian. Many natural law theorists adhere to it as strongly as their Kantian associates do. It would be equally dogmatic, of course, to assume in advance that there is never a point in systematizing moral intuitions of a given kind into a legalistic code. In some passages, Baier comes close to this form of dogmatism.

One area in which the efforts of natural law thinkers have actually done some good, I believe, is in reflecting on the conditions of just warfare, where there is every reason to desire a self-consistent, systematically developed, and widely followed legalistic code. Hugo Grotius, the international lawyer and a major figure in the early modern history of natural law ideas, was also a great systematizer of just-war criteria. His successes in this delimited area are still influential to a degree far exceeding the influence of his ethical theory, taken as a whole. And rightly so. Because Baier does not discuss examples of this kind, her objections to the use of legal imagery in ethics sometimes seem more sweeping than anything I would be willing to accept. The prudent policy is to take each case on its merits, systematizing a region of discourse only where this serves a legitimate practical purpose. If natural lawyers wish to systematize moral discourse as a whole, they ought to reflect on the possibly disproportionate unintended consequences of the attempt.

Baier raises especially telling questions about the unintended consequences of teaching ethical theory. Natural law theorists often portray themselves as defenders of civilization against the evil forces of scepticism, nihilism, and relativism. Yet, as Baier points out, courses on the varieties of ethical theory, from natural law to utilitarianism, are 'a very effective way to produce a moral skeptic'.[31] This would not be so if ethical theory in fact tended to supply the sort of systematic adequacy and metaphysical reassurance it seeks. As Alasdair MacIntyre has often argued, the theorists are quite good at poking holes in one another's theories. The cumulative effect of the poking is not only embarrassing for theorists claiming that there are substantive moral principles evident to the natural light of human reason, it is also demoralizing for students who have been led to believe that the rational legitimacy of moral discourse ultimately depends on the systematic rendering and defence of such principles. No wonder courses in ethical theory tend to produce sceptics, nihilists, and relativists.

Natural law theories typically involve not only an anti-sceptical attempt at systematic representation of the naturally knowable features of the moral law but also a realistic theory of moral truth designed to rebut nihilism and relativism. This is where the contest between positive and negative ethical theories is most directly engaged. A theory of moral truth aims to explain what it is (if anything) for a true moral sentence to be true or what (if anything) makes a moral sentence true. Realistic theories do this by postulating something 'real' or 'natural'—something the existence of which does not depend on human artifice—and then defining truth as a relation of correspondence to that something. Metaphysical interpretations of the moral law or the eternal law are candidates for this explanatory role often favoured by natural lawyers. Can my minimalist explications of higher law be used to support the moral realist's claim that moral truth is a relation of correspondence to the real? No, for my explications have presupposed the notion of moral truth. It would be circular to use such concepts of eternal law to explain moral truth.

On my interpretation, it goes without saying that true moral sentences correspond to the eternal law, for the concept of eternal law merely takes the concept of truth ordinarily applied to moral sentences and combines it with a vague notion of improved vocabularies and a particular ideal for the construction of deductive systems. Such a concept is suitable for some uses in moral discourse, but it can hardly play the explanatory role natural law theorists assign to it in their sort of moral realism. So far as I can see, the only way to obtain a concept fit for that theoretical role is to make one's ethical theory dependent on questionable metaphysical commitments.

Even the most patient reader may well be perplexed at this point in my argument. Several paragraphs back, I sounded suspiciously like a natural law realist, attacking all attempts to reduce moral truth to a function of what the powerful command, what one's peers accept, or what one is justified in believing. My claim was that such reductive analyses of truth neglect or eradicate the cautionary use of 'true'. Natural law realists make the same claim in the hope of holding out for truth as correspondence to something fixed, given, and unchangeable.

Now, however, I am expressing the suspicion that realist explanations of moral truth are not any better. Anti-realists express the same suspicion. Because they share my suspicions about the metaphysical commitments of realistic ethical theory, they either provide something other than correspondence for moral truth to consist in or else abandon the idea that acceptance of a moral sentence involves commitment to its truth. This is where the reductive treatments of truth appear. One kind of anti-realist analyses truth in terms of a watered-down substitute for truth-as-correspondence, and then proposes to go on using the concept in this diluted sense. Moral truth, it might be said, is nothing more than conformity to the implicit social contract or conventions of one's group. The other kind of anti-realist turns the reductive analysis into a rule for eliminating the concept from moral discourse. And yet I have, since the first paragraph of this essay, been employing the concept of moral truth in the undiluted way that realists do—cautionary use and all. In fact, I have stressed that the (undiluted) concept of moral truth is presupposed by my explications of lawhood. My position seems to alternate paradoxically between affirmation and denial of realism.

The paradox dissolves when one distinguishes between accepting the various uses of 'true' as legitimate moves within ordinary moral discourse and accepting a theoretical explanation or definition of moral truth. My claim is that the theoretical explanations take you into the Serbonian bog. This claim leaves me free to view the various uses of 'true' as innocent until proven guilty. The rejection of those uses advocated by one sort of anti-realist is also in the Serbonian bog, for it shares the realist assumption that the legitimacy of those uses depends on the success of the realist's explanation. All of these positions get the relation between ethical theory and ordinary linguistic practice wrong. They assume that the legitimacy of the practice depends on the success of a particular kind of theoretical explanation.

Realism and anti-realism are theories competing to give the best answer to the same question: is moral truth to be treated by the ethical theorist (*a*) as a relation of correspondence to something real (like the non-minimalist's eternal law) that is higher and better than the artificial codes we construct, (*b*) in terms of a watered-down substitute for correspondence-to-the-real (like warranted assertibility or conformity to convention), or (*c*) as an illegitimate notion because there is nothing of the right kind for moral sentences to correspond to? Realists opt for *a*, anti-realists divide between *b* and *c*.[32] I am tempted to answer the question by saying 'none of the above', but this might create the impression that I am preparing the way for yet another theoretical explanation of what makes moral truths true. It is less misleading to say that I reject the question. The problem with the question, and the factor that limits the possible range of answers, is the special sort of explanatory task it implicitly assigns to the 'ethical theorist'.

I am not objecting to what Baier calls descriptive anthropology —'an account of our customs and styles of justification, criticism, protest, revolt, conversion, and resolution'.[33] Such an account, carried out with tools borrowed from philosophers of language like J.L. Austin and Donald Davidson, as well as from the historians and sociologists, might teach us a great deal about how the term 'true' functions in moral discourse. Nor do I object to the idea that such an account might, in some significant sense, be theoretical and explanatory. It can be expected to include, for example, both a semantics and a pragmatics. I have no qualms about theory as such, nor any desire to reify the distinction between description and explanation, as some Wittgensteinians have done. I am objecting, however, to the idea that we need a theory of moral truth in a sense that transcends the result of both descriptive anthropology and ordinary moral deliberation. Descriptive anthropology tells us how the term 'true' functions in moral discourse. Ordinary moral deliberation tells us which moral sentences we have good reason to deem true *in medias res*. I see neither the need for more than this nor the likelihood that trying for more will end outside the Serbonian bog.

We acquire the concept of truth by participating in language games in which the term 'true' is used. Thus we discover very early on that the term has a use implying acceptance, as in the sentence 'What King said about the injustice of segregation is true.' To believe that a given proposition is true is (at least) to accept the proposition. To say that a given proposition is true is to express one's acceptance of it and perhaps to do such other things as endorse, proclaim, or admit it. The term also has more specialized metalinguistic uses, as in the Tarskian formula ' "S" is true if and only if S'.[34] And it has the cautionary use to which I have already referred.

Now suppose that you have mastered all of these uses, in moral contexts and others. Suppose further that you have developed a reflective account of them. You know what pragmatic force the term 'true' adds to this or that speech act, you know how to put the term to full use in Davidsonian semantics, and you know how to distinguish the use of the predicate 'is true' from that of certain other predicates (like 'is justified'). In short, you know how to behave competently with the term and you know everything the various compartments of descriptive anthropology can tell you about its behaviour. It follows that not only have you acquired the concept of truth, you understand it. There is nothing missing that a theory of moral truth would supply. A theorist may desire a concise definition of the concept. But surely this neat result would merely be a summing up of whatever details of linguistic behaviour one's descriptive anthropology has managed to discover. Moreover, experience shows that not all concepts admit of definitions that are both informative and concise. Some terms are too varied in their uses to be readily summarized in a definition. Others are so central to our discursive practices that one would not know how to define them without employing the very concept one is trying to define. 'True' resists definition for both of these reasons. It is therefore best left undefined.

Arthur Fine is one of several philosophers with whom I share this conclusion about truth.[35] A brief discussion of his work in the philosophy of science should help clarify the similar tack I am taking in moral philosophy.[36] His work has critical, diagnostic, and prescriptive components. The critical component is a set of arguments against the leading contemporary versions of realism and anti-realism in the philosophy of science. The diagnostic component traces each of these versions to the same root causes. The prescriptive component advises us how to avoid the difficulties of both realism and anti-realism—namely, by adopting what Fine calls 'the natural ontological attitude'.

As one might expect, the critical component of Fine's work relies heavily on arguments realists and anti-realists have already made against one another. For example, the cumulative effect of his presentation is considerably strengthened by allusions to arguments Larry Laudan and Bas van Fraassen have made against realism. When Fine puts these together with some related arguments of his own, he is able to make a convincing case for the conclusion that the most widely respected recent defences of realism are question-begging. The major claim of those defences is that realism provides the best explanation for the progress of science. So Fine supplements his case with historical commentary on relativity and quantum theory as 'living refutation of the realist's claim'.[37]

When Fine turns to the anti-realists, he first considers those he calls 'truthmongers', who retain truth as a concept central to the scientific enterprise but define it in epistemic terms. The leading contemporary forms of truthmongering, Fine says, can all be understood as portraying 'the truth of a statement P as amounting to the fact that a certain class of subjects would accept P under a certain set of circumstances'.[38] These forms vary according to the constraints they place on the subjects and circumstances in question. The most plausible form takes the subjects to be perfectly rational and the circumstances to be those in which all evidence has finally been uncovered by the procedures of rational enquiry. The result is a definition of truth as ideal rational acceptance. We can think of this theory as starting out from the uses of 'true' that imply acceptance, treating these as paradigmatic, and then trying to enrich the notion of acceptance until the metalinguistic and cautionary uses are accounted for as well. The theory is more plausible than other forms of truthmongering because it seems to accord better with the cautionary use of 'true'.

But even the most plausible form of truthmongering is unsuccessful. Even if all the evidence were in and our perfectly rational agents were weighing it, they would still have choices to make in striking a balance between simplicity and strength in the explanatory systems they devise, and there is no assurance whatsoever that a single system would emerge as *the* best. Lewis was rightly careful, when defining empirical lawhood, to leave open the possibility that there are numerous *true* deductive systems achieving a best combination of simplicity and strength. Think of how many best combinations there might be if the false systems are not ruled out of the competition from the start, as in Lewis's definitional procedure. The truthmonger, who is attempting to define truth, has no means for excluding false deductive systems from the start without begging the question. So it seems clear that ideal rational acceptance is likely to yield far too many truths, some of which will be incompatible with one another.

Fine links this acceptance-oriented form of truthmongering to behaviourism, alludes to the standard charges of reductionism that have been successfully prosecuted against the behaviourists, and then gives a compressed but powerful argument of his own to show that acceptance theories generate an unacceptable endless regress. The only way to stop the regress, it turns out, is to use the concept of truth in a sense at odds with the truthmonger's theory. In a suggestive footnote, Fine proposes a number of other ways to display the gaps between the behaviour of 'true' and that of the favoured conceptions of acceptance.[39] Sensing that he would be beating a dead horse, he goes no further with his criticisms of truthmongering, and turns his attention to the empiricists. Here he aims to undermine empiricist reasons for limiting truth-talk to the observable. His criticisms focus on whether the distinction between the observable and the non-observable can be made out clearly and on whether there is any non-arbitrary reason to see that distinction as carrying the significance empiricists want to ascribe to it.

It should be obvious that the theorists discussed by Fine are answering a multiple-choice question exactly analogous to the one I have located at the centre of ethical theory. His realists can be paired with mine, his truthmongers with my diluters, his empiricists with my disposers of moral truth. Are Fine's critical arguments conclusive? He would be the first to say no. As he puts it, 'One can always dodge the arguments and, where that fails, bite the argumentative bullets.'[40] In controversies of this sort, even especially compelling critical attacks on a position often force its advocates to do nothing more than return to the drawing-board in the hope of devising new and improved armour. If one cannot take precisely the same position while wearing the new armour, the new position will be called sophisticated, the former one naïve. For this reason, Fine switches from the critical to the diagnostic mode. He argues that conflict between realists and anti-realists has a discernible pattern that allows us to explain why theorists suffering defeat in battle tend to retreat only long enough to repair their armour instead of giving up the fight. If each side always finds weapons capable of piercing the opposition's new armour, why not conclude that the positions being defended are ultimately indefensible? Why see each new defeat as temporary and reversible?

The scientific realist, Fine says, sees science as looking out on reality, striving 'to grab hold of significant chunks of its definite structure'. Truth is pictured as the desired relation between certain bits of scientific language and the significant chunks. Believing the truth is conceived as successful grabbing. The trouble comes in trying to make sense of this picture without presupposing the notion of truth being explained. The picture becomes trivial when truth is presupposed, incoherent or mysterious when truth is not presupposed. For any particular version of this picture produced so far, anti-realists have succeeded in exposing the trouble. So the truthmongers, convinced that no such picture can be corrected, have encouraged us to turn around, 'to look back at our own collective selves, and at the interpersonal features that constitute the practice of the truth game'.

We are invited to focus on the mundane roots of truth-talk and its various mundane purposes and procedures. Concepts having to do with acceptance provide a rich setting for all these mundane happenings. If we then take truth just to *be* the right sort of acceptance, we reap a bonus for, when we bring truth down to earth in this way, we obtain insurance against the inherent, metaphysical aspects of realism.[41]

The truthmongers, Fine says, seek security 'by sheltering for awhile in a nest of interpersonal relations. But it would be a mistake to think that we will find truth there.' That is to say, truth cannot be reduced to some feature of that nest, even an idealized feature. The behaviourist arguments for the reduction are not good ones. The truthmongers 'seem to have taken shelter in that corner mainly in reaction to realism'.[42]

The dialectic linking these two positions thus exhibits the following pattern:

Realism reaches out for *more* than can be had. Behaviorism reacts by pulling back to the 'secure' ground of human behavior. In terms of that it tries to impose a limit, short of what realism has been reaching for. The limit imposed by behaviorism, however, is simply *less* than what we require. So realism reacts by positing something more, and then reaches out for it again. What we can learn from this cycle is what makes it run, and how to stop it.[43]

The thing that makes the cycle run is an assumption both sides share—the idea that truth is a 'substantial something', the sort of thing 'for which theories, accounts, or even pictures are appropriate'. The diagnosis follows: realists and truthmongers are both searching for the substantial something that truth is. They share the assumption that it must be a substantial something, something that can be the fitting object of an explanatory theory. To search for such a something is to engage in a metaphysical quest, to enter the Serbonian bog where armies whole have sunk. Next, then, comes the Burkean prescription: shun the quest. Avoid the bog. Stop the cycle. Give up the idea that truth must be a substantial something.

This is not the same prescription the empiricist gives. Fine does not advise that we stop employing the concept of truth in connection with scientific theories or in specifying the aim of scientific enquiry. Empiricism still poses as having reasons of a special theoretical sort for permitting the use of 'true' in some contexts and not in others. But these reasons have not proved any more defensible than the realist metaphysics of the correspondence theorists or the behaviourist metaphysics of the truthmongers. And here too there is a commonality linking the debating partners, for empiricists share with their opponents the desire to explain at a very high level of generality what the scientific enterprise is all about. The methodological strictures that empiricists place on the use of the term 'true' derive from the explanation they favour. Yet from Fine's point of view, it is not clear why science needs an explanation of the kind realists and anti-realists are all trying to give. If the explanation is not needed, and if the attempted explanations have all fared poorly, why bother?[44]

Fine's 'silence is golden' policy does not counsel complete silence in philosophy of science. It leaves plenty of room for what Baier calls descriptive anthropology. As for the concept of truth, 'Its uses, history, logic, and grammar are sufficiently definite to be partially catalogued, at least for a time'. So it is possible to improve one's reflective understanding of the concept. 'But it cannot be "explained" or given an "account of" [in the sense that pretends to transcend descriptive anthropology] without circularity. Nor does it require anything of the sort.'[45] To rest content with descriptive anthology while allowing actual scientific practice to determine which sentences should be counted as true hypotheses is to adopt the natural ontological attitude. I am recommending the same attitude to moral philosophers.

Natural law theory in its traditional form was intertwined with the realist metaphysics of traditional natural philosophy. It sought to provide a kind of correspondence to the real that would explain what makes moral sentences true. The idea seemed plausible so long as natural philosophy conceived of the cosmos in a moralized, teleological fashion. But when the teleological cosmos gave way to the impersonal and infinite universe of modern science, scientific and ethical realism tended to break apart, and ethical theorists predisposed toward realism had to work hard at finding something suitably real and natural for moral sentences to correspond to. In this context, scientific realists often looked upon their ethical counterparts with suspicion, and diverse forms of anti-realism were proposed for ethics. The new plausibility of anti-realism in ethical theory derived from the sense that the world, as currently understood, was able to do something for scientific sentences that it was powerless to do for moral sentences—that is, make them true.

Many theorists decided that something less cosmological, something having to do with *human* nature or practical reason or collective intersubjectivity, would have to be substituted for the traditional correspondence relation if the notion of moral truth was to be retained. Some of the resulting programmes, which I am calling anti-realist, called themselves natural law theories, but they were hardly of the traditional kind. Ethical anti-realists —including both scientific realists and empiricists—began arguing with one another over whether the notion of moral truth should be redefined or dropped altogether. There arose new forms of ethical realism (such as intuitionism, utilitarianism, and value theory) to take up the third side of the triangular debate. Meanwhile, traditional natural law theory became increasingly nostalgic in tone and quixotic in performance. It was treated more and more dismissively by the anti-realist opposition as an exemplification of some fairly obvious fallacy and by its realist successors as a quaint relic from a prescientific age.

It is high time for moral philosophy to rethink its relation to the philosophy of science. If Fine and others like him have correctly diagnosed the debates over truth endemic to the latter, and the familiar philosophical pictures of science deserve rejection, then those pictures can no longer serve as fixed points of comparison and contrast for the analysis of moral discourse. Doubts of the form, 'But what could there be for moral sentences to correspond to?' and 'What would it be to observe that murder is wrong?' lose a significance they once had. If philosophers of science follow Fine's advice and stop asking the question of what sort of relation to a special something makes a given sentence true, the old reasons for wondering what on earth (or in heaven) could make a *moral* sentence true will collapse. And in their absence, the ordinary language user's disposition to say 'It's true that murder is wrong' will seem perfectly in order—which is to say, neither metaphysically tainted by philosophical realism nor in need of being taken at something other than face value. The natural ontological attitude, says Fine, is to take science and its characteristic uses of 'true' at face value, without the overlay of philosophical interpretation provided by something grander than descriptive anthropology. This attitude promises to break up the triangular debate in which natural law theory participates and to restore moral discourse to respectability. The threat of unfavourable contrasts with science disappears—and along with it the rationale for viewing natural law theory as a chivalrous knight defending the honour of morality against its decadent modern detractors. In fact, the line of demarcation between science and ethics begins to fade away.

Thus Fine says that the natural ontological attitude is 'basically at odds with the temperament that looks for definite boundaries demarcating science from pseudoscience, or that is inclined to award the title "scientific" like a blue ribbon on a prize goat'.[46] When Fine's attitude is applied to ethics, it tends not only to restore one's confidence in moral truth but also to rehabilitate the thought that moral and scientific truth are inseparably intertwined. Why? Not because the teleological cosmos has been reconstituted. One reason is that when we try to refrain from big pictures and instead try to make sense of science in the fine-grained way, it will become impossible to avoid appraising the human purposes, virtues, communities, and social consequences that figure in the stories of scientific endeavours we will need to tell. Another reason is that it once again becomes natural to admit that moral truths depend (though not in the systemic and deductive way natural lawyers have sometimes claimed) on what the world and human beings are in fact like. If it were not true, for example, that members of our species have a tendency to bleed and experience pain when cut, certain acts that are cruel and vicious would not be. If firing nuclear missiles caused no more damage than a large grenade, many sentences belonging to the ethics of war would change truth values. Counterfactuals like these preserve what is worth saving from the natural law doctrine of the *ordo quem ratio non facit*.[47]

In this chapter, I have tried to demonstrate the possibility (and suggest the desirability) of standing back from natural law theory without falling backwards into the arms of another ethical theory. I began by assessing the significance, value, and metaphysical costs of several conceptions of higher law, drawing especially on van Fraassen's extensive sceptical arguments against analogous conceptions in the philosophy of science. I then criticized two distinct undertakings that have gone by the name of natural law theory—one related to the quest for system, the other related to worries over the status of moral truth. I called on Bernard Williams annd Annette Baier for help in criticizing the first and on Arthur Fine for help in criticizing the second.[48]

But I have also tried to distinguish suspicions about the theoretical projects of natural lawyers from the doubt that relatively unphilosophical references to a higher law, like those found in Burke's speeches, are intelligible and legitimate fixtures of moral discourse. Nothing I have said entails striking the locutions of Sophocles and King from our lexicon. When a great poet or social critic decks out the cautionary use of 'true' in a memorable image and empowers the search for this-worldly betterment, the moral philosopher is wise to leave well enough alone.

NOTES

© Jeffrey Stout 1992. I wish to thank David Bromwich, Robert George, Russell Hittinger, Richard Rorty, and an anonymous referee for commenting on the first draft of this chapter.

1. Translated by Robert Fagles in *Sophocles: The Three Theban Plays* (New York: Penguin Books, 1984), 82.
2. 'Letter from Birmingham City Jail', in *A Testament of Hope: The Essential Writings of Martin Luther King, Jr.*, ed. James Melvin Washington (San Francisco: Harper & Row, 1986), 293.
3. *Summa Theologiae*, Ia IIae, q. 90, a. 4.
4. Ibid., q. 91, a. 1.
5. Ibid., q. 91, a. 2, Ia IIae, q. 90, a. 4.
6. Any attempt to seek moral guidance from the order of nature was bound to fail, from a Kantian point of view, for at least two reasons: first, as a violation of moral autonomy, and second, because of the fact that scientific enquiry into the laws of nature had largely abandoned a teleological conception of nature. If the objective order of nature as we experience it is essentially devoid of meaning and purpose, if science contemplates a world of matter in motion where Aquinas had once contemplated a world of Aristotelian substantial forms, how can there be a law of nature with moral implications?
7. For an account of some of the relevant historical background, see Charles Taylor, *Sources of the Self: The Making of the Modern Identity* (Cambridge, Mass.: Harvard University Press, 1989), chs. 14–16.
8. Bas C. van Fraassen, *Laws and Symmetry* (Oxford: Clarendon Press, 1989), 6–7.
9. Quoted ibid. 40.
10. Quoted in David Lewis, *Counterfactuals* (Cambridge, Mass.: Harvard University Press, 1973), 73. See F.P. Ramsey, *Foundations of Mathematics* (London: Routledge & Kegan Paul, 1931), 242.
11. See *Laws and Symmetry*, ch. 3, for van Fraassen's extensive critical discussion of Lewis on lawhood. As will become clear, van Fraassen does not accept Lewis's account of laws of nature. Nor does he accept any other. He counts Lewis's as the most nearly successful of an ultimately unsuccessful lot. He surveys the best of that lot in chs. 3–5, and argues a strong case against the very idea of laws of nature in ch. 8. An important point emerges along the way: that the idea of laws of nature is now much more important to philosophers than it is to scientists. Of course, if van Fraassen's conclusions are accepted,

it will cease being an important idea to philosophers of science as well. Is this a death knell for the idea of laws of nature in the culture as a whole? Does not the best contemporary epistemological and scientific thinking owe more to Pascalian probability than to the idea of laws of nature?

12. *Counterfactuals*, 73, italics in original.

13. Ibid., italics in original.

14. Ibid. 74. I discuss Lewis's *Encyclopedia* and certain other matters related to the topic of this paper in an essay entitled, 'On Having a Morality in Common', in Gene Outka and John P. Reeder, Jr., eds., *Prospects for a Common Morality* (forthcoming).

15. Cf. van Fraassen, *Laws and Symmetry*, 41–2.

16. Ibid. 42.

17. David Lewis, 'New Work for a Theory of Universals', *Australian Journal of Philosophy*, 61 (1983), 343–77; van Fraassen, *Laws and Symmetry*, 43.

18. For a discussion of the vagaries of the concept of a moral language, see my *Ethics after Babel: The Languages of Morals and Their Discontents* (Boston: Beacon Press, 1988), ch. 3. I should add that for present purposes the distinction between moral and non-moral can be drawn in virtually any way you please. Because of my holistic inclinations in the philosophy of language, I would not want to place too much weight on the distinction or to draw it in terms of the use of particular words that are sometimes thought to be distinctively action-guiding.

19. Lewis identifies propositions with sets of possible worlds and defines sentences as expressible propositions. See *Counterfactuals*, 45–7. I prefer to define propositions as interpreted sentences and to view sentences, like the languages in which they are cast, as human artefacts.

20. I would count Martin Heidegger, Donald Davidson, and Richard Rorty as parsimonious. See especially Rorty's essay, 'Were Newton's Laws True Before Newton?' (forthcoming).

21. I borrow the phrase 'cautionary use' from Richard Rorty, 'Pragmatism, Davidson and Truth', in Ernest LePore, ed., *Truth and Interpretation: Perspectives on the Philosophy of Donald Davidson* (Oxford: Basil Blackwell, 1986), 333–55.

22. The quoted phrases come from Burke's speeches in support of Hastings's impeachment. See *Edmund Burke: Selected Writings and Speeches*, ed. Peter J. Stanlis (Gloucester, Mass.: Peter Smith, 1968), 390, 406. The excoriation of natural law theorizing begins with his early parody, *A Vindication of Natural Society*, and extends throughout Burke's career. Needless to say, Burke was attacking mainly the

most prominent 18th-cent. forms of natural law theory, though I
believe his criticisms have much wider application.

23. For a dismissal of Burke as a shoddy theorist and turncoat, see
Alasdair MacIntyre, *Whose Justice? Which Rationality?* (Notre Dame,
Ind.: University of Notre Dame Press, 1989), 8, 217–19, 229, 353. For
an interpretation that plays down the references to a higher law, see
C.E. Vaughan, *Studies in the History of Political Philosophy*, ii (Man-
chester: Manchester University Press, 1925), ch. 1. For an attempt to
explain away the abhorrence of theory, see Peter Stanlis, *Edmund
Burke and the Natural Law* (Ann Arbor, Mich.: University of Michigan
Press, 1958).

24. The context is as follows: 'These are deep questions, where great
names militate against each other, where reason is perplexed, and
an appeal to authorities only thickens the confusion: for high and
reverend authorities lift their heads on both sides, and there is no
sure footing in the middle. The point is the *great Serbonian bog,
betwixt Damiate and Mount Casius old, where armies whole have sunk.* I
do not intend to be overwhelmed in that bog, though in such
respectable company.' From Burke's 'Speech on Conciliation with
the Colonies', in *Selected Writings and Speeches*, 170, italics in original.
The allusion is to *Paradise Lost*, ii. 592.

25. Bernard Williams, *Ethics and the Limits of Philosophy* (Cambridge,
Mass.: Harvard University Press, 1985), 72.

26. Ibid. 74.

27. Ibid.

28. Ibid. 116–17.

29. Annette Baier, *Postures of the Mind* (Minneapolis: University of
Minnesota Press, 1985), 232.

30. Ibid. 208.

31. Ibid. 234.

32. Most theories advertising themselves under the label 'natural law'
are realist, but some modern varieties influenced by Kantian con-
structivism (called deontological by Lloyd Weinreb and minimalist
by Russell Hittinger) may belong to the first type of anti-realism.

33. Baier, *Postures of the Mind*, 232.

34. Rorty calls the first sort of use the 'endorsing use' and the second the
'disquotational use'. See 'Pragmatism, Davidson, and Truth', 334–5.

35. Donald Davidson and Richard Rorty have also reached conclusions
like mine and Fine's, and I have been influenced by both. Unfortunately, a very confusing debate has arisen over whether Davidson
should be read as a correspondence theorist, a coherence theorist, or
as a 'no-theory' theorist, and he has complicated matters further by
choosing various cryptic self-descriptions. Rorty, while never accused

of being a correspondence theorist, has sometimes identified himself with anti-realist reductions of truth to warranted assertibility or to what would be believed at the end of enquiry. It would be too daunting a task to sort out the relationships between my views and theirs in the remaining pages of this essay. For relevant works by Davidson, see the essays collected in his *Inquiries into Truth and Interpretation* (Oxford: Oxford University Press, 1984). For his claim that we should take the notion of truth as primitive, see 'A Coherence Theory of Truth and Knowledge', in Lepore, ed., *Truth and Interpretation*, 308. For two of Rorty's more careful recent attempts to avoid reductive definitions of truth, see 'Pragmatism, Davidson and Truth', cited above, and 'Is Natural Science a Natural Kind?' in Ernan McMullin, ed., *Construction and Constraint: The Shaping of Scientific Rationality* (Notre Dame, Ind.: University of Notre Dame Press, 1988), 49–74. For my criticisms of Rorty's less careful moments, see *Ethics after Babel*, ch. 11, where I refer to the position I am taking here as modest pragmatism.

36. Arthur Fine, *The Shaky Game: Einstein, Realism and the Quantum Theory* (Chicago: University of Chicago Press, 1986), esp. chs. 7 and 8.
37. Ibid. 122.
38. Ibid. 138.
39. Ibid. 141 n. 4.
40. Ibid.
41. Ibid. 139, italics in original.
42. Ibid., 140. A few sentences later on the same page, Fine identifies the relevant sort of behaviourism with 'the idea that if the working practices of the truth exchange are the practices of acceptance, then acceptance is what truth is *all* about, and *nothing but* acceptance' (my italics). It is important to see that it is the reductionist character of the behaviourism that causes the problem. There is nothing wrong with lavishing one's attention on the working practices or with holding that descriptive anthropology gives us exactly the kind of reflective understanding we need of the concept of truth. The trouble comes when the working practices are thought to be capable of referring only to themselves. As Fine puts it on p. 142, 'To be sure, the antirealist is quite correct in his . . . recommendation to pay attention to how human beings actually operate with the family of truth concepts. Where he goes wrong is in trying to fashion out of these practices a completed concept of truth as a substantial something, one that will then act as a limit for legitimate human aspirations.'
43. Ibid. 141–2, italics in original.

44. Fine makes this point as follows: 'But science is not needy in this way. Its history and current practice constitute a rich and meaningful setting. In that setting questions of goals or aims or purposes occur spontaneously and *locally*. For what purpose is a particular instrument being used, or why use a tungsten filament here rather than a copper one? . . . These sorts of questions have a teleological cast and, most likely, could be given appropriate answers in terms of ends, or goals, or the like. But when we are asked what is the aim of science itself, I think we find ourselves in a quandary . . .' (p. 148, italics in original).

45. Ibid. 149.

46. Ibid.

47. For a discussion of this doctrine from a perspective sympathetic to traditional natural law theory, see Russell Hittinger, 'Varieties of Minimalist Natural Law', *American Journal of Jurisprudence*, 34 (1989). Hittinger and I are putting pressure, from opposite directions, on natural law theorists who would like to get by without making the extensive metaphysical commitments of traditional Thomism. Hittinger would like to persuade natural law theorists to return to something resembling the Thomistic metaphysical scheme, whereas I am recommending trying to get by with as little dependence on metaphysics as possible. But if I understand him correctly, Hittinger shares my conviction that a return to metaphysical claims about the nature of human action and its perfection in the virtues would drastically limit the role one could reasonably expect a natural law theory to play in a pluralistic society. (See Hittinger's essay in the present volume.) He is content to have the theory play a role within a religious community already committed to the metaphysics the theory requires. I do not accept the metaphysics, but I respect the modesty of Hittinger's hopes for his theory.

48. I am not claiming that these authors would approve of what I am doing with their unwitting assistance. Williams would surely oppose much of what I have said in approval of Fine. Williams's doubts about systematicity do not prevent him from offering an ethical theory of the second sort, a theory that plays out a form of ethical anti-realism against a background of scientific realism. See *Ethics and the Limits of Philosophy*, chs. 8 and 9.

PART II
NATURAL LAW AND LEGAL THEORY

5

Natural Law and the Separation of Law and Morals

NEIL MACCORMICK

Some books make a radical impression upon the reader by the boldness and novelty of the theses they state; to write such a book is a rare and difficult achievement. It is scarcely easier, though, and no less rare, to make a radical impression by a careful restatement of an old idea, bringing old themes back to new life by the vigour and vividness with which they are translated into a contemporary idiom. That has been the achievement of John Finnis's *Natural Law and Natural Rights*,[1] a book which for British scholars has brought back to life the classical Thomistic/Aristotelian theory of natural law. A theory which more than one generation of thinkers had dismissed as an ancient and exploded fallacy kept alive only as the theological dogmatics of an authoritarian church was rescued from a whole complex of misunderstandings and misrepresentations. At the same time, it was exhibited as a thoroughly challenging account of law, fully capable of standing up to the theories which were regarded as having refuted and superseded it, while taking into account and accepting into its own setting some of the main insights or discoveries of these theories.

I suppose that I ought to have seen all this coming, for John Finnis launched some of his key ideas in postgraduate seminars that a group of us were responsible for presenting in Oxford in the late sixties. Still more should I have foreseen it when, in the early seventies, Finnis made a series of visits to Edinburgh as external examiner in jurisprudence, and in the course of outings for fresh air along the shore at Cramond or up the Braid Hills, he sketched the way his work was shaping. Even then, the penny did not drop for me, and it was only when a typescript arrived in early 1978 from Malawi for comment and advice that I at last grasped what was going on, and what it meant. I have seldom

read a work of philosophy with a greater sense of excitement and
discovery than that which I experienced on a first breathless run
through the pre-first edition of *Natural Law* (as I shall henceforward
abbreviate it). It remains for me an intellectual landmark; one of
those few books which bring about a permanent change in one's
understanding; a shift in one's personal paradigm.

My first task here is to outline what have become for me the
key points in the Finnisian position. Then I shall go on to reflect
upon the implications they have for a view of law 'beyond
positivism and natural law',[2] that is, after we abandon as misleading the false oppositions of view conjured out of the old
caricature of natural law. The key points are these five: (1) first,
what I shall call the thesis of 'natural law and the separation of
law from morals'; (2) secondly, the thesis of 'the necessary moral
aspiration of law-giving', according to which those who exercise
legislative power must at least represent themselves as pursuing
a social common good, however far they fall short of doing so in
reality; (3) thirdly, the 'practical reason' thesis, according to
which the same human capability of applying reason to practical
issues is essentially and similarly involved both in legal activity
and in moral deliberation; (4) fourthly, the thesis of 'the essential
formal features of law'—minimal respect for legality as a part
of the very being of law; (5) finally, the theses about 'the good
and the right', concerning the priority of the good over the right
and the irreducible plurality of human goods. I shall deal with
these in that order, adding a concluding section to summarize
what becomes of the supposedly fundamental opposition of
natural law theory and legal positivism, and how in general I
now view the law and morality debate, given my warm
response to *Natural Law*.

1. NATURAL LAW AND THE SEPARATION OF LAW FROM MORALS

For long, the leading jurisprudential image of natural law theory
presented it as defined by the thesis that unjust laws are necessarily non-laws. This thesis was taken to be coupled with a
theory of the derivability of principles of justice from observation
of nature (whether human nature or the nature of things, or

both), this theory in turn very probably involving an illegitimate derivation of 'ought' from 'is'. In general, there was a suspicion of a failure to draw adequate lines either way as between the morally desirable and the legally obligatory. Further, the relative clarity and knowability of positive law stood in contrast with the much disputed question of the nature and status of moral values and principles. So natural law involved a propensity to make appeal to that which is obscure and disputable from that which is at least capable of being established in a much clearer way by such methods as legislation and judicial precedent.

Positivist theories of law, by contrast, while acknowledging that law and morality have many parallelisms of terminology and of topics for concern, such as duties to refrain from violence, to deal honestly, to respect people's property, and possessions, to keep sexual impulses under proper control, nevertheless hold that law can be explained, analysed, and accounted for in terms independent of any thesis about moral principles or values. This is because in some way or another the validity and the content of law depend upon social practices or usages. The transformation of practice and usage into normative law may indeed require the mediation of some methodological or epistemological principles; but, if so, these are themselves independent of moral judgement. Thus it is clear that positivism as a position in legal theory stands for 'the separation of law and morals', to recur to a famous phrase.[3]

This does not entail that positivists are amoralists, or uncon-cerned about the moral quality of the positive law. On the contrary, many have been ardent reformers or critics of established law, and perhaps the single most influential British law reformer of all time, Jeremy Bentham, was (not by mere coincidence) the intellectual progenitor of legal positivism in its British, indeed anglophone, forms. In fact the positivists' claim is that the mere existence of a law as such is no guarantee whatever of its moral (or other) merits as a law. Nor is it a guarantee that obedience to the law's demands is morally obligatory or even morally permiss-ible. The quality of much law may be such that a good human being should work tirelessly for its reform or abolition, and of some, it may be such as to demand disobedience in the last resort. Law is not due automatic moral respect, but watchful and jealous scrutiny from a moral point of view. Yet none of this

implies doubt or denial that bad law really is law. Its being law is
an issue of social fact, not one of moral value. For some positivists,
indeed, a ground for concern about the practical tendencies of
natural law has been that any equation of the legal with the
moral, any suggestion that whatever is legal really has some
moral ground, may lead to a dilution of this attitude of watchful
and critical jealousy lest the law which exists make demands
which ought not to be made.

Finnis's theory of natural law, however, does not deny the
thesis of the separation of positive law from morality in the form
in which I have just ascribed it to unnamed positivists (if a name
be demanded, let me unblushingly name my own, thereby
evading all risk of the charge that I have invented a view which
nobody has ever held; slim though my expertise may be, there is
one theoretical position as to which it will not brook denial). For
Finnis, the classical doctrine is not that there is a simple and
universal all-or-nothing moral criterion for the validity of every
law in every legal system, transcendentally superadded to whatever may be each system's explicit internal criteria of validity of
law. That 'an unjust law is no longer legal but rather a corruption
of law' is indeed a teaching of St Thomas; but, as Finnis stresses
to powerful effect, it is not a thesis about the validity of law in the
technical sense. Validity in this sense has to do with the observance of proper procedures by persons having appropriate competence. Of course there may be legislation properly enacted by
competent authorities which falls far short of or cuts against the
demands of justice. The validity of the relevant statutory norms
as members of the given system of law is not as such put in doubt
by their injustice. The legal duties they impose, or the legal rights
they grant, do not stop being genuinely legal duties or legal
rights in virtue of the moral wrongfulness of their imposition or
conferment. They are, however, defective or substandard or
corrupt instances of that which they genuinely are—laws, legal
duties, legal rights.

This corruption or defectiveness does indeed weaken, and in
grave cases simply negates, any moral case for obedience (to laws
or duties) or respect (for rights). In being a defective law, an
unjust enactment is, in a practical moral perspective, at best
defectively obligatory, whether or not in the perspective of legal
analysis it is a valid imposition of legal obligation. The UK

Parliament has recently enacted legislation, initially for Scotland alone, subsequently (and with effect a year later) for England and Wales also, which impose a new form of local taxation, replacing the old system of 'rates' (which were a form of property tax upon immoveable property based on the notional rental value of the property). The new tax, the 'Community Charge', imposes a flat rate charge at an amount determined by the local authority upon every adult resident of each local authority area regardless of the income or wealth of the payer, save in so far as a reduced charge is exigible from certain categories of particularly poor persons. If in its whole context this is (as I for one think it) a plain case of a seriously unjust enactment, the Finnisian account must be that any moral duty to pay is at best an attenuated one, notwithstanding that the enactments in question are unimpeachably valid as a matter of law, and that the content of the Acts includes centrally a legal duty to pay the statutorily prescribed charge. But the positivistic theory I have in view yields just the same conclusion —the law is a valid law, but if the duties it imposes are duties in violation of the demands of justice, it will follow that the moral issue whether or not to comply is prima facie an open one.

Up to this point in the argument, there is then no serious difference between the 'positivist' and the proponent of 'natural law', despite all the generations of controversy directed to this very point of the 'existence' of the unjust law 'as such'. Some natural lawyers may flatly deny the existence of an unjust law, but by no means all do; and Finnis has put it beyond denial that the mainstream of the natural law tradition (now flowing bounteously through his own books) affirms the possible existence of such laws, while denying or downgrading their morally compelling quality and insisting on their essential defectiveness as law. On the other hand, while there may be some positivists who will deem the unjust law as fully obligatory as any other, nevertheless the mainstream, at least in the English-speaking world, unequivocally asserts the lack of moral obligation of the unjust law.[4] Indeed, it can be claimed that the positivistic attitude actually facilitates a sharpened awareness of the always present potential conflict of the legal and the moral.

So what was all the fuss about then? Not entirely nothing—for at the very least, the positivists have highlighted a boundary for natural law theory, setting up useful signposts and perimeter fences against the risk of overstated versions of jusnaturalism which slip fallaciously from the idea of corrupted or defective law to that of invalid law. Moreover, the positivistic programme of analytical enquiry into the conceptual structure of legal thought and the presuppositions of legal validity, the concepts of legal sources, and all the rest of it has borne good fruit, such indeed that (as Finnis again shows, equally by example and by precept) modern work in the natural law tradition can be considerably enriched by drawing on the resources of analytical positivism. In so far as both schools of thought warn us that from the moral point of view bad laws are only weakly obligatory, and in extreme cases entirely lacking in obligatory quality, and urge us to be vigilant about the injustice that may be done in the name and forms of law, their united voice is the more impressive for the dividedness of their theoretical starting-points.

Still, the fact that a natural lawyer can share in the affirmation of positivism's main point (namely, the conceptual independence of legal validity from moral value or moral merit), does not eliminate difference, and from that difference those attached to the positivist tradition ought to learn much. For there can be other essential connections between the legal and the moral apart from those which positivism has set out to deny; and these very connections may be built into a sound understanding of just those social sources from which positivists quite correctly see positive law as deriving. This warns us how tendentious has been the title of the present section of this chapter, and leads on into its second section.

2. THE ESSENTIAL MORAL ASPIRATION OF LAW-GIVING

As Finnis has argued, most social institutions and practices are intelligible only in the light of some point, some value, some specially appropriate excellence we ascribe to them. Books are not simply numerous sheets of printed paper encased between coloured covers, education is not simply whatever imparting of facts goes on in places called schools or colleges, music not any human contrivance of sequenced sounds, and so on. In all these cases, an explanation of what counts as a book, as education, as a piece of music, depends on explicit or implicit adoption of a view (however controversial) as to what would count as good or sound or focal examples of the genus under consideration. A view about this depends on one's explicit or implicit sense of what values should be realized in this form, and this implies the holding of some view about the kind of general good(s) the practice or institution is supposed to serve. In the light of focal or paradigm cases, other weaker or more problematic cases may be brought in by closer or more remote analogy, the relevance of analogies being at least partly conditional on what one takes to be the values or excellences proper to the best examples of the genus or genre. Another way of putting this might be to say that all such concepts belong in Ronald Dworkin's class of 'Interpretive Concepts', or have the 'purposive' character ascribed by L.L. Fuller to all distinctively human institutions. In their broad thrust, Finnis's, Dworkin's, and Fuller's arguments on this point do not seem to me to be open to dispute.

All this helps us to understand the possibility of framing criteria for judging what counts as belonging to a relevant class. Can a pile of bricks, or a splosh of colour on canvas, or a cube of crushed cars be seriously considered as works of art—sculpture or painting? Criteria are called for, but they cannot be value-free. What is at issue is whether the objects in question relate at all to relevant values. What is necessary is not to go straight to one's own value judgements. What is necessary is rather to consider what intentions we can impute to the maker or collocator of the object—do they include an intention to appeal significantly to the aesthetic sense of viewers of the object? Is the object itself closely or remotely analogous to others which we regard as plainly and indisputably objects produced with that intention, and successful in light of it? Given affirmative answers to these questions, we can accept the objects as paintings or sculptures, even if, having passed our own value judgement, we regard them as hopeless failures in these categories (after all, they as failures may yet be more interesting than other clearer cases of art which are no more than painstaking but merely derivative work, lacking in inspiration or originality).

Different again is our response to what we deem essentially fraudulent presentations, where the 'artist' indeed purports to have relevant intentions, but we for our part judge the artistic posturing to be mere pretence, aimed at tricking the gullible public. Even the fraudulent case, however, is one which is intelligible only by reference to that which it pretends to be. Always, there is an implicit 'claim to correctness', a pretension that one is seriously bent upon realizing relevant values, when one purports to be, or is, engaged upon any socially or humanly meaningful performance.[5]

The same applies to law. It is of course not a defining feature of law, nor a condition of legal validity, that the provisions of statutes or the holdings of case-law be actually just or have some actual tendency to secure or promote some public (social) good or benefit (what Finnis refers to as the 'common good'). Yet as both Robert Alexy and I have pointed out, there would be a pragmatic self-contradiction involved if a legislature enacted a Bill expressly purporting to be for the implementation of unjust discrimination.[6] It is not accidental that we have Acts called 'Administration of Justice' Acts, but no 'Administration of Injustice' Acts. This is not to say that none of the legislation we have administers injustice; nor is it to say that legislators must sincerely believe in its justice, its expediency, or its 'correctness' in any other dimension (maybe even some of those who voted for the Community Charge legislation had doubts as to its justice, or its expediency, or both); it is merely to say that, however things may stand on all these points, the idea of legislation passed without even a pretension to correctness is a kind of absurdity. When the Emperor Caligula threatened to make his horse a consul, this was a way of humiliating the Senate by reminding them that they would have to treat the purported 'nomination' and 'election' as formally correct, even though no one could possibly believe in this pretended correctness—an extreme version of the tale of the emperor's new clothes. If there were not an implicit absurdity, there would not be the humiliation.

A related point, which I have made more extensively elsewhere,[7] concerns the notion of punishment necessarily invoked by criminal legislation. On any theory of punishment which takes due account of the ineluctably expressive and symbolic aspect of punishment (punishment as expressing on behalf of the state an attitude of deep disapprobation toward the conduct criminalized by the law), it cannot but be the case that laws imposing punishment ought by virtue of their very nature to criminalize only such deeds as merit such an expression of such an attitude. Laws which invoke a morally loaded institution like punishment cannot avoid becoming morally loaded themselves. Laws which penalize innocent conduct are thus necessarily perversions of law. For example, to punish people for taking part in something so blameless as interracial marriage is necessarily to stigmatize it as morally impure. That is what is so deeply objectionable about anti-miscegenation laws.

The general conclusion is that laws, like other social institutions, are fully intelligible only by reference to the ends or values they ought to realize, and thus by reference to the intentions that those who participate in making or implementing them must at least purport to have. This does not entail any acceptance of substantive moral criteria as criteria of legal validity, but it does involve acknowledging the moral quality of the relevant ends and values, namely justice and the public good. It is as true of law that justice and the promotion of public good within the constraints of justice are the particular goods that make it intelligible to us as a congeries of institutions and practices as it is true of art that its particular point is the communication of aesthetic experience through creative originality. It is thus the case that laws we judge unjust or detrimental to the public good are on that very account laws that we judge essentially deficient examples of the genus to which they belong, even though we may also judge them to belong validly to that genus.

On the one hand, therefore, we have to acknowledge that there is indeed a necessary connection between law and morality hitherto unnoticed by positivists, albeit perfectly consistent with the other 'separation' on which they have insisted. On the other hand, however, it has to be conceded that the connection in question does not protect us from very much. The problems of the real world do not seem often to arise from people passing legislation which they only pretend to think just, while secretly intending some nefarious purpose. Even less do they revolve around the open and unapologetic espousal by legislators of measures they openly characterize as unjust and inexpedient. They have a great deal more to do with the holding of perverse moral opinions and the legislative implementation of these. That such laws lack the special virtue of law is of no avail where the legislature and its constituency mistakenly and sincerely, but perhaps quite passionately, believe they act well and wisely.

If there are wicked or misguided people who hold power, they will doubtless enact wicked or misguided principles into law. To teach them that legislation ought always to evince essentially moral aspirations will be of no avail, for they will be quite ready to agree and to point out how ardent they are in pursuit of exactly such aspirations. The only way to get rid of their wicked law will be by getting them out of power or by persuading them to change their moral and political convictions. The fact that there are certain moral aspirations which are conceptually intrinsic to law (though not conditions of its validity) could never stop perverted opinions about relevant values being transformed into perverted laws. A stark warning is provided by the fact that some of the leading jurisprudential ideologues of Nazism in Germany were denouncers of positivism, and some even took themselves to be propounding a purified version of natural law doctrine (involving, *inter alia*, such obscenities as assertion of the natural human and moral superiority of the Aryan race and other such nonsense).[8] The mistake they made was not that of thinking morality relevant to law-making; it was that of identifying their hideous views about the healthy sentiments of the people with the demands of justice and morality.

Still, the positivist who denies the conceptual dependency of legal validity upon moral value cannot use the arguments which avail to that end against the altogether different thesis that certain moral aspirations are intrinsic to the very concept of law. All the more so if weight is given to the powerful arguments put by H.L.A. Hart for holding the 'internal point of view' of the members of a group to be necessary for any explanation of what it is for a rule to exist.[9] Those who are committed to an enterprise give it the character it has, and those who wish to understand and to study social phenomena in a more detached, non-committal, 'external' perspective must nevertheless make themselves imaginatively aware of the attitudes which infuse those phenomena in the view of the participants. This is prerequisite to understanding, though not necessarily the whole of it. This hermeneutic[10] approach, however, seems to make the Finnisian conclusion inevitable, vigorously though Hart still defends a different view.[11]

Before one finally acquiesces in the thesis of the necessary moral aspiration of law-giving, one yet has to face a new and rather serious objection. It is one thing to claim that an ideal legislator ought to be committed to justice and the public good in her/his acts of legislation. But it may be the case both that human legislators are not unanimous in their moral opinions, and all the more that the citizens subjected to the law are not completely or at all in agreement with each other or with any of the legislators. In this case, that is, in reality, there is therefore no possibility that in a multi-member legislature all who vote—even all who vote in the majority on any issue—fully agree about the justice or expediency of the legislation they join in enacting. A requirement of perfect unanimity (such as prevailed, I believe, in the ancient Polish Parliament) would practically preclude the passage of any legislation at all. But resort to majority voting and party whips and all the devices which make possible legislation as we know it under representative democracy seems to cut against the very possibility of Alexy's 'claim to correctness' being honestly made by any legislator. Majority votes rest on compromise, and compromise may sit uneasily with the claim that it is justice one is doing.

A classic example is provided by the framing of the Constitution of the United States in 1787. The framers found it necessary to compromise on the issue of slavery, and subsequently judges who themselves held slavery to be abhorrent and unjust nevertheless held also that the duties of their constitutional station required them to administer faithfully the laws regarding slavery.[12] Without a compromise on slavery, the Union would not have been formed. But what the compromise did was precisely to compromise the commitment to justice of those who were personally opposed to slavery as a grave injustice. On any reasonably rigorous test of the 'claim to correctness' as a claim about a belief in the justice of what one does, they would have resoundingly failed it. Yet if the United States of America have not got a full-blown Constitution, who has? Is the answer that they only got one *really* in 1865, or in 1954, but perhaps had none at all or, more plausibly, had only a corrupt or substandard one till then (as indeed anti-slavery Americans maintained in the times before the War of 1861–5)?[13]

Before we go too far down that line of argument, we had better recall that (whatever judgement we in the end pass about the compromises of 1787) a spirit of compromise is far from undesirable in any system of government by consent. Human beings, legislators included, may hold their convictions about justice and the public good with passionate conviction, the passionate conviction which can be the enemy of compromise and tolerance. In extreme cases, this can be admirable; and depth or strength of conviction is always impressive. It can only be for the worse when the best lack all conviction and the worst are full of passionate intensity. But whoever is afflicted with passionate intensity, he or she is apt to have no truck with compromise, and even to have difficulty in summoning up a spirit of real tolerance for opposed views. And what then can become of democracy and constitutional government? Do not these above all require willingness to compromise and to be mutually tolerant, first on the part of the legislators, secondarily (but scarcely less) on the part of the citizen electorate?

Thus a positivist who is willing to be persuaded that the very idea of law has implicit in it a certain aspiration towards certain values, and that serious respect for these values is essential to authenticity in law-making, will do well to demand greater care than the present chapter has so far shown in delineating the relevant values. My students, who in this have a caution I do not exactly share, tell me that such a positivist ought also to be very chary indeed about accepting too readily Finnisian claims about the self-evident quality of basic judgements of value; for a belief in the self-evidence of one's judgements (the same would go for a belief in their divine certification) can also be an enemy of tolerance for those who see matters differently. However that may be as to self-evidence, I do believe (without being able to argue the point adequately here) that one of the historic roots of positivism's appeal has been that by freeing the concept of law from dogmatic attachment to any particular moral philosophy or theory of justice, one creates intellectual and political space for tolerance and democratic pluralism. This may help to explain a fact which many find paradoxical, namely that the generation of thinkers who spent the War of 1939–45 struggling against Nazism and Fascism and against all the time-servers who held that the law ought to be obeyed whatever the law was and whoever had made it to whatever ends and by whatever means, nevertheless stood firmly for positivism, rejecting the pleas of those like Gustav Radbruch who argued in Germany for a return to natural law as the necessary bulwark against the errors and crimes of the Nazi period.

The upshot, anyway, must be to hold that while a regard for some conception of justice and the public good must be involved in anything that we could recognize as law, any acceptable conception of justice and the public good within democratic constitutionalism must include some principle of toleration as a second-order principle of justice, and some element of compromise as an essential element of the public good. Wherever law purports to have some form of constitutionalist-democratic legitimation, these are requirements for the adequacy of that legitimation. That is to say, the issue of the morally obligatory quality of the law's requirements is affected by the conception of justice and the public good held by the legislators, not merely by their acting on some conception of it. Upon this point, it seems to me, a well-known thesis of Philip Soper's calls for significant revision. I have in mind his idea that a ground (perhaps only quite a weak one) of the prima-facie obligatoriness of law arises from the respect due to the attempts made in good faith by governors and legislators to provide for justice and the common good (as they see it) through the legislation they enact. My present argument suggests that essential to the force of this point would be endorsement by governors and legislators of principles of tolerance and compromise.[14]

In fact, it appears that the question of political obligation still has to be handled as a special question depending on particular qualities of particular laws, lawgivers, and constitutional arrangements. That a law is a law does not entail that one has an obligation to comply with it, just because of what it is, nor just because of the sincerity of those who enacted it (sincere Nazis, perhaps?). That laws have always some tendency to promote some kind of social order may involve some weak prima-facie moral obligation since one usually has an obligation to one's neighbours both to keep the peace and to support it. The special character of constitutionalist democracy entails that laws passed with a sincerely held claim to the special conception of correctness here involved do have the character of engaging a quite strong prima-facie obligation of compliance, from a moral point of view. But this is because constitutionalist democracy engages people in mutual moral obligations as obligations of mutual fairness, subject to mutual tolerance within wide limits of tolerance.

However that may be, the possibility of a complex understanding of justice which includes a requirement of tolerance and thus also a willingness to compromise (the good of compromise and mutual tolerance being included in a complex conception of the public good) allows us after all to conclude that the 'claim to correctness' can indeed be satisfied even in the setting of a pluralistic democracy. Compromise and tolerance within certain limits can in fact be a part of rather than the enemy of an acceptable sense of justice, and can make it at least permissible sincerely to assent to legislation which one regards as partly unjust. No claim need be made that this is the only conceivable sense of justice; but so long as it is a genuine one, we are not forced into the paradox of concluding that one necessary feature of law is incompatible with democracy.

3. PRACTICAL REASON

There is, then, a significant, albeit weak, connection of law with morality, on account of the essential moral aspiration of lawgiving. Apart from the analogy of other social practices and institutions drawn in the last section and used to buttress the assertions there made about law, is there any other ground why this should be so? Again, we can draw in similar terms upon the work both of Finnis and of Alexy to pursue this point. For it has to be acknowledged that law and morality do not only share a vocabulary and a set of concerns; the concerns they share are supremely practical concerns for human beings, material to the issue of how we are to live, each for ourself and all together. The common vocabulary of 'ought' and 'must', 'right' and 'wrong', 'duties', 'obligations' and 'rights', is a common judgemental vocabulary concerned to focus upon aspects of situations which call for decision and action, and where the judgement of certain lines of action determines what one can justify doing (even if not what in the end one does). The issue is what to do? What can rightly be done?

These are matters which do and must engage our passions and emotions, our desires, hopes, and fears; they do and must engage our secondary feelings for each other through empathy or sympathy, and through the sympathetic imagination. Without feelings of our own and a capability to feel in some way the feelings of others, we could still perhaps be marvellous calculators or even computers, but we could neither be moral agents nor be human beings. Nor is it only feeling that we evince in our practical concerns; we are also practical reasoners, and reasoning is necessarily more than merely instrumental. Reason is inevitably involved in any attempt to constitute momentary ends into some coherent system or order, enduring through time and availing in common among persons. Reason is involved in the universalization and checking of particular projects, and weighing them in the setting of an aspirationally coherent way of life.[15] There is a real analogy (though no identity) of moral with legal reasoning; above all, both are truly modes of reasoning. Reason in these spheres is intrinsically practical.

What then is the difference between practical reason as manifested in legal practice and practical reason as displayed in the moral life? The answer lies in the elements of publicity, authority, and determinacy special to law. Always the last resort moral judgement is that of an individual moral agent judging for her or himself after reflection on whatever advice, consultation, regard for convention or consensus or tradition or religious teaching is for her or him most persuasive or even authoritative. Always the last resort legal judgement, however, is that of a public tribunal acting as the responsible authority in such matters for a political community by reference to a publicly established and relatively clearly statable set of norms or standards which are represented both as being the norms or standards of that community and as implementing some conception of justice within it.

Why must we have both such sets of judgements? So far as concerns the moral judgements, there is no possibility for rational creatures with our emotional make-up to do without them. For each of us, practical dilemmas are continually arising which call for decision in the light of values to be served and pursued, commitments to be undertaken and subsequently either observed or neglected. Whatever we do is done under judgement of our neighbours and peers—and our superiors and inferiors as well. We in turn respond to their judging and doings and judge in our turn. Notwithstanding the biblical 'Judge not that ye be not judged', we really have no escape from this. Whatever be the principles and values in terms of which we judge in our interpersonal dealings and concerning our own most fundamental aspirations, these are, truly, our morality. There is no escaping the necessity of it; but if there is no escaping it, there is equally no escaping the impossibility of living by this alone.

The fact is exactly that we also have to have law on account of the incurable defects of an imaginary situation in which we all live together socially (and politically and economically), and yet each live according to individual standards of judgement and as judges of ourselves and every other. Not even the most assiduous cultivation of a sense of common tradition would be sufficient to achieve co-ordination of judgements, never mind of modes of conduct. As Finnis well remarks, even a community of angels would face co-ordination problems soluble only under the authority of some common public rules. Or in Alexy's terms we should say: however thoroughly we might construct the rules and forms of general practical discourse, we should always find that for some crucial interpersonal dilemmas the result of reasoned practical deliberation will be indeterminate. The reasonable practical reasoner must therefore conclude that some agencies have to be established for settling common public rules and standards and common authoritative judgements about their meaning and about the possibility of breach of them. That is, it is reasonable to institutionalize law, legal judgement, and legal reasoning.

But if such are the justifying reasons for our resort to law, they are also restrictive reasons as to the kinds of law it is reasonable to have. Law is for the reasonable regulation of conflict and settlement of disputes. Hence whoever purports to exercise legal authority, whether as lawmaker or as judge, has to do so at least upon a colourable claim of doing so reasonably, that is in accordance with some conception of justice and the public good. Someone who openly claimed to rule only by brute power and without regard to any rational scheme of value could not be understood to be ruling through, far less under, law. The thesis that there is such a thing as practical reason and that law belongs to the exercise (however defectively) of practical reasonableness is therefore of fundamental importance. It is the basis of the claim that there is a necessary connection between law and morality: they connect by virtue of both being modes of exercise of practical reason, at the same time as they differ in being different modes of it, having different criteria of validity for the norms or rules they apply.

One important corollary of all this is that every system of

positive law necessarily contains some non-positive norms. These are norms of sound reasoning. No student of legal reasoning can in the end doubt this. For although one part of the study of legal reasoning concerns the examination and rational reconstruction of local and particular rules, for example, rules about precedent or the interpretation of statutes and of constitutional provisions and constitutional law, yet there are also parts of it which, although one can (and should) explain and illustrate them through illustrations and examples culled from particular systems of positive law, nevertheless do not owe their standing as norms of reasoning to any process of enactment or authoritative determination, and could not be deprived of it by intelligible enactment to the contrary. Examples are: that if a rule is acknowledged as valid, and if facts in a case fit the conditions of the rule, then unless there are present implicit exceptions or grounds for overriding the rule, it ought to be applied; that if a certain decision can properly be given in a certain case, then materially the same decision must also be proper in any materially similar case, and hence the implications and consequences of the particular ruling considered in universalized form are relevant to its justification; and that consistency and coherence of decision over time ought to be pursued in any given jurisdiction.[16] Law belongs to the realms of the reasonable by virtue both of its own character and of the part it plays in the life of human communities; not by virtue of anyone's authoritative decision. As such, it is governed in action by norms of sound practical reasoning, as much when these are broken as when they are well observed. For when they are plainly broken, the purported justification of a decision is seen to be no justification at all.

4. THE ESSENTIAL FORMAL FEATURES OF LAW: LEGALITY AND MORAL VALUE

All that has been said so far clears the way for acknowledging the moral relevance of the forms of law. The argument from practical reason establishes the rational necessity of some sort of legal order in any human community. But it also has implications for the form this must take. To put it shortly, there must be some observance of the 'Rule of Law'. The best modern account of this is that given by L.L. Fuller, whose account is in its main points confirmed both by Finnis and by Joseph Raz.[17] For there to be law at all, there have to be rules of a reasonable degree of generality and clarity; they must be published to their addressees and be prospective in effect; there should be reasonable constancy and mutual consistency in the rules over time, and they must set standards with which it is possible to comply; and finally, given that there are rules which have such characteristics in some reasonable balance, the conduct of legal officials should be substantially congruent with the announced rules. These, according to Fuller, are principles with two aspects: first, they are such that their by-and-large observance by governmental authorities is essential to the practical working of any legal system; second, they are themselves principles of legislative morality, amounting to a distinctive 'Inner Morality of Law'. Legality is thus one form of or element in moral good.

At one time, I was inclined to agree with H.L.A. Hart that Fuller's principles, even if in some measure essential to the existence of legal systems as systems of rules, are merely technical requirements of legal efficiency, not any sort of 'morality'. For they appear to be in themselves morally neutral.[18] After all, they can in principle be as well observed by those whose laws wreak great substantive injustice as by those whose laws are in substance as just as can possibly be. Laws which exclude women or black people from public office or professional practice or from the right to vote can, for example, fulfil all of Fuller's stipulations; indeed, their efficiency as means of unjust discrimination might well be enhanced by careful observation of the stipulated principles. Conversely, as to the congruency of official conduct with announced rule, there is surely everything to be said for arbitrary exceptions and cheating exemptions which at least save some lives, where the rule evaded is one which does wickedness to people, as in the case of rules which required the dispatching of human beings to death camps. So not merely does adherence to the Fullerian principles fail to guarantee morally desirable outcomes; sometimes the morally preferable outcome requires breach of a significant one of them.

True as these observations are, they overlook the possibility that some ways of organizing human affairs can have positive value, and that this value can be moral value, even in situations in which there are countervailing moral values, even overriding

ones. There is always something to be said for treating people
with formal fairness, that is, in a rational and predictable way, setting public standards for citizens' conduct and officials' responses
thereto, standards with which one can choose to comply or at
least by which one can judge one's compliance or non-compliance,
rather than leaving everything to discretionary and potentially
arbitrary decision. That indeed is what we mean by the 'Rule of
Law'. Where it is observed, people are confronted by a state
which treats them as rational agents due some respect as such. It
applies fairly whatever standards of conduct and of judgement it
applies. This has real value, and independent value, even where
the substance of what is done falls short of any relevant ideal of
substantive justice. Where—say in the death camp case—one
approves of unprincipled exceptions and cheating exemptions
that save lives, even at random, one ought (I believe) to concede
that those who don't escape have suffered an extra injustice; they
are both being murdered and are being unfairly picked on
within a class of people who all ought not to be discriminated
against, and who, being innocent, ought not to be killed. It is a
mark of a world gone mad that one can welcome something itself
evil (arbitrariness on top of wickedness) as a partial mitigation of
the greater evil. In lesser cases of lesser injustice, or of more
doubtful injustice, it is easier to recognize that the value of
fairness-through-legality can be a partly redeeming value, even
where one's overall judgement is that the substance of what is
done remains unfair. A 'Community Charge' may be an unjust
tax, but a fairly administered one is less objectionable than one
subject to secret exceptions or arbitrary favouritism or the like.

A telling example of the value people do practically attach to
the observance of legality has been provided by recent developments in the Warsaw Pact countries. At all stages of the revolu-
tions against one-party Communist governments, there has been
expressed *inter alia* a clamant and persistent demand for a res-
toration of the Rule of Law, and this has been plainly a moral
demand. Those who have protested against and denounced the
arbitrary rule and arbitrary self-preferences of presidents like
Ceausescu and party officials like Honecker have not been asking for technically efficient law. They have been demanding the
instatement in public life of basic elements of fairness, fairness
upon which people can be agreed even while they differ sharply

about the more substantival demands of justice. People can reasonably differ, for example, about the extent to which private property and a market economy are requirements of justice, or instruments of inequality and therewith of injustice. But even subject to that disagreement, they can agree that whatever property and contract regime is fixed by law, the situation will be better—better in moral terms—if the regime is applied fairly and openly and in accordance with the Rule of Law. A claim (such as Hart makes) that legality is mere efficiency could very properly be disputed here. Matters of due process or natural justice do not commonly enhance efficiency from a managerial or governmental point of view. If it's true that legal efficiency is at stake, this surely tells us something about the character of law and the special value of *law's* efficiency. That it has moral value, and that its absence is morally evil, is what our fellow Europeans have been telling us since 1989. I hear them, and believe them.

In this respect then, again because of the link with practical reason, there is an important link between the legal and the moral, in the sense that the realization of the value of legality inherent in the very nature of legal regulation is of moral value, albeit not of absolute or overriding moral value in all situations. Law can provide part of the content of public morality. To conclude this section, we should note also that there are ways in which it also provides part of the content of private morality.

It is a thought at least as old as David Hume's *Treatise of Human Nature*[19] that personal virtues like honesty, or 'justice' as Hume called it, presuppose some 'artificial' allocation of rights, particularly rights of property. I can't refrain from dishonest interference with your assets unless you have some assets. For most purposes this postulates legally defined notions of possession and property. Other aspects of honesty in business deals, in contract, in taxation do or may involve essentially legal determinations of relevant duties and relationships. Any practical morality that we can imagine is bound to involve at least most-purpose respect for rights as conferred by law, coupled with the possibility of arguing as vigorously as you will for reform and redistribution, or even revolutionary expropriation. But the fact that one makes such arguments cannot (save in exceptional cases, if then) justify one in invading the rights of others as they stand under law. This follows from the practical need to ascribe authority to some common code, and thus to respect the obligations and rights which arise under it. It is remarkable how little of common everyday morality is left with any substantial content if we imagine away the positive law. We depend on legal arrangements as ways (always imperfect, of course) of solving our co-ordination problems. From a moral point of view, this usually stops us from legitimately acting outside the scheme of co-ordination ourselves.

5. THE GOOD AND THE RIGHT

All that has been written here so far assumes our capacity to form value judgements, and indeed to share apprehensions or intuitions or opinions on that which is good for human beings. If we had no sense of the good, we should have no sense of direction for the pursuit of any steady ends or aims; equally, no sense of what to shun or avoid as bad. Thus we should have no sense of right and wrong, for the wrong is precisely that which ought to be shunned; the right, that which may, or in some cases must, be done. Wrong/not wrong ('all right') is a basic binary opposition marking the line we draw at some point on the scale of the bad or not-so-good, or of failure in will to the good. Without any conception of good and evil, we should lack any possible content for our sense of the right or the wrong.

A real strength of *Natural Law* is the author's refusal to accept the priority of the right over the good in practical deliberation (though by counting practical reasonableness as a good of the same level as all the others, he seems to make it too easy to derive the right from the good). Also powerful is his argument that our capability to apprehend the good is at that simple and fundamental level of awareness at which we simply have to acknowledge the self-evident character of the goodness of life's goods. Ulterior proof or derivation is impossible in the case of first premises, although 'retorsive' arguments can perhaps be made to show that any argument against the basic goods would become self-defeating.

The other essential element in Finnis's account of the good is that it comprises a plurality of basic goods which are mutually incommensurable. For an individual or a community to achieve a good life, or a good way of life, there is required a balance among several goods, not a simple aggregation of a single good, whether

Benthamite pleasure or more modern preference-satisfaction. There should always be some considerable regard for every basic good, and there can never justifiably be action directly against one; but beyond that, it is a question of balance and judgement to secure a reasonable mix of all aspects of the good.

It is sometimes said that a liberal vision of society is irretrievably self-contradictory, since it assumes a pluralism of values, with every person his or her own judge of what is valuable to him or her, while at the same time demanding the institution of a state to hold the ring among competing individuals on terms that are neutral as between all their views of what is good. All sorts of antinomies and tensions, even 'contradictions', can be detected in the law of a supposedly liberal state—for example, between individualistic and altruistic values in tort law, or between strictly deontological retributivism and rules and practices in the criminal law oriented towards reform or deterrence or prevention, and so on.

Suppose, however, that the fundamentals of practical reason and moral experience are or include some discernible and distinct basic goods which are intrinsically incommensurable, and which can reasonably be pursued, both individually and communally, through a great plurality of ways of life, of which each in itself is perfectly reasonable, but not all are necessarily mutually compatible. In this case, there will indeed be a role for states which can facilitate interpersonal co-ordination by determining upon a reasonable body of law which as far as possible leaves individuals free to pursue the good as they judge it within the bounds of reason, but subject to necessary interventions both in the case of conflict between in-themselves-reasonable ways of acting and living, and in the more obvious case of failure or refusal to conform to laws as determined. Even in this case, there may be competing and partly incompatible, as well as incommensurable, aspects of the good involved in the remedial or punitive action applicable in response to illegal actings.

On this view, the presence of antinomies or tensions within the constitutional and legal orders of a liberal state would not have to be considered as evidence of some deep-seated and ultimately-to-be-fatal contradiction in any possible liberal ideology or constitutional blueprint. They might simply be inevitable (and not particularly regrettable) features of the human predicament. We just do as human beings confront a plurality of goods, and a plurality of visions of how to bring these goods together in a good life and a good political order. These rival visions are the stuff of deliberation and debate—debate which thrives on mutual but respectful contradiction, with a possibility but not inevitability of some supervening dialectical synthesis. A political order which fosters debate will inevitably yield richly contradictory political theories, without its necessarily being the case that each (or all but one) of these theories is in itself manifestly untenable. Only a kind of intellectual perverseness would force one to read this pluralism of ideas as a proof of the indefensibility of liberalism; its very existence is, in a way, its own best defence.

An attractive, even if not conclusive, defence of liberalism against some of what appear at first sight powerful objections to it is thus facilitated by insistence on the diversity and incommensurability of aspects of the good. The neutrality demanded of the state is then neutrality as between rival versions of the good, not some kind of rather fantastical neutrality as between good and evil. An argument along these lines has recently been advanced by Joseph Raz.[20] But of course, it is not only liberalism which could draw aid and comfort from such a theory—so could many varieties of conservatism, or of republican communitarianism, or of social democracy, or democratic socialism. Really, what is excluded is totalitarian government (including majoritarian totalitarianism), with the subordination of all phases and forms of life to one authoritatively elaborated and imposed vision of the good. Conversely excluded is resort to any simple version of the argument from contradiction, where what is truly at issue is diversity of the good, and hence the necessity to make difficult choices among genuine goods, while trying to keep all aspects of the good genuinely in play in the social and political forum.

For my part, as is doubtless obvious by now, I find the points Finnis takes and some of the ulterior conclusions derivable from his points to be extremely persuasive. At the very least, the argument for and from diversity of the good captures well the phenomenology of political and moral deliberation, and indeed of scholarly reflection (who is unaware of the rational strength and intellectual attractiveness of views wholly or partly incompatible with his/her own?). The good is neither simple nor one-dimensional; and any concrete decision on what is right or wrong presupposes some conception of what is good and bad.

Still, I remain uneasy with the ipsedixitism of the claim of self-evidence tied to a bald listing of seven basic goods. I have particular difficulty with the thesis that practical reasonableness functions both as a good on a par with the other basic goods and as the source of the principles we require when it comes to ordering our pursuit of any goods. It seems to me more probable that any list of basic goods we produce will be a construct achieved by the application of practical reason to actual and possible aims and interests we impute to individuals. The ideas of Jürgen Habermas and Robert Alexy on rational practical discourse here seem to me helpful, in suggesting how we might abstract out of concrete aims and wishes general categories of the good in terms of ends whose adoption would satisfy felt needs and interests in a potentially universalizable way.[21] Such a project does not have to make any unacceptable 'methodologically individualistic' assumptions about people; it need not assume that our most basic desires and interests are purely endogeneous, owing nothing to the communal and social contexts from which in large measure we derive our sense of self. We are all indeed 'contextual individuals', and it is as contextual individuals that we can be envisaged as participants in rational discourse. Hence such discourse does not invent goods or ends in abstraction from people as they appear in historical and social settings, but reflects on the question which of the values we hold are capable of being rationally deemed objective in those settings. In this way, and odd as it may seem, I think that there are points of interesting convergence between the approach of Alexy and Habermas, and ideas derivable from the work of Hume and Smith to which I also owe some allegiance.

Thus, to conclude this section of the present chapter: there is great weight both in the thesis that rights and the right presuppose goods and in the thesis that there is an irreducible plurality of aspects of the good. This has strong and important implications in respect of leading arguments in political theory; but Finnis's own account of the basic goods works from what still seems to me an unacceptable version of meta-ethical cognitivism, notwithstanding some very powerful arguments recently advanced in clarification of the position by Robert George,[22] and further rehearsed in the present volume. I remain in search of a different and more constructivist account of the good, while desiring to deploy arguments from the plurality of goods in ways similar to Finnis's. I am by no means sure that I can have this cake and eat it too; I retain a sense of real puzzlement over these issues, and cannot claim to put forward any final view of my own.

6. ON LAW AND MORALISM

A few years ago, in the Seegers Lectures at Valparaiso University, I set forth what I rather tentatively called 'A Moralistic case for A-Moralistic Law?'[23] There, I argued compendiously for a version of the positivistic case on the conceptual separation of law from morals, and for a version of the liberal case against a direct legal enforcement of moral values, what I called (and call) a case for restricted 'establishment of morals'. What was original in that set of arguments, if anything was, came out of my suggestion that both the argument about the conceptual law–morality distinction and the argument about the proper uses of legal coercion rely upon practical—moral—rather than purely epistemic considerations.[24] It is for moral reasons that we should seek to avoid confusing legal and moral issues, and that we should abstain from using the law simply to enforce whatever we hold to be of moral value. There is only a restricted range of moral duties which it is morally acceptable to enforce legally.

The present essay has arisen from an invitation to reflect upon *Natural Law and Natural Rights* ten years on, as a contribution to discussions of natural law from several points of view. As must be clear, *Natural Law* is a work for which I have the highest regard, and one by which I feel myself greatly influenced. Whether the extent of that influence has been such as to leave me with a consistent overall theoretical position is no doubt a question of small moment to others than myself. Still, I do think that the two theses of the Seegers Lectures are fully compatible with, and indeed supported by, the ideas derived from *Natural Law* which form the main part of the present chapter. Whether and how far my reading of Finnis is an eccentric one is for others to decide. I am sure that there are aspects of his own position which are fundamental from John Finnis's point of view, but which I have either passed over in silence here, or explicitly or implicitly denied. Nor can I impute to him agreement with these other theses of my own.

It is, however, of significance that for him as much as for anyone claiming a positivistic stance, the question of legal validity is firmly distinguished from that of moral value. The idea that this follows from the practical force of both moral and legal thought is a point of great importance which I think must be accepted by any thinker in this field. And the same practical reason which gives us ground to think it desirable to have systems of law, which include relatively clearly statable rules derived from legislation and other sources, also gives us ground to desire that these rules be applied as a relatively distinctive code, and elaborated through legal reasoning which, as a form of practical reasoning, belongs to the same genus as moral reasoning but to a different species of it. For this reason, we may insist that courts of law are courts which properly deal with law as a body of practical rules and principles distinct from moral principles. Legal reasoning should be permeable to moral reasoning; and, in particular, consideration of those aspects of justice to which law necessarily aspires should inform all legal reasoning. But the law best fulfils the moral aspirations implicit in it by abstaining from any direct across-the-board enforcement of moral values. Acceptance of many themes and ideas from natural law theory as John Finnis has reshaped it does not preclude our continuing to insist on the conceptual distinction of the legal and the moral or on the forcefulness of the case for insisting upon limits to the extent to which law can rightfully be used to implement moral values beyond those derivable from duties of justice. It would be far closer to the truth to say that a revaluation of the reciprocal interdependency as well as mutual differentiation of law and morality gives particular strength to the case for those views rather than justifying their abandonment.

I have alluded throughout this chapter to positivism and to natural law theory in ways which hark back to the traditional textbook opposition of these positions. As a matter of the history of legal ideas it remains important to see how that supposed opposition arose and how the controversy was conducted. But I for one regard the issue of mutual opposition as now closed and unfruitful. There are elements from works in both schools which any sound theory of law has to embrace. And within each school ideas have been advanced which ought to be rejected, not because of the school in which they were advanced, but because of their fallaciousness. The tasks ahead are those of pressing forward with analysis and critique of legal ideas and institutions, and with studies of practical reason and practical discourse in legal, moral, and political spheres. Such work is not well done if it does not draw on the work and wisdom of our predecessors. And it would be foolish and arbitrary to reject work or wisdom because of the 'school' to which we choose to assign it.

For almost twenty years now I have had the honour to be the incumbent of what I suspect is the only surviving chair of 'Public Law and the Law of Nature and Nations' anywhere in the world. When I started out I was still of the view that theories of the 'law of nature and nations' belonged more to the history books than to the serious business of contemporary legal philosophy. A better acquaintance with the history of the books has over the years taught me better and helped me to broaden the canvas and scope of my juristic enquiries. A telling moment in this better appreciation of the particular duties of my particular station has been the reading of (and rereading of and reflection upon) *Natural Law and Natural Rights*.

NOTES

© Neil MacCormick 1992. This chapter was prepared during the Spring Semester of 1990 when I had the very good fortune to be Anne Green Visiting Professor at the University of Texas School of Law; it was improved by helpful conversations there, and in seminars at the Law Schools of the University of Michigan and Arizona State University and the Philosophy Club of Southern Methodist University; I am particularly grateful to Bill Powers, Philip Soper, Jeffrie Murphy, Steven Sverdlik, and other colleagues too numerous to name who took part in these seminars. I am also very grateful to Robert George as editor.

1. (Oxford: Clarendon Press 1980); hereinafter, detailed references are omitted since the whole present essay is a response to Finnis's book as a whole.

2. Ota Weinberger, 'Beyond Positivism and Natural Law Theory', ch. 7 of N. MacCormick and O. Weinberger, *An Institutional Theory of Law* (Boston: D. Reidel Pub. Co., 1986).

3. See H.L.A. Hart, 'Legal Positivism and the Separation of Law and Morals', *Harvard Law Review*, 71 (1958–9), 598; now also ch. 2 of Hart, *Essays in Jurisprudence and Philosophy* (Oxford: Clarendon Press, 1983).

4. Most notably, H.L.A. Hart, in *The Concept of Law* (Oxford: Clarendon Press, 1961), 205–7; cf. J. Raz, *The Authority of Law* (Oxford: Clarendon Press, 1979), N. MacCormick, *H.L.A. Hart* (London: Edward Arnold, 1981).

5. The idea of the 'claim to correctness' is borrowed from Robert Alexy's *Theory of Legal Argumentation*, trans. R. Adler and N. MacCormick (Oxford: Clarendon Press, 1988); see esp. 104–8, 127–30, 191–4, 214–20.

6. See R. Alexy, 'On Necessary Relations between Law and Morality', *Ratio Juris*, 2 (1989), 167–83; MacCormick, 'Law, Morality and Positivism', ch. 6 of MacCormick and Weinberger, *Institutional Theory*.

7. See N. MacCormick, *Legal Right and Social Democracy* (Oxford: Clarendon Press, 1982), ch. 2.

8. A. Kaufmann, 'National Socialism and German Jurisprudence from 1933 to 1945', *Cardozo Law Rev*, 9 (1988), 1629–49; cf. M. Reimann, 'National Socialist Jurisprudence and Academic Continuity', ibid. 1651–62.

9. H.L.A. Hart, *The Concept of Law* (Oxford: Clarendon Press, 1961), 54–6, 82–8.

10. For a development of the claim that Hart's approach is essentially hermeneutic, see MacCormick, *H.L.A. Hart*, chs. 2–4, 13.

11. See H.L.A. Hart, *Essays in Jurisprudence and Philosophy*, Introduction, 13–14.

12. This point has recently been brought home to me with particular vividness by Sanford Levinson in his *Constitutional Faith* (Princeton NJ: Princeton University Press, 1988), 86–8.

13. See ibid. 76–7, 186–7.

14. See Philip Soper, *A Theory of Law* (Cambridge, Mass.: Harvard University Press, 1984), 77–83.

15. See MacCormick, 'The Limits of Rationality in Legal Reasoning', ch. 9 of MacCormick and Weinberger, *Institutional Theory*.

16. See MacCormick, *Legal Reasoning and Legal Theory* (Oxford: Clarendon Press, 1978), chs. 5–9. At the time of writing that book, I had become aware of the non-positive character of the reasoning norms I discussed, but not of the full significance of their non-positive character.

This was one of the many benefits of reading Alexy's directly contemporary *Theorie der juristischen Argumentation* (Frankfurt-on-Main, 1978), of which the English translation is cited at n. 5, above.

17. See L.L. Fuller, *The Morality of Law* (New Haven, Conn.: Yale University Press, 1964), ch. 2; cf. Finnis, *Natural Law*, 270–6, and J. Raz, *The Authority of Law* (Oxford: Clarendon Press, 1979), ch. 1.

18. See Hart, *The Concept of Law*, 202–4; 'If this is what the necessary connexion of law with morality means, we may accept it. It is unfortunately compatible with very great iniquity' (p. 202); see also Hart, 'Legal Positivism and the Separation of Law from Morals', and *Essays in Jurisprudence and Philosophy*, ch. 16.

19. Many editions; see bk. III, pt. 2, *passim*.

20. J. Raz, *The Morality of Freedom* (Oxford: Clarendon Press, 1986).

21. See J. Habermas, *Moral Bewusstsein und kommunikatives Handeln* (Frankfurt-on-Main, 1983), esp. pp. 74 ff; also, 'Morality and Ethical Life', *Northwestern University Law Review*, 83 (1988–9), 38–53, and Alexy, *Theory of Legal Argumentation*.

22. See Robert P. George, 'Recent Criticism of Natural Law Theory', *University of Chicago Law Review*, 55 (1988), 1371–429.

23. See MacCormick, 'A Moralistic Case for A-Moralistic Law?', *Valparaiso University Law Review*, 20 (1985), 1–4.

24. But see Philip Soper, 'Choosing a Legal Theory on Moral Grounds', *Social Philosophy and Policy*, 4 (1987), 31–48. In the light of this telling criticism, I have to qualify my position; it remains the case that there is a good moral argument for 'amoralistic' conception of law; but not one which of itself excludes a more morally laden conception.

6

Natural Law and Legal Reasoning

JOHN FINNIS

Moral reasoning, legal reasoning, and their interrelationships can scarcely be understood reflectively without attention to two different sources of ambiguity. The source is, in each case, well known: the distinction between reasons and feelings; and the distinction between doing (the shaping of one's own 'existence' by one's choices) and making (the exercise of technique by activity on some form of 'cultural' object or method). But the distinctions are commonly not well understood, and the traps they lay for the analysis of morality and adjudication are usually neglected.

I

We are animals, but intelligent. Our actions all have an emotional motivation, involve our feelings and imagination and other aspects of our bodiliness, and can all be observed (if only, in some cases, by introspection) as pieces of behaviour. But rationally motivated actions also have an intelligent motivation—seek to realize (protect, promote) an intelligible good.

So our purposes, the states of affairs we seek to bring about, typically have a double aspect: the goal which we imagine and which engages our feelings, and the intelligible benefit which appeals to our rationality by promising to instantiate, either immediately or instrumentally, some basic human good. While some of the purposes we employ intelligence to pursue may be motivated ultimately by nothing more than feeling, others are motivated ultimately by (an understanding of) a basic human good. The idiom in which 'reason' refers to purposes—'the reason he did that', equivalent to 'his purpose in doing that'— fails to mark this distinction. But none of common speech's related terms—'purpose', 'goal', 'intention'—is free from the same ambiguity. So I stipulate that when I speak of 'reasons' in this chapter, I refer (except when discussing technical reasons) to reason(s) as giving ground for intelligent action motivated ultimately by a basic human good (more precisely, by the intelligible benefit promised by the instantiation of a basic good).[1]

An account of basic reasons for action should not be rationalistic. Human flourishing is not to be portrayed in terms only of exercising capacities to reason. As animals, we are organic substances part of whose well-being is *bodily life*, maintained in health, vigour, and safety, and transmitted to new human beings. To regard human life as a basic reason for action is to understand it as a good in which indefinitely many beings can participate in indefinitely many ways, going far beyond any goal or purpose which anyone could envisage and pursue, but making sense of indefinitely many purposes, and giving rational support to indefinitely many goals.[2]

This sense of '(basic) reason for action' holds for all the other basic human goods: *knowledge* of reality (including aesthetic appreciation of it); *excellence in work and play* whereby one transforms natural realities to express meanings and serve purposes; *harmony between individuals and groups* of persons (peace, neighbourliness, and friendship); *harmony between one's feelings and one's judgements and choices* (inner peace); *harmony between one's choices and judgements and one's behaviour* (peace of conscience and authenticity in the sense of consistency between one's self and its expression); and *harmony between oneself and the wider reaches of reality* including the reality constituted by the world's dependence on *a more-than-human source of meaning and value*.

Such a statement of the basic human goods entails an account of human nature.[3] But it does not presuppose such an account. It is not an attempt to deduce reasons for action from some pre-existing theoretical conception of human nature. Such an attempt would vainly defy the logical truth (well respected by the ancients)[4] that 'ought' cannot be deduced from 'is'—a syllogism's conclusion cannot contain what is not in its premisses. Rather, a full account of human nature can only be given by one who understands the human goods practically, i.e. as reasons for choice and action, reasons which make full sense of supporting feelings and spontaneities.

An account of practical reasonableness can be called a theory of 'natural law' because practical reasoning's very first principles are those basic reasons which identify the basic human goods as ultimate reasons for choice and action—reasons for actions which will instantiate and express human nature precisely because participating in those goods, i.e. instantiating (actualizing, realizing) those ultimate aspects of human flourishing.[5]

II

To the extent that legal reasoning derives from and participates in practical reasonableness, a sound theory of legal reasoning must differ from some theories now current. At the heart of 'Critical Legal Studies', for example, is a denial that there are any objective human goods. Of the four reasons (all bad) which Roberto Unger offers for denying that there are objective human goods, the argument closest to his heart, I think, is that by affirming that there are such goods one 'denies any significance to choice other than the passive acceptance or rejection of independent truths . . . [and] disregards the significance of choice as an expression of personality'.[6]

But, in reality, it is the diversity of *rationally* appealing human goods which makes free choice both possible and frequently necessary. Like every other term concerning human activity, 'choice' is afflicted, in common idiom, by ambiguities originating particularly[7] in the distinction between reason and feeling. In its strong, central sense, free choice is the adoption of one amongst two or more rationally appealing and incompatible, alternative options, such that nothing but the choosing itself settles which option is chosen and pursued.[8] Many aspects of individual and social life, and many individual and social obligations, are structured by choice between rationally appealing options whose rational appeal can be explained only in terms, ultimately, of basic human opportunities understood to be objectively good (though variously realizable). No sound sense can be made of 'objectivity' and 'truth', here or elsewhere, otherwise than in terms of rational judgement, open to all relevant questions.

But if the basic human goods, for all their objectivity and truth, open up so much to free choice, what can be the basis for identifying choices which, though rational, ought to be rejected because unreasonable, wrong, immoral?

Moral thought is simply rational thought at full stretch, integrating emotions and feelings but *undeflected* by them. Practical rationality's fundamental principle is: take as a premiss at least one of the basic reasons for action, and follow through to the point at which you somehow bring about the instantiation of that good in action. Do not act pointlessly. The fundamental principle of moral thought is simply the demand to be fully rational: in so far as it is in your power, allow nothing but the basic reasons for action to shape your practical thinking as you find, develop, and use your opportunities to pursue human flourishing through your chosen actions. Be entirely reasonable.[9] Aristotle's phrase *orthos logos*, and his later followers' *recta ratio*, right reason, should simply be understood as 'unfettered reason', reason undeflected by emotions and feelings. And so undeflected reason, and the morally good will, are guided by the first moral principle: that one ought to choose (and otherwise will) those and only those possibilities whose willing is compatible with a will towards the fulfilment of all human persons in all the basic goods, towards the ideal of integral human fulfilment.

Take a simple, paradigmatic form of immorality. Emotion may make one wish to destroy or damage the good of life in someone one hates, or the good of knowledge; so one kills or injures, or deceives, that person just out of feelings of aversion. It is immoral, because hereabouts there is a general, so to speak methodological, moral principle intermediate between the most basic principles of practical reason (the basic goods or reasons for action, and the first moral principle) and particular moral norms against killing or lying. This intermediate moral principle, which some call a mode of responsibility,[10] will exclude meeting injury with injury, or responding to one's own weakness or setbacks with self-destructiveness.

Perhaps more immediately relevant to political and legal theory is the intermediate moral principle requiring that one act fairly: that one not limit one's concern for basic human goods simply by one's feelings of self-preference or preference for those who are near and dear. Fairness (and its paradigmatic formulation in the Golden Rule) does not exclude treating different persons differently; it requires only that the differential treatment be justified either by inevitable limits on one's action or by intelligible requirements of the basic goods themselves. I shall say more (VII below) about the legitimate role of feelings in making fair choices in which one prioritizes goods (or instantiations of basic goods) by one's feelings without prioritizing persons simply by feelings.

There are other intermediate moral principles. Very important to the structuring of legal thought is the principle which excludes acting against a basic reason by choosing to destroy or damage any basic good in any of its instantiations in any human person (VI below). A basic human good always is a reason for action and always gives a reason *not* to choose to destroy, damage, or impede some instantiation of that good; but since the instantiations of human good at stake in any morally significant choice are not commensurable by *reason* prior to choice, there can never be a sufficient reason not to take that reason-not-to as decisive for choice. Only emotional factors such as desire or aversion could motivate a choice rejecting it.

Of course, the basic reasons for action, as the phrase suggests, present one with many reasons for choice and action, many reasons to . . . And since one is finite, one's choice of any purpose, however far-reaching, will inevitably have as a side-effect some negative impact on (minimally, the non-realization of) other possible instantiations of this and other basic goods. In that sense, every choice is 'against some basic reason'. But only as a side-effect. In the choices which are excluded by the intermediate moral principle now in question, the damaging or destruction or impeding of an instantiation of a basic good—the harming of some basic aspect of someone's existence and well-being—is chosen, as a means, i.e. *as part* of the description of the option adopted by choice. Whereas the first intermediate principle excludes making such damage or destruction one's end, the present principle excludes making it one's means. The concepts of (the) end and means (defining an option) come together in the conception so fundamental to our law: intention.[11]

III

Even so rapid a sketch begins to make clear that a theory of natural law, while primarily a theory of human goods as principles of practical reasoning, must accommodate within its account—as practical reasoning itself must take into account—certain features of our world.

Among these features are the reality of free choice, and the significance of choices as lasting in the character of the chooser beyond the time of the behaviour which executes them; and the distinction between what is chosen as end or means (i.e. as intended) and what is foreseen and accepted as a side-effect (i.e. an unintended effect). Again, there are such basic facts as that which Robert Nozick overlooked in declaring that (virtually) everything comes into the world already attached to someone having an entitlement over it—the reality being, on the contrary, that the natural resources from which everything made has been made pre-exist all entitlements and 'came into the world' attached to nobody in particular; the world's resources are fundamentally common and no theory of entitlements can rightly appropriate any resource to one person so absolutely as to negate that original communality of the world's stock.[12]

A further feature of the world to be accommodated by a sound natural law theory is the distinction between the orders of reality with which human reason is concerned. In attending to this set of distinctions, we shall be noticing the second of the two sources of ambiguity I mentioned at the outset.

Almost any interesting human state of affairs instantiates the four orders of reality with which human reason is concerned. Consider, for example, a lecture. (1) One hears the *sounds* produced by the speaker's vocal chords: there is an order of nature which we in no way establish by our understanding but which we can investigate by our understanding, as in the natural sciences or (as right now) in metaphysics. (2) One hears the speaker's *expositions, arguments, and explanations* and brings one's understanding into line with them (if only to the extent necessary to reject them as mistaken): there is an order which one can bring into one's own enquiries, understanding, and reasoning, the order studied by logic, methodology, and epistemology. (3) One hears *the lecturer*, who (like the audience) is freely engaging in an activity and thereby participating in a human relationship: there is an order which one can bring into one's own dispositions, choices, and actions—one's *praxis*, one's doing, one's *Existenz*—the 'existential' order studied by some parts of psychology, by biography and the history of human affairs, and by moral and political philosophy. (4) One hears the *English language* and statements ordered by an expository or rhetorical technique, making and decoding the formalized symbols of a language and the less formalized but still conventional symbols and expressive routines of a cultural form and technique: the order one can intelligently bring into matter which is subject to our power, so as to make objects such as phonemes, words, poems, boats, software, ballistic missiles and their inbuilt trajectories—the order of *poiesis*, of making, of culture—studied in the arts and technologies, and in linguistics and rhetoric.[13] (Corresponding to these four orders are four irreducibly distinct senses of 'hearing'.)

Almost every form of reductionist deformation in social (say, political) theory, and many destructive misunderstandings in almost every aspect of, say, legal theory, can be traced to oversight of the complexities and ambiguities created by the irreducible distinctions between these four orders—whose irreducibility to one another is disguised by the fact that each in a sense includes all the others.

The distinction particularly relevant to legal theory is that between the third (existential, moral) order and the fourth (cultural, technical) order. Few morally significant choices can be carried out without employing some culturally formed technique; and no technique can be put to human use without some morally significant choice. But every technique has an integral, fourth-order intelligibility which can be fully explicated without referring to the morally significant choices by which it might be put to use and the moral principles of practical reasonableness pertinent to such choices.

Amongst the ambiguities created by the distinctions between the third and fourth orders is the ambiguity of the term 'rational choice'. It has (at least) three important, distinct senses:

(1) choice which is fully reasonable, complies with all the requirements of practical reasonableness, and is thus morally upright;

(2) choice which is rationally motivated in the sense that its object has been shaped by practical intelligence and has rational appeal, even if it is in some respect(s) motivated ultimately by feeling rather than reason, feelings which have to some extent fettered and instrumentalized reason, and is therefore unreasonable and immoral, though rational;

(3) decision and action which is technically (technologically) right, i.e. is identifiable according to some art or technique

as the most effective for attaining the relevant technical objective—typically, the decision for which there is, within this technique (e.g. this game), a dominant reason which can be commensurated with the reasons for alternative options and which includes all that these offer and some more.

Sense 3 is the only sense in which economists and exponents of 'game' or 'decision' theory commonly use the phrase 'rational choice'. I have used the terms 'rational' (and its cognates) and 'choice', in Section II above, in sense 2 (or senses 1 and 2) but never in sense 3. Here is rich opportunity for misunderstanding.[14] In senses 1 and 2, what makes rational choice necessary is the incommensurability of the intelligible goods and bads involved in alternative options; if options were fully commensurable, alternatives could be identified as unqualifiedly superior and inferior, and the unqualifiedly inferior would lose its rational appeal, fall out of rational deliberation; rational choice would be unnecessary and, in a significant sense, impossible (VI below). But in sense 3, rational choice is possible *only* when one option can be identified as unqualifiedly superior.

IV

Legal reasoning and rationality has, I suggest, its distinctiveness and its peculiar elusiveness because, in the service of a third-order, existential, moral, and chosen purpose—of living together in a just order of fair and right relationships—there has been and is being constructed a fourth-order object, 'the law' (as in 'the law of England'). This is a vastly complex cultural object, comprising a vocabulary with many artfully assigned meanings, rules identifying permitted and excluded arguments and decision, and correspondingly very many technical routines or processes (such as pleading, trial, conveyancing, etc.) constituted and regulated according to those formulae, their assigned meanings, and the rules of argument and decision.

This cultural object, constructed or (as we say) posited by creative human choices, is an instrument, a technique adopted for a moral purpose, and adopted because there is no other available way of agreeing over significant spans of time about precisely how to pursue the moral project well. Political authority in all its manifestations, including legal institutions, is a technique for doing without unanimity in making social choices—where unanimity would almost always be unattainable or temporary—in order to secure practical (near-)unanimity about how to co-ordinate the actions (including forbearances) of members of the society.[15]

Legal reasoning, then, is (at least in large part) technical reasoning—not moral reasoning. Like all technical reasoning, it is concerned to achieve a particular purpose, a definite state of affairs attainable by efficient dispositions of means to end. The particular end here is the resolution of disputes (and other allegations of misconduct) by the provision of a directive sufficiently definite and specific to identify one party as right (in-the-right) and the other as wrong (not-in-the-right).

Hence the law's distinctive devices: defining terms, and specifying rules, with sufficient and necessarily artificial clarity and definiteness to establish the 'bright lines' which make so many real-life legal questions *easy questions*. Legal definitions and rules are to provide the citizen, the legal adviser, and the judge with an algorithm for deciding as many questions as possible—in principle every question—yes (or no), this course of action would (or would not) be lawful; this arrangement is valid; this contract is at an end; these losses are compensable in damages and those are not; and so forth. As far as it can, the law is to provide sources of reasoning—statutes and statute-based rules, common law rules, and customs—capable of ranking (commensurating) alternative dispute-resolutions as right or wrong, and thus better and worse.

Lawyers' tools of trade—their ability to find and use the authoritative sources—are means in the service of a purpose sufficiently definite to constitute a technique, a mode of technical reasoning. The purpose, again, is the unequivocal resolution of every dispute (and other question for just decision) which can be in some way foreseen and provided for. Still, this quest for certainty, for a complete set of uniquely correct answers, is itself in the service of a wider good which, like all basic human goods, is not reducible to a definite goal but is rather an open-ended good which persons and their communities can participate in without ever capturing or exhausting the good of just harmony. This good is a moral good just in so far as it is itself promoted and respected as one aspect of the ideal of integral human fulfilment. As a moral good its implications are specified by all the moral principles which could bear upon it.

Thus there emerges the tension around which Ronald Dworkin's work on legal reasoning revolves.

V

Dworkin seeks to resolve the tension between law's and legal reasoning's character as a culturally specified technique of attaining predictable answers to problems of social co-ordination and its character as, in each of its decisive legislative, executive and judicial moments, a moral act participating in justice (or injustice). His attempted resolution fails, I think, to grasp the real nature and implications of that tension.

In judicial reasoning as portrayed by Dworkin, two criteria of judgement are in use; as we shall see, there is between these two criteria a kind of incommensurability analogous to the incommensurability between the human goods involved in morally significant, rationally motivated choices. One of these criteria or dimensions belongs to what I have called the third (moral) order or rationality, and the other to the fourth (technical) order. The first dimension Dworkin calls 'fit': coherence with the existing legal 'materials' created by past political decisions, i.e. with legislation and authoritative judicial decision (precedent). The second dimension he now calls 'justification'.[16] And he tries to show that a *uniquely* correct ('the right') answer is available in 'most' hard cases.

One can deny this last thesis without committing oneself to any scepticism about the objectivity of human good(s) or of correct judgements about right and wrong. Nor need one's denial be predicated on the popular argument which Dworkin is rightly concerned to scorn and demolish—the argument that disagreement is endemic and ineradicable. (For disagreement is a mere fact about people, and is logically irrelevant to the merits of any practical or other interpretative claim.) Nor need a denial of Dworkin's one-right-answer thesis rest on the fact that no one has the 'superhuman' powers of Dworkin's imaginary judge.

Even an ideal human judge, with superhuman powers, could not sensibly search for a uniquely correct answer to a hard case (as lawyers in sophisticated legal systems use the term 'hard case'). For in such a case, the search for the one right answer is practically incoherent and senseless, in much the same way as a search for the English novel which is 'most romantic and shortest' (or 'funniest and best', or 'most English and most profound').

Assuming with Dworkin that there are two 'dimensions' or criteria of judicial assessment, we can say that a case for judicial decision is hard (not merely novel) when not only is there more than one answer which is not in evident violation of an applicable rule, but also the answers which are in that sense available can be ranked in different orders along each of the relevant criteria of evaluation: for novels, their brevity and their English-ness (or humour, or profundity, or . . .); for judicial judgements their fit with previous legislation and precedent, and—let us grant (not concede) to Dworkin—their *inherent* moral soundness.[17] In such a case there is found what theorists of 'rational choice' (in sense 3) call 'intransitivity', a phenomenon which such theories confessedly cannot really handle:[18] solution A is better than solution B on the scale of legal fit, and B than C, but C is better than A on the scale of 'moral soundness'; so there is no sufficient reason to declare A, or B, or C the overall 'best judicial decision'. If the rank order was the same on both dimensions, of course, the case was not a hard one at all, and the legal system already had what one always desires of it: a uniquely correct answer.

In his works before *Law's Empire*, Dworkin tried to overcome this incommensurability of the dimensions or criteria of assessment by proposing a kind of lexicographical (in Rawls's terminology 'lexical') ordering. Candidates for the 'best account' of the law of England in 1980 must fit the then existing English legal materials adequately, and of those which satisfy this threshold criterion, that which ranks highest on the other criterion (moral soundness) is overall, absolutely, 'the best', even though it fits less well than (an)other(s).[19] But this solution was empty, since he identified no criteria, however sketchy or 'in principle', for specifying when fit is 'adequate', i.e. for locating the threshold (of fit) beyond which the criterion of soundness would prevail. (It was like being told to search for the funniest novel among those that are 'short enough'.) Presumably, candidates for the one right answer to the question 'When is fit adequate?' would themselves be ranked in terms both of fit and of soundness. An infinite regress, of the vicious sort which nullifies purported rational explanations, was well under way.

In *Law's Empire*, Dworkin abandons the simple picture of a lexical ordering between these two criteria. We are left with little more than a metaphor: 'balance'—as in 'the general balance of political virtues' embodied in competing interpretations or accounts of the law (of England (in 1990)). But in the absence of any metric which could commensurate the different criteria, the instruction to balance (or, earlier, to weigh) can legitimately mean no more than 'Bear in mind, conscientiously, all the relevant factors, and *choose.*' Or, in the legal sphere, 'Hear the arguments, sitting in the highest court, and then *vote.*'

In understanding practical rationality in all its forms, one should notice a feature of the experience of choice. *After* one has chosen, the factors favouring the chosen option will usually seem to outweigh, overbalance, those favouring the rejected alternative options. The option chosen—to do x, to adopt rule or interpretation y—will commonly seem (to the person who chose, if not to onlookers) to have a supremacy, a unique rightness. But this sense of the supremacy, the rightness of one (the chosen) option will not alter the truth that the choice was not rationally determined, i.e. was not guided by an identification of one option or answer as 'the right one'. (And this does not mean that it was irrational; it was between rationally appealing options.) Rather, the choice established the 'right' answer—i.e. established it in, and by reference ultimately to, the dispositions and sentiments of the chooser.[20] When the choice in a hard case is made by (the majority in the) highest appeal court (a mere brute fact), the unique rightness of the answer is established not only by and for the attitude of those who have chosen it, but also for the legal system or community for which it has thus been authoritatively decided upon, and laid down as or in a *rule.*

VI

The incommensurability of Dworkin's two dimensions or criteria for judicial judgement has significant similarities to the incommensurability of the goods (and reasons) at stake in alternative options available for morally significant choice in any context.

The moral and political rationality which underpins (though does not exhaust) legal rationality cannot be understood without an understanding of incommensurability.

Incommensurability, the absence of any *rationally* identified metric for measuring, or scale for 'weighing', the goods and bads in issue, is much more pervasive and intense than one would imagine from the simple Dworkinian picture of legal reasoning along the two dimensions of legal fit and moral soundness. One meets incommensurability in humble contexts, such as having to choose between going to a lecture, reading a good book, going to the cinema, and talking to friends. One meets it in relation to grand social choices, such as whether to reject or renounce a nuclear deterrent:[21] exploring such a choice will amply illustrate the impotence of all forms of aggregative reasoning towards morally significant choice—choice outside the purely technical or technological task of identifying the most cost-efficient means to a single limited goal.

The reasoning most characteristic of technical rationality is 'cost-benefit analysis', comparing the costs of alternative options with the probable benefits.[22] This can be carried through with full rationality only when (*a*) goals are well defined, (*b*) costs can be compared with some definite unit (e.g. money), (*c*) benefits can also be quantified in a way that renders them commensurable with one another, and (*d*) differences among means, other than their efficiency, measurable costs, and measurable benefits, are not counted as significant. None of these conditions is fulfilled in moral reasoning.

Indeed, morally significant choice would be unnecessary and, with one qualification,[23] impossible if one option could be shown to be *the best* on a single scale which, as all aggregative reasoning does, ranks options in a single, transitive order. If there were a reason (for doing *x*) which some rational method of comparison (e.g. aggregation of goods and bads in a complete cost-benefit analysis) identified as rationally preferable, the alternative reason (against doing *x*), being thus identified as rationally inferior, would cease to be rationally appealing in that situation of choice. The reason thus identified as dominant, as unqualifiedly preferable, and the option favoured by that reason, would be rationally unopposed. There would remain *no choice* of the sort that moral theories seek to guide. For, the morally significant choices which moral theories seek to guide are between alternative options which have rational appeal.

To identify options as morally wrong does not entail identifying one option as (morally) uniquely right. Indeed, even when one option can be judged the only (morally) right option for a given person (a moral judgement which only that person's prior commitments and dispositions will make possible), this entails only that the alternative, immoral options are not fully reasonable. It in no way entails that these alternative options are irrational, i.e. lack rational appeal in terms of genuine, intelligible human goods which would be secured by the immoral options and sacrificed by the morally upright option. Thus rationally motivated, morally significant choice remains possible—indeed characteristic of the human situation—even in the perhaps relatively uncommon case of the moral 'one right answer (option)'.

But when technical reasonings identify one option as uniquely correct, i.e. as dominant, they do so by demonstrating that it offers *all that the other options offer and some more*; it is unqualifiedly better. The other options then lack *rational* appeal. Such deliberation ends not in choice—in the rich, central sense of that ambiguous term—but rather in insight, 'decision' (not choice, but rationally compelled judgement), and action.

One of morality's principles, I have said (II above), excludes acting against a basic reason by choosing to destroy or damage any basic human good in any of its instantiations in any human person. For these instantiations are nothing other than aspects of human persons, present and future, and human persons cannot rationally be reduced to the commensurable factors captured by technical reasoning. These instantiations of human good constitute *reasons against* any option which involves choosing (intending) to destroy or damage any of them. The significance of the incommensurability of goods involved in such morally significant options is that no reason *for* such an option can be rationally preferable to such a reason against. And the same is true of the *reason against* an option which is constituted by that option's unfairness.

What, it may be asked, are the grounds for regulating one's choice according to the reason-*against* rather than by any reason-*for*? Once again, they cannot be stated without reference to some features of our world, the fundamental context of all human choosing. Options which there are reasons *for* my choosing are infinite in number. Being finite, I simply cannot do everything, cannot choose every option for which there are reasons. But I can refrain from doing anything; I can respect every serious reason-against. So, an unconditional or absolute affirmative duty (duty *to . . .*) would impose an impossible burden and be irrational; but negative moral absolutes (duties *not* to . . .), if correctly stated with attention to the distinction between intention and side-effect, can all be adhered to in any and every circumstance.

Moreover, many human goods (e.g. the lives of others) are gifts, givens, which we can destroy or damage, but cannot create. Here, too, is a ground of the intelligible asymmetry between reasons-for and reasons-against. Nor does the priority, within their ambit, of reasons-against give morality as a whole a negative cast, or elevate 'moral purity' to the rank of a supreme goal. The first limb of practical reason's first principle remains that human good is to be done and pursued. Its second limb is that evil is to be avoided. But a full respect for and adherence to the absolute duties to forbear from evil leaves open a wide field of (more numerous) individual and social positive responsibilities.

VII

The moral absolutes give legal reasoning its backbone: the exclusion of intentional killing, of intentional injury to the person and even the economic interests of the person,[24] of deliberate deception for the sake of securing desired results, of enslavement which treats a human person as an object of a lower rank of being than the autonomous human subject. These moral absolutes, which *are* rationally determined and essentially determinate, constitute the most basic human rights, and the foundations of the criminal law and the law of intentional torts or delicts, not to mention all the rules, principles, and doctrines which penalize intentional deception, withdraw from it all direct legal support, and exclude it from the legal process.

The rationality of all these moral and legal norms depends upon the incommensurability of the human goods and bads at stake in morally significant options for choice. This incommensurability has further implications of importance to legal reasoning.

The core of the moral norm of fairness is the Golden Rule: 'Do to others as you would have them do to you; do not impose on others what you would not want to be obliged by them to accept.' This has two aspects. First: practical rationality, outside the limited technical context of competitive games, includes a rational norm of impartiality. This norm excludes not all forms and corresponding feelings of preference for oneself and those who are near and dear, but rather all those forms of preference which are motivated only by desires, aversions, or hostilities which do not correspond to intelligible aspects of the real *reasons* for action, the basic human goods realizable in the lives of other human beings as in the lives of oneself or those close to one's heart.

The Golden Rule's second aspect is this. Although fairness is thus a rational norm requiring one to transcend all rationally unintegrated feelings, its concrete application in personal life presupposes a commensuration of benefits and burdens which reason is impotent to commensurate. For, to apply the Golden Rule one must know what burdens one considers too great to accept. And this knowledge, constituting a pre-moral commensuration, cannot be by rational commensuration. Therefore, it can only be one's intuitive awareness, one's discernment, of one's own differentiated *feelings* towards various goods and bads as concretely remembered, experienced, or imagined. This, I repeat, is not a rational and objective commensuration of goods and bads; but once established in one's feelings and identified in one's self-awareness, it enables one to measure one's options by a rational and objective standard of inter-personal impartiality.

Analogously, in the life of a community, the preliminary commensuration of rationally incommensurable factors is accomplished not by rationally determined judgements, but by *decisions* (choices). Is it fair to impose on others the risks inherent in driving at more than 10 m.p.h.? Yes, in our community, since our community has by custom and law *decided to* treat those risks and harms as *not too great*. Have we a rational critique of a community which decided to limit road traffic to 10 m.p.h. and to accept all the economic and other costs of that decision? Or not to have the institution of trusts, or constructive trusts? No, we have no rational critique of such a community. But we do have a rational critique of someone who drives at 60 m.p.h. but who, when struck by another, complains and alleges that the mere fact that the other's speed exceeded 10 m.p.h. established that other's negligence. Or of someone willing to receive the benefits (e.g. the tax benefits) of trusts but not willing to accept the law's distinction between trust and contract in his bankruptcy.

And, in general, we have a rational critique of one who accepts the benefits of this and other communal decisions but rejects the burdens as they bear on him and those in whom he feels interested. In short, the decision to permit road traffic to proceed faster than 10 m.p.h., or to define trusts just as English law does, was rationally underdetermined.[25] (That is not to say that it was or is wholly unguided by reason; the good of human bodily life and integrity is a genuine reason always practically relevant, and the rational demand for consistency with our individual and communal tolerance or intolerance of other—non-traffic— threats to that good provides some rational criteria for decision. And similarly with the trust, whose rationality defied many legislative attempts, for centuries, to suppress this peculiar double ownership.) Still, though rationally underdetermined, the decision to permit fast-moving traffic, once made, provides an often fully determinate rational standard for treating those accused of wrongful conduct or wrongfully inflicting injury. Likewise with trusts, in bankruptcy.

In the working of the legal process, much turns on the principle—a principle of fairness—that litigants (and others involved in the process) should be treated by judges (and others with power to decide) *impartially*, in the sense that they are as nearly as possible to be treated by each judge as they would be treated by every other judge. It is this above all, I believe, that drives the law towards the artificial, the *techne* rationality of laying down and following a set of positive norms identifiable as far as possible simply by their 'sources' (i.e. by the fact of their enactment or other constitutive event) and applied so far as possible according to their publicly stipulated meaning, itself elucidated with as little as possible appeal to considerations which, because not controlled by facts about sources (constitutive events), are inherently likely to be appealed to differently by different judges. This drive to insulate legal from moral reasoning can never, however, be complete.

Incommensurability has further, related implications for legal reasoning. It rules out the proposed technique of legal reasoning known as Economic Analysis of Law. For it is central to that technique that every serious question of social order can be resolved by aggregating the overall net good promised by alternative options, in terms of a simple commensurating factor (or maximand), namely wealth measured in terms of the money which relevant social actors would be willing and able to pay to secure their preferred option. Equally central to Economic Analysis is the assumption, or thesis, that there is no difference of principle between buying the right to inflict injury intentionally and buying the right not to take precautions which would eliminate an equivalent number of injuries caused accidentally.[26] A root and branch critique of Economic Analysis of Law will focus on these two features of it.

Less fundamental critiques, such as Dworkin's (helpful and worth while though it is),[27] leave those features untouched. Indeed, Dworkin's own distinction between rights and collective goals (the latter being proposed by Dworkin as the legitimate province of legislatures) is a distinction which uncritically assumes that collective goals can rationally be identified and preferred to alternatives by aggregation of value, without regard to principles of distributive fairness and other aspects of justice—principles which themselves constitute rights, and which cannot be traded off, according to some rational methodology, against measurable quantities of value.[28]

VIII

In sum: much academic theory about legal reasoning greatly exaggerates the extent to which reason can settle what is greater good and lesser evil. At the same time, such theory minimizes the need for authoritative sources. Such sources, so far as they are clear, and respect the few absolute moral rights and duties, are to be respected as the only reasonable basis for judicial reasoning and decision, in relation to those countless issues which do not directly involve those absolute rights and duties. A natural law theory in the classical tradition makes no pretence that natural reason can identify the one right answer to those countless questions which arise for the judge who finds the sources unclear.

In the classical view, expressed by Aquinas with a clear debt to Aristotle,[29] there are many ways of going wrong and doing wrong; but in very many, perhaps most situations of personal and social life there are a number of incompatible *right* (i.e. not-wrong) options. Prior personal choice(s) or authoritative social decision-making can greatly reduce this variety of options for the person who has made that commitment or the community which accepts that authority. Still, those choices and decisions, while rational and reasonable, were in most cases not required by reason. They were not preceded by any rational judgement that *this* option is *the* right answer, or the best solution.

NOTES

© John Finnis 1992.

1. For my use here of 'purpose', 'goal', 'feeling', 'benefit', 'motivated', and 'basic human good', see Germain Grisez, Joseph Boyle, and John Finnis, 'Practical Principles, Moral Truth, and Ultimate Ends', *American Journal of Jurisprudence*, 32 (1987), 99–151 at 99–110.

2. See John Finnis, Joseph Boyle, and Germain Grisez, *Nuclear Deterrence, Morality and Realism* (Oxford: Oxford University Press, 1987), 277–8; John Finnis, *Natural Law and Natural Rights* (Oxford: Clarendon Press, 1980), 84–5, 100.

3. See John Finnis, *Fundamentals of Ethics* (Oxford: Oxford University Press, 1983), 20–2; Finnis, 'Natural Inclinations and Natural Rights . . .', in L. Elders and K. Hedwig, eds., *Lex et Libertas* (*Studi Tomistici* 30, Libreria Editrice Vaticana, 1987), 43 at 43–9.

4. So Aristotle's principal treatise on human nature is his *Ethics*, which is an attempt to identify the human good, and is, according to its author, from beginning to end an effort of practical, as opposed to theoretical, understanding (see e.g. *Nicomachean Ethics*, 1. 1. 1094ª26–ᵇ12 with Aquinas' commentary); Finnis, *Fundamentals of Ethics*, 24. Aristotle's *Ethics* is not derivative from some prior treatise on human nature, not even his *De Anima*.

5. In Aristotle, 'natural' (as in 'natural right' or 'right by nature') also connotes objectivity or truth: see *Fundamentals of Ethics*, 24.

6. Roberto Mangabeira Unger, *Knowledge and Politics* (New York: Free Press, 1975), 77. On this, and the other arguments, see Finnis, 'On "The Critical Legal Studies Movement" ', in J. Eekelaar and J. Bell, eds., *Oxford Essays in Jurisprudence: Third Series* (Oxford: Oxford

University Press, 1987), 144–65 at 163–5; or in *American Journal of Jurisprudence*, 30 (1985), 21–42 at 40–2.

7. But not exclusively; ambiguities arise here also from various phenomenal and cultural sources; so movements can be said to be 'chosen' and 'free' just in so far as they are not subject to physical constraints, or external constraint, or social constraints; and so on.

8. On free choice and its conditions, see e.g. Finnis, Boyle, and Grisez, *Nuclear Deterrence*, 256–60; Joseph Boyle, Germain Grisez, and Olaf Tollefsen, *Free Choice: A Self-Referential Argument* (Notre Dame, Ind.: Notre Dame University Press, 1976); Aquinas, *De Malo*, q. 6, a. un.

9. See Grisez, Boyle, and Finnis, *Nuclear Deterrence* , 119–25.

10. Thus *Nuclear Deterrence*, at 284–7. In *Natural Law*, 100–13, I call them 'basic requirements of practical reasonableness', and in *Fundamentals of Ethics*, 69–70, 74–6, I call them 'intermediate moral principles'.

11. On intention, see Finnis, 'Intention and Side-Effects' in R. G. Frey and Christopher Morris, eds., *Liability and Responsibility: Essays in Law and Morals* (Cambridge: Cambridge University Press, 1991), 32–64; for the relation between the analysis of action here sketched and the mode of responsibility which excludes choosing to destroy, damage, or impede any instantiation of any basic human good, see *Nuclear Deterrence*, 286–90.

12. Robert Nozick, *Anarchy, State and Utopia* (Oxford: Blackwell, 1974), 160; Finnis, *Natural Law*, 187. Cf. the principle of eminent domain, or the way in which laws of insolvency, while quite reasonably varying from country to country, are all structured around some principle of equality amongst creditors or within ranks of creditors. But the most obvious implication is the principle that in conditions of great scarcity and deprivation, goods become once again common just to the extent necessary to allow those in danger to appropriate what they need to avert e.g. starvation; this moral principle can qualify even the legal definition of theft, whether directly or via the concept of (dis)honesty: J.C. Smith, *Justification and Excuse in the Criminal Law* (London: Stevens, 1989), 50–2.

13. For an elementary account (differently enumerated), see *Natural Law*, 136–8, 157; for profound exposition, explanation, and reflection concerning the four orders, see Germain Grisez, *Beyond the New Theism: A Philosophy of Religion* (Notre Dame, Ind.: Notre Dame University Press, 1975), 230–40.

14. See Finnis, 'Concluding Reflections', *Cleveland State Law Rev.*, 38 (1990), 230–50 at 235–8.

15. See further Finnis, *Natural Law*, 231–7; Finnis, 'The Authority of Law in the Predicament of Contemporary Social Theory', *Notre Dame*

Journal of Law, Ethics and Public Policy, 1 (1984), 115–37; Finnis, 'Law as Co-ordination', *Ratio Juris*, 2 (1989), 97–104.

16. See Ronald Dworkin, *Law's Empire* (Cambridge, Mass.: Harvard University Press, 1986), 255. This term seems confusing, since both dimensions are, on his account, necessary to justify a judicial decision. His previous name for the second dimension, (inherent substantive moral) 'soundness', was better: see Dworkin, *Taking Rights Seriously* (Cambridge, Mass.: Harvard University Press, 1978), 340–1. Still, the labels adopted by Dworkin have the merit of making it clear that fit, although relevant precisely because a necessary condition for securing certain moral and political goods and requirements such as community and integrity, is itself a matter of historical fact, namely, the facts about what judgements and decisions have been made by the relevant institutions in a given society over a given span of time, and the extent to which some actual or hypothetical judgement or decision corresponds in content to earlier judgements and decisions.

17. Throughout this discussion of Dworkin's dimensions of assessment, I shall take for granted his assumption that 'morality' and 'moral soundness' refer to a 'dimension of assessment' which can sometimes be rightly (in some sense of 'right' relevant to judicial duty) subordinated to some other criterion or criteria (such as 'fit'). But the truth here is different, though not simple: morality always trumps every other criterion of choice, though not in such a way as to make immoral choice irrational; but the truth conditions of any moral truth(s) relevant to a judge include facts about fit; if the facts about fit cannot (on moral standards of judgement) be reconciled with morality, one is in a *lex injusta* situation, as to which see Finnis, *Natural Law*, ch. 12.

18. In 'game theory'—a vast and sophisticated body of reasoning about situations of ordinary life (e.g. 'bargaining') conceived *as if* they had the simple, unitary-goal, self-interested structure of a competitive game—the first axiom is that of transitivity: if a is better than b and b is better than c, then a must be better than c; if x is worse than y and y than z, then x is worse than z; etc., and similarly for comparative predicates other than 'is better than' or 'is worse than', e.g. 'is preferable to'. See H.D. Luce and H. Raiffa, *Games and Decisions* (New York: Wiley, 1957), ch. 1. Clear-headed masters of game theory acknowledge that in real life *in*transitivities abound: a is better than b in one respect (e.g. proximity to school), and b is better than c in another respect (e.g. physical amenities), but since the two bases of comparison (proximity and amenities) are not commensurable with each other, it does not follow that a is better than c in any respect, let

alone unqualifiedly better. So Luce and Raiffa are reduced to saying: 'We may say that we are only concerned with behavior which is transitive, adding hopefully that we believe this need not always be a vacuous study' (ibid. 25). On the same page they acknowledge the typical cause and effect of intransitivities: a topic or situation forces 'choices between inherently incomparable alternatives. The idea is that each alternative invokes "responses" on several different "attribute" scales and that, although each scale may itself be transitive, their amalgamation need need not be.'

19. See e.g. Dworkin, *Taking Rights Seriously*, 340–2.

20. See Grisez, 'Against Consequentialism', *American Journal of Jurisprudence*, 23 (1978), 21–72 at 46–7.

21. See Finnis, Boyle, and Grisez, *Nuclear Deterrence, Morality and Realism*, 207–72. Joseph Raz, *The Morality of Freedom* (Oxford: Oxford University Press, 1986), 321–66, explores incommensurability with some similar conclusions.

22. There are other forms of reasoning in the fourth, cultural order, e.g. aesthetic. Here, makers are not guided by any goal adequately identifiable independently of the efficacious means which they might calculate and adopt for achieving it; artistic creation thus outruns technique. Instead, such makers, responding to the sensible particularity of the matter on or with which they work, are each guided by a 'sense' of the object, a sense which cannot be articulated otherwise than by producing the object, yet which somehow serves to measure the adequacy of any particular attempt. There is interaction between the process of creation and this imaginative 'conception' or 'intuition' or 'anticipation' of the object; the anticipation may be refined and altered, even radically, without however disappearing, during the process. To assess the artistic, aesthetic worth (goodness or badness) of the final product involves an aesthetic appreciation of the unity between 'what the work is trying to say' and 'how the work is saying it'; the aesthetic understanding does not come to rest at either pole; nor does it use criteria wholly prior and external to the composition itself. Provided that a composition has a kind of inner unity, clarity, integrity, it can have an aesthetic worth which can govern and reshape, rather than be governed by, pre-existing standards generalizing the features of previous aesthetic objects which by their own inner unity, clarity, integrity established *for themselves* their artistic worth.

23. The qualification: there may be choice between (say) two options, one of which is rationally motivated, but the other of which, though shaped in its structure of means by intelligence, is ultimately motivated *only* by feeling. But this is not the sort of choice with

which moral reasoning is concerned, although the struggle against temptations arising from emotional motivations is undeniably of moral significance.

24. English law claims not to recognize the principle that an intent to injure is sufficient to make unlawful an otherwise lawful action: *Bradford Corporation* v. *Pickles* [1895] AC 587; *Allen* v. *Flood* [1898] AC 1. But the significance of this claim is greatly reduced by (i) the doctrine, established in *Quinn* v. *Leathem* [1901] AC 495 and *Crofter Hand Woven Harris Tweed* v. *Veitch* [1942] AC 435, that an agreement to do acts which harm the plaintiff with the predominant intention of harming him is a tort even if the acts themselves are otherwise lawful, and by (ii) the further doctrines which give actions in tort to those who are harmed by a wrongful act, e.g. of fraud, inducing or threatening breach of contract or interference with contract, etc., when that act is intended to harm them, even when they would otherwise have no action in respect of the fraud, intimidation or breach of or interference with contract; see e.g. *Lonrho plc* v. *Fayed* [1991] 3 All E.R. 303 (HL). Moreover, the foundational character of the doctrine in *Bradford Corporation* v. *Pickles* and *Allen* v. *Flood* is put in question by the fact that in American common law it has been rejected: see James Barr Ames, 'How Far an Act May Be a Tort Because of the Wrongful Motive of the Actor', *Harvard Law Review*, 18 (1905), 411–22; and *Prosser on Torts* sect. 130. Moreover, the House of Lords' adoption, in the 1890s, of the principle that motive alone cannot make an individual's act unlawful was deeply confused by a flawed analysis of action and intention. (1) There was a fundamental failure to distinguish feelings from reasons for acting; e.g. Lord Watson expressed the principle as: 'when the act done is, apart from the feelings which prompted it, legal, the civil law ought to take no cognizance of its motive' ([1898] AC at 94). (2) Correspondingly there was a failure to see that acts should be described, identified, in terms of the ends and means identified in the deliberations which shaped the options amongst which the actor chose, and so must distinguish clearly between ends or means and side-effects; the argument which the Lords rejected in 1898 included within 'malice' a purpose to 'benefit oneself at the expense of one's neighbour'—which confuses the case where loss to the neighbour is the object (and financial benefit to self no more than a welcome side-effect) with the case where financial benefit to self is the object (and loss to the neighbour no more than a foreseen, perhaps even a welcome side-effect); the Lords rejected the argument without identifying the radical ambiguity.

25. Of course, this does not mean that it was 'indeterminate' in the

strong sense of the word which the Critical Legal Studies Movement uses so vaguely and uncritically, i.e. indeterminate in the sense of being wholly unguided by reason. (See Finnis, 'On "The Critical Legal Studies Movement" ', 147, 157–61.) For the good of bodily life and integrity is a genuine reason always practically relevant; and some further rational criteria for decision are provided by facts about human reaction-times and susceptibility to impact, and by the rational demand for consistency with our individual and communal tolerance or intolerance of *other*—non-traffic—threats to that good.

26. See Finnis, 'Allocating Risks and Suffering', *Cleveland State Law Rev.*, 38 (1990) 193–207 at 200–5.

27. Dworkin, *A Matter of Principle* (Cambridge, Mass.: Harvard University Press, 1985), pt. IV.

28. See Finnis, 'A Bill of Rights for Britain? The Moral of Contemporary Jurisprudence', *Proc. Brit. Acad.* 71 (1985), 303–31 at 318–22.

29. See Aquinas, *Summa Theologiae*, Ia IIae, q. 95, a. 2; Aristotle, *Nicomachean Ethics*, 5. 10. $1134^{b}19$–$1135^{a}6$; Finnis, *Natural Law*, 281–90, 294–5.

7

The Irrelevance of Moral Objectivity

JEREMY WALDRON

1. OBJECTIVITY AND REALISM

No one should infer from the title of this chapter that objectivity in the sense of fairness, impartiality, or even-handedness is being called irrelevant or unimportant in law or anywhere else. The sense of 'objectivity' I mean is less familiar than that. It is the sense invoked when people claim that some moral judgements are objectively true, while others are objectively false.

Those who make this claim about objective truth and falsity are called 'moral realists'—or at least, that's what they are called by philosophers. I'm sure most non-philosophers find this term bewildering: I imagine 'moral realist' has Machiavellian reson-ances in the minds of many people, or that it connotes what we might call the ethics of Thrasymachus. Those who teach moral philosophy to law students often have to spend time explaining that 'moral realism' has very little in common with 'legal realism', and indeed that it contradicts it in several respects. The legal version is much closer to what 'realism' means to the ordinary person—namely, the sense in which 'Let's be realistic' means something like 'Let's be cynical.' At any rate, 'moral realism' is what philosophers call the thesis that there are such things as objective moral truth and objective moral falsity; and 'anti-realism' is the term for the denial of that thesis. Since moral realism is an important component of natural law jurisprudence, it is worth taking some time to explore its implications for law, legality, and adjudication.

The realist's belief in moral objectivity can be stated technically as follows:

> There are facts which make some moral judgements (that is, some statements of value or principle) true and others false, facts which are independent of anyone's beliefs about the matters in question.[1]

Anti-realists deny this. They deny that there is a moral reality which determines the truth or falsity of the judgements people make. They say: *there are only moral judgements and the people who make them.* Some of the judgements that are made we like, and some we don't like. Some we repudiate and some we cherish. Some we ignore, and some we ride out to kill for. But there are no objective matters of fact which justify these attitudes or which make any of the judgements correct or any of them incorrect.

Anti-realists differ in what they go on to say about the idea of truth. For some, talk of the truth or falsity of a moral judgement is as sensible as talking of the truth or falsity of an exclamation like 'Long live liberty!' or 'Down with Mrs Thatcher!' For others, the predicates 'true' and 'false' are not meaningless, so much as redundant. To say, 'It is true that abortion is wrong' is just a particularly ponderous way of aligning oneself with the judgement 'Abortion is wrong.' It adds nothing to a simple repetition of that judgement. This is what is sometimes called a 'disquotational' theory of truth: disquotational because it makes the proposition ' "*p*" is true' mean the same as '*p*' (without the double quotation marks).[2] Either way—whether we reject the idea of truth for moral judgements or read it disquotationally—the idea of an objective matter of fact which makes a moral judgement true or false, and which a moral judgement purports to represent or to which it purports to correspond, is rejected.

In this chapter, I want to raise questions about the relevance to legal decision-making of the debate between moral realists and their opponents. In particular, I want to raise these questions in the context of a legal system governing a society in which there are unresolved disagreements or oppositions on all or most major moral issues. In other words, I want to raise questions about the relevance of moral realism to legal decision-making in a society like our own.

2. LEGAL POSITIVISM AND MORAL JUDGEMENT

Legal positivism can be understood as a view about what legal decision-making involves, or it can be understood as a view about what legal decision-making *ought* to involve: I shall call the former 'descriptive', and the latter 'normative', positivism. Cutting across this is another distinction between positivism as a thesis in general jurisprudence—a thesis about law as such—and positivism as a thesis in particular jurisprudence—a thesis about some particular legal system (or a particular part of some legal system).

Common to all of these is the positivist conception of law. According to that conception, law can be understood in terms of rules or standards whose authority derives from their provenance in some human source, sociologically defined, and which can be identified as law in terms of that provenance. Thus statements about what the law is—whether in describing a legal system, offering legal advice, or disposing of particular cases—can be made without exercising moral or other evaluative judgement. The judgement is simply one of social fact. That is not true, of course, of law-*making*, for legislation is almost always the exercise of moral or political judgement. But once a legal rule is laid down, no further exercise of such judgement is required for its identification or application.

Descriptive positivism maintains that this is what law *is*—law as such (perhaps by definition), or law in (say) the United States or in England. Now in regard to those particular legal systems, descriptive positivism is almost certainly false. This is partly because many of the rules and standards identified by the best available tests of positive law actually require those who administer them to exercise moral judgement. And it is partly because there are inevitably such gaps in positive law and such indeterminacy in the meanings of the legal rules as to make their administration in fact impossible without the exercise of moral judgement. I shall not waste time defending these claims; everyone is familiar with the evidence. Some jurists try to evade these points by definitional manœuvre: they say that the existence of a legal rule which requires the exercise of moral judgement is incompatible only with 'positive' positivism, not with 'negative' positivism;[3] and they say that the existence of gaps and indeterminate meanings in a given set of positive rules indicates only that we may run out of law in some systems and have to switch to political decision-making, not that legal decision-making itself takes on a moral or political character. As far as I can tell, the motive behind such moves is to secure a victory in the descriptive debate for a position *called* 'legal positivism', no matter what that position turns out to be.

As a descriptive or a definitional thesis, legal positivism is meta-ethically neutral. It takes no position on the nature of moral judgement. It is compatible with moral realism and with moral anti-realism. All it says is that legal decision-making is one thing, moral judgement another.

Normative positivism is a different matter. This is the thesis that the law *ought* to be such that legal decisions can be made without the exercise of moral judgement. Or, if we don't want to state it in the language of obligation: it is the thesis that it would be *a good thing* for the law to be as the descriptive positivist thinks it is. Normative positivism is itself a moral claim: it is a moral claim about the making of moral claims. It identifies the contamination of legal decision by moral judgement as a disadvantage; it says that we lose something of value thereby. It is by far the most interesting form of legal positivism (and indeed it is hard to imagine how a positivist definition of the concept of law could be sustained, without eventually having resort to some such normative thesis). Gerald Postema has argued convincingly that normative positivism was the legal philosophy of Thomas Hobbes, David Hume, and Jeremy Bentham.[4]

The striking thing about normative positivism is the way it views putative cases of moral decision-making in law. For the descriptive positivist, such cases are threats or counter-examples: they have to be reclassified or explained away if the descriptive thesis is to be maintained. Her normative counterpart, however, views them in a different light. They are unsatisfactory aspects of the law to be condemned and minimized. The legal system is to be reformed so that moral decision-making, by judges or officials, is eliminated as far as possible.

Why? The reasons in Hobbes's, Hume's, and Bentham's jurisprudence had to do with the desirability of certainty, security of expectation, and knowledge of what legally empowered officials were likely to require. If the decisions of an official turned on the exercise of her moral judgement, there would be no telling what she might come up with. From the point of view of the citizen trying to organize her life, the official's decisions would be arbitrary.

In modern jurisprudence, 'arbitrary' has at least three connotations, all of them bad. Sometimes it means 'unpredictable', and that, as I said, was the charge that particularly worried Bentham and other thinkers in the mainstream of British positivism. Sometimes it means 'unreasoned', as when a decision is made on the basis of whim or reflex prejudice rather than on the basis of argument. Now these are not the same. A judicial decision can be unreasoned without being unpredictable: we may know, for example, that a judge is a 'knee-jerk' conservative on some range of issues. But it needs to be emphasized also that a legal decision can be unpredictable without being unreasoned. We may know that the judge is going to reason morally (by her own lights) but not know what her moral framework will be. Or even if we do know that she is, for example, a utilitarian, we may be unable to predict her decision because we do not know enough about her reasoning powers or about the information available to her.

A third sense of 'arbitrariness' has become particularly important with regard to American constitutional law. Some feel that even if judges are making moral decisions as reasonably and as predictably as they can, still their decisions lack *legitimacy*. It is for the people or the legislators they have elected to make that sort of decision; it is not for the judges to take the determination of social principle and social value into their own hands.[5] In this democratic sense, 'arbitrary' means something like 'without authority or legitimacy'.

For reasons like these, normative positivists oppose and seek to minimize the amount of moral decision-making exercised by judges and other (unelected) officials in the legal system.

Those who disagree with them in this sometimes refer to themselves as proponents of the idea of *natural law*. Now in modern Anglo-American jurisprudence, 'natural law' is the term used most often for opposition to descriptive or definitional positivism. Natural lawyers deny that law consists of positive rules; they insist that the whole concept of law and the application of particular laws inevitably implicates moral principles and moral values. But if they add, 'and a good thing too', they become opponents not only of descriptive, but of normative positivism as well. These natural lawyers deny that there is anything arbitrary about judges' making moral decisions; indeed they welcome the introduction of values and principles into this area of public life.

Many, but not all, of those who oppose normative positivism, are also moral realists. One exception seems to be Ronald Dworkin.

Dworkin emphatically denies that there is anything wrong with judges incorporating moral and political views into their judgements. He thinks it is unavoidable, and he thinks it an integral part of what good adjudication requires.[6] He insists that such judgements be reasoned, and he repudiates both the democratic charge of illegitimacy and the Benthamite worry about unpredictability. But he has indicated many times that he is not a moral realist (in the sense defined at the beginning of this chapter), or at least that he does not think the debate about moral realism worth participating in.[7] Other opponents of normative positivism, however, *are* moral realists, and indeed the term 'natural law' is sometimes reserved for the position that conjoins moral realism with opposition to positivism in one or other of its forms.[8] That is an understandable usage, since outside analytic jurisprudence, 'natural law' is often used to refer simply to the facts which, according to a moral realist, make judgements of value true or false.

Dworkin apart, is there anything natural or understandable about the connection between moral realism, on the one hand, and opposition to normative positivism, on the other? Is there reason to expect a normative positivist to be anti-realist? Should we expect someone who believes in moral objectivity to think that moral decision-making by judges and other legal officials is a good thing? I am going to argue for a negative answer to these questions.

The attractions of an affirmative answer are fairly obvious. According to realists, those who are sceptical about moral objectivity present moral judgements as simply the arbitrary expression of emotion. Cut loose from any independent criterion of truth or objectivity, judgements about right and wrong become purely matters of private opinion. They become as whimsical and as contingent as the feelings and commitments of those who make them. Your judgement is as good as mine, because there is no true or false of the matter. Now these sound like exactly the accusations that lead jurists in the direction of normative positivism. If an individual's moral judgement is just the idiosyncratic expression of her attitude, then it is unpredictable, unreasoned, and lacks authority; in a word, it is *arbitrary*. Those who want to eliminate arbitrariness from law, therefore, have good reason to be normative positivists if anti-realism is true. If anti-realism is false, however, then moral judgements regain the status of truth claims, and they require all the authority, reasonableness, and predictability that that entails. With that status they can be allowed back into the law. So—the common view concludes—moral realists are likely to feel much more comfortable than anti-realists in allowing judges to make moral decisions.

That is the view I want to attack. That is the difference moral realism is supposed to make in jurisprudence which I shall argue it should not make. In the three sections that follow, I shall make some general points about realism and anti-realism in moral philosophy, before resuming my argument, in Section 6, to the effect that moral decision-making in law is likely to be as arbitrary (in all three senses) for a moral realist as for any opponent of moral objectivity.

3. QUASI-REALISM AND THE NO-DIFFERENCE THESIS

Some philosophers argue that the issue of moral objectivity is irrelevant generally, not merely with regard to the law.[9] Ronald Dworkin toys with this view, in his response to those he calls 'external skeptics': 'We use the language of objectivity, not to give our ordinary moral . . . claims a bizarre metaphysical base, but to *repeat* them, perhaps in a more precise way, to emphasize or qualify their content.'[10] Maybe we use it, he says, to indicate our seriousness, or our belief that the claim we have made has ramification for the lives of everyone, not just our own. But, he goes on,

[T]here is no important difference in philosophical category or standing between the statement that slavery is wrong and the statement that there is a right answer to the question of slavery, namely that it is wrong. I cannot intelligibly hold the first opinion as a moral opinion without also holding the second. Since external skepticism offers no reason to retract or modify the former, it offers no reason to retract or modify the latter either. They are both statements within rather than about the enterprise of morality . . . I hasten to add that recognizing the crucial point I have been making—that the 'objective' beliefs most of us have are moral, not metaphysical, beliefs, that they only repeat and qualify other moral beliefs—in no way weakens those beliefs or makes them claim something less or even different from what they might be thought to claim. For we can assign them no sense, faithful to the role they actually play in our lives, that makes them not moral claims. If anything is made less important by that point, it is external skepticism, not our convictions.[11]

Notice that this is distinct from the disquotational conception of truth referred to earlier. Someone might hold a disquotational theory of truth in moral contexts, but still think that the question of moral objectivity was a robust and important philosophical issue. Dworkin, however, seems to suggest in this passage that it is a non-issue (though elsewhere on the pages from which I have quoted he indicates that it might be an interesting debating topic 'for a calm philosophical moment, away from the moral or interpretive wars').[12]

The view that there is no significant difference at all between realism and anti-realism (about morality, or anything) seems difficult to sustain, without a general attack on metaphysics and on the whole business of discussing the meanings of words and the sorts of things that exist. Realists claim that there are real properties corresponding to the predicates 'good' and 'right', and that no one understands the meaning of these terms unless they grasp that. Anti-realists say that the use of evaluative predicates can be understood without invoking any ideas along those lines at all. If that does not count as a philosophical disagreement, nothing does.

A more modest version of the no-difference position is Simon Blackburn's thesis of 'quasi-realism'.[13] Though Blackburn insists that there is a live philosophical issue between realists and their opponents, he denies that anti-realism does any violence to the way we ordinarily think about ethics and morality. Quasi-realism, he says, is the enterprise of 'trying to earn our right to talk of moral truth, while recognizing fully the subjective sources of our judgements, inside our own attitudes, needs, desires, and natures'.[14] In carrying through this programme, Blackburn has contributed enormously to the debate about moral objectivity by answering some of the cruder criticisms and disarming some of the sillier caricatures of emotivist and other anti-realist positions. But I think it is a mistake to promise that one can produce an anti-realist counterpart for *everything* ordinary moralists want to say. For even if ordinary moral discourse is not systematically infected with a false metaphysics, it has been so influenced in the minds of many of its practitioners by a belief in moral objectivity, particularly the objectivity of Divine Command, that it is unlikely to have remained entirely free of metaphysical distortion. It may be wiser for the anti-realist to remain neutral on the question of whether ordinary ways of talking about morality make sense. (One disadvantage of Blackburn's term 'quasi-realism' is that it indicates a willingness to let the realists dictate the terms of the discussion, so that the anti-realist struggles along, showing that she too can keep up with realist idioms.)

A couple of other considerations reinforce this point. First, it is simply no longer true that ordinary moral discourse is characterized unambiguously by realist-sounding talk of truth and falsity, logic and argument, reasonable and unreasonable positions. Some is and some isn't. For every stern preacher who talks about the reality of obligation, there is a gum-chewing sophomore who says that all moral views are just matters of opinion and there's no ultimate standard. The ordinary talk one hears is infected as much with relativist idioms as with truth-claims.[15] Moral realists often *say* that their meta-ethic gives a better account of what people ordinarily think about morality. But that's because they are not listening to what actually gets said in our culture, or they are filtering or discounting some of it already on the basis of the very theory they take themselves to be supporting with this evidence. Their theory may offer a better account of their own moralizing and that of their chums. But ordinary moral discourse, as I hear it, is a meta-ethical Babel. It is the job of a philosopher to try and sort that out, not to promise in advance to accommodate as much of it as she can.

Second, we should remember that 'realism' and 'anti-realism' are terms that pick out *types* of meta-ethical view, not particular theories. There are several different anti-realist theories (Humean projectivism, emotivism, prescriptivism, conventionalism, existentialism, etc.). Though a given anti-realist might feel some common cause with all such views ('It's us against the realists'), in fact she will reject all but one of them.[16] Similarly, there are many different versions of moral realism (ranging from naturalism through moral rationalism to some version of God and hellfire); and, again, one presumes that a given realist will reject all but one of these. Many modern realists do not want to associate themselves, for example, with any view that defines 'right' and 'wrong' in terms of the will of God. But it seems likely that if any realism has shaped the way we talk about morals in ordinary discourse, it is this one. Since even their philosophical opponents reject that, it seems crazy for an anti-realist to promise that her theory can cope with and explain the legacy of Divine Command conceptions in our moral feelings and our moral vocabulary.

4. THE PANIC ABOUT EMOTIVISM

All the same, it is worth reiterating here the points that Blackburn and others have made in answer to some criticisms of anti-realism, particularly emotivist versions of anti-realism.[17] Their points do not fulfil the quasi-realist promise that emotivism can accommodate all realist idioms in ordinary discourse. But they are a useful antidote for a certain panic that realists seem to feel about the consequences of adopting an emotivist approach. Since emotivism remains the most interesting sceptical view, it is worth dealing with that panic before we look at the implications that moral realism and anti-realism have for the law.

Emotivists are often accused by their opponents of not taking morals seriously, of making morality merely a matter of whim, of suggesting that our moral judgements are as capricious and as arbitrary as our feelings about the people, situations, and actions being judged. The implication is that realists are able to take their moral commitments more seriously than emotivists because they regard them as a response to some matter of objective fact rather than a product of contingent feeling.

But the idea of taking one's moral judgements seriously needs a little scrutiny. Taking one's judgements seriously might mean (*a*) being ready to act on them, being moved by them, having them play an important role in practical life and action, and actually doing what one judges to be right (even when tempted not to). Or it might mean (*b*) being unwilling to budge—in debate and argument—from the moral claims one makes, sticking with one's judgements, refusing to countenance the possibility of changing one's view, and so on.

Now I take it that what the realists have in mind when they talk about being serious about one's moral judgements is something like *b* as opposed to *a*. If a moral judgement is an accurate report of a matter of fact, then one who regards herself as a reliable

observer should stick with her report—sternly, strictly, sonor-
ously, or whatever—and refuse to be tempted to adopt a more
seductive-sounding but factually less accurate position. But actually, nobody is particularly interested in this form of moral
steadfastness, or at least in this form taken alone. What attracts us
to the idea of taking morals seriously is not someone sticking to a
particular view (a moral description, a moral characterization) in
the face of temptation away from it. What attracts us is someone
being prepared to *act* on a moral judgement. We are attracted by
a person's being practically and not just theoretically steadfast.
The moral person we admire has the ability to be *moved* by the
good, not just the ability accurately to detect and report its
presence.

Now, it is a well-known feature of moral judgements that their
sincere adoption indicates a commitment to action. Emotivists
have a ready explanation of this: since moral judgements are
expressions of emotion, and since (by definition) emotions move
us (albeit in complicated ways), then obviously one who makes a
moral judgement that x is good is moved to act in favour of x,
since that disposition is precisely what her judgement evinces.
Realists, on the other hand, have a notoriously difficult time with
this feature of moral language. Since moral properties are just
factual properties on their account, it is hard to see why their
recognition should indicate any willingness to act in any particular way.

This difficulty is often used as the basis of an independent
argument against realism—one aspect of Mackie's so-called 'argument from queerness'.[18] I do not want to use it, in this chapter, as
a line of argument in its own right, for I believe the realist has an
answer. She simply denies the assumption that knowledge of the
good is necessarily motivating.[19] But it is worth seeing how it
affects the present issue—of whether realists take their moral
views more seriously than emotivists do.

We have seen that the realist is embarrassed by having her
moral seriousness characterized in terms of b rather than a,
above. Now the more she tries to escape from this embarrassment, the more she runs into the difficulty posed by the argument
from queerness. To move from b to a, it has to be the case that
accurate perception of moral facts disposes one to act morally.
But for that to be the case, moral facts do have to be presented as

something queer—and not 'queer' in the sense of unusual or odd (like giraffes or neutrinos), but 'queer' in the sense that it looks as though the metaphysical account of them has been cobbled together in an *ad hoc* way purely to meet this difficulty. It looks, then, as though we should turn to emotivism if we want a meta-ethic that shows how people take their morals seriously—at least in a sense of 'seriously' that is of some practical interest.

Underlying the attack on emotivism, there is a constant insinuation by the realist that people's emotions are flighty and contingent—too much under their control and too subject to self-serving manipulation to be an appropriate foundation for morality.[20] But even the realist has to concede that *something* in our moral practice is as fickle and manipulable as emotion. If it is not our moral judgements, then it is our motivation to act on those judgements. Since in the end it is how people act that really concerns us, the realist cannot claim any advantage here.

There are also things to be said about the implied account of emotions in this discussion. Realists seem to crave a foundation for our moral commitments in something more stable than what Thomas Nagel has referred to as 'fortuitous or escapable inclinations'.[21] But in fact that is not a sensible way to characterize many deep emotions, which are strong, steady, and remarkably resistant both to deliberate change and the vicissitudes of circumstance. Think, for example, of parental love and concern. Why should the feelings that find expression in moral judgement not be more like that, than like a whimsical taste for cookies, a whoop for a football team, or an afternoon's inclination to take a nap? Realists become awfully prone to caricature when they hear the term 'emotion' in a meta-ethical theory. They say things about human feelings—their alleged crudity, simplicity, fickleness, and inarticulacy ('boo!' and 'hooray!')—in order to lampoon the opposing position which they would (one hopes) never dream of saying about them in any other context where feelings were being discussed. (Does anybody think that one's emotional attachment to one's child is best captured by 'Hooray for Sam!'? If not, why should anyone think that an idea as crude as that must be the emotivists' best candidate for what is expressed in a moral commitment?)

We should remember also what is being compared with what. The realist is of course tempted to say that we are comparing the fickleness of an individual's feelings, on the one hand, with the solidity of hard moral fact, on the other. But that is a mistake. What is being compared with the alleged fickleness of emotion is not the solidity of moral facts themselves, assuming there are such things, but the solidity or fickleness (whichever it is) of people's *beliefs* about moral facts. Even if there are such objective facts, there is certainly no privileged, easy, or uncontroversial access to them; there is certainly no mode of belief which is straightforwardly and indubitably reflective of the facts' solidity. We know that there are psychological phenomena like self-deception, wilful blindness, deceit, capricious and unpredictable misapprehension, and illusion with regard to other matters of fact. People can mislead themselves and others, and change their minds deliberately or arbitrarily back and forth as easily when they are surveying the world of tangible middle-sized objects, as when they are taking on or sustaining an emotional commitment. Evidently the realist is not entitled to assume that our beliefs about moral facts are any steadier in regard to these vicissitudes than our factual beliefs generally. But once that is conceded, the contrast with the fickleness and unreliability of 'mere' emotions evaporates.

Perhaps, in the end, what worries the realist is the *contingency* of judgement and feeling on the emotivist account. Not contingency in the sense of fickleness; we have already dealt with that caricature. But contingency in the sense that emotivism makes moral judgements *depend* on the wrong sort of thing. The emotivist seems to think that everyone must be prepared to say the following about her own moral sensibility:

> I only make the moral judgements I do (at whatever level) because of how I feel. If I felt differently I would make different moral judgements.

But that characterization can be misleading, for the 'because', and the counterfactual that go with it, are ambiguous.

If the 'because' is supposed to connote simple causality (i.e. 'Among the causal antecedents of some moral judgement I make are some feelings of mine'), then the emotivist is indeed committed to it: that indeed is what it is for a judgement to be expressive of a feeling. (As a matter of fact, the realist could accept that as well, since on her account the attitudinal genesis of a judgement does not detract at all from its status as a descriptive bearer of truth-value.) But the 'because' of causality is not the 'because' of justification or reason-giving. The emotivist is emphatically *not* committed to saying that her own feelings *justify* the judgements that she makes. When I condemn an action, I usually do so in virtue of some feature F that it has (the action's cruelty, for example, or its hurtfulness), and I may express that relation in the counterfactual: 'If the act had not been F, it would not have been wrong.' Critics sometimes accuse the emotivist of thinking that the feature of arousing a negative emotion in the speaker is the paradigm value for F. But, as Simon Blackburn argues, emotivists are not committed to that at all:

The counterfactual 'If we had different attitudes it would not be wrong to kick dogs' expresses the moral view that the feature which makes it wrong to kick dogs is our reaction. But this is an absurd moral view, and not one to which [an emotivist] has the least inclination. Like anyone else he thinks that what makes it wrong to kick dogs is that it causes them pain. To put it another way: he approves of a moral disposition which given this belief [about the dogs' pain] as an input, yields the reaction of disapproval as an output; he does not approve of one which needs belief about our attitudes as an input in order to yield the same output, and this is all that gets expression in the counterfactual.[22]

5. MORAL DISAGREEMENT

The impulse to anti-realism in ethics has many sources. For some, it is simply that emotivism or prescriptivism provides what appears to be the best account available of what is going on when moral judgements are made and thought about and followed. They do not come into meta-ethics with any particular sceptical axe to grind. They just start from the position (which everyone acknowledges) that moral judgement has *something* to do with attitude, feeling, and the determination and guidance of action, and they build up their account from that. Having developed their analysis, they then discover that there is simply no room for any notion of moral truth and moral objectivity, and they put those ideas quietly aside.[23]

Others are led to anti-realism more directly, from their reflections on the intractability of moral disagreement. There seem to be disagreements or oppositions about almost everything in ethics—about values, principles, virtues, deserts, God, the nature of the good life, our obligations to one another, the appropriate way to deal with conflict, politics, democracy, rights, the respect due to humanity in all its forms, our relations to the animals, and on and on—and there is no consensus at all about how such disagreements may be resolved.[24] Of course the existence of disagreement does not imply the truth of anti-realism. But it is not entirely crazy to explore the anti-realist option in the face of disagreements as apparently irresolvable as these.

It may be worth expanding on this last point. The differences that exist in people's moral, ethical, and political views were taken famously by J.L. Mackie to be the basis of one of two main arguments supporting moral scepticism: 'radical differences between first order moral judgements make it difficult to treat those judgements as apprehensions of objective truths.'[25] Certainly they make it difficult to treat *all* the different views as apprehensions of objective truths, but I take it Mackie's point is that they make it difficult to treat *any* moral views in that way. Given what morality is and what it is for (given the sort of fact it must be, if it is a matter of fact), how could there be objective truths and falsity certified by the way the world is, and yet so much disagreement?

Realists' reactions to this argument differ. Nicholas Sturgeon writes that it is 'one argument for moral skepticism that I respect even though I remain unconvinced',[26] while Michael Moore insists that it is

subject to the crushing rejoinder that the mere fact of disagreement among the judgments of people hardly shows there is no fact of the matter to be agreed upon. People within a culture, and people in different cultures, may disagree about all sorts of things, such as whether the winds are influenced by the earth's rotation, or whether the moon is made of rock. The simple fact of disagreement for certain sorts of belief cannot itself show that there is no fact of the matter being argued about. To think otherwise is to confuse intersubjective agreement with objectivity.[27]

Now Moore is correct about the logical gap between disagreement and there being no objective fact of the matter. But he writes as though *this is all that needs to be said* about moral disagreement in order to avoid embarrassment for the realist.

And it isn't: moral disagreement remains a continuing difficulty for realism, even if it doesn't entail its falsity, so long as the realist fails to establish connections between the idea of objective truth and the existence of procedures for resolving disagreement.

If we disagree about whether the moon is made of rock or cheese, both of us will say that the matter could be settled if someone actually went there and tasted it. If we disagree (to use Moore's less trivial example) about the impact on wind of the earth's rotation, we look to meteorology and physics for complicated suggestions for sorting this out. Now moral realists have pointed out, quite properly, that scientific methodology is enormously complicated and subtle: the simple positivist image of indubitable observation-statements that either refute or confirm a disputed hypothesis is naïve and uninteresting, and it does not count at all against moral realism that there is nothing similar available in ethics. Still, our conception of reality in science is associated with the whole complex apparatus of methodology, heuristic, observation, and experimentation. We know how to proceed in the face of disagreement. The point is that there is nothing equivalent in morals, nothing that even begins to connect the idea of there being a fact of the matter with the idea of there being some way to proceed when people disagree.

The point has to be stated carefully. I am not saying that there is no procedure or methodology in ethics that commands *universal* assent; there is no such procedure in science either. Astronomers say one thing, astrologers another.[28] But at least in mainstream science, there is a broad conception of method acknowledged by a large group of practitioners, all of whom regard that acknowledgement as something independent of the scientific disagreements they have with one another. No doubt the conception is loosely defined and controversial in places. No doubt also, the group excludes some of those who purport to practise science. Still it is understood by its members, at any rate, and by a substantial consensus in the culture at large, to include the protagonists in a large number of important disagreements. In other words, a single (albeit loosely defined) conception of method for settling disagreements is shared by a significant group of people who regard themselves as engaged in serious disagreement. And what is more, disagreements do get settled by this method, and when they do not, we can often refer to the terms of the method to explain why.

Among moralists, there is nothing remotely comparable. What tends to happen is that each main view comes along trailing its own theory of what counts as a justification: utilitarians have one view, Kantians another, Christian fundamentalists yet another, and so on. Aristotelians, Nietzscheans, Marxists, traditional conservatives like Burke, liberals like Rawls, feminists like Gilligan— all acknowledge that the disagreements between them are important (if any are). Yet unlike their counterparts in the scientific community, they share virtually nothing in the way of an epistemology or a method with which these disagreements might in principle be approached.

If two utilitarians disagree about social policy, they can refer that disagreement to the complex apparatus of modern consequentialism: different levels of moral thought, different models of inter-personal comparability, strategic and game-theoretical models, sophisticated points about moral mathematics, and so on. But all of this counts for nothing if the moral disagreement is between a utilitarian and a deontologist, or between Bentham and Nietzsche. Perhaps a utilitarian who is also a moral realist will maintain that the basic propositions of her theory are true and those of her deontological opponent false. She will claim that the development of utilitarian ethics beginning in the late eighteenth century is progress towards the truth, and that it represents an improvement in our moral sensibility over the systems that preceded it. She will say, too that the Nietzschean is making some sort of appalling mistake. *But there is nothing she can say to support these claims*—indeed, nothing she can say about how a statement of this kind could be found to be true, how people might be mistakenly convinced that it was false, and so on.

Modern moral realists are simply disingenuous about this lacuna. Mark Platts, for example, writes that (on the realist view he espouses) 'moral judgments are viewed as factually cognitive, as presenting claims about the world which can be assessed (like any other factual belief) as true or false, and whose truth or falsity are as much possible objects of human knowledge as any other factual claims about the world.'[29] But how exactly are we to assess the truth or falsity of a moral judgement? What does the assessment involve? What procedures? What methodology? We are never told. For a proposition to be a possible object of knowledge, it is not sufficient for it to be capable of being true and being believed to be true: there must also be some gesture in the direction of justification for the true belief in question, and in particular a non-trivial sense of justification that would have some connection and sensitivity to the distinction between the genesis of true belief and the genesis of false belief.

Platts says that '[w]e detect moral aspects of the world in the same way we detect (nearly all) other aspects: by looking and seeing'.[30] But in non-moral cases, where two people disagree about something (say, the colour or size of an object) and each of them claims to have based her belief on visual detection, we can supplement the simple epistemology of 'looking and seeing' with a whole apparatus which we agree on and which explains mistake, illusion, and perspective—a whole paraphernalia which connects the epistemology to complicated procedures for distinguishing truth from falsity, accuracy from error, and which is rooted eventually in a physiological and psychological account of perception.[31] There is nothing comparable in ethics.

Platts also writes: 'By a process of careful attention to the world, we can improve our moral beliefs about the world, make them more approximately true.'[32] He adds that this process of improvement has no end-point, nothing that counts as final certainty. But he fails to say anything about what 'care' is or involves in this context. Again, in straightforward cases of 'looking and seeing', an account can be given: 'Look at an object from several angles before you pronounce on its shape, because angle of vision affects shape perception in the following way . . .'. We give an account of what it is to be careful which has an agreed and independent basis in our theory of perception. Nothing similar is agreed on in ethics, and nothing at all along these lines is offered by Platts.

By their own lights, moral realists ought to be very concerned that they have nothing to offer in the way of a method for approaching moral disputes. Consider what Michael Moore has written about what he thinks of as the sad predicament of the moral sceptic:

A skeptic will regard his own values with embarrassment, for they hold out a promise on which he thinks he cannot deliver. His value judgments, that is, purport to be descriptive in form. For example, he may say such things as, 'killing is wrong,' a statement that seems capable of being true or false. Moreover, others expect that when he says these things, he has reasons with which he can demonstrate the truth of such propositions, reasons that others will find persuasive. Yet his skepticism tells him that none of this is true. He is merely playing a peculiar form of language game when he makes his value judgments. Accordingly, when he wishes to engage in honest debate and not merely to issue propaganda, he will qualify his value judgements with 'I think,' or 'of course, it's only my opinion.' He will try to cancel the promissory note as he issues it, because he believes he cannot otherwise pay it.[33]

As a matter of fact, many anti-realists deny that their (or anyone else's) moral judgments hold out such a promise. 'Error Theorists' (such as Mackie) believe they do, but non-cognitivists (such as R.M. Hare) do not.[34] Be that as it may, certainly *realists* believe this about *their own* moral judgements. But since they are quite unable to 'demonstrate the truth' of their judgements or show how they correspond to moral reality, they should be the ones in all honesty to qualify them with 'Of course, it's only my opinion' and so on. For though they insist that there is some fact of the matter, they offer us nothing which would help distinguish a mere arbitrary opinion from a well-grounded belief.

6. MORAL JUDGEMENT AND ADJUDICATION

Let us turn now finally to the law, and to the desirability of moral decision-making by judges and other officials in legal contexts.

We know there is moral disagreement in society and that even those who believe that there are right answers in these controversies are unable to agree about how we might arrive at them. In the face of all this disagreement, how should a judge or other official behave? How should she respond to the fact that many of the people whose lives are affected by her decisions, and many of the other officials in whose company she must make her decisions, hold views on issues of social and political morality that are radically at odds with her own?

In particular, given everything that has been said so far, what difference would the truth of moral realism make to her dilemma? The main misgiving, we recall, is about the *arbitrariness* of moral decision-making by judges: arbitrariness in the sense of unpredictability, irrationality, and democratic illegitimacy. This is what normative positivists fear about judicial moralizing. Are their fears likely to be allayed at all by a belief in moral objectivity? Is it an apprehension that arises only on account of the emotivist theory of ethics?

Michael Moore, for one, seems to believe that the answer to these last two questions is 'Yes.' Judges have to believe in objectivity, he claims, in order to dispel the suggestion of arbitrariness in their moral judgements. They cannot afford to be sceptics:

Judges are subject to [the] debilitating psychological consequences of skepticism no less than the rest of us. The institutional role may even intensify these effects, for judges must not only make value judgments, but also impose them upon other people. If one's daily task is to impose values on others, to think that these are only one's own personal values doubtlessly makes the job hard to perform at all. To foist personal values onto hapless litigants is not for many temperaments a satisfying role.[35]

But in the light of what we have said, this now seems completely wrong-headed. Even if scepticism is rejected, even if there *are* moral facts which make true judgements true and false judgements false, still the best a judge can do is to impose her *opinion* about such facts on the 'hapless litigants' who come before her. They will have beliefs and opinions of their own on the matter, and even if they too become card-carrying moral realists, they will no doubt continue to ask why the judge's view of the facts should prevail over theirs. For, obviously, the truth of moral realism (if it is true) does not validate any particular person's or any particular judge's moral beliefs. At best, it alters our understanding of the character of a moral disagreement without moving us any closer to an understanding of who is right and who is wrong.

We saw earlier that Moore thought an anti-realist, if she is honest, ought always to 'qualify [her] value judgments with "I think," or "of course, it's only my opinion" ', and he seems to think this will embarrass the judge because, in the same breath, she will be imposing the views she is qualifying in this way on people who disagree with her. In fact, it is quite unclear why Moore thinks this retiring posture is either appropriate for or distinctive of the anti-realist position. For one thing, if an anti-realist is going to be coy about her value-judgements in a way that is meta-ethically transparent, she ought to be saying, not 'I think', but 'I feel'. She ought to characterize her judgement not as a personal opinion (for her opponent will ask: 'Opinion about what?') but as some sort of complicated affect. Talk of opinion is appropriate when there is some *matter of fact* about which people disagree. It is not necessarily appropriate in cases of contrary emotions.

But then the next point is obvious. Since, on any account, there is moral disagreement, and since we do not agree even in principle on any way of settling such disagreements, a judge who is assigned the task of making moral judgements ought to be saying, 'I think', and 'Of course, it's only my opinion', *even if realism is true*. If she pays any attention to the fact that she is not the only person in society with an opinion on the issue she is addressing, she will certainly be conscious of some arbitrariness in her opinion's prevailing, whether she is a realist or not.

Consider the three aspects of arbitrariness we mentioned earlier: worries about the unpredictability, the irrationality, and the democratic illegitimacy of judicial moralism.

6.1. *Unpredictability*

Does moral realism make any difference to the predictability of those judicial decisions that involve a moral element? If some version of emotivism is true, there will be a modicum of empirical predictability. We know, for example, that Rehnquist is a conservative and Thurgood Marshall something of a liberal, and political scientists use this as a basis for fairly reliable predictions about the attitudes they will express and the positions they will take, without assuming anything in the way of moral objectivity. What would moral objectivity add to this?

Without an epistemology, the answer I think is 'nothing'. The only basis for predicting what a judge's beliefs will be about the moral facts today is the record of her beliefs about them in the past, and as we have seen, something similar to this form of predictability is already available even if realism is false. Maybe if realists came up with a psychology of moral perception, predictability could be improved. We know that in the presence of a red patch, most observers who are not blind will detect redness (and we can explain why), and we know that if an elephant wanders into the courtroom, the judge along with everyone else is likely to report, 'There goes an elephant.' If responses to the presence of moral value were as predictable as this, then maybe realism would have something to offer in the way of dispelling arbitrariness. But no modern realist wants to associate herself with such an epistemology. Very few regard perceptions of value as on a par with colour discriminations or the discrimination of large visible objects. And any who did would find herself having to denigrate her moral (as opposed to her meta-ethical) opponents as colour-blind, on such a wide front as to deprive the analogy with sense-perception of any usefulness at all in dealing with inter-personal disputes.[36]

6.2. *Irrationality*

It might seem as though the worry about irrationality is the one where realism clearly has the advantage over moral anti-realism. After all, realists say that moral judgements are reasoned reports of the presence of moral properties, while anti-realists explicitly deny this.

But the worry about the irrationality of judicial moralizing is not about what judges say, but about what they do. It is a concern about whether they are prepared to argue or assemble reasons for their views, or whether they simply announce them flatly, saying that though they cannot argue about virtue or vice, they know it when they see it. And here it seems that anti-realist and realist accounts of moral judgement are simply on a par.

Some realists do take the flat 'I know it when I see it' approach to the detection of moral value. They will *say* it is a perception (and in principle correctable etc.), but that has no impact on the way they argue. The counterpart of this position is the emotivist who *simply* expresses or gives vent to what she takes to be her attitude on some issue. She too may draw attention to the mutability of her disposition, and even express a favourable attitude towards that. But again, it does not affect how she argues. Often—and I suppose this is some evidence for quasi-realism—it will be impossible to distinguish such a realist judge from such an anti-realist on the bench.

On the other hand, some emotivist may articulate her moral

judgement on a particular issue in terms of the ramification of some more general attitude that she has. She may indicate for example that she cares about human starvation in all its forms, and so in this particular case she is going to act to protect some plaintiff from the possibility of starvation. In this case, she has something that looks quite like what a realist would call *a reason* to offer in support of her particular verdict. The verdict is not simply there starkly staring at us, as an arbitrary moral reflex. Once again, if the question about arbitrariness is, 'Is the moral judgement simply posited, or does it derive from more general considerations?', then such an emotivist is no worse off than the realist in terms of the way she regards her moral dispositions.

6.3. *Democratic Illegitimacy*

Particularly in American constitutional adjudication, a judge has sometimes to assert her view of what is right over the view taken by a legislature or electorate. There are considerable difficulties in explaining the democratic legitimacy of this.

The theory that moral and political views are merely matters of attitude is often associated with an uneasiness about permitting judges to strike down legislation in spite of its democratic credentials. Those who have been persuaded of some anti-realist view such as emotivism have often presented this as though it allowed the simple preferences of nine judges to prevail over the preferences of the mass of voting citizens or their elected representatives. If it is simply preferences versus preferences, or attitudes versus attitudes—if there is nothing objective about any of them—then surely the only thing to do (the argument goes) is to let the numbers count. Emotivism, therefore, is often taken as a reason for opposing constitutional review.

Now there *are* good reasons for opposing the judicial review of legislation, but they are not these.[37] To see this, consider again how little difference the recasting of the judges', legislators', and voters' moral views in *realist* terms would make. If realism is true then what the judge is imposing on her fellow citizens is not something which is merely a subjective preference of hers, but something which is a belief of hers about the moral facts. That looks reassuring until we remember that what the judge's view is opposed to is, equally, not the subjective preferences of legislators and voters, but *their* beliefs about the moral facts. As before, in the absence of any account of how one could tell which of two conflicting beliefs about the moral facts is more accurate, the imposition of one person's or a few people's beliefs over those of the population at large still seems arbitrary and undemocratic.

The issue comes down to comparing like with like. If moral realism is true, then judges' beliefs clash with legislators' beliefs in moral matters. If realism is false, judges' attitudes clash with legislators' attitudes. What we must not allow the realist defender of constitutional review to say is that it is a case of judge's beliefs clashing with legislators' attitudes. She is not entitled to be realist only about those whom she favours as decision-makers.

The sense one often gets from discussions that attempt to legitimize constitutional review is that the judge is an elevated moral deliberator holding views of principle while the demos and its representatives are stuck at the level of articulating their sordid interests and their shabby prejudices. There may be points to be made about the extent to which the political decisions of different agents are governed by their own narrow self-interest; maybe judges work in an institutional setting that leaves them less concerned with self-interest in their decision-making than directly elected politicians have to be.[38] But even if this is true, it has nothing to do with realism or anti-realism about morality. If the institutional setting is such as to taint a legislator's moral position with narrow self-interest, then the very same constraints are likely to influence the *beliefs* that she holds about (moral and other) matters of fact. Once again, we must remember that attitudes are not the only things that can be affected by interest. We are all familiar with wilful blindness, self-deception, and so on in uncontroversially factual areas, and of course there is no reason to expect that this will be diminished (indeed—depending how you approach the connection between moral judgement and motivation—every reason to expect it to be enhanced) in the area of moral fact. Some defenders of judicial review may argue that judges have greater expertise in moral matters than ordinary citizens, so that their beliefs and their reasoning are more likely to be reliable. But we have already noticed that moral realists can produce no epistemology to match their ontological commitments. Without an epistemology —and an epistemology which is, at least to some extent, less controversial than the knowledge claims it covers—there cannot be a theory of expertise. Thus the epistemic inadequacy of moral realism is far-reaching: in practical matters, it deprives realists of almost everything that they might want to say or argue for in the name of objectivity.

I have argued that the moral realist is no better off than the emotivist in supporting the legitimacy of judicial review. The converse holds also: the emotivist is no worse off than the realist in this regard. The case for judicial review must be won or lost on the moral merits of the matter, on the basis of moral arguments about fairness, justice, and democracy. And that is likely to be an area where there is no less disagreement (again, disagreement that can be analysed in either of these ways) than on the merits of the decision itself.

To sum up, then. If realism is false, then what clash in the courtroom and in the political forum are people's differing attitudes and feelings, and there will seem something arbitrary about any one of them prevailing over any of the others, when none can be 'certified', so to speak, on any credentials other than the fact that some people find it congenial. If realism is true, then what clash in the courtroom and in the political forum are people's differing beliefs (hunches, hypotheses, speculations, prejudices) about moral matters of fact. But that these are beliefs about matters of fact does not detract in any way from what will *still* seem to be a certain arbitrariness in one prevailing over any of the others. Since the realist abjures the sort of foundationalist epistemology that might make some such beliefs self-certifying and since she is unable to secure support for any other epistemology that might serve as a basis for a theory of error, a theory of review, or a theory of expertise, all we have is a set of different persons' conflicting beliefs. Exactly as in the case of attitudes, none of these can be 'certified' as superior or naturally prevalent on any credentials other than the fact that some people find it congenial. Either we have the arbitrariness of just taking one attitude over others equally eligible, or we have the arbitrariness of just taking one belief over others equally eligible. But arbitrariness is there, on either meta-ethical account.

7. CONCLUSION

Why did natural lawyers ever imagine the contrary? I can only think that they were seduced by the idea that facts themselves might operate as constraints on the arbitrariness of judicial decision. Liberals and conservatives alike are concerned that judges should not think of themselves as free agents when they make their decisions, at liberty to determine the fate of the litigants as they please. They should think of themselves as constrained rather than unconstrained decision-makers.[39] But if a judge's decision contains an essential moral element, and if moral realism is false, then the sense of constraint disappears. Outcomes are determined by the judge's subjective preference, and to the extent that her attitudes are under her control, she can make any decision she likes. (And the question of why she, rather than anyone else, should be the one who is allowed to do what she likes in this area, is invited.) If, on the other hand, moral realism is true, then there is a right answer to whatever questions of principle the judge puts to herself. We are apt to think of this as some sort of comfort: the right answer is there, so the judge is constrained after all.

But the existence of a right answer, if there is one, is so far a mere matter of ontology: there is some fact of the matter that makes one answer the judge might give true, and another that she might offer false. But making true and making false are not things that facts do to judges. The facts don't reach out and grab the decision-maker, preventing her from deciding capriciously, or dictating themselves to her in any unavoidable way. Making true and making false are semantic relations, and for all that any realist has told us they have nothing whatever to do with the social, psychological, or political determinants of the judge's decision-making. Facts don't constrain us in the sense of constraint in which we are interested in politics. That there is a right answer 'out there' (or wherever) certainly means that a judge is not making a fool of herself when she goes out ponderously in search of it. But its existence doesn't drive her to pursue it, let alone determine that she will reach it. Different judges will reach different results even when they all take themselves to be pursuing the right answer, and nothing about the ontology of the right answer gives any of them a reason for thinking her own view is any more correct than any other.

In the end it is moral disagreement, not moral subjectivity, that gives rise to our worries about judicial moralizing. And since realists have almost nothing of interest to say about the resolution of moral disagreement, they have nothing to offer to allay these concerns. Their thesis adds nothing to the natural law case against normative positivism.

NOTES

1. Some realists insist that the facts referred to in this formulation must be 'external' or 'mind-independent'; but this is too strong, since many realists do not want to deny that there would be no moral facts if conscious agents like ourselves did not exist, nor do they need to deny that reference to beliefs is sometimes included in the truth-conditions of moral propositions (e.g. 'It is wrong to offend some-one's deeply held beliefs'). The formulation I have used in the text is suggested in Ralph Walker, *The Coherence Theory of Truth* (London: Routledge, 1989), 3.

2. Of course, this works only for those languages in which a proposition can be referred to using a term formed by putting quotation marks before and after the terms normally used to express that proposition. Notice also that, for a realist, the proposition ' "p" is true' is *equivalent* to 'p' (the former is true in all and only the cases in which the latter is true). What distinguishes the disquotationalist is that she thinks the two propositions are not only equivalent but *identical in meaning*.

3. See Jules Coleman, 'Negative and Positive Positivism', in his collection, *Markets, Morals and the Law* (Cambridge: Cambridge University Press, 1988).

4. Gerald J. Postema, *Bentham and the Common Law* (Oxford: Clarendon Press, 1986). Jules Coleman has objected that normative positivism infuses morality into the concept of law, and thus commits 'the very mistake positivism is so intent on drawing attention to and rectifying' (Coleman, 'Negative and Positive Positivism', 11). Postema exposes the confusion of this objection clearly: Postema, *Bentham*, 328–36.

5. In recent American variation on this theme, it is (or was) for the Founding Fathers of the Republic, not the current judges, to make fundamental judgements of moral and political value.

6. There has been some confusion in the past as to whether the moral element in Dworkin's ideal of adjudication involves reference to the conventional morality of the community or judgement in moral matters by the judge herself *in propria persona*. His most recent discussion, however, makes it clear that although the judge should pay some attention to the former as a consideration of political fairness, her judgements about justice should be her own best estimation of what that value requires. See Ronald Dworkin, *Law's Empire* (London: Duckworth, 1986).

7. Ibid. 82–3. See also the beginning of Sect. 3 below.

8. See Michael Moore, 'Moral Reality', *Wisconsin Law Review* (1982), 1061.

9. For a discussion, see Nicholas Sturgeon, 'What Difference Does it Make Whether Moral Realism is True?', *Southern Journal of Philosophy*, 24 (1986), 115.

10. Ronald Dworkin, *Law's Empire*, 81.

11. Ibid., 82–3.

12. Ibid. 82. See also p. 80: 'There is an ancient and flourishing philosophical debate about whether external skepticism, particularly external skepticism directed to morality, is a significant theory and, if it is, whether it is right.'

13. The most general statement of quasi-realism is found in Simon Blackburn, *Spreading the Word: Groundings in the Philosophy of Language* (Oxford: Clarendon Press, 1984). Its application to ethics is indicated clearly in his essays, 'Rule-Following and Moral Realism', in S. Holtzman and C. Leich, eds., *Wittgenstein: To Follow a Rule* (London: Routledge, 1981), esp. 174 ff., and 'Errors and the Phenomenology of Value', in Ted Honderich, ed., *Morality and Objectivity: a Tribute to J.L. Mackie* (London: Routledge, 1985).

14. Blackburn, *Spreading the Word*, 197.

15. Hence the widespread panic—inflamed by Alan Bloom and others—that a whole generation has grown up in American colleges talking and thinking nothing but relativist thoughts about morality.

16. For example, the most sensible and powerful criticisms of emotivism came from R.M. Hare, who was an anti-realist of a different stripe, not from any realist opponent. See esp. R.M. Hare, *The Language of Morals* (Oxford: Clarendon Press, 1952), ch. 1.

17. Emotivism is the theory that moral terms like 'good', 'right', and 'wrong' contribute nothing in the way of descriptive meaning to the statements in which they occur. They are linguistic devices for the

expression of attitude, and for the evocation of similar attitudes in their audience. The most provocative statement of emotivism is still the one found in A.J. Ayer, *Language, Truth and Logic* (Harmondsworth: Penguin Books, 1971), ch. 6. There are, however, philosophically more sophisticated accounts in David Hume, *A Treatise of Human Nature* (Oxford: Oxford University Press, 1888), bk. iii, pt. 1, and Charles Stevenson, *Ethics and Language* (New Haven, Conn.: Yale University Press, 1944).

18. J.L. Mackie, *Ethics: Inventing Right and Wrong* (Harmondsworth: Penguin Books, 1977), 40: 'An objective good would be sought by anyone who was acquainted with it, not because of any contingent fact that this person, or every person, is so constituted that he desires this end, but just because the end has to-be-pursuedness somehow built into it. Similarly, if there were objective principles of right and wrong, any wrong (possible) course of action would have not-to-be-doneness somehow built into it.'

19. See e.g. Moore, 'Moral Reality', 1122–3. See also David O. Brink, *Moral Realism and the Foundations of Ethics* (Cambridge: Cambridge University Press, 1989), 37–50. Brink calls this position 'externalism'—i.e. the link between moral judgement and action depends on some independent or external motivation. For an 'internalist' response by the realist ('Why should it not just be a brute fact about moral facts that . . . their clear perception does provide sufficient grounding for action?'), see Mark Platts, 'Moral Reality', in Geoffrey Sayre-McCord, ed., *Essays on Moral Realism* (Ithaca, NY: Cornell University Press, 1988), 295.

20. See the interesting discussion in Sabina Lovibond, *Realism and Imagination* (Minneapolis: University of Minnesota Press, 1983), 1–9.

21. Thomas Nagel, *The Possibility of Altruism* (Princeton, NJ: Princeton University Press, 1970), 6, quoted in this connection by Lovibond, *Realism and Imagination*, 4.

22. Blackburn, 'Rule-Following', 179.

23. I suspect this is how R.M. Hare was led to an anti-realist position; certainly that is how it appears from *The Language of Morals*.

24. Realists sometimes suggest that to acknowledge the existence of disagreement is to concede that moral judgements make truth-claims. But that is unimportant. What matters is that the adherents of various moral positions regard one another as opponents, and each may regard herself as an opponent of the others. Someone who has an independent reason for saying that moral judgements make truth-claims will describe these oppositions as 'disagreements about the (moral) facts'. Others may describe it as 'disagreement' in a

looser sense (as when you and I 'disagree' about which restaurant to visit). Still others may eschew the language of disagreement altogether and just talk of opposition. Nothing hangs on this.

25. Mackie, *Ethics*, 36. The second argument is 'the argument from queerness', to which I alluded in the previous section.

26. Nicholas Sturgeon, 'Moral Explanations', in Sayre-McCord, *Essays on Moral Realism*, 229.

27. Moore, 'Moral Reality', 1089–90.

28. See Alan Gewirth, 'Positive Ethics and Normative Science', *Philosophical Review*, 69 (1960), 311.

29. Platts, 'Moral Reality', 282.

30. Ibid. 285.

31. Partly what this means is that we can give an account of (the subjectivity of) perception that is 'objective' in the sense discussed by Nagel in *The View from Nowhere* (New York: Oxford University Press, 1986), 5.

32. 'Moral Reality', 285.

33. Moore, 'Moral Reality', 1063.

34. Compare Mackie, *Ethics*, 35, with R.M. Hare, *Moral Thinking: Its Levels, Method and Point* (Oxford: Clarendon Press, 1981), 80.

35. Moore, 'Moral Reality', 1064.

36. This, by the way, is the appropriate way to deal with John McDowell's analogy between moral predicates and the terms for secondary qualities: John McDowell, 'Values and Secondary Qualities', in Honderich, *Morality and Objectivity*, 110.

37. See Jeremy Waldron, 'Rights and Majorities', in John W. Chapman and Alan Wertheimer, eds., *NOMOS XXXII: Majorities and Minorities* (New York: New York University Press, 1990), 44.

38. Again, I doubt this. To the extent it is true in America, I suspect it is a matter of self-fulfilling prophecy with regard to legislatures ('Let's leave the issues of principle for the courts to decide').

39. There is a useful discussion of this concern, as well as an explosion of the pretentions of moral philosophy in this regard, by Mark Tushnet in *Red, White and Blue: A Critical Analysis of Constitutional Law* (Cambridge, Mass.: Harvard University Press, 1988).

8

Law as a Functional Kind

MICHAEL S. MOORE

Natural law has for a long time had a bad press. It is supposed to be the sort of spooky stuff that Bentham derided when he hooted at natural rights as not being just simple nonsense, but 'nonsense on stilts'.[1] Oliver Wendell Holmes's own brand of ethical scepticism and legal positivism led him to characterize the natural law as a 'brooding omnipresence in the sky',[2] rather like the northern lights apparently, but without the lights. The prevalence of such views has for some time made it the case that 'to be found guilty of adherence to natural law theories is a kind of social disgrace'.[3]

Recently the experience of announcing a natural law view has become a little less like removing one's hat and revealing one's antennae for all to see. This greater acceptance is partly due to the increased acceptance of moral realism within philosophy.[4] Since a natural lawyer about law is also (necessarily) a moral realist about morality, this greater acceptance of the moral metaphysics of natural law has removed some of the 'spookiness' attitude toward natural law theories. But part of this reaction to natural law remains even for those cured of metaphysical *naïveté* about morality. To such persons, the natural lawyers' assertion that a necessary connection exists between law and morality seems obviously false even if not metaphysically outrageous. It is this latter rejection of natural law—the rejection of the thesis that law and morality are necessarily connected—that I wish to examine here.

The jurisprudence that interests me is that natural law jurisprudence which grew up after the Second World War and which may be seen as being in part a reaction to the atrocities done by the Nazis in the name of German law. Natural law jurisprudence since the Second World War argues for the relational thesis distinctive of natural law on the following basis: (1) general jurisprudence studies the nature of law in general; (2) the essence of law in general is to be found in law's functions (or ends), not in its distinctive structures (or means); (3) such function of law is . . . [some value that is both a true moral value and can be served by law uniquely so that value can be said to be law's distinctive end]; (4) given the end of law and given human limitations in achieving that end, the structural attributes law must possess to fulfil its function include the possession by law of legitimate practical authority obligating citizen obedience; (5) law can possess legitimate practical authority obligating citizen obedience only if in content it is not too unjust; therefore, (6) for something to be law at all it must necessarily not be unjust, the natural lawyer's conclusion.

Such an argument obviously opens up large areas where much must be said to be clear, let alone convincing. I shall proceed in the following way. Beginning at the end of the foregoing argument, I shall first examine the conclusion (6). In the first part of the chapter I thus clarify what I understand a natural law theory of law to assert. In Section 2 I turn to the beginning of the argument (1), examining the presuppositions about the nature of jurisprudence contained in the idea that jurisprudence studies law in general. In Section 3, I examine the idea of functional attributions, taking the functional organization of the human body as my point of departure, and seek to show how jurisprudence is best carried on in functionalist terms (2). Section 4 constitutes a preliminary view of the difficulties attendant on marrying a functionalist methodology in jurisprudence to the natural law thesis. In this part I describe the tension that exists between giving law a functional characterization (3), on the one hand, and discovering amongst law's structural features that authoritativeness of its norms that makes unjust 'laws' no laws at all (4), (5). In this chapter I shall not undertake the further tasks of defending my own view of the end of law, nor of arguing for a structural realization of some such end of law that includes as one of law's features that it obligate obedience. My essay is thus preliminary and expository, not itself a defence of a natural law view.

1. WHAT IS A NATURAL LAW THEORY OF LAW?

As I shall use the phrase, a 'natural law theory' contains two distinct theses: (1) there are objective moral truths; and (2) the truth of any legal proposition necessarily depends, at least in part, on the truth of some corresponding moral proposition(s). The first I shall call the moral realist thesis, and the second, the relational thesis.

It is the relational thesis that interests me in this chapter, and so I shall not outline how one might defend the moral realist thesis.[5] What does need saying here, however, is how often 'natural law' is used to label the moral realist thesis by itself.[6] There are four related usages of 'natural law' of this sort that require mention just to dispel confusion.

One is as a synonym for moral realism itself. Lawyers often use the phrase 'natural law' to refer to any 'objectivist' meta-ethical position. Such generic meta-ethical objectivism is more precisely known as moral realism. A 'natural lawyer' in this broadest meta-ethical sense holds that the truth of any moral proposition lies in its correspondence with a mind- and convention-independent moral reality. 'Natural law' in this sense is committed to two meta-ethical theses: (*a*) moral qualities such as justice exist (the existential condition); and (*b*) such qualities are mind- and convention-independent (that is, their existence does not depend on what any individual or group thinks—the independence condition).[7]

Sometimes 'natural law' is used by lawyers and others to refer to a particular species of moral realism. One such more particular usage of the phrase can be seen by attending to the distinction between 'naturalists' and 'non-naturalists' in ethical philosophy. A non-naturalist believes that there are mind- and convention-independent moral qualities to which true moral propositions correspond, but believes that these qualities are 'non-natural', that is, they do not exist in the natural world. Such qualities may be related in various ways to natural ones, or they may not, but in any case they are not identical to those natural qualities nor are the expressions referring to such non-natural qualities equivalent to or synonymous with expressions referring to natural qualities. Moreover, existing as they do in a non-natural realm, such non-natural qualities must be known in some supra-sensible way, which usually leads theorists of this stripe to posit a special faculty of intuition (leading to a common epistemic label for this metaphysical position, 'intuitionism').[8]

A naturalist believes none of these things. Rather, he believes that moral qualities such as culpability do not exist in any realm different from the natural realm in which such properties as causation and intentionality exist. Moral qualities are simply natural qualities of a certain kind, just as intentionality is a natural quality of a certain kind (that is, a quality of mind). With this distinction in mind, 'natural law' can be seen as sometimes being used to refer to that kind of meta-ethics that is naturalist, rather than non-naturalist, in its realist metaphysics.[9]

Sometimes a further refinement is intended by the usage of 'natural law'. Sometimes the phrase refers to a particular kind of naturalistic moral realism, namely, one finding moral qualities to be identical to or supervenient upon only one kind of natural facts, the facts of human nature. This is the 'wired in' view of natural law, holding that there is a universal and discrete human nature, and that the nature of that human nature determines what is morally right. The human nature referred to here may be teleological, so that it is cast as the natural function of mankind; or it may be a more contemporary anthropology, using only non-teleological descriptions of universal human traits. In addition, such human nature may be thought to possess epistemic power within each human being, so that each has a natural access to moral truth; or it may be thought to possess motivational power within each human being, so that each can not only see the good but has some natural inclinations to pursue it. We might call any and all of these variations, 'human nature naturalism'.[10]

A fourth exclusively meta-ethical usage of 'natural law' is to refer to that species of naturalistic moral realism associated with many religious traditions.[11] On this view, the nature of moral qualities like goodness is given by their having been commanded by God. This is a naturalist realist view because it asserts the (human) mind- and convention-independent existence of moral qualities and because it makes them depend on the natural fact of divine command.

These four meta-ethical senses of 'natural law' are worth mentioning only because the phrase is so often taken to be used in those senses. Yet the natural law theory of law I defend is committed only to the first of these senses of natural law—the moral realist sense—and not to naturalism, human nature naturalism, or religious naturalism. One can be as atheistic and as non-naturalist in one's metaphysics as one pleases and still be a natural lawyer in my sense. (For this reason some have suggested that a better label for my kind of view would be the 'moral law theory of law', but for reasons I shall mention later the traditional label is best.)

It bears the emphasis of repetition that subscription to 'natural law' in any of the meta-ethical senses of the phrase is insufficient to be a natural lawyer in my sense. The natural law that interests lawyers asserts not only the meta-ethical thesis of moral realism but also the relational thesis. One could thus be a 'natural lawyer' in the meta-ethical sense of being a moral realist yet not be a natural lawyer in legal theory. This would be the combined view that there are mind- and convention-independent moral truths but that such truths are irrelevant to the truth conditions of legal propositions. Legal positivists often hold just this combination of views.[12]

A moral realist view is thus not sufficient to be a natural lawyer. Some have argued that it is not even necessary.[13] Such people argue that natural law does not require that the truth conditions of legal propositions depend on moral truth but only on there being certain moral *beliefs* conventionally accepted in the society whose law it is. One might think, for example, that the truth of the singular legal proposition, 'This segregated school system violates the Equal Protection Clause of the Four-teenth Amendment', depends on a moral belief of most Americans (namely, a belief that segregated schools are immoral because it is violative of each person's moral right to equality).

There is nothing incoherent about this view; my only point here is that it is not a natural law view. For given its convention-alism about the morals to which law relates, such a view is really a kind of legal positivism: what is legally required does not depend on what is morally right, but only upon a certain kind of social fact, namely, whether a group of people have the requisite moral beliefs. That segregated schools are wrong is a moral fact; that most Americans now believe that they are wrong is a social fact, which this kind of legal positivist would add to facts about Supreme Court utterances in order to have a value-free theory of law. Such a positivist is as much a natural lawyer's opponent as is the more traditional kind who seeks to keep even shared moral beliefs out of his theory of law.

Having said what a theory of natural law is not, it is time to say what it is. The relational thesis distinctive of a natural law theory of law asserts that there is some necessary connection between law and morality. In clarifying this thesis we need to say more about the two things being related—law, morality—and then about the relation asserted to exist between them.

Take law first. Clarity demands that we distinguish two dimensions of generality of law. The first can be seen by referring to Herbert Hart's fruitful distinctions about law in his 1958 debate with Lon Fuller.[14] In the context of discussing the *law* from which morality is separated (according to legal positivism), Hart distinguished: (*a*) *law*, in the sense of legal system, from (*b*) *laws*, in the sense of the individual statutes or common law rules that may exist in a legal system, from (*c*) the *law of a case*, in the sense of that singular proposition of law that decides a particular case.

The distinction between laws and the law of a case can be seen in terms of the (logical) generality of the legal proposition involved. When we use the word 'laws', we refer to those standards describable by what I shall call general legal propositions. There is commonly a legal rule, for example, that a non-holographic will must be subscribed to by at least two witnesses in order to be valid. A general legal proposition is one which asserts the content of such a rule, thus: 'All non-holographic wills must be subscribed to by at least two witnesses to be valid.' A singular legal proposition, by way of contrast, picks out a discrete individual, event, or state of affairs, and predicates of it some legal attribute. For example: 'This will (referring to a particular document executed by a particular testator) is valid.' The difference between the two kinds of legal propositions is a matter of logical form. A general proposition uses universal quantifiers (for example, 'all wills') while a singular proposition singles out (by use of definite referring expressions) one particular thing in the world for legal characterization. In the example given, 'this will' picks out one particular thing in the world.

Judges need singular legal propositions in order to decide cases. In a will contest, what decides the case is the truth of singular propositions such as 'this will is valid' or, 'this will is invalid'. The truth of certain general legal propositions has a bearing on the truth of such singular legal propositions; but it is the truth of the latter that decides particular cases because it is only the latter kind of propositions that refer to the particular party or transaction before the courts in individual cases. I thus call the law expressed by such singular legal propositions the 'law of the case'.

Law is a yet more general notion than laws. Here, one's concern is about the conditions that must be present before law as such is present. The questions, 'When is there law?', or 'Does this society have law?', or 'When do we have the Rule of Law?', are invariably questions about when there is a legal system.[15] I shall accordingly call the systemic notion *law*.

A second dimension of generality has to do with the distinction between general and particular jurisprudence.[16] General jurisprudence studies law (laws, laws of cases) in the abstract, without regard to any particular legal system. General jurisprudence is thus often described as 'external' because the phenomena with which it deals, and the viewpoint from which it deals with them, are external to any particular legal system, including the one in which the observer lives. Particular jurisprudence is in this sense internal, for it studies law (laws, laws of cases) as those phenomena occur within some one particular legal system and from the vantage-point of actors (lawyers, judges, citizens) within that legal system. Particular jurisprudence is thus a culture-bound enterprise while general jurisprudence is not.

Anyone who asserts or denies a connection between law and morality must specify with what generality he is talking about law in each of these dimensions of generality. The natural law jurisprudence that I wish here to examine primarily asserts the connection of morality to law to exist at the most general level of each of these two dimensions. That is, such jurisprudence talks about the connection of morals to the existence conditions of law as such, and not, for example, to the American legal system. Moreover, this primary focus is on law in the sense of legal system, not laws or the singular laws of particular cases. The primary relational thesis of the theory is that the truth conditions of the statement 'law exists' include the truth conditions of certain corresponding moral propositions.

I say that this is the *primary* relational thesis of the theory because there are secondary relational theses, namely: (*a*) the truth conditions of the statement 'X is a law' include the truth conditions of the corresponding moral statement 'X is just', and (*b*) the truth conditions of the statement 'X is the law of some case' include the truth conditions of the corresponding moral statement, 'X is just'. These are secondary relational *theses* to the primary thesis, and not mere corollaries, because there are independent arguments establishing the truth of (*a*) and (*b*) that give them a meaning broader than they would have as corollaries alone. None the less, these are *secondary* relational theses because they are partly corollaries of the primary thesis: since the existence of laws of cases and of laws presupposes that there is a legal system to which such laws of cases and laws belong, the moral existence conditions of law will also be among the moral existence conditions for laws and laws of cases.

There is also of course a like trickle-down effect from a natural law *general* jurisprudence to a natural law *particular* jurisprudence. If law as such can exist only if certain moral criteria are satisfied, then law in America exists only when such criteria are satisfied too. Such particular relational theses are thus *secondary* theses too. They are *theses*, not mere corollaries, because in many legal systems there are additional ways that morality enters the existence conditions for laws and laws of cases that are peculiar to that legal system. In America, for example, the existence of judicial review and of a value-laden, written Constitution results in much 'natural law' constitutional law. These particular connections heavily colour how morality is related to law in the American legal system in ways not following from the general connection of morality to law. None the less, the natural law jurisprudence discussed in this chapter focuses on the general connection between law as such and morality, not the particular jurisprudence of specific cultures.[17]

Turning now to the nature of the thing, morality, to which law is related by natural law theory, less needs to be said. Nothing here needs to be said regarding the metaphysical status of the morality to which law is related—that question is already dealt with by the moral realist thesis of natural law theory. Rather, the question is what boundaries there are to morality so that the relational thesis can be made more precise.

This is a more difficult question than it may appear. If moral facts are as factual as any other fact—which, crudely put, is what the moral realist thesis asserts—how do they differ from other facts, such as the fact that an action was motivated by a desire to see another suffer? Is this less a moral fact than the fact that the action was sadistic in its motivation? Less than the fact that the action was cruel? Less than the fact that the action was wrong? Which of these are moral properties of the action, and which are properties of a non-moral kind? Non-naturalist moral realism has an easy answer (easy to state, at least, although hard to analyse) to this query: the moral properties are the non-natural ones. For those of us who are naturalist realists, however, that easy answer is unavailable. For naturalist realism, moral properties are either type-identical to natural properties, or they supervene upon them. Neither possibility gives rise to any clear answer to our 'moral borders' question.[18]

A tempting answer may be in terms of the illocutionary act-potential of the words used to refer to moral properties. This speech act criterion works like this: words that in their typical use not only describe a property but express an evaluation of the object possessing it are evaluative words, and the properties they refer to are moral properties.

This is close, but too tied to conventional features of language use—change the illocutionary act-potential of a word, and thereby effect a change in morality? I doubt it. It is better to focus on the prescriptive element of evaluations: a moral property not only gives us a reason to believe that it exists, like any other property; a moral property also has 'has-to-be-doneness' built into it in the sense that its existence gives rational actors a reason to act (to pursue it if it is good, retard it if it is bad). A moral property gives rational actors an objective reason to act.

Saying this may not seem to resolve our 'borders' problem about morality. Objective reasons to act can be self-regarding or other-regarding, prudential or non-prudential, reasons of autonomy or reasons of deontology, agent-neutral reasons or agent-relative reasons. Are all these to count as *moral* reasons, and thus the properties that give rise to them to count as *moral* properties? By the notion of morality that interests me, the answer is yes. The morality to which law is necessarily related of course includes properties like justice and injustice, equality, right and wrong, entities like rights and duties—the properties and entities that give obligation-reasons, reasons of deontology, or morality in its narrowest sense. Yet I also mean to include non-obligation-imposing properties such as the virtues, which give each of us reasons to pursue them even if not obligating us to do so.

Further, we should include properties giving us only prudential reasons to promote and retard them—properties like painfulness, our own as well as others.

We need a notion of morality that is as broad as practical rationality itself because that poses the interesting question to a natural law theory of law. Is some norm law despite its not being a dictate of practical rationality, or can a norm be law only if in content it conforms to the dictates of practical rationality for the persons that the norm purports to bind? That I take to be the interesting question of debate between legal positivism and natural law, and a sense of 'morality' narrower than 'practical reasonableness' only distorts that debate.

Broad as it is, this sense of morality is narrow enough to exclude the purely subjective and instrumental 'oughts' that Lon Fuller's critics were so fond of throwing up at him as *reductios*. It does not include the 'ought' of Hart's murderous poisoner who, on learning of the failure of his poison, says, 'I ought to have given her a second dose.'[19] Such 'oughts' are wholly instrumental; they are means to the satisfaction of the subjective desires of an evil person; such a person has no *objective* reason to have given his intended victim a second dose, not even an objective reason of prudence.[20] Such oughts, accordingly, are not part of the morality to which law is related.

Our third and last clarification of the relational thesis of natural law was to describe the relation asserted to exist between law and morality. There are three possible relations that a natural law theorist might think exist here. The strongest is to assert an identity in legal and moral properties and thus an equivalence in legal and moral propositions. If 'slavery is unjust' is true, then 'slavery is legally prohibited' is true too, on this view. Such a view makes the justness of a norm *sufficient* for that norm's status as law.

This is a very strong or pure view of the relation between law and morality, for it makes law depend on nothing other than morality. Statutes can at most be evidence of laws; court decisions, only evidence of the law of the cases decided; constitutions, only evidence of the foundations of a legal system. Although Cicero, Blackstone, and other natural law thinkers on occasion said such things, and although such a strong version of natural law would be required to describe the prosecutions at Nuremberg as prosecutions under non-retroactive *law*, this is not the view post-Second World War natural law jurisprudence has defended.

A much weaker view would make law (laws, laws of cases) always depend on morality, in the sense that the morality or immorality of a norm would always be *relevant* to its legal status. But this weak natural law view would not assert that the justness of a norm—say one prohibiting criminal conduct—was *sufficient* to constitute that norm into a law, nor would this view even assert that the justness of a norm was *necessary* for that norm's legal status. Rather the justness of a norm would only be 'criteriologically' relevant.[21]

My own view of the relation is stronger than this. My view is Augustine's view, that the justness of a norm is *necessary* to its status as law, but that law and morality are not identical. Just because some action is immoral and just because a norm prohibiting that action would be just, does not mean that action is illegal. This 'less than pure' natural law view leaves room to include institutional history—facts like legislatures passing statutes, courts deciding cases—as relevant to a norm's legal status. On the other hand, my Augustinian view rejects the weak or criteriological view of the relation. The Augustinian view has a bite to it lacking in the weaker view, for on the Augustinian view the justness of a norm is *necessary* to its status as law. Or, to use Augustine's much quoted language, an unjust law is no law at all.[22] Similarly, an unjust court decision is not the law of the case so decided, an unjust political system, not a legal system at all. These are strong enough conclusions to be counter-intuitive to many.

There is one last clarificatory hurdle to be cleared before getting on to the argument, and that concerns the nature of the necessity claimed here. It is sometimes said that there may well be a *contingently* necessary relation between law and morality, but that such contingent necessity is not what the natural lawyer needs. He needs, it is further said, that it be *analytically* necessary—part of the meaning of 'law'—that law be connected to morality in the way just specified.

There is a grain of truth to this charge, so let me extract it before throwing the rest away. The legitimate point is that natural law as a legal theory cannot be established by doing particular jurisprudence alone. This is true even if the particular jurisprudence that is done is done for all the cultures there are or have been in the world. Suppose every legal culture has (or had) the following characteristics: for every plausible moral argument there is a plausible constitutional law argument, and vice versa; there is judicial review, so that every statute or case decision is subject to being overturned if contrary to the constitutional law (which is by hypothesis the same in content as morality). In such circumstances, it could be said of each culture that an unjust law is not a law of the system and that an unjust decision does not determine the law of the case decided. Even so, the natural lawyer's relational thesis would not have been made out, because it would not have been shown that law (or laws and laws of cases) itself is connected to morality in the requisite way. One has to do general jurisprudence in order to make out the natural lawyer's relational thesis (or its opposite, the legal positivist's thesis of the separation of law and morals).

Some sense of 'necessity' is thus involved in saying that, *necessarily*, law cannot be too unjust and still be law, and 'contingent necessity' is no kind of necessity at all. Such 'contingent necessity' is based on what is sometimes called an accidental generalization. An accidental generalization is a generalization that is true of a finite sample size of things but that is not necessarily true because of the nature of the kind of things making up the sample. 'All American lawyers are under seven feet tall' is, as far as I know, true about the hundreds of thousands of American lawyers that exist. Yet the generalization is not necessarily true because it does not answer correctly the crucial counterfactual question, 'If someone were over seven feet tall, would he not be a lawyer?' There is, in short, no necessary connection between size and being a lawyer, only an accidental connection. Similarly, to observe that all legal systems we have seen invalidate laws that are contrary to morality does not support the counterfactual (would there be law without this connection to morality?) needed to apply the generalization to all legal systems that could exist, and not just those that have existed.

So some sense of necessity is required. *Analytic* necessity, however, is not what the natural lawyer needs to establish, because few if any words have a meaning supporting analytic relations.[23] 'A bachelor is an unmarried man' may be an analytically necessary truth, but I would hardly defend 'an unjust norm is not law' as having the same nature.

Saul Kripke's notion of 'metaphysically necessary' is the sense of necessity needed by the natural lawyer here.[24] Unlike the semantic notion of analytic necessity, a metaphysically necessary truth is a truth only dependent on how the world is and not upon the conventions of human language use. 'Water is H_2O' is (as far as we know) a metaphysically necessary truth because something wouldn't be water if it weren't H_2O. Put another way, one atom of oxygen bound to two of hydrogen gives the essential nature of water. Such essence is *not* fixed by what English speakers mean when they say or think to themselves, 'water'. Such an essence is to be found in the nature of the kind of thing that water is. We have theories about such essential natures, but theories can be wrong; definitions (analytical truths), which purport to fix such essences by conventional stipulation, could not be wrong.

A natural lawyer should say that the essence of law is such that it includes justice, among other things. *Necessarily*, that is, if some system, norm, or decision is unjust, it is not *legal*. Not as a matter of conventional usage of the word 'law' (analytical necessity); not as a matter of universal social practices (contingent necessity); but as a matter of the nature of one of the things that exists in the world, namely, law.

2. THE STRUCTURE OF GENERAL JURISPRUDENCE: FOUR JURISPRUDENTIAL DEBATES

2.1. *The (Im)Possibility of General Jurisprudence*

Before getting to the nature of and justification for functionalist general jurisprudence, we need to deal with certain debates about jurisprudence more generally. The first is the debate whether general jurisprudence in any form is possible. The argument is that an historically situated human observer (i.e. any of us) cannot get external to her own legal culture in order to think about (either descriptively or normatively) 'law in general'. The most such an observer can do, this view continues, is to interpret one's own legal culture, and one will only mislead oneself and others if one parades the results of such internal interpretation as if it were an external description or evaluation of something more general than, say, *American* law.

Ronald Dworkin's recent work is critical of general jurisprudence in this way.[25] Dworkin's 'you can't be doing anything different from what I'm doing, which is particular jurisprudence' claim is based mostly on epistemological scepticism but partly on the positive claim that law is an interpretive concept (that demands therefore on interpretation of a single culture's legal system).

Against general epistemological scepticism, little can be said here.[26] The positive claim is jurisprudentially more interesting. An interpretive concept for Dworkin is a concept towards which we take the 'interpretive attitude'.[27] The interpretive attitude, in turn, is mainly marked by regarding some practice as authoritative for one's decisions in the sense that there is some point or value served by making one's decisions depend on interpretations of some authoritative practice (or 'text').[28] The point or value justifying judges in taking the interpretive attitude towards statutes, for example, might plausibly be thought to be the furtherance of democracy (assuming that the statutes in question issue from a democratic legislature).

The problem with this positive claim lies in its justification of the interpretive attitude for legal theorists as well as for judges, for there is an important disanalogy between the reasoning of judges and the reasoning of legal theorists. It is just not very plausible to think that jurisprudence is interpretive in the way that much of the legal reasoning done by judges when they decide cases is interpretive, for what is distinctive about interpretive reasoning is the authority granted to some text as one decides particular cases. And what authority is possessed by the practices of Anglo-American judges for me as a legal theorist? When I seek to articulate the best way for judges to justify their decisions, how are those judicial practices in any way authoritative for me, as a kind of text that I must respect? Granted, there are persuasive normative arguments making certain texts authoritative for *judges* when they decide cases; but what are the analogous arguments making those judges' practices authoritative for me when I seek to articulate the best theory of how judging should be done? Why should I care if none of them, all of them, or some of them, for example, actually look for the psychological intentions of the framers in applying the United States Constitution? No matter what the practices of American judges might be in this regard, I would argue (and have argued) that the framers' intentions are irrelevant to both the right answer, and the right way to justify what is the right answer, in constitutional cases.

Of course, one can target normative arguments at particular audiences, and when one does so it is often a good rhetorical strategy not to bend too much the practices of your targeted audience as you seek to persuade them to mend their ways. Perhaps the authoritativeness of Anglo-American legal practice for Dworkin comes to no more than that. But such considerations have to do with the pragmatics of presentation of a theory of legal reasoning, not with there being some intrinsic mandate that jurisprudence be limited to interpreting some culture's legal practices. Such pragmatic considerations hardly require some kind of 'interpretive' jurisprudence that is limited in its ambitions to providing interpretations of some one legal culture's practices; such considerations only constitute a practical limitation on how one presents general jurisprudence to certain audiences.

Alternatively, perhaps the point only is that general jurisprudence must be worked out not only in the ideal case but also as applied to the less than ideal world. To be practical, general jurisprudence must take into account certain features of existing legal cultures because those features themselves are morally relevant. It matters, for example, to what degree a legislature or a constitutional convention is truly democratic because such representativeness affects the degree of respect to which legislative or constitutional enactments are entitled.

Yet this defence of interpretivist and therefore particularist jurisprudence is ill-conceived because it in no way defends the authoritativeness of some culture's legal practices for a legal theorist. The only point this argument establishes is that when general jurisprudence is applied to some culture it must take into account the features of that culture that make a difference. The point is the same as that to be made to an observer generally: when describing or evaluating the practice of slavery in Athens, take into account whatever features of Athenian culture (limited alternative economic opportunities?) are relevant. In neither case does such context-sensitive application of one's moral or scientific theory mandate the authoritativeness of any set of practices, legal or otherwise.

2.2. *Descriptive versus Normative General Jurisprudence*

General jurisprudence is often divided between descriptive jurisprudence and normative jurisprudence. A descriptive jurisprudence seeks to describe law and in so doing employs a concept of law that such jurisprudence does not create. A normative jurisprudence, by contrast, does not seek to employ a concept of law already formed but rather, to stipulate a meaning to 'law' that we ought hitherto to employ. The first seeks to tell us what law (or our concept of law) is, whereas the other seeks to tell us how law ought to be conceived.

Normative jurisprudence most typically gives moral reasons why we ought to conceive of law in one way or another. Legal positivist conceptions of law, for example, are often accused of making persons who accept them too obeisant to legal authority; natural law conceptions are accused of breeding both reactionaries and anarchists.[29] In either case, the reason given to adopt a concept of law is a moral one. Normative reasons can also be of a non-moral kind, however. Instrumentalists about theoretical terms in social science take there to be no reality dictating how such terms are to be used; rather, we must create a concept like law to suit our explanatory and predictive purposes. Following this instrumentalist perspective out in jurisprudence will result in a normative jurisprudence, for such jurisprudence will purport to tell us how we *ought* to conceive of law, even though the reasons backing the 'ought' are of a non-moral kind.[30]

Both kinds of normative jurisprudence should be put aside as being incapable of answering the debate between legal positivism and natural law.[31] The natural lawyer asserts that there is a necessary connection between law and morality, and neither kind of normative jurisprudence can support or rebut that claim. To give moral reasons for *inducing* belief in the natural law theses is not to give reasons to believe those theses. Put another way: the good or bad consequences of someone believing some proposition to be true have nothing to do with the truth of the proposition. The question the natural lawyer poses is whether or not natural law is true. He is not concerned with whether our believing such theses

to be true will have good or bad consequences. The latter calculation may affect to whom he tells his natural law theory, but it
cannot affect whether he believes the theory to be true.

Theory-building reasons of social science likewise cannot
answer the natural lawyer's question. Even if we *ought* to adopt a
certain concept of law for, say, increased-predictability-of-judicial-
decisions reasons, that cannot affect whether and how law *is*
related to morality. For our newly defined construct—let us call it
'schmaw'—does not refer to law; in fact (on instrumentalist
views of scientific theories) it doesn't refer to anything at all.
Schmaw does not exist, but the term 'schmaw' is a logical place-
holder in some predictive calculi of social science. How law is
related to anything is untouched by the success of social scientists
in framing some construct like 'schmaw'.

So ours is a quest in descriptive general jurisprudence. I next
shall consider how this enterprise is best carried on.

2.3. *Describing Law versus Describing a Social Concept of Law*

Most often descriptive general jurisprudence adopts a conventionalist theory of meaning in its quest to analyse law.[32] A
conventionalist about meaning believes that words like 'tiger',
'gold', 'malice', and 'law' refer to their respective things in the
world only via a conceptual intermediary. That is, what determines what the word 'gold' refers to—gold—is our *concept* of
gold. There are thus three things, on this view of meaning: gold,
the thing, 'gold', the word, and 'gold', the concept.

Most often a concept takes the form of a list of criteria for a
thing to be gold,[33] for example, 'yellow, precious, malleable,
metal'. Anything that satisfies such a list must (analytically must)
be gold, and anything lacking these properties must not be gold.

On this view of meaning general jurisprudence becomes a
study of 'the *concept* of law' or 'the *concept* of a legal system'—to
paraphrase the titles of the best-known books of this genre.[34] For
on this view of meaning one studies the nature of the thing, law,
by studying our concept of law (remembering that law is whatever our concept of law fixes it as). In rejecting the claim that
natural law theory's relational thesis is an analytic truth I have
already implicitly rejected this approach to jurisprudence. It is
now time to make this rejection explicit.

The alternative theory of meaning under which I shall proceed asserts that our concepts do not determine the reference of terms like 'gold' or 'law'. Rather, the theory is one of 'direct reference' whereby 'law' refers to law without some third thing intervening. The meaning of 'law', on this theory, is given by the nature of the thing referred to—law—and not by some concept of law that fixes (by linguistic convention, or 'analytic necessity') what can be law.

The theory of direct reference has been defended elsewhere at length with respect to natural kind terms like 'gold' or 'tiger'.[35] Whether such a theory of meaning properly applies to artefactual words like 'pencil', 'lawyer', or 'law' is more controversial, for such kinds of things are often thought to lack any natural essence that can guide the meaning of such terms.[36] What is included in the class of such things, one might think, is wholly a matter of our conventions, conventions that can be fully stated as *concepts* (lists of properties) of pencil, law, etc.

Often those who adopt the conventionalist line on words like 'law' confuse two different ways in which conventions might be relevant to the meaning of 'law'. Such persons often confuse conventions being part of the nature of a thing, on the one hand, with our linguistic conventions (concepts) fixing that nature as a matter of analytic necessity, on the other. Take the phrase 'co-ordination solution', as it is used by game theorists. A co-ordination solution is a convention that forms around some salient feature of a co-ordination problem. But that does not mean that the kind of thing that can be a co-ordination solution is fixed by our linguistic conventions (concepts) about the correct use of the phrase, 'co-ordination solution'. We study the nature of co-ordination solutions as a matter of better or worse theory; we do not study them only by attending to the concept of co-ordination solution in use in our language.

My own view is that the only things whose nature is fixed by our concepts are 'things' that do not exist—Pegasus, the twentieth-century kings of France, and the like. There are no things referred to by such terms, so such words' meaning can only be given by their concepts. Pencils, law, co-ordination solutions, etc., do exist and thus can have a nature that gives the meaning of their respective words.

Accordingly, I shall not seek to tease out a concept of law.

General jurisprudence should eschew such conceptual analysis in favour of studying the phenomenon itself, law.

2.4. *Law as a Nominal versus Functional Kind*

The immediately foregoing remarks will seem more controversial than they are until it is realized what has been left open by them. Specifically, the possibility they leave open is that law is a nominal kind. A natural kind is a thing that exists in nature as a kind without human contrivance. Natural kinds have a nature that makes them kinds even if no human makes use of that nature or even discovers or labels it. A nominal kind, by contrast does not exist as a kind in nature, although its particular specimens may exist. Indeed, a nominal kind is *nominal* in the sense that as a kind its only nature is given by the common label attached to its various specimens.

Consider Figueroa Street, the north–south street in Los Angeles often listed as the longest municipal street in the world. Figueroa streetness is a good candidate for being a nominal kind not just because it was created by man (or at least a related species, Angelenos) but because there is no nature to Figueroa streetness that determines whether any given bit of asphalt or concrete is or is not part of it. Whether some bit of asphalt partakes of Figueroa streetness wholly depends on human convention: how were the Los Angeles maps and street signs posted?

If law were a nominal kind like Figueroa streetness then there would be no unified nature to seek in descriptive general jurisprudence. General jurisprudence would become the study of whatever was *called* 'law' by native speakers of English as they observed their own and others' societies. The attempt would be to distil universal characteristics possessed by all things so labelled

I implicitly rejected this sociological conception of general jurisprudence when I rejected 'contingent necessity' as the kind of necessity needed by the natural lawyer. Let me now make the rejection more explicit and more defensible. In the first place, I doubt that there would be a conceivable enterprise called general jurisprudence if law were a nominal kind like Figueroa streetness. For all that unifies the bits of pavement that together form Figueroa Street is the symbol, 'Figueroa Street', attached to each bit. When we change cultures and change language, we give up the unifying symbol. 'Law' is not a word in French or German; of course, 'droit' and 'Recht' are, but how could one say that these mean what we mean by 'law' when there is no *nature* to law that droit and Recht share? General jurisprudence could only be a language-specific study, so that there would be an English general jurisprudence, a French general jurisprudence, etc.

One might agree with this last point and simply give up on general jurisprudence on the ground that, indeed, it has no subject-matter, law being a nominal kind without a nature susceptible of cross-cultural study. One is thus not forced by this argument to view law as other than a nominal kind.

More conclusive argument against thinking that law is only a nominal kind may be found if we repair to other artefactual terms. Consider the term 'mower'. The Seventh Circuit Court of Appeals in the United States had to consider recently whether a haybine that both cut the hay and conditioned it was a mower within the meaning of a statutory exemption of 'one mower' for a farmer in bankruptcy. As Frank Easterbrook noted, haybines are not *called* 'mowers'; they are called 'haybines'. If mower were a nominal kind, this linguistic fact should have been the end of the case. Yet the court correctly decided that the symbol attached to haybines was not determinative because mowers had a nature:

[N]either is it appropriate to say that the statute concerns only machines called 'mowers'. . . . 'mower' is not limited to the thing called a mower today, or even the thing called a mower in 1935. A statutory word of description does not designate a particular item . . . but a class of things that share some important feature.[37]

As Easterbrook concluded, in order to apply the statutory word, 'mower', he had to discover 'what a mower *is* . . .'.[38]

What is the nature of a mower, if 'mowerness' is not merely a nominal kind? It is not very plausible to think that mowers have some essential structural features, features without which they would not be mowers. Technological advances have changed the structural features of mowers considerably, and will continue to do so—and will not those instruments for the mowing of hay still be *mowers*? An affirmative answer suggests that the essence of mowerness is given by function and not by structure. Anything that mows hay is a mower, whatever its structural features turn out to be. (Think of the common answer to the question, 'Do you have a dishwasher?', given by pointing to one's children and saying, 'I have two of them.')

I call kinds like mowers functional kinds. Unlike nominal kinds, items making up a functional kind have a nature that they share that is richer than the 'nature' of merely sharing a common name in some language. Unlike natural kinds the nature that such items share is a function and not a structure. A stomach, for example, could have a silicon-based chemistry and be cubical in shape (rather than carbon-based and roundish) and still be a stomach because it performs the first-stage processing of nutrients distinctive of stomachs.

Whether law is a functional kind is not obvious. One cannot simply say that law is created by *purposive* human activity and that therefore law is 'purposive' (i.e. a functional kind), as Lon Fuller used to do.[39] This glosses all the interesting questions. I shall accordingly examine the question (of what kind of kind law is) in two stages: first, we need to be clear how functions are attributed to parts of systems and how systems themselves are assigned functions, and to illustrate this I shall talk about the functional organization of the human body. Second, we need to apply this analysis to legal systems and see what sense we can make of the idea that legal systems serve a function.

3. FUNCTIONALIST JURISPRUDENCE

3.1. *Health and the Functions of the Human Body*

'The function of the human heart (or the heart's beating) is the circulation of blood.'[40] This seems to be a true statement, but my enquiry is into what we mean when we assign such a function to body parts or processes. Most obviously, we at least mean that one of the things the heart does—one of the consequences of its beating—is that the blood circulates. Whatever else we mean, we do mean to assert this much when we discover functions of things.

Often this is all that function statements are taken to assert. Joe Raz, for example, in his discussion of the functions of law, means only to discuss the *effects* of law.[41] The function of a thing for Raz is just its effects, which he taxonomizes as being either direct or indirect. More generally, social scientists often use function language in this limited way, saying for example that the *function* of certain ceremonial dances in certain tribes is the relaxation of group anxieties; all they apparently mean is that such dances have such effects. Similarly, much of the current research into the function of sleep is purely an empirical research into the *effects* of sleep—does it sweep away unnecessary memories of the day (Hughlings Jackson), allow us to dream and thus to discharge drive energies (Freud), prevent or combat fatigue (Claparede, Coriat), or even 'knit up the ravelled sleeve of care' (Shakespeare)?[42]

Such usages of 'function' are misleading, because all we have done when we isolate the effects of something else is to discover *possible* functions for that thing. The function it actually has will be one of those consequences, but it will not be all of them.

In the heart example, we cannot simply mean that one of the effects of one of the heart's activities is that blood circulates when we give that as the heart's function. For hearts do many things— such as occupying space in the chest cavity and putting upward pressure on the peristaltic gut—and even when we focus on their beating activity to the exclusion of others, that beating has many consequences besides the circulation of blood. Such beating produces noise in the chest cavity, for example.

None of these other consequences is the function of the heart, so we must mean something more determinate when we say that its function is to circulate the blood. Similarly, when we discover the functions of sleep, we will not have simply catalogued all the effects sleep in fact causes. (Otherwise, we should include as a possible function of sleeping the maintenance of the mattress industry, the provision of opportunities for night-time burglaries, etc.)

One temptation may be to think that of all the consequences of an activity like sleeping or heart-beating, we honour as its function only those consequences the designer had in mind when he made such things. This solution leads very quickly to the teleological argument for God's existence, for with hearts and human bodies there is no *human* designer to have intended some effect; so if a designer's intention is needed in order for a function to exist, and if hearts and sleep have functions, then there must be a Grand Designer.

Those of us who are not theists reject such a conclusion and therefore must reject the premiss that leads to it (namely, that functions are the intended effects of a system's designer). Another temptation may be to think that the function of something is the consequence either actually brought about, or intended to be brought about, by the average human user of that thing. The function of a hammer is to drive nails because that is the usual intention with which it is used, on this view. While such conventionalist ascriptions of function may be all that is meant on some occasions for artefacts like hammers, this can't be what we mean about hearts and sleep; for neither the beating of our hearts nor our sleeping are acts we will and thus are not done by us to achieve further intentions. The function of sleep thus cannot be the consequence we typically intend to achieve by going to sleep.

My answer to our problem is different from the preceding two answers, relying on designers' or users' intentions. To find an activity's function, we sort through all the consequences of that activity in light of an hypothesis both about there being some larger system in which the activity occurs and about that system having an overall goal. The heart's beating and sleeping are both activities within (or of) the system we call the human body. We think such a system itself has a function or goal, namely, physical health. Such a system-wide goal is aided by some consequences of a heart's beating and by some consequences of sleeping, and not by others. We call the former the function of the heart or of sleep.

This selection amongst the consequences of sleep or of the heart's beating is thus in part guided by a further causal judgement: not only must the circulation of blood be caused by the heart's beating, but the circulation of blood must itself cause maintenance of that state of the system that is its goal (here, health). But this is only part of the story about discovering what is the function of what. Also needed, of course, is some way of picking out what is the overall goal of the system.

Finding the goal of the human body cannot itself use the same strategy we just detailed in selecting the function of sleep or of hearts. The finding of ever larger systems, with ever larger goals, has to stop somewhere. There are two leading possibilities for how we discover the overall goals of some system: we either find that the system naturally tends to maintain itself in some state of equilibrium despite widely disequilibriating conditions; or we discover that of all the human goods there are some but not others that either are or can be served by the system in question. The first is a value-free enterprise while the second is value-laden.

With regard to the first of these possibilities, there are cybernetic mechanisms with feedback loops that maintain various natural or man-made systems in certain states. We call such states homoeostatic states. The subsystem of the human body that maintains constant inner body temperature despite widely varying environments is one example. One can study such systems and meaningfully index what one learns around the maintenance of this naturally occurring end state. The function of dilating capillaries in the skin would then be said to be the ridding of inner body heat, the function of perspiration the same, etc. In no sense does this kind of function assignment require an evaluation by the investigator. Both the discovery of a goal for the system, and the discovery of the causal contribution of each part of the system to its attainment of its goal, are matters of hard, scientific fact.

Most of the time, however, this is not how we assign functions. Most of the time we are evaluating something as good when we say what it is good for (i.e. what its function is). In such cases we consult our list of all the good things there are and ask, which of these, if any, does/can this system promote? Physical health is on just about everyone's list of goods ('when you have your health, you have . . .' etc.). Physical health is the good that the human body can contribute—it can't contribute justice or liberty or economic well-being—so physical health is the goal of the human body.[43] When we attribute functions to body parts or processes based on their causal contributions to physical health, we are positively evaluating such parts and processes. 'The heart's beating is good for circulation which is good for physical health, and physical health is good', is the evaluation that lies behind the innocent statement, 'the function of the heart is to circulate blood'.

The evaluative nature of such goal attribution is easily missed in the case of physical health because there is such widespread agreement on health's desirability. Freedom from death, distress, or disability—the 'three Ds' typical in definitions of negative health—are seen to be good by just about everybody.[44] Move to mental health, however, and the disagreement becomes larger, particularly about the level of mental capacities that are healthy to have. Since mental health guides the functional organization of the mind just as physical health guides the functional organization of the body, disagreement about the goodness of various ideas of mental health makes more evident the normative nature of mental function attributions.

Let me now draw this together in a way that can be applied to functional jurisprudence. Suppose we are ignorant of modern medicine or biology, but we have a sense that perhaps the human body is a functional system. The steps we should take as we test our intuition should go like this.

1. We isolate some parts or processes that we are relatively certain are parts or processes of the system. These are provisional hunches only, because we know that if we are right about the system as a whole—it is a functional kind, a kind whose essence is given by its function and not by its structure—we could be wrong about any particular structure actually belonging to the system. In the example I have been using, we start with the heart and sleeping as a part or activity of the human body.

2. We isolate the effects of the activities of the heart, or the effects of the activity of sleeping. This is our list of possible functions for each of these parts or activities.

3. We ascertain of all the human goods which one or ones could be served by the human body. Physical health being such a good, we hypothesize that physical health is the goal of the body, i.e. what the body is good for.

4. In light of such a hypothesis about the goal of the human body, we discover which of the various activities of the heart, and which of the various effects of sleep, themselves causally contribute to the maintenance of the body in the state of health. These activities and effects are the functions of the heart and of sleep.

5. We continue the same four-step analysis both from the 'bottom up' and from the 'top down'. The bottom-up strategy picks other parts or processes we are relatively sure belong to the human body and probes their effects for any contribution to health. Such a procedure may modify what we think physical health to be. The top-down strategy begins with our increasingly well-defined notion of health and looks for parts or processes

that must exist if the overall goal of health is to be maintained. Such a procedure may throw out certain parts of the body that are not essential in that they perform no function (e.g. 'love-handles', the bits of waist fat that serve no function but which we none the less label in (humorously) functional terms).

At the end of our multiply iterated four-step procedure we will have written a comprehensive medical textbook on the human body. The overall system will be subdivided, not by structural principles, but by functional ones, so that we will have major subsystems such as the 'limbic system', the 'reticular system', etc. Such subsystems will themselves be divided into subsubsystems, etc., so that eventually each essential (structural) feature will have its (functional) place in the teleological organization of the body. Such a textbook is a book in applied ethics because it asserts (or more often, presupposes) the goodness of health and then charts in detail the unique ability of the human body to realize that good. The same, I shall now argue, is true of jurisprudence textbooks when properly written, except that both the good the legal system obtains, and the means of its attainment, are of course quite different from the function and structure of the human body.

3.2. *Law as a Functional Kind*

As Phil Soper has noted, 'in the case of the concept of a legal system, most modern theorists agree that it is function that provides the clue to the latent principle [essence]'.[45] Suppose we share the intuition that law (legal systems) is a functional kind. Functionalist jurisprudence, rightly conceived, should play out that intuition in the five steps just outlined.

1. What are, provisionally at least, features of law? There is no poverty of suggestions in this regard. We might plausibly think that law is marked by coercive sanctions and the habit of obedience that such sanctions induce in people.[46] Alternatively, we may fasten on to the idea that law regulates its own creation,[47] or that law is marked by the existence of a special secondary rule that legitimates all other rules as rules of law.[48] We may think that 'law has authority', and mean by that either that law is actually morally obligating,[49] or that law is *regarded* by its citizens and/or

judges as obligating,[50] or that from the point of view of the legal professional law is obligating.[51] Yet again, we may fasten on to those features often called the rule of law features—characteristics such as general, prospective, public, clear, stable, consistent rules that only command the possible and which officials apply when they adjudicate citizens' claims.[52] Others have thought that law is marked by formal features, such as the continuity of legal entities over time, the treating of past acts as having authority now, the gapless nature of law, or its ability to generate an authoritative rule without there being some other rule authorizing it,[53] whereas still others think that law is most uniquely marked by its justification of present state coercion by past political decisions or by its inherently controversial nature.[54]

Each of these has been presented as being a feature of law as such. Each is plausible enough to be selected as the place to begin in seeking the function law serves and the structures needed to realize that function. For ease of illustration, let us pick a simple feature, that a legal system is marked by its citizens at least believing that its norms have legitimate practical authority over them.

2. We now need to isolate the typical effects of such (provisionally) structural feature of law. We might suppose, for example, that the effects of citizen belief in the authoritativeness of law include (*a*) that it makes citizens less willing to think for themselves in moral matters; (*b*) that it frees citizens' time for more leisure activities; (*c*) that it increases rebelliousness in children, who by virtue of such widespread belief must revolt against the law as well as against parents in order to develop into autonomous adults; (*d*) that it allows the solution of co-ordination problems because the perceived authoritativeness of laws will make them salient features of any co-ordination problem faced by citizens. This list could of course be drawn out considerably even from this one feature of law.

3. In order to say what is the function of citizens' believing law to be authoritative, we next need some hypothesis about the general goal of law. As with structural features of law, there is again no dearth of plausible suggestions here. Law, it has been suggested, has as its goal the subjecting of human conduct to the guidance of rules;[55] the enhancement of the liberty and autonomy of persons through the opportunities for choice law

can create when it has predictable legal sanctions;[56] the promotion of the common good, which on one conception of it, is that way of realizing substantive human goods made possible by life in a community;[57] the maximization of the common good in another sense, namely the aggregative sense that aggregates the preferences of citizens into a social welfare function;[58] the promotion of the common good in yet another sense, namely, the goods of individuals which as individuals each has in common with other individuals;[59] the enhancement of simple survival for individuals;[60] attaining integrity in government, a desirable mode of government's achieving substantively good results through comprehensive, coherent, and equality-respecting means;[61] the maintenance of peace and order;[62] the peaceable settlement of disputes between citizens;[63] social control not by actual obligation or by force but by prima-facie obligation.[64]

To get a handle on such a list requires nothing less than a full theory of the good and the right. One has to know, that is, what is objectively good and one has to know the permissible means of reaching it through action. Then one can decide which of this list are goods and thus which could be what a legal system is good for.

John Finnis's comprehensive *Natural Law and Natural Rights* illustrates this insight nicely. In the early chapters Finnis lays out his view of the seven good things and the nine conditions of practicable reasonableness that constrain any moral person's attainment of those seven good things. Finnis needs such a fully described moral theory in order to pick out the distinctive goal of law, which Finnis urges to be the 'common good'. The common good as Finnis conceives it is 'a set of conditions which enables the members of a community to attain for themselves reasonable objectives, or to realize reasonably for themselves the value(s), for the sake of which they have reason to collaborate with each other . . .'.[65] The common good is thus not for Finnis the good each individual has which is the same as the good of everyone else. Although Finnis is a moral realist, his view of morality allows there to be different answers to how persons should lead their lives that are equally good. The law, as Finnis sees it, is uniquely situated to co-ordinate these different visions of the good life allowing each to realize his/her own vision.

Consider, by contrast, Lon Fuller's once held view that legal theorists did not have to develop a full theory of the good and the right in order to ascertain the unique good of law. Fuller purported to discover an 'internal morality of law' that allowed him to ground his famous eight structural features (publicity, generality, etc.) as being necessary to law.[66] Yet the goal that Fuller's truncated morality produced was the colourless, neutral goal of subjecting human conduct to guidance by rules. As many of Fuller's contemporary critics pointed out,[67] there is nothing intrinsically good about that goal. By itself, guiding persons by rules cannot be the goal of law because, by itself, guiding persons by rules is not a good.

Suppose one has a full theory of the good and the right. And suppose that one has enough of an idea of the structural characteristics of a legal system to sort through that full moral theory and to isolate which good(s) are those uniquely achievable through law. One could then hypothesize which of the suggested goals of law is in fact its goal.

For illustration, let me continue with Finnis, since his system is so completely worked out. Finnis argues that the common good is a good—it consists in (i) the good of co-ordinating conflicting individual goods for mutual benefit, (ii) the good of co-ordinating individual goods when doing so has intrinsic merit (as in play), and (iii) the good of co-ordinating when that realizes the goods of friendship and love.[68] Finnis further argues that this threefold common good is the unique good law can achieve and thus is law's goal.

4. Armed with a view of the goal of law, one can then isolate which of the effects of certain features of law are those features' functions. In Finnis's case, this would be to pick the consequence, co-ordination, as the function served by law being believed to be authoritative by its citizens. Such co-ordination, and not citizens' obeisance or children's patterns of rebelliousness, would be the function served because such co-ordination itself causes the common good to be realized.

5. Having a provisional theory of the goal of a legal system and the functional and formal features of some parts of such a system, functionalist jurisprudence then repeats steps 1–4 for each plausible part of a legal system, asking in each case whether such a part could perform a function in the attainment of the goal of law. Working from the bottom up is to start with a feature such as

coercive sanctions and ask whether this feature is a necessary part of law (necessary in the sense of necessary to attain the goal of law). Sanctions, for example, are not an obviously necessary feature of law if the goal of law is the common good in Finnis's sense, because co-ordination problems do not require sanctions for their solution.[69] Working from the top down is to start with the goal of the legal system and seek to discover what structures one would need in order to realize such a goal. Herbert Hart, for example, once speculated that a goal of the legal system on which everyone could agree was survival and that from such a goal one could infer that law would have to have a 'minimum content' of criminal prohibitions and property entitlements.[70]

4. FUNCTIONALIST JURISPRUDENCE AND NATURAL LAW

We now should ask whether the enterprise just described will inevitably result in a natural law theory. In exploring this question I shall explore along the way other doubts about the enterprise.

One broadside objection would deny that functionalist jurisprudence carried on along the lines outlined above *could* yield a natural law result. The argument is that in functionalist jurisprudence there can be no *necessary* connection of law to morals because no structural features are necessarily law. Herbert Hart voiced a moderate form of this objection in his consideration of 'natural law with a minimum content'.[71] Hart correctly noted that even conceding *arguendo* that survival is good and that survival is a goal of the legal system, it still requires assumptions about human nature to generate conclusions about the shape of law. Hart's example: if we each had an armoured exterior rendering us invulnerable to physical attacks by our fellows, the criminal prohibitions needed would be quite different from those needed by us quite vulnerable persons.

Marshall Cohen once put Hart's point more bluntly. In objecting to defining law by whatever structural features maximally realize the goal of law, Cohen objected that 'Means are not logically entailed by ends'.[72] Cohen's example: political office is often obtained through the means of party service, military glory, and intellectual eminence; yet no one would define 'political office' in terms of these typical means of obtaining it.[73]

Both Hart and Cohen mistake the necessity claimed by natural

law (or by any sensible theory of law). They thought that to give
the nature of law was to produce an analytic definition (concept)
of 'law' so that law's structural features (including its relation to
morality, if any) would be analytically necessary features of law.
As I argued before, this is a mistake. Legal theorists engaged in
general jurisprudence only need point to a metaphysical necessity
about the nature of law. And while Hart is certainly right that
functionalists need to plug in certain assumptions about human
nature, these human nature claims are (if true) metaphysical
necessities too. Given these (metaphysically necessary) truths
about human nature, and given the (metaphysically necessary)
truths about morality that make some goal of law good, then law
(metaphysically) must have certain structural features. Such non-
analytic necessity about law's structural features is enough for
any legal theorist, natural lawyer or otherwise.[74]

A second objection to functionalist jurisprudence focuses on
the dependence of any structural feature being a feature of *law* on
the selection of an ultimate goal for law. The idea is that even if
familiar criminal prohibitions are necessary to preserve survival,
that does not make such prohibitions necessary to law as such.[75]
But this objection forgets what it is that functionalist jurisprudence claims about the goal of law: the claim is that law's essence
is given by that goal, not by any structural feature. Therefore any
structural feature necessary to attain law's goal *is* law in any
sense that the functionalist need defend. The only way this
essentialist claim of the functionalist can be forgotten is by
focusing on examples like Hart's, where a goal is picked for law
(survival) only because of widespread agreement on its desirability[76] and not because such a good is the good law can
uniquely achieve.

This raises a third objection to functionalist jurisprudence:
there is no universal agreement on an end for law.[77] This objection
can be put aside quickly. The last thing a moral realist means by
objectivity is universal agreement. Moral realism is not the
doctrine that certain values, such as the value of law, are universally agreed upon. Rather, it is the claim that such values exist and
that their existence does not depend on what we or any group of
people think. Agreement about the ends of law is not to be
expected, but neither is the issue of agreement relevant. In this
context it is a red herring.

A fourth and more serious objection about functionalist jurisprudence would be the objection that it just assumes that law
serves a goal (that is, that law is a functional kind). Not only is
this unsupported, but as a natural law theory it is question-
begging because functionalists assume from the start that law
must serve some good. No surprise that they then end up with a
theory of law asserting that law is necessarily connected to
morality (i.e. to something good).[78]

There are two aspects to this objection that need separating.
One is a circularity charge to functionalist jurisprudence as such,
independent of whether such jurisprudence reaches a natural
law conclusion; the other is the question-begging charge directed
against functionalist jurisprudence in so far as it purports to
yield a natural law conclusion. As I now propose to show, to
answer the circularity charge will be to answer the question-
begging charge as well.

The circularity part of the objection can be fleshed out like this.
A functionalist about law starts with some feature he takes to be a
feature of a legal system (call it feature 'X'), and then seeks X's
function. Yet he can't know whether X is or is not a feature of law
without knowing the goal of law, for the goal determines what is
functionally necessary to its realization (i.e. is law). On the other
hand, he cannot know the goal of law—nor even whether law has
a goal—until he knows which of all the goods there are is the
good that law can uniquely serve, but to know this he has first to
know what law's structural features are.

Strange as it may sound to say it, the circularity of functionalist
jurisprudence is not a defect of that mode of analysis but a virtue.
For if the epistemic credentials claimed by the analysis were any
stronger than they are, they would have to be false. As it is, such
credentials are exactly analogous to those obtaining anywhere
where one claims to know anything.

Consider our knowledge of the existence of a natural kind like
gold, together with our knowledge of the kind's essential nature
(gold's atomic structure) and of its instances (pieces of gold).
How might someone come to know whether there is in the world
some kind of thing that we can call gold, what its nature was, or
what its instances were, if he began in ignorance on all these
matters? He might come across some initial examples, say some
bits of iron pyrites (fool's gold). He might later come across many

other individual bits of yellow, metallic stuff, and decide to label
the whole class 'gold'. This at the moment is a highly provisional
hypothesis, because he is hypothesizing that all the members of
the class of things that he has encountered share some essential
nature even though he doesn't know what it is. He could be
wrong about this, as the case of jade illustrates; but he provisionally thinks that there is a kind, gold.

He next seeks to discover gold's essential nature, and develops
various theories. Such theories are constructed in light of everything else that he knows (say, about other elements of the
periodic table) and in light of such theories' ability to include as
gold the instances of the stuff he has so far encountered.

Suppose eventually he reaches our theory of gold, that it is an
element with such and such an atomic structure. He will then
turn that theory back on to the examples that suggested it to see
whether or not they are truly instances of gold. As I have posed
this little story, it turns out that his initial examples are not
instances of gold at all.

There is no natural stopping-point in this process any more
than there is a natural starting-point in the acquisition of knowledge about anything. Theories of the nature of a kind, hypotheses
that there is a kind, hypotheses about what are the instances of a
kind, are just that, theories and hypotheses. They are always
subject to improvement and even replacement. At any point in
time the most one gets is a kind of 'reflective equilibrium'—
which is enough certainty to justify worrying about something else.

Consider another illustration of this non-foundationalist epistemology, the currently fashionable 'interpretivism'. In Dworkin's
hands, for example, interpretivism begins by focusing on some
'pre-interpretive data'.[79] Such data is pre-interpretive in the
sense that one hypothesizes that this data is part of the law
before one has (by interpretation) justified that claim. Dworkin's
example in jurisprudence: start with the idea that law is inherently controversial at a theoretical level.[80] Next, one seeks the
point or value of law, which Dworkin calls our interpretation or
conception of law. For Dworkin, this is integrity. Then, one
applies back on to the data that generated it this theory of law's
point to justify what are and are not features of law. This results
for Dworkin in a general description of law's structural features,
what Dworkin calls our *concept* of law: law is marked by its use of

political decisions made in the past to justify present state coercion.[81] With this more complete picture of law's structural features, Dworkin then more fully justifies his 'interpretation' (or 'conception') of law's point or function: law as integrity is the conception of law making law's structural features (given by our 'concept' of law) the best they can be.

Thus, even those who began their jurisprudential careers sceptical of functionalist jurisprudence[82] have ended up engaged in such jurisprudence, however unwittingly. The reasons for this are twofold: first, knowledge of any kind, natural or functional, will be non-foundationalist ('circular') in the way indicated. Second, law's nature as a functionalist kind forces those who would study it to do so in the functionalist way. Law does seem to be good for something more than it seems to have a structural essence, and playing out this intuition in the way indicated is to verify or falsify this intuition.

Does this beg any questions about natural law? Only in the sense that a physical scientist 'begs' questions about the relation of gold to atomic structure by his theory that that is the nature of gold—which is to say, not at all. The theory that law is a kind and that its nature is given by such and such a goal is just that, a theory, falsifiable as is the atomic theory of gold. It is not a foundational assumption about law's nature that begs the question, 'Is law related to morality?' True, if law is a functional kind then necessarily law serves some good and thus, necessarily, law is in that way related to morality. But this is a discovery, not a posit, of functionalist jurisprudence.

I have saved the best objection for last. This is the opposite of the question-begging objection just considered. Now the objection is that functionalist jurisprudence cannot result in a natural law theory. An observation of Ruth Gavison's begins this objection: 'It is true that a description of a thing that is defined by its function must affirm that it has some minimal capacity to perform the function, but such functional attributions are morally evaluative only if the function itself has a determinate moral value. Nothing will be called a knife if it could not cut; yet knives are not inherently good or bad.'[83]

Lon Fuller's functionalist jurisprudence well illustrates this pitfall. Early in his career[84] Fuller likened a legal system to a steam-engine in that both were functional kinds; this, he thought, meant that there could be no clear separation of the questions, 'Is X a steam-engine?' and 'Is X a good steam-engine?', for the reason that Gavison mentions: to be a steam-engine at all is to perform the function of steam-engines to some degree. Gavison's point is that the goodness of a good steam-engine need not be moral goodness but only an instrumental goodness. One can, as noted earlier, be a *good* poisoner in the instrumental sense of 'good'.

Fuller's functional jurisprudence was peculiarly open to this charge, because much of the time Fuller proclaimed that the overall goal of law was simply the subjecting of human conduct to the guidance and control of general rules.[85] This by itself is not very plausibly thought to be among the things that are intrinsically good. If such an instrumental good were the only thing law was good for, then like a knife or a steam-engine such an instrument can equally well be used for good or for evil.[86] Yet it is not difficult to think of intrinsic goods that are plausibly served by those aspects of law (generality, prospectivity, publicity, etc.) on which Fuller focused. Liberty and autonomy come most easily to mind, for Fuller's rule of law virtues allow citizens more predictability of when law will sanction their behaviour and such increased predictability enhances planning ability and hence liberty and autonomy. Alternatively, such features may plausibly be supposed to serve the good of co-ordination and collaboration.[87]

Liberty, autonomy, and the common good (in the co-ordinative sense) are genuine moral goods. If these are the goals of law, then for a system to be a *legal* system there must be some moral goodness in these dimensions. This by itself would support a weak version of the natural law relational thesis, for what would be said is that the existence of a legal system in part depends on its moral worth (in the dimensions of liberty, autonomy, and the common good).

This would be a weak version of the natural law relational thesis because the goods of morality other than those that are the goals of law are not related to the existence conditions for a legal system. It is thus still possible that a legal system exists (because it is sufficiently promotive of law's distinctive goods) and yet that it is patently unjust. As Hart observed, systems can be highly respective of individual liberty (assuming *arguendo* that is the good at which law aims) and still possessed of great iniquity in every other dimension of morality.[88]

There is thus something of a dilemma facing any functionalist jurisprudence that has a natural law theory as its conclusion. On the one hand, functional jurisprudence seeks some distinctive end that law serves. The very idea that law is a functional kind depends on there being some such good that law can uniquely serve. That is what allows the functionalist to define law by its (functional) ends, and not by its (structural) means. Law cannot have as its distinctive good 'all things that are good' without ceasing to be a functional kind.

Yet the natural law conclusion sought by functionalist jurisprudence seems to demand that law have as its goal nothing less than all the goods there are. For short of such a comprehensive goal for law, law seems 'compatible with great iniquity'.

Lon Fuller's mode of confronting this dilemma was highly problematic. Fuller assumed that any system that promoted law's goal had to promote all other goods as well. As Fuller put it throughout his work,[89] his was the faith that if you do things the right way (i.e. seek law's goal, its 'internal morality'), you'll end up doing the right things. That requires a stronger faith in the interconnectedness (within human nature) of the various motivations to promote all the goods there are than I can sustain.[90]

A better mode of confronting this dilemma is to seek some goal for law that does have connections to all the goods there are and yet is not simply 'all the goods there are'. This is Finnis's strategy in so far as he assigns law the goal of the common good, which is not another of the seven good things Finnis thinks there are; yet the common good consists in the seven goods in so far as we can obtain them through co-ordination and community. Dworkin's implicit response to the dilemma is the same. He posits a goal of law, integrity, which is not one of the four political goods there are (distributive justice, fairness, procedural fairness, fraternity). Integrity is thus distinct, a separate end distinctively law's; yet integrity is connected to all legitimate political aims (the above four goods). Integrity purports to be both intrinsically good and the good uniquely served by law, and yet it purports to be linked to all goods such that its denial denies them as well.

Whether these responses by Finnis and Dworkin to the dilemma fare any better than Fuller's I shall leave to another occasion.

Important here is to see that some such resolution is necessary if a functionalist jurisprudence is going to lead to a natural law theory of law.

I shall close with a few remarks on how functionalist general jurisprudence may also generate a natural law theory of laws and of laws of cases. Suppose the functionalist who is also a natural lawyer has made her case about law. That is, it is shown that law has a distinctive goal, that goal is intrinsically good, and that good can be realized only if all other goods are also realized to some degree. A sufficiently unjust system will in that case not be a legal system.

This natural law conclusion about legal systems will have a trickle-down effect on laws and laws of cases. If the unjustness of a society precludes it from having a legal system, then that unjustness will also preclude it from having any laws or laws of cases. No law, no laws, and no case-laws. As much Fuller would have had the post Second World War German courts decide; they should invalidate the Nazi informer statutes, not on the ground that such statutes were themselves unjust, but on the ground that there was no legal system in place in Nazi Germany. The same would be true for the judgements of Nazi courts: they should not be given *res judicata* effect because such judgements could not represent the laws of the cases purportedly decided by them if there was no legal system.

To this limited extent the functionalist who has made out his natural law theory about law has also made it out about laws and laws of cases. Yet natural law theory is typically more ambitious than this for laws and laws of cases. About laws, the natural lawyer's relational thesis is that the degree of *their* injustice (not the overall injustice of the legal system of which they are a part) determines their status as laws. The functionalist thus needs some argument about laws that is independent of the argument about law if he is to establish his secondary relational thesis about laws.

About laws, the crucial issue between legal positivist and natural law theories is whether laws necessarily obligate to be laws. If the answer is yes, as Augustine asserted, then laws must be relatively just to be laws—for only morality can obligate. If the answer is no, as Bentham proclaimed, then it is perfectly possible that unjust norms can both fail to obligate and yet be laws.

The functionalist in jurisprudence who wishes to defend the natural law theses about laws must thus show that laws necessarily obligate. This can be done by a functionalist only by showing that the end of law is served by laws obligating obedience to their terms by citizens and judges. The function of law, in other words, must be such that law's structure possesses this feature.

Consider Finnis's end for law for purposes of illustration. If law exists in order to promote the co-ordination of the differing goods of individuals (the 'common good'), then laws may be thought to need acceptance by citizens as authoritative (obligating) in order to serve their co-ordinating function. For laws that are believed to be obligating are strongly salient features of any co-ordination problem and thus can serve as such a problem's solution. Finnis, however, needs to show more than this to make out his natural law thesis about laws. Laws need to *be* obligating—not just believed to be obligating by citizens—in order for the natural law relational thesis to be true. And this structural feature does not seem necessary for laws to serve their co-ordinating function. To make it necessary, Finnis would have to argue that citizens will not maintain their belief in the obligating character of laws unless they believe that the laws are just, and they will not maintain any long-term belief that the laws are just unless those laws *are* just.

There are problems with this chain of reasoning. Why do laws need to be accepted as authoritative by citizens in order to have the salience needed to solve co-ordination problems—couldn't sanction-backed rules that are not believed to be obligating be equally salient? Also, asserting that long-term beliefs in justice are supportable only if the objects of belief *are* just, is to assert a strong causal thesis about moral qualities, namely, they inevitably cause belief. Although a moral realist should think that moral qualities do cause belief, it is not very plausible to assert it so strongly; there can be (and are) numerous factors that cause people to hold false beliefs about morality permanently.

Finnis appears to believe that he can sidestep a defence of these troublesome points by adverting to his notion of 'central' or 'focal' meaning.[91] The central case of 'law' for Finnis is seen only from the internal point of view of an actor asking, 'How does *that* (some norm that purports to be a law) affect my obligations?' The necessary obligatoriness of laws to be laws stems from the conceptual primacy of the question asked from such internal point of view, for Finnis. Yet whatever the merits of this defence of the natural lawyer's crucial structural claim about laws, it is not a defence based on functionalist grounds. This is not a defence preceding *from* law's co-ordinating function *to* law's obligatory nature; rather, this defence abandons functionalist jurisprudence for a direct argument that the essence of law (law's 'focal meaning' or 'central case') lies in its obligating character.

Whatever the problems Finnis would have in defending the natural law thesis as the level of laws, I mention it for illustration only. Consider now the thesis at the level of the laws of cases. The laws of cases can have two different sources: (1) in authoritative general rules or other standards, such as statutes; or (2) in the reasoning by analogy from prior particulars that are regarded as having been authoritatively decided. The first source requires interpretive legal reasoning in order to discover the law of some case, and the second source requires non-interpretive (or common law) reasoning in order to discover the law of some case.[92] Let me consider each type of case-law separately.

With regard to interpretive case-law, Lon Fuller famously argued for 'purposive interpretation' in his 1958 debate with Herbert Hart.[93] Statutes, Fuller argued, should be interpreted by their purposes, so that a fully operational truck mounted on a pedestal as a war memorial in a park should not be considered a vehicle for purposes of a statute forbidding vehicles in the park—no matter how much such a truck was a standard instance of the word 'vehicle' in ordinary English. Hart responded that a legislature's purpose could be evil and that purposive interpretation was no guarantor of the justness of the law of the case that resulted. Could not Nazi judges have interpreted Nazi statutes regarding the Jews in a way that furthered the purposes of such statutes?[94]

If the natural lawyer has made out his relational thesis at the level of laws, then the answer to Hart's question must be no. If laws must be obligating to be laws, and if they must be just to be obligating, then the purpose that guides interpretation of such laws cannot be evil. Imagine a statute motivated exclusively by an immoral purpose. For example, the legislature requires margarine-makers to dye their product red solely because butter-makers do not want competition with their product. Suppose that dyeing margarine red in fact causes a real good to be achieved, perhaps the prevention of its consumption by those deathly allergic to it. Purposive interpretation of such a statute would then not be guided by the purpose (motive) of the legislature that passed the statute. Rather, such interpretation would ignore that psychological question altogether and engage in moral reasoning: how can the moral good that is the purpose (function) of the statute best be served?[95] The law of the case that results from this latter kind of purposive interpretation will be dependent upon morality in just the way the natural lawyer asserts. If the judgement of a case is unjust, it is not the law of that case, but a judicial mistake.

Now consider common law reasoning. Here we cannot rely on the necessary justice of laws to argue for the necessary justice of laws of cases, because there are no laws in common law reasoning. (There is law, but no laws.) Instead, the natural law argument here proceeds from the goal of common law reasoning, which is equality. (One must of course have some overall goal to law that makes equality the goal of this kind of laws of cases, but I leave that to the side for now.) Equality requires that like cases be treated alike, the requirement of formal justice. How one determines the likeness that morally entitles litigants to like treatment is the crucial question. I have elsewhere argued that equality is an intelligible good only if one judges likeness as including all and only morally relevant features.[96] If this is so, then the law of a common law case depends on all of morality, for only all of morality can answer the question of relevant likeness. This does not mean that the decisions of past cases have no bearing on the content of the common law; only that the directions of like treatment such cases demand are determined by a moral judgement about relevant similarity. This is enough to make out the natural law thesis for this kind of law of the case.

COMMENT: WALDRON ON REALISM

Jeremy Waldron's thoughtful chapter in this volume makes two criticisms of the moral realist half of natural law as I define it: (1)

that moral realism is false; and (2) that it doesn't matter whether moral realism is true or false. I shall here respond briefly to the second criticism.

The criticism goes like this. Moral realism is a metaphysical position. It is not an epistemological theory. My own non-foundationalist epistemology differs not at all from the non-foundationalist epistemology of those with quite different moral metaphysics. Therefore, my moral realist cannot present any arguments or evidence to resolve any case not equally well presentable by the anti-realist, even if the metaphysical claims for the arguments differ. Disagreements will be as persistent, as irresolvable, no matter if we or the disputants think we are disagreeing about conventions, about the true nature of morality, or even if we are not really disagreeing except in the sense that we are expressing opposed attitudes. For politics, this argument concludes, the real pay-offs lie in the ability to discover, justify, and convince our opponents of the error of their ways (epistemo-logy), not in convincing them that there is something about which they could be in error (metaphysics).[97]

Ronald Dworkin shares much of this argument. Yet, when Dworkin too scorns realism for its inability to deliver 'a thunder-ing metaphysical knockdown demonstration no one can resist who has the wit to understand'[98] he is caricaturing moral realists' positions. Metaphysics is not a source of new evidence, a new method of discovery, argument, or proof. Metaphysical beliefs are only beliefs about what it is the evidence we all possess evidences. Realists believe that the various features of our moral experience—our willingness to reason about moral questions, our expectation that moral judgements are backed by reasons, our sense that moral judgements give reasons for belief as well as for actions, our search for answers in the face of indeterminate conventions, the fact that we have moral beliefs (and not simply attitudes)—are best explained by the realist thesis that a mind-independent moral reality exists. Realists (at least *qua* realists) do not contend that they have discovered a new kind of experience that, when made known, will convince the unbelievers of the goodness of justice, the evil of intolerance, etc. The realists' meta-physical contention is only that the realists' theses make better sense of the experience most of us at various times experience.

How, then, can such a metaphysical position make a difference?

In just the way I indicated in a series of earlier articles:[99] moral realism can make sense of some of our adjudicatory practices—and thereby give us a reason to continue them, or modify them, as the case may be—that moral conventionalism and moral scepticism cannot. Consider but one example, the practice of judicial review in American constitutional law in so far as that review is exercised in interpreting the Bill of Rights and the Civil War Amendments. A moral realist can see those Amendments as referring to pre-existing moral rights all persons possess. When a moral realist judge today invalidates the expression of majority will that a statute presumptively represents, he does so in the name of something beyond his power to change and beyond the power of a societal consensus to change. His warrant for going against the majority is not that *his feelings* are different than the majority's, nor is it that some super-majority's past consensus is different from the present consensus a statute represents. His justification for judicial review is straightforward, and so is his mode of practising it: he will seek to discover the true nature of the rights referred to by building the best theory he can muster about the nature of equality, the nature of liberty, etc.

The sceptic and the conventionalist must both scramble if they are to find any justification for judicial review. The conventionalist judge, if he is a contractarian about the authority of the Constitution, might say that the particulars actually present in the minds of the framers can be used to invalidate subsequent legislation, because that was the super-majority's 'deal'. The equal protection clause, for example, is then interpreted to prohibit anything closely resembling the Black Codes of the Reconstructionist South in 1868, but otherwise is empty of any (non-race-based) equality-producing interpretations. If such judges are not contractarians, they must suppose some deep or hidden consensus of today's values that eluded the legislature that passed the statute that is in question.

Waldron's non-conventionalist judge is in the most difficult justificatory stance of all. If Waldron's emotivist judge is a contractarian about the Constitution's authority, he will be like Ely's judge who wants to follow the intent of the rule-maker even when the rule-maker, believing in ghosts, passes a rule regulating the behaviour of ghosts.[100] How do you follow the rule when you, unlike the rule-maker, don't believe ghosts exist? How do you make sense of even *trying* to follow the rule when you know that if the rule-maker believed what you believe about ghosts—namely, that they do not exist—he would never have passed the rule to begin with?

Waldron's emotivist judge is on no easier ground if he is not a contractarian about the Constitution's authority. If such a judge thinks that the Constitution has authority because by and large it coincides with what he feels is right, then his warrant for judicial review is the same as Holmes: granted, Holmes said, these are only *my* feelings, but since no one else's (no matter how numerous) are any better, I'll impose mine and not theirs.[101]

The short of it is that the justification of judicial review is a wild and unseemly scramble for any but a moral realist. Waldron thinks not, because he thinks the fact of disagreement about what rights persons possess makes judicial review as problematic for the realist as for anyone else. Waldron rightly points out that legislatures, too, may be operating with theories of equality and theories of liberty in seeking to legislate in conformity with the Fourteenth Amendment. Waldron thus thinks that the question of why a judge's differing moral beliefs should control is as pressing for the moral realist as for anyone else.

The answer lies in the moral realist's ability to say that there is something (in the nature of equality or of liberty) about which the judge *could be* right. That possibility at least leaves it open to then go on and argue that selection procedures for judges, and institutional differences between courts and legislatures, make judges better epistemic authorities about the rights persons possess than are legislatures. These further arguments are familiar: (1) judges are better positioned for this kind of moral insight than are legislatures because judges have moral thought experiments presented to them everyday with the kind of detail and concrete personal involvement needed for moral insight. It is one thing to talk about a right to privacy in general, another to order a teenager to bear a child she does not want to bear. One might well think that moral insight is best generated at the level of particular cases, giving judicial beliefs greater epistemic authority than that possessed by legislative beliefs on the same subject. (2) Judicial training is training in principled generality, so that even at the most abstract level one might think judges have the advantage. Moral rights, on such a view, are more safely left in the hands of those who can work out their content in a principled manner. (3) The institutional features of judicial office—notably job security—make judges better able to focus their deliberations on the moral aspect of any problem, putting aside all the questions of political expediency with which legislators must grapple. For this reason only judges can afford to take the long view that moral insight demands. (4) The judicial temperament may be more suited to assessing moral questions than is the temperament of those who are legislators. By temperament, I mean both the actual psychology of those who become judges rather than legislators, and the culture of each institution that inculcates and reinforces that psychology. Even-handedness, freedom from bias and prejudgement, neutrality, are the distinctively judicial virtues. They are also the virtues of the 'ideal observer' in moral theory, that postulate of some moralists about who can best gain insight into morality's truths.

Whatever one thinks of these familiar points about the comparative epistemic advantages of judges over legislators with respect to morality, the crucial point relevant here is that Waldron's emotivist theorist cannot even start this argument. For the emotivist, there is no question to ask about whether a court or a legislature is better equipped to describe the rights persons actually possess because, for the emotivist, people don't actually possess any rights. Emotivists like Waldron can certainly express their own feelings in terms of rights talk, but the last thing that could justify judicial review would be that courts are better than legislatures at discovering and applying Waldron's (or anyone else's) feelings.[102]

A conventionalist is not quite as bereft of any way to even begin the institutional comparison as is the emotivist, for the conventionalist can argue that courts are best at idealizing conventions so that they have maximal coherence ('integrity'), for example. Still, the conventionalist runs into the familiar question: what sense does it make to constrain a democratic majority by rights themselves given content by that same majority's interpretation of those rights? Why would one expect a court better to reflect consensus than a democratic legislature? Such questions are perhaps not unanswerable, but the conventionalist's metaphysics in any case make his defence both different and less persuasive than the realist's defence of judicial review.

NOTES

© Michael S. Moore 1992. Versions of this paper were presented to the faculty Ad Hoc Workshop at the University of Pennsylvania Law School, to the Philosophy of Law Reading Group, Greater Philadelphia Philosophy Consortium, and to the 1990 annual meeting of the Midwest Political Science Association, Chicago. I am indebted to the many participants for their helpful comments, and particularly indebted to Chris Boorse, John Finnis, Ruth Gavison, Robert George, Heidi Hund, Ken Kress, Stephen Morse, and Ed Rock for their separate comments. Special thanks go to Jeremy Waldron, my co-teacher of the jurisprudence seminar at University of California, Berkeley, from which much of this paper sprang, for his friendly disagreements with much that the paper asserts.

1. Jeremy Bentham, *Anarchical Fallacies*, in *Works* (Edinburgh: W. Tait, 1843), ii. 501.
2. *Southern Pacific Ry.* v. *Jensen*, 244 U.S. 205, 222 (1916).
3. H. Voegelin, 'Kelsen's Pure Theory of Law', *Political Science Quarterly*, 42 (1927), 268–76, at 269.
4. Bill Lycan reports that he found himself 'preaching to the choir' in a recent defence of moral realism, contrary to the more typical reaction in the past that regarded moral facts as 'right up there with Cartesian egos, moxibustion, and the Easter Bunny . . .', William Lycan, *Judgement and Justification* (Cambridge: Cambridge University Press, 1988), 198.
5. A defence of the moral realist thesis may be found in Moore, 'Moral Reality', *Wisconsin Law Review* (1982), 1061–1156; Moore, 'Moral Realism as the Best Explanation of Moral Experience', unpublished manuscript, Jan. 1989.
6. See e.g. the many papers discussing 'natural law' in Sidney Hook, ed., *Law and Philosophy* (New York: New York University Press, 1963), where what is discussed is some variant of moral realism.
7. These two theses—of existence and independence—are distinctive of realism in any domain, be it morality, psychology, mathematics, etc. See Moore, 'The Interpretive Turn: A Turn for the Worse?', *Stanford Law Review*, 41 (1989), 871–957, at 874–81.
8. The *locus classicus* of non-naturalist realism is G. E. Moore's *Principia Ethica* (Cambridge: Cambridge University Press, 1903).
9. It is this sense of 'natural law'—as naturalist realism—that generates the much overblown discussion in 20th-cent. ethics of the 'naturalistic fallacy'. For a discussion, see Moore, 'Moral Reality'.

10. Perhaps the best reason to dispense with the label, 'natural law', is the assumption that a natural lawyer is committed to human nature naturalism in her meta-ethics. Because some natural lawyers such as Aristotle and Aquinas were committed to human nature naturalism makes the confusion understandable but no less a confusion.

11. See e.g. Kai Nielsen, 'The Myth of Natural Law', in Hook, ed., *Law and Philosophy*, 129 ('If there is no God . . . the classical natural law theory is absurd . . .').

12. As Herbert Hart noted in his classic description of legal positivism. Hart, 'Positivism and the Separation of Law and Morality', *Harvard Law Review*, 71 (1958), 593–629. Legal positivism, as Hart points out, is a legal theory; it is not committed to non-cognitivism in meta-ethics nor, indeed, to any meta-ethical position. Still, as Hart did not point out, one motive for seeking a 'pure' theory of law— that is, a theory holding law to be uncontaminated by morality—is the fear that morality is irrational and that law cannot be scientific if it is tied to morality. Kelsen and Holmes were both partly motivated to their legal positivism by this fear.

13. See e.g. Theodore Benditt, *Law as Rule and Principle* (Stanford, Calif.: Stanford University Press, 1978), who argues for what he calls 'natural law' based on there being a necessary connection between law and conventional morality. Ronald Dworkin has throughout his career flirted with conventionalism about the morality to which law is related. See Dworkin, 'Philosophy, Morality, and Law—Observations Prompted by Professor Fuller's Novel Claim', *University of Pennsylvania Law Review*, 113 (1965), 668–90, at 688–90; Dworkin, *Taking Rights Seriously* (Cambridge, Mass.: Harvard University Press, 1978), 95, 125–6. 129, 134–5, 159–66; Dworkin, *Law's Empire* (Cambridge, Mass: Harvard University Press, 1986), 73. I and many others have noted this conventionalism before. Moore, 'Metaphysics, Epistemology, and Legal Theory', *Southern California Law Review*, 60 (1987), 453–506; Moore, 'A Natural Law Theory of Interpretation', *Southern California Law Review*, 8 (1985), 277–398, at 298–300; L. Alexander, 'The Empire Strikes Back', *Law and Philosophy*, 6 (1987), 419–38; H. Hurd, 'Relativistic Jurisprudence: Skepticism Founded on Confusion', *Southern California Law Review*, 61 (1988), 1417–509, at 1458–9; J. Finnis, 'On Reason and Authority in *Law's Empire*', *Law and Philosophy*, 6 (1987), 357–80. To the extent that Dworkin is a conventionalist about the morality to which law is related, he is not a natural lawyer, despite his own occasional self-labelling in these terms. (Dworkin, ' "Natural" Law Revisited', *University of Florida Law Review*, 34 (1982), 165–88.)

14. Hart, 'Positivism', 600–1. The distinctions in the text are not quite the way Hart described them.

15. So argued in Joseph Raz, *The Concept of a Legal System*, 2nd edn. (Oxford: Oxford University Press, 1980).

16. There are often several distinctions elided together under the labels 'general jurisprudence' and 'particular jurisprudence'. See e.g. J. W. Harris, *Legal Philosophies* (London: Butterworths, 1980), 4, where Harris has the distinction turn on the generality of the concepts analysed and not on the culture-free or culture-bound nature of the enterprise.

17. The exception again is Dworkin, who apparently eschews general jurisprudence. See text at nn. 27–9, below.

18. See Moore, 'Moral Realism'.

19. H. L. A. Hart, 'Book Review—*The Morality of Law*', *Harvard Law Review*, 78 (1965), 1281–96, at 1286.

20. The attentive reader will have noticed that I not only presuppose that each of us has reasons to act that we in no sense subjectively desire—'objective reasons'—but that satisfaction of desire is not itself among the objective reasons of practical reasonableness. For defence of both points, see Tom Nagel, *The View From Nowhere* (Oxford: Oxford University Press, 1985), 169–71.

21. On criteriological theories generally, see Moore, 'The Semantics of Judging', *Southern California Law Review*, 54 (1981), 151–295, at 214–21.

22. Augustine, *De Libero Arbitrio*, 1. 5. 11. There is an ambiguity that affects considerably just how strong this Augustinian view is. The ambiguity turns on whether we count only the unjustness of the content of a purported legal norm when we are assessing its legal validity, or we count also other considerations of morality (such as the unfairness of surprising reliance on the norm, the injustice caused by the encouragement of lawlessness by civil disobedience by others, etc.) when we ask, is this norm unjust? The latter view can be much weaker than the former, depending on how much weight is attached to the secondary moral considerations that might make a norm unjust-in-content nevertheless overall just. Aquinas appeared to have adopted the second, weaker view, as would I. A. C. Pegis, ed., *Basic Writings of Saint Thomas Aquinas* (New York: Random House, 1945), ii. 795 (*Summa Theologica*, Ia IIae, q. 96, a. 4); J. Ross, 'Justice Is Reasonableness: Aquinas on Human Law and Morality', *The Monist*, 58 (1974), 86–103, at 103.

23. See Moore, 'Semantics'.

24. Saul Kripke, *Naming and Necessity*, 2nd edn. (Cambridge, Mass.: Harvard University Press, 1980).

25. Dworkin, *Law's Empire*; Dworkin, 'Legal Theory and the Problem of Sense', in R. Gavison, ed., *Issues in Contemporary Legal Philosophy* (Oxford: Oxford University Press, 1987). I discuss this aspect of Dworkin's thought in 'The Interpretive Turn', 947–56.

26. See generally 'The Interpretive Turn'.

27. Dworkin, *Law's Empire*, 47.

28. Ibid. See below, Sect. 4, where I give an alternative interpretation of Dworkin's interpretivism that makes it (to my mind, at least) much more plausible but at the cost of reducing it to functionalist general jurisprudence.

29. The arguments of Lon Fuller and Herbert Hart, respectively, in Fuller, 'Positivism and Fidelity to Law—A Reply to Professor Hart', *Harvard Law Review*, 71 (1958), 630–72; Hart, 'Positivism'. See generally P. Soper, 'Choosing a Legal Theory on Moral Grounds', in J. Coleman and E. F. Paul, eds., *Philosophy and Law* (London: Basil Blackwell, 1987).

30. Hart suggests such a social-science-construct approach to juris-prudence in various places in *The Concept of Law* (Oxford: Oxford University Press, 1961), but he does not apparently follow the method in the book. See generally Moore, 'Introduction' to the Legal Classics edn. of *The Concept of Law* (Birmingham, Ala.: Gryphon Pub., 1990).

31. As also noted by John Finnis, *Natural Law and Natural Rights* (Oxford: Oxford University Press, 1980), 24–5. See also Philip Soper, *A Theory of Law* (Cambridge, Mass.: Harvard University Press, 1984), where at 171, n. 13, Soper urges that 'one must take care not to confuse the question of what is important about law with the question of what is important in deciding whether to classify something as law'. Despite this warning, Soper himself appears to mix normative arguments about how we ought to classify law (at 158–60) with his nominally non-normative, essen-tialist search for the nature of law (at 25).

32. On conventionalist theories of meaning, see Moore, 'Natural Law', 291–301.

33. Alternatively, some think that a concept is conventionally fixed by paradigmatic examples. See e.g. W. Gallie, 'Essentially Contested Concepts', *Proceedings of the Aristotelian Society*, 56 (1956), 167–98. Arguably, Herbert Hart shared this 'paradigm case' view of con-cepts. See Hart, 'Positivism', 607–8, where Hart discusses 'standard instances'; see also Hart, 'Ascription of Responsibility and Rights', *Proceedings of the Aristotelian Society*, 49 (1949), 171–94, where Hart thought it 'absurd' to seek criterial definitions of legal concepts. None the less, Hart's own theory of law in *The Concept of Law* is

statable as a definition of law (in terms of two individually necessary, jointly sufficient conditions, general citizen obedience of the
primary rules and adoption of the internal attitude by officials
towards the secondary rule of recognition). On this, see P. Hacker,
'Hart's Philosophy of Law', in P. Hacker and J. Raz, eds., *Law,
Morality and Society* (Oxford: Oxford University Press, 1977).

34. Hart, *The Concept of Law*; Raz, *The Concept of a Legal System*.
35. Moore, 'Natural Law'; Moore, 'Semantics'.
36. See e.g. S. Munzer, 'Realistic Limits on Realist Interpretation',
    Southern California Law Review, 58 (1985), 459–75; Schwartz, 'Putnam
    on Artifacts', *Philosophical Review*, 87 (1987), 566–74; D. Patterson,
    'Realist Semantics and Legal Theory', *Canadian Journal of Law and
    Jurisprudence*, 2 (1989), 175–9. Compare Hilary Putnam, *Mind,
    Language, and Reality* (Cambridge: Cambridge University Press,
    1975), 242–5; Moore, 'Semantics', 217–18; Moore, 'Natural Law', 300–
    1; Brink, 'Semantics and Legal Interpretation (Further Thoughts)',
    Canadian Journal of Law and Jurisprudence, 2 (1989), 181–91; Leo
    Katz, *Bad Acts and Guilty Minds* (Chicago: University of Chicago
    Press, 1987), 82–96.
37. *In re Erickson*, 815 F.2d 1091, 1092 (7th Cir. 1987).
38. Ibid. at 1093.
39. Fuller consistently elided 'purpose' in the sense of mental state
    with 'purpose' in the sense of function in his rush to conclude that
    law is purposive. See e.g. Fuller, 'Human Purpose and Natural
    Law', *Natural Law Forum*, 3 (1958), 68–76. Because of this and like
    confusions, Hart's jurisprudential epitaph for Fuller was accurate
    (if a bit brutal); 'The author [Fuller] has all his life been in love with
    the notion of purpose and this passion, like any other, can both
    inspire and blind a man . . . I wish that the high romance would
    settle down to some cooler form of regard. When this happens, the
    author's many readers will feel the drop in temperature; but they
    will be amply compensated by an increase in light.' Hart, 'Book
    Review', 1296.
40. This example, and the analysis that follows, are presented in
    greater detail in Moore, *Law and Psychiatry: Rethinking the Relation-
    ship* (Cambridge: Cambridge University Press, 1984), 26–32.
41. J. Raz, 'The Functions of Law', in Raz, *The Authority of Law* (Oxford:
    Oxford University Press, 1979).
42. These and other theories as to the function of sleep are explored in
    Ernest Hartmann, *The Functions of Sleep* (New Haven, Conn.: Yale
    University Press, 1973).
43. See Moore, *Law and Psychiatry*, 190–4. Chris Boorse has long
    disagreed with me on this. See Boorse, 'On the Distinction Between

Disease and Illness', *Philosophy and Public Affairs*, 5 (1975), 49–68; Boorse, 'Wright on Functions', *Philosophical Review*, 85 (1976), 70–86; Boorse, 'What a Theory of Mental Health Should Be', *Journal of Theory of Social Behavior*, 6 (1976), 61–84; Boorse, 'Health as a Theoretical Concept', *Philosophy of Science*, 44 (1977), 542–73. One can only settle the long-standing debate between myself and Boorse on the basis for function assignments on a piecemeal basis. About function assignments within physical medicine, Boorse's and my own method largely overlap in the functions they assign body parts because the health we value is by and large the health our bodies normally tend to achieve anyway, given aeons of natural selection. Still, the overlap is not perfect: we value capacities that make obesity dysfunctional even though there is no natural tendency to maintain *healthy* (i.e. not dysfunctional) weight; indeed, the body's natural tendency to store energy in the form of fat we find to be quite dysfunctional and thus unhealthy.

44. This definition of health will be found in Robert Spitzer and Jean Endicott, 'Medical and Mental Disorder: Proposed Definition and Criteria', R. Spitzer and R. Klein, eds., *Critical Issues in Psychiatric Diagnosis* (New York: Raven Press, 1978). My own fine-tuning of the definition is in Moore, 'Definition of Mental Illness', in *Critical Issues*; and in *Law and Psychiatry*, 210–16.

45. Soper, *A Theory of Law*, 170, n. 9. See also Soper, 'Legal Theory and the Problem of Definition', *University of Chicago Law Review*, 50 (1983), 1170–200, at 1187, n. 62.

46. John Austin's and Jeremy Bentham's view. For a modern discussion of each, see Hart, *Concept of Law*, 18–76, and Hart, *Essays on Bentham* (Oxford: Clarendon Press, 1982), 127–43.

47. Kelsen's slogan. Hans Kelsen, *General Theory of Law and State* (Cambridge, Mass.: Harvard University Press, 1949), 124, 126, 132, 198, 354.

48. Hart, *Concept of Law*.

49. Finnis, *Natural Law*.

50. Soper, *A Theory of Law*.

51. Raz, *The Authority of Law*.

52. Lon Fuller, *The Morality of Law*, 2nd edn. (New Haven, Conn.: Yale University Press, 1969).

53. Finnis's five formal features of law in *Natural Law*, at 268–70.

54. Dworkin's 'concept' of law in *Law's Empire*.

55. Fuller, *Morality of Law*.

56. F. A. Hayek, *The Road to Serfdom* (London: Routledge & Kegan Paul, 1944), 54. This is also most clearly the value that makes best sense of Fuller's eight desiderata for law. See Finnis, *Natural Law*,

at 272; Hart, 'Book Review', 1291; M. Radin, 'Reconsidering the Rule of Law', *Boston University Law Review*, 69 (1989), 781–819; and A. Gianella, 'Thoughts on the Symposium: The Morality of Law', *Villanova Law Review*, 10 (1965), 676–8, for reconstructions of Fuller along these lines.

57. Finnis, *Natural Law*. Arguably Fuller too had some co-ordinative goal in mind for law when he said that law provides 'firm base lines for human interaction' (*Morality of Law*, 209, 210, 223, 229), that it enables men to collaborate effectively (*Anatomy of Law* (Westport, Conn.: Greenwood Press, 1968), 6), and that it allows for that 'collaborative articulation of purpose' ('A Rejoinder to Professor Nagel', *Natural Law Forum*, 3 (1958), 83–104) Fuller thought essential to moral insight.

58. Richard Wasserstrom, *The Judicial Decision* (Stanford, Calif.: Stanford University Press, 1961), 10–11.

59. One of Finnis's senses, although not his main one, in *Natural Law*, 155.

60. Hart, *Concept of Law*, 188.

61. Dworkin, *Law's Empire*.

62. e.g. Hobbes, *Leviathan*.

63. Karl Llewellyn, *The Bramble Bush* (New York: Oceana Publications, 1930), 12.

64. Soper, *A Theory of Law*.

65. Finnis, *Natural Law*, 155.

66. Fuller, *Morality of Law*.

67. Hart, 'Book Review', *supra*; Dworkin, 'Professor Fuller's Novel Claim'; Dworkin, 'The Elusive Morality of Law', *Villanova Law Review*, 10 (1965), 631–9; Marshall Cohen, 'Law, Morality, and Purpose', *Villanova Law Review*, 10 (1965), 640–54. For a contemporary expression of this criticism, see Radin, 'Reconsidering The Rule of Law'.

68. Finnis, *Natural Law*, 139–47.

69. On this, see Leslie Green, 'Law, Co-ordination, and the Common Good', *Oxford Journal of Legal Studies*, 3 (1983), 299–324. Compare Finnis, 'Law as Co-ordination', *Ratio Juris*, 2 (1989), 97–104.

70. Hart, *Concept of Law*, 189–95; Hart, 'Positivism', 622–3.

71. Ibid.

72. Cohen, 'Law, Morality, and Purpose', 623, n. 19.

73. Ibid. 649.

74. The assumptions about human nature that must be made in order for functionalist jurisprudence to yield determinate answers about law's structural features are what incline me to retain the otherwise misleading label, 'natural law theory of law'. Human nature enters

here, in the determination of what is instrumentally necessary for the attainment of law's good; human nature does not enter in to determine what is intrinsically good.

75. For such an objection, see Nielson, 'The Myth of Natural Law', in Hook, ed., *Law and Philosophy*, 136–8.
76. Both Hart and Nielson explicitly discuss such goals as survival because of their popularity, not because of their plausibility as distinctively legal goals. See ibid. 136–7; Hart, *Concept of Law*, 187–8.
77. Hart, 'Positivism', 623.
78. I am indebted to Stephen Morse for seeing this objection clearly. See Frederick Olafson, 'Essence and Concept in Natural Law Theory', in Hook, ed. *Law and Philosophy*, 237, for an apparent form of the objection.
79. Dworkin, *Law's Empire*, 65–6. My interpretation of Dworkin's interpretivism is alternative to that earlier given. Earlier, I took Dworkin to be claiming that jurisprudence is interpretive in the sense that there was some authoritative text for legal theorists whose theories were therefore interpretations of that text. Now, I construe Dworkin to be eschewing the need for any text; such 'interpretivism' proceeds rather by seeking a 'point' or value to the existence of law (not a point or value to regarding some legal practices as authoritative for theorists—true interpretation). The difference is that such textless 'interpretivism' is just functionalist general jurisprudence under a quite misleading label, for like the functionalist Dworkin seeks a goal for law and lets that goal guide what structural features are part of law.
80. Ibid., pp. vii, 3–15. See particularly p. 13: '[L]aw is a social phenomenon. But its . . . function . . . depend[s] on one special feature of its structure. Legal practice, unlike many other social phenomena, is *argumentative*.'
81. Ibid. 93, 110.
82. Dworkin, 'Does Law Have a Function? A Comment on the Two-Level Theory of Decision', *Yale Law Journal*, 74 (1965), 640–51. In this criticism of Dick Wasserstrom's functionalist jurisprudence, the early Dworkin regarded 'the assumption of a fundamental social goal as chimerical, even as a legislative standard'. Ibid. 648.
83. R. Gavison, 'Natural Law, Positivism, and the Limits of Jurisprudence: A Modern Round', *Yale Law Journal*, 91 (1982), 1250–85, 1266–7.
84. Fuller, *The Law in Quest of Itself* (Boston: Beacon Press, 1940), 10–11.
85. Fuller, *Morality of Law*, 53, 107, 115, 122, 130, 146, 150, 162.
86. The first of the two main criticisms commonly levelled at Fuller's

functionalist jurisprudence. See Hart, 'Book Review'; Dworkin, 'Professor Fuller's Novel Claim'; Cohen, 'Law, Morality, and Purpose'.

87. Finnis so appropriates Fuller's eight desiderata of law. *Natural Law*, 270–3.

88. Hart, *Concept of Law*, 202; 'Book Review', 1287. See also Kenneth Stern, 'Either-or or Neither-nor', in Hook, ed., *Law and Philosophy*, 249–50, where Stern urges that the best mousetrap is not necessarily one that is best in trapping mice (a mousetrap's function); rather, the best mousetrap may be one that is pretty good at catching mice *and* that serves other values best, e.g. one with a safety catch that prevents human harm.

89. Fuller, 'What the Law Schools Can Contribute to the Making of Lawyers', *Journal of Legal Education*, 1 (1948), 189–204, at 204; Fuller, 'Fidelity to Law', 636, 643, 661; Fuller, 'A Reply to Professors Cohen and Dworkin', *Villanova Law Review*, 10 (1965), 655–66, at 661–6. Fuller, *Morality of Law*, 152–86, 223–4.

90. This was the second major criticism of Fuller's functionalist jurisprudence: even if law's 'internal morality' (law's goal) was intrinsically good, one could achieve that moral good without necessarily achieving any other goods (Fuller's 'external morality of law'). For a limited resuscitation of Fuller on this point, see Finnis, *Natural Law*, 273–6.

91. Personal communication, 7 Jan. 1990. On 'focal meaning', see Finnis, *Natural Law*, ch. 1.

92. I defend the view that statutory reasoning is interpretive in Moore, 'Natural Law Theory of Interpretation', and I defend the view that common law reasoning is non-interpretive in Moore, 'Precedent, Induction, and Ethical Generalization', in L. Goldstein, ed., *Precedent in Law* (Oxford: Oxford University Press, 1987).

93. Fuller, 'Fidelity to Law'.

94. Hart, 'Positivism'.

95. I argue for this kind of purposive interpretation in 'Semantics' and in 'Natural Law Theory of Interpretation'.

96. Moore, 'Precedent'.

97. Similar criticisms are directed at the relevance of my moral metaphysics by others. See e.g. R. Smith, 'The New Institutionalism and Normative Theory: Reply to Professor Barber', in *Studies in American Political Development*, 3 (1989), 74–87; S. Brubaker, 'Republican Government and Judicial Restraint', *Review of Politics*, 49 (1987), 570–2; Brubaker, 'Conserving the Constitution', *American Bar Foundation Research Journal* (1987), 261–80; S. Fish, 'Dennis Martinez and the Uses of Theory', *Yale Law Journal*, 96 (1987), 1773–810.

98. Dworkin, *Law's Empire*, 85.
99. See generally Moore, 'Moral Reality'; Moore, 'A Natural Law Theory of Interpretation'; Moore, 'Precedent, Induction, and Ethical Generalization'; Moore, 'The Interpretive Turn: A Turn for the Worse?'; Moore, 'Do We Have an Unwritten Constitution?', *Southern California Law Review*, 63 (1989), 107–39; Moore, 'Three Concepts of Rules', *Harvard Journal of Law and Public Policy*, 14 (Summer 1991).
100. John Hart Ely, *Democracy and Distrust* (Cambridge, Mass.: Harvard University Press, 1980), 39.
101. O. W. Holmes, 'Natural Law', *Harvard Law Review*, 32 (1915), 40–8.
102. I see three not entirely consistent responses to this argument in Waldron's paper. The first denies that if emotivism is true then those of us who design legal institutions (or recommend to others how they should design them) cannot make the institutional comparisons suggested. Even if emotivism is true, Waldron might respond, we still can evaluate positively certain rights being protected and compare how well judges (*vis-à-vis* legislatures) protect them. We might call this the 'everything-goes-on-as-before' response. The problem with this response lies in the simultaneous doublethink that it requires. On the one hand, we (who are justifying judicial review as system—designing theorists) say of judges that their 'beliefs' about 'moral rights' are in reality not beliefs about any things; rather, judges express their emotions in their talk of 'moral rights'. On the other hand, we allow ourselves to cast our feelings as if they were beliefs about rights that really exist. It is this bifurcation that allows us emotivist-system designers to duplicate the moral realist's calculation with one of our own: will the feelings of judges be more likely or less likely than the feelings of legislators to promote . . . what? Not *our* feelings, but the moral rights of persons. This is the doublethink that I find both psychologically unintelligible and epistemically unjustifiable. Psychologically, how can it be that we see only too well the true meta-ethical status of judges' and legislators' moral 'beliefs' while not seeing the same meta-ethical status of our own? Epistemically, what could justify inducing such wilful blindness in ourselves, even if it were psychologically possible? Is it that one cannot admit that *our* feelings about rights are only feelings—that is, that they lack cognitive content—without altering how we feel about rights?

A second response would admit that in making the institutional comparison we see clearly the meta-ethical status of our own moral 'beliefs' about 'moral rights', yet deny that we are in any way demotivated by that meta-ethical insight. Granted, these are only our feelings, but that doesn't make us care any less about designing institutions so that they maximize the number of decisions that respect our feelings. Yet this clear-sighted emotivist system-designer seems to undervalue democracy. Only if like Holmes we are willing to have our attitudes on these matters prevail even when we are in the minority, should we design institutions so that they are more likely to produce outcomes favouring our feelings. Yet since these are only feelings, why should we have our way if a majority of our fellow citizens have different feelings? We, like the judges whose power of judicial review we are justifying, need moral realism to make sense of our undemocratic impositions.

Waldron's third possible response is to build on the doubts about expertise in matters of morality expressed in his paper. Here he might deny that judges could be better moral deciders than legislators because, he might think, no one has enhanced powers of moral insight. Yet, this response is in danger of presupposing that realism is false on its way to concluding that the truth or falsity of realism is irrelevant. For the only reason I see for doubting that Nazis, sadists, the quick-tempered, the non-empathetic, the non-universalizing, etc., are worse than their opposites in reaching true moral judgements, is to deny that there are any true moral judgements. For by my armchair inductive study, the former groups are obviously worse judges of what morality demands because they get it wrong so often. Even if Waldron were right that there is no checking procedure for moral truth as there is for scientific truth—which I also deny—the ability to compare outcomes of certain persons or procedures allows us to verify who or what are better harbingers of moral truth. If Waldron is to deny the possibility of making the suggested institutional comparison he must deny this, but to do so he has to deny that *we* ever know any moral truths. This sceptically based objection to the relevance of moral realism confirms something Nicholas Sturgeon also has noted: why is it that only moral sceptics think that moral metaphysics doesn't matter?

PART III
NATURAL LAW, JUSTICE, AND RIGHTS

9

That 'Nature Herself Has Placed in our Ears a Power of Judging': Some Reflections on the 'Naturalism' of Cicero

HADLEY ARKES

Those of us who grew up with the legends of Franklin Roosevelt were impressed with a series of visual images that came along with the hagiography: they were scenes from the Depression and the Second World War, which offered the dramatic setting for the special mission and story of Roosevelt. Among the pictures from the Depression, we remember the scene of bitter farmers, banding together to resist the sheriff, who was charged to act as an agent of a bank in foreclosing on a family farm. A companion scene was drawn from the run on the banks in the first days of the Roosevelt Administration: a crowd of desperate depositors was massed outside the doors of the bank, hoping to get in and retrieve what they could of their savings before the bank went under.

The banks figured prominently in these scenes as threatening institutions. If they were not corporate villains themselves, they were institutions that reflected an economic system that bore destructively on ordinary people. Over the years I would come to learn how much selection went into the history that was shaped and edited by the historians in praise of Roosevelt, and one of the curious omissions in that history is that none of the critical writers drew on the character of a bank as an institution and sought to connect these two sets of scenes. Or at least I am not aware of any commentator or artist who offered a creative juxtaposition and sought to connect the constituencies that were connected by the banks. With a touch of imagination, there might have been a painting showing the embattled farmers, massed for resistance . . . against the crowd of depositors, who were anxious to retrieve their savings, which had been lent out to the farmers by the banks. Of course, we will hear many artful words about corporate interests and the skilful manipulation of accounts, so that it becomes impossible to know whether there was any money out there but the money invented by the bank. But that account becomes too clever by half: the money deployed as loans depends on the assets that are built up in large part by depositors, who leave their money with the prospect of earning a return. At a certain point, the refusal of the farmers to repay their loan or yield some other asset marks a refusal to give back the money that was extracted from depositors. Those who would hold back from repossessing the property of the farmers would, in effect, dispossess the property of the depositors. The difference is that the farmers are left in possession of their farms; the depositors who lent their money are left with nothing.

During the New Deal, the Supreme Court elicited the contempt of intellectuals and writers when it resisted schemes for the cancellation of debts. To the reformers on the left, the Court merely showed a stodgy want of imagination in resisting novel schemes to cope with an economic crisis. And the Court itself spoke in muted tones; it rarely found the moral language that would offer the most compelling account of the principles it was trying to defend. At no point, in the careful writing of the jurists, did we find the issue reduced to its stark moral terms, as it was in this brief passage by Cicero in *De Officiis* ('Of Duties'). What is the meaning, he asked, of an 'abolition of debts, except that you buy a farm with my money; that you have the farm, and I have not my money?'[1]

For Cicero, it was plain that schemes for the abolition of debt did not become 'legal' or warranted because they were covered with the trappings of law; they had to be understood, without shadings or cavilling, as legalized forms of theft. The taking of property could be obscured through layers of legislation, by passing the property through intermediaries and institutions. But none of this flexing of the legislative art could efface the brute underlying fact: namely, that property was taken from one person and transferred for the benefit of another, without a justification. The recipient might indeed be in desperate want of money, but there was still the need to show just why those who were compelled to give up their property bore any distinct or special responsibility for the plight of those in need—a responsibility that could justify the liability that was being focused on them now, to bear the burden of supplying a remedy. Without that justification, there was a danger of rendering insecure the ground on which people claimed, for their personal use, the fruits of their own work. A policy that called that kind of ownership into question would begin to dismantle the intricate system of relations that supported production, employment, investment, saving. And a scheme that was advanced, in public, to serve the interests of the poor would have the practical result of visiting its most destructive consequences upon the people who were most vulnerable and dependent.

In the record of our experience, there have been few cases more vivid—or more confirming of Cicero's argument—than the experience of the United States in the 1780s, in the crisis that led to the adoption of the Constitution. That crisis was produced by a wave of movements to cancel debts. In Massachusetts, the times were marked by Shays' Rebellion, and what the Founders saw in the pattern of events was an incapacity, in the separate states, to preserve the conditions of justice: in the circumscribed arena of politics in the states, it was far easier for a dominant local interest to gain a majority, and to seek its ends at the expense of a minority. But even before the Founders responded with a polit- ical remedy, the season of attacks on debts and creditors quickly brought its own sanction: those with money to lend would simply not put their property at hazard, under conditions in which debts could be cancelled. Or they would charge a premium that would make loans vastly more expensive—and far harder to obtain. Justice George Sutherland would later note that the 'bonds of men whose ability to pay their debts was unquestion- able could not be negotiated except at a discount of thirty, forty, or fifty per cent'.[2] The effect was a massive drying up of invest- ment and credit. And it stood to reason that this state of affairs had to be far more injurious to people who did not have money to lend—people who were dependent, for their livings, on the investment and the business that were fuelled by the money of others.[3]

As Cicero would have described the situation, an immoral policy begat ruinous consequences. The swiftness and certainty of those consequences was, in fact, an integral part of the under- standing held, by Cicero, that these schemes of legislation were violating nothing less than 'laws of nature'. And therein lies a refined problem in the argument over natural law. But before I cross that threshold, I would back up for just a moment: I suggested that Cicero would not have been taken in by the forms of 'social legislation'; he would not have been distracted by the forms of legislation and prevented from seeing the act of theft that they disguised, because he was not burdened, in his view of the world, with the lens of the modern 'positivist'. That is to say, he was not willing to find the source of law or lawfulness in the fact that a measure was proclaimed with the authority and power of a sovereign. He understood that, behind the power of statutes and edicts, was the natural law, which gave us the measure of the things that were right or wrong, just or unjust.

Cicero readily understood, of course, that there was a difference between the universal law and the laws that had to be tailored to particular places and peoples. He also understood that there was a difference between the exacting standards of the moral law and the standards that seemed as morally strenuous as the local inhabitants in any place could abide. But he also understood that the civil laws had to find their ground in deeper principles of judgement; the principles that guided our understanding of the things that were right and wrong. And so it may be, as Cicero says, that people who sell houses and property are not obliged, by the local laws, to reveal the defects in the property to the buyers. 'Such a method of procedure', he wrote, 'is neither by custom accounted morally wrong nor forbidden either by statute or by civil law; nevertheless it is forbidden by the moral law.'[4] As Cicero acknowledged, 'The civil law is not necessarily also the universal law'; but he insisted, nevertheless, that 'the universal law ought to be also the civil law'.[5] For Cicero, the civil law was not the measure of right and wrong; and therefore, it could not supply a moral justification for any piece of legislation to note that it was enacted in a thoroughly 'legal' way.

Cicero was free, then, to look past the forms, to the moral substance of legislation; and if he did not find the measure of rightness in convention and statute, he would purport to find the source of law in nature, or in that 'Reason which is in Nature, which is the law of gods and men'.[6] The sense of nature began, in other words, with the awareness of beings who were marked, distinctly, by the capacity for speech and reason. I have had the occasion already to explain, with some detail, the implications that unfolded from a similar understanding, in Aristotle, of the 'nature' that was distinctly human.[7] I have also mapped, with some care, the moral system that unfolded, for Kant, out of the nature of a 'rational creature as such'. Aristotle and Kant could both appeal to the nature of beings possessed of reason; they could draw, at critical places, on the same understanding; and yet they could produce moral teachings with notably different properties. Those who know the texts will know that followers of the two writers may be gravely divided in their understanding of the sources and reach of the moral laws, the place of 'experience', the existence of 'categorical' rights and wrongs, and the claims of prudence.

Cicero was quite emphatic in his conviction that 'Nature' was the source of law, but that still left open a serious question about the brand of natural law that he sought to expound. And no small part of the differences engaged here would be found in the different answers to the question of just how one arrived at the understanding of 'human nature'. Do we form our understanding of nature as an *inductive generalization*: do we begin with human beings as we encounter them in our experience, and then draw generalizations about humans and their characteristic behaviour, based on the sample of humans we have seen? And if that record of experience contains ingredients such as incest, infanticide, slavery, and genocide, as practices with remarkable endurance, would we be obliged to incorporate them in our understanding of the life that is 'natural' for human beings?

Our inclination has been to identify the 'truly human' with the 'better part of our natures'. But in that event, we must imply some understanding of the imperatives of 'reason', or the 'logic of morals', which can supply a standard of moral judgement quite apart from the spotty record of our species. Beyond that, the generalizations that are drawn from induction can never give us anything more than a statement of probability. If the Founders had been stating merely an inductive generalization in the Declaration of Independence, they could have proclaimed, at best, that '*most* men are created equal', or that *most* humans have the capacity to give and understand reasons.[8] As Lincoln rightly observed, the Founders 'did not mean to say all [men] were equal in color, size, intellect, moral developments, or social capacity'. They understood perfectly well the pattern of inequalities that was manifest in the human record. But they did not intend to offer merely a statement of probability, or an inductive generalization, when they insisted that 'all men are created equal'. As Lincoln recognized, they understood that they were expressing an abstract, universal truth, that would be 'applicable to all men and all times'.

The American Founders referred, in this respect, to 'self-evident truths'. Hamilton described them more precisely in the *Federalist* as those 'primary truths, or first principles, upon which all subsequent reasonings must depend. These contain an internal evidence which, antecedent to all reflection or combination, commands the assent of the mind.'[9] Philosophers in our own day may speak instead of apodictic or necessary truths. But in either event, the people who use these terms have in mind propositions with the force of axioms or first principles. Those propositions can then be the source of other propositions, deductively drawn, and as Thomas Reid observed, 'whatever can, by just reasoning, be inferred from a principle that is necessary, must be a necessary truth'.[10] It makes a profound difference, for any system of moral philosophy, that it claims to speak through necessary and universal propositions, as opposed to propositions that are merely contingent or problematic. We may be maddeningly uncertain, in particular cases, as to whether we are dealing with a moral question, or we may be unclear about the principles that bear on the case at hand. But if it becomes clear, say, in any case, that a punishment of death is being visited on people solely on account of their race, it makes a critical difference that the wrongness of genocide does not hinge on climate or locale or the distribution of local opinion. Nor would it hinge on the question of whether some people—or even most people—happen to benefit, in substantial, material ways, from the commission of this wrong. If we can speak of wrongs that are grounded in necessary truths, then we would have a logical ground for the recognition of wrongs that are *categorical* and not merely contingent.

I would recall this issue here because it touches a question at the core of the argument over natural rights. Aristotle recognized the difference between things that were right or wrong in themselves, and things that were merely right or wrong as means to other ends.[11] For example, it is not inherently right or wrong to practise the art of driving a car. Whether it is right or wrong depends on the end to which that art is directed—whether in driving to work at a legitimate business, or driving a get-away car for the Mafia. But the chain of instrumental 'goods' would merely lead on to an infinite regress, unless the chain could find a terminus somewhere, in an understanding of the ends that are legitimate or illegitimate, good or bad. And yet, it has been widely thought that Aristotle's understanding of 'final' ends does not partake of the stringency that affects Kant's understanding of 'categorical' rights and wrongs. Some followers of Kant in our own day are quite emphatic that the use of nuclear weapons would be categorically wrong, and they would not threaten the use of these weapons even if it were necessary to resist a totalitarian power such as Nazi Germany. In contrast, certain votaries of Aristotle would insist on a claim of prudence, which would make it justified to contemplate even indiscriminate killing, if that were the only way of resisting an 'immeasurable evil', such as Nazi Germany.

At issue here is a refined problem that marks some of the most intractable puzzles in natural law. I am not prepared to claim that Cicero had managed to solve this enduring problem, which stands at the centre of natural rights and the claims of moral truth. But I think he did mark off a path of argument rather different from the paths that have become familiar to us, and if I can offer here an account of that argument, there is a fair chance of illuminating something more of the terrain that surrounds the path of argument.

There are passages in *De Officiis* in which Cicero takes a decisive position to insist on principle and override the claims of prudence. He takes, in other words, a hard position on 'categorical' rights and wrongs, which would rival the pretensions of the most fortified Kantians. But his position becomes all the more remarkable when we appreciate the fact that he had set the ground for his move by putting himself at odds with Aristotle and Plato on the place of speculative knowledge. As a consequence, he could reach a kind of Kantian position only by making a pivot so wide that it could hardly be attributed to a subtle misstep. With Plato and Aristotle, Cicero was inclined to find the core of human nature in the character of human beings as 'social' animals; the only animals that were suited, by nature, to live in a *polis*. But

Cicero would carry the logic of that argument just one step further, with a quick reversal on Aristotle and Plato: the two ancient masters held that there was nothing higher than speculative knowledge or contemplation—that is to say, the absorption in philosophy, or the understanding of things, as an end in itself, an activity pursued with no other motive than a respect for its own, intrinsic goodness. And yet, Cicero was prepared to argue that the core of our nature supplied also the standard for judging the order, or ranking, of the things we might know. In this vein, he would argue that 'those duties are closer to Nature which depend upon the social instinct than those which depend on knowledge.' And among the objects of our wisdom or knowledge, the knowledge that bears on our social obligations would be higher than knowledge that is merely theoretical. The knowledge to which Cicero accords the foremost place is the 'knowledge of things human and divine, which is concerned also with the bonds of union between gods and men and the relation of man to man'.[12] But Cicero then places his accent on the service of human needs, or the safeguarding of human interests. From that angle, the knowledge that has a practical effect, in serving the needs of humans, must be 'ranked above speculative knowledge'. ('Ea . . . actio in hominum commodis tuendis maxime cernitur; pertinent igitur ad societatem generis humani; ergo haec cognitioni anteponenda est.')[13]

A reader trained in modern texts may begin to see, in these arguments, the rudiments of an argument that finds, in the 'community' (or the 'people' or the 'Volk') the ultimate ground of morality. All the more surprising, then, is the turn taken by Cicero when he insists, nevertheless, that 'there are some acts either so repulsive or so wicked, that a wise man would not commit them, even to save his country'.

Posidonius has made a large collection of them; but some of them are so shocking, so indecent, that it seems immoral even to mention them. The wise man, therefore, will not think of doing any such thing for the sake of his country; no more will his country consent to have it done for her.[14]

After a decorous interval, Cicero was willing, much later in the text, to speak of the unspeakable, and speak with the concreteness of cases. He recalled that Themistocles had conceived a plan for striking at the Spartan fleet when the ships were drawn up at shore at Gytheum. Themistocles would have had agents moving in stealth to set the ships afire. It was too impolitic to offer the plan in the public forum, and so Themistocles proposed that the people appoint a representative to consider his counsel. The assembly appointed Aristides, who listened to Themistocles' plan and reported back to the assembly. Aristides confirmed that the plan would be quite expedient, but that it was anything but morally right. On the strength of that advice—and knowing, apparently, nothing more—the assembly rejected the scheme of Themistocles.[15]

In a second example, offered still later, Cicero recalled an incident that arose in the Roman war against King Pyrrhus. Pyrrhus 'had declared war on the Roman people, and in the course of the war, a deserter had come from the camp of Pyrrhus to the camp of Gaius Fabricius. The deserter offered this proposition: that with a suitable award, he would return to his camp and administer a poison to the king. Fabricius refused the offer and sent the deserter back to his own camp; and his dispatch of the turncoat was commended by the Senate. Cicero went on to remark that

if the mere show of expediency and the popular conception of it are all we want, this one deserter would have put an end to that wasting war and to a formidable foe of our supremacy; but it would have been a lasting shame and disgrace to us to have overcome not by valour but by crime the man with whom we had a contest for glory.[16]

I do not think we can regard Cicero as anything less than earnest in his teaching, but the writing in *De Officiis* contains many dramatic swings and reversals, which are evidently meant to draw the reader into the puzzle of the contradictions. Cicero takes the safety and well-being of the public as an interest that overrides the claims of private dignity and the fastidiousness of a personal moral code.[17] And yet, we are to infer that Cicero would permit one's own citizens to die in large numbers rather than striking, by stealth, at the arms or the ships of an enemy. In our own time, even a man of the most stringent moral rectitude might have authorized the poisoning of Hitler if he had reason to believe that this one move could have saved millions of innocent lives, in the battlefields and the gas chambers. Was Cicero really appealing here to principles of morality, which could be applied categorically, applied without shadings or qualifications, in all varieties of cases? Or was he affecting the seriousness of a categorical imperative for propositions that merely expressed a curious understanding of sportsmanship, within the circles of gentlemen?

Of course, even Immanuel Kant was not willing to make such a dramatic departure from prudence in his respect for categorical duties. Kant was willing to accommodate a concern for the safety of the public, which could permit a certain release from an overly rigorous application of moral principles, in places where a strict adherence to the rules might be destructive of the very ends of moral judgement. One suspects that Cicero would have made a similar concession to prudence before he drew his final judgement in cases of this kind. And in fact, in *De Officiis*, he offers a strand of argument that may lead his reader in a notably different direction. Cicero remarks, in Book 3, that there are no duties to tyrants. Indeed, he said, it was not opposed to nature and morality if that 'pestilent and abominable race should be exterminated from human society':

[F]or as certain members are amputated, if they show signs themselves of being bloodless and virtually lifeless and thus jeopardize the health of the other parts of the body, so those fierce and savage monsters in human form should be cut off from what may be called the common body of humanity [*humanitis corpore*].[18]

In the other passages I cited, the safety of the public was radically subordinated—one might almost say, shockingly subordinated—to the commands of a stringent morality. To that extent, the claims of the 'social bond' would seem to be overridden by a morality whose imperatives may not be compromised. But in the passage on the killing of the tyrant, the demands of that strict morality are reconciled with the claims of the social bond. The assassination of a tyrant may serve to improve the bonds of society; and the reconciliation is accomplished through the notion of the polity as a 'common body'.

I hold back from referring to a 'metaphor' of the body, for as difficult, as fraught with implausibility as the scheme may be, Cicero's moral theory depends on the reality or experience of the 'social body'. The harmony or dissonance of society is to be felt palpably or measured. The ontological standing of the 'social body' becomes the centrepiece, I think, in Cicero's 'naturalism'.

And through that naturalism, through that reality of the social body, Cicero seeks to resolve those thorny, enduring tensions in moral philosophy: the tension between the right and the expedient, between the categorical and the contingent.

Cicero readily admitted that there may be a tension between the commands of morality and the things that *appeared* expedient. But Cicero seemed driven to hold, as a persistent, emphatic theme, that what was morally right was in fact expedient: the course of rightness was the course that served our interests. There may be obvious benefits at hand for acting in a low manner, but Cicero maintained, nevertheless, that there was no tension, finally, between the claims of principle and the 'social interest'. A modern reader might be inclined to translate Cicero here in the familiar terms of 'rule utilitarianism': that in the long run, a policy of expediency will bring its own costs, and a policy of rectitude will bring its own, tangible goods. Or we may be inclined to think in a more religious or metaphysical style, that the gains of morality will be absorbed in our souls, even if our bodies and our interests languish in the material world. Cicero was no doubt willing to draw to his own argument any credulity that these perspectives could claim among his own readers. But I don't think he was willing to settle for either one of these constructions. He was not willing to defer the gains and costs to the indefinite future, and he was not willing to allow that the injuries of immorality, the injuries to our character, were consigned to a domain of the soul quite removed from our experience. The novelty of his argument hinged on his success in going beyond these convenient devices and familiar arguments, which were ultimately of course evasions of the main problem.

In Book 3 of *De Officiis*, Cicero observed that 'Nature's laws do forbid us to increase our means, wealth, and resources by despoiling others'.[19] Cicero understood that men commonly heard voices other than the voice of equity, the voice that constantly urged upon them the discipline of justice and self-restraint. They heard the voice that moved them to covet, or even to appropriate for themselves, the possessions of their neighbours. They may suffer the distraction of confusing the expedient with their own good, 'for with a false perspective they see the material rewards but not the punishment—I do not mean the penalty of the law, which they often escape, but the heaviest penalty of all, their own demoralization'.[20] The translator of this Loeb edition chose to render this passage with the term 'demoralization', a word we often identify these days with a debilitating loss of confidence. In that vein, we can speak of a certain demoralization among the Vietcong or the Mafia, even if we are unwilling to concede that either one of these organizations is directed to a decent or moral end. Neither one, therefore, could be at serious risk for suffering a de-moralizing, a crippling haemorrhage of its morality. In the original passage, Cicero wrote, *sed ipsius turpitudinis*—which would be closer, I think, to saying 'but their own, worsening turpitude'—their becoming morally worse. That state of affairs may be quite real even if the miscreants continued to look quite chipper and prosperous. But the effects would be felt more palpably, and be seen more readily, in the network of social relations that marked the ties of 'society'. One could no doubt find the characters who became more attractive with their effrontery and daring; who made from their plunder a fortune, and from their performance a social success. And yet, in Cicero's sober reckoning, theft was 'fatal to social life', and it could be regarded as more contrary to nature than death itself. Death comes in the course of nature, and a community survives the death, or replacement, of its members. But if theft became a rule of action, if it were converted from a crime into a rule of injustice, 'the bonds of human society must inevitably be annihilated'.[21] Analogies to the body were quite familiar in classical philosophy, and Cicero appealed to those analogies here; but I think Cicero was offering an account that moved beyond analogies. He was writing, I think, with a literal seriousness that touched the ground of his moral understanding:

Suppose, by way of comparison, that each one of our bodily members should conceive this idea [of theft for its own advantage] and imagine that it could be strong and well if it should draw off to itself the health and strength of its neighbouring member, the whole body would necessarily be enfeebled and die; so, if each one of us should seize upon the property of his neighbours and take from each whatever he could appropriate to his own use . . . .[22]

Cicero was no stranger to the artful uses of metaphor, but it would be a mistake to assign this passage to the flight of metaphor, for it was an expression, as I have suggested, of the 'naturalism' he had really incorporated in his understanding. If injustice became a rule of action in any domain, if theft and looting, say, became a way of life—that everyone was expected to do it, that no one thought he could afford to fail to do it—then Cicero expected a real withering of the social body. It might be the equivalent of a wince, the natural reaction to a discordant note. Or it might take the form of a withholding of trust, a withdrawal from other people, perhaps even the resort to outright warfare. But the reactions, he thought, would move beyond metaphor; there would be a palpable effect, seen in our faces and our bodies, and felt, noticeably, in a community of souls embodied.

In his work on 'The Orator', a work dedicated to Marcus Brutus, Cicero devoted an extended section, near the end of the work, to the rhythm of language offered by the speaker. In a manner befitting a veritable doctor of oratory, Cicero considered the varieties of metres and the ends to which they were suited. He remarked, in this vein, that the iambic rhythm is most like a speech, more like reality, and that helped to explain why this rhythm was used so often in fables or stories. On the other hand, 'the dactylic hexameter is better suited to a lofty and magniloquent subject'. Cicero went on to report that Ephorus, a notable orator—hence, a man whose opinion was worth regarding on the subject—'inclines to the paeon, or dactyl, but avoids the spondee and trochee'.[23] Writers came late in recognizing the uses or importance of rhythm. Cicero claimed that Herodotus had no idea of rhythm, and the ancient writers who had much to say about oratory said nothing on the subject of rhythm. Metaphors arose from ordinary speech, or daily conversation, but 'rhythm was not drawn from a man's own house, nor had it any connexion of relationship to oratory. And therefore it was later in being noticed and observed, bringing as it did the last touch and lineaments to oratory.'[24]

Rhythm was an adornment to oratory; it was a device to enhance the effect, or advance the purpose, of the speech. It could also be measured on the scale of decorum: one would not use portentous speech, with grave, dignified rhythm, for the sake of endorsing a trivial cause or staging a burlesque—just as one would not use weighty or grave music to accompany a bit of slapstick. A 'spondee' was a foot of two long syllables, and as

Cicero wrote, 'It appears somewhat dull and slow; still it has a
certain steady march not devoid of dignity.'[25] And yet, rhythm
was no mere cosmetic, just as music itself was not merely a
cosmetic of sound, a device for framing the acts of men with
agreeable sounds in the background. It may indeed be reduced
to that at times, as it is in the muzak of our supermarkets and
elevators. But music and rhythm were also bound up with the
logic and order of mathematics; a logic that found a deep reson-
ance in our souls. And that is why people can recognize a
striking, discordant sound at once, even if they are untutored in
music, even if they know nothing of the grammar of notation. In
the same way, people may have, locked away in their souls, the
natural awareness of rhythm. For Cicero the evidence was displayed quite amply in the experience of the theatre. 'When
verses are being repeated,' he wrote, 'the whole theatre raises an
outcry if there is one syllable too few or too many':

Not that the mob knows anything about feet or metre; nor do they
understand what it is that offends them, or know why or in what it
offends them. But nevertheless nature herself has placed in our ears a
power of judging of all superfluous length and all undue shortness in
sounds, as much as of grave and acute syllables.[26]

Even for an assembly of the uncultivated, with people un-
schooled, 'nature herself has placed in [their] ears a power of
judging', and there was no reason to believe that this power of
judging was confined to matters of rhythm. There was more
reason to believe that this understanding reached other subjects,
which drew on that same logic, 'placed in our ears'. For those
who are drawn to the mysteries contained in our language, there
is a suggestive connection between music and the law. The
nature and function of the law is to *bind* people to a common law;
the root of 'law' is in the Latin *ligare*: to bind. The words for law
are drawn from the words for tendons, or cords, and there was an
early mixing, in imagination, of the cords of the body, the cords
of the lyre, the cords of the law. George Hersey has sought to
collect the clues of these tropes, or puns, in his book on *The Lost
Meaning of Classical Architecture*:

The myth about Orpheus . . . whose lyre charms beasts, actually records
the moment when law was first introduced into the society that invented
that myth. After explaining that words for law are derived from words

for tendons, that is, the sinews of the body politic, Vico continues, 'and that nerve, or cord, or force that formed Orpheus's lyre' became 'the union of the cords and powers of the fathers, whence derived public powers.' Vico is here building on tropes of *corda*, which means tendon or sinew, lyre string, and also the musical chords those strings sound when played. The musical harmony of Orpheus's lyre introduces social harmony, in turn, for the earlier laws were poems (for example, the *Iliad* and the *Odyssey*), which taught the Greeks about the deeds of their ancestors and the edicts of their gods. Thus law and morality were first conceived of as a body of ancestral edicts preserved in works of art. By the same token, the beasts Orpheus charmed are not real beasts but lawful mankind's barbarian ancestors, who lived before the first laws were chanted.[27]

Cicero readily understood that the harmonies of music and the harmonies of law bore a relation to the harmonies of mathematics. All of them found their root in a logic immanent in nature. Cicero bore no illusions about the corruptions that were also contained in human nature: he understood the appeals of venality and self-deception, and he recognized, too, that certain wrongs may be too refined for people in the bulk to fathom. But at a certain level, also, he seemed to understand—and he sought, I think, to teach—that a discordant law was as instantly known and felt by a public of ordinary men as a discordant note was instantly recognized by a common audience. And when he held that certain wrongs simply snapped the social bonds, I think he meant, quite literally, that certain wrongs produced the political or social effect of a public wince: there would be a palpable recoil, a withdrawal of acceptance and trust; and a string of such events would produce a discernible effect on the social body, or the body politic. There would have to be a certain withering of trust, credit, co-operation; a gradual narrowing of the willingness to enter joint ventures, to take on common commitments, to risk one's life or fortune for people who were not of one's own family. As I read Cicero now, I think the maxims of our public life were maxims that expressed this primeval, natural sense of justice. Edmund Burke once remarked that 'refined policy is ever the parent of confusion'. When Cicero spoke and wrote of the principles of justice, he seemed to understand that the maxims of public and private honesty were written so plainly on our souls that they naturally produce a social recoil when they are violated.

It may be true that the wicked can prosper, and Cicero was no more inclined to deny that fact than any other urbane man of his age. But he also understood, with a sober realism, that the systematic violation of certain principles of justice will have an almost immediate effect in impairing, or contracting, our common life.

I return, with this thread, to the scenes I recalled at the beginning of this chapter: embattled farmers, during the Depression of the 1930s, prepared to resist a sheriff who is about to foreclose on a mortgage. In that time of hysteria, the political class showed a willingness to respond with an array of improbable measures. Traditional canons of equity, and even an ordinary sense of the workings of the world, seemed to be suspended in the desperate search for a remedy, or in the low cleverness of politicians in making a gesture toward a remedy. Politicians were enjoined to think boldly, and one of the more radical measures, cast off by the genius of Congress, was the Frazier–Lemke Act of 1934. This legislation was put forth under the broad power of the Congress to enact uniform laws on bankruptcy. But even a jurist as open to inventiveness as Justice Brandeis could find, in this legislation, features that pushed novelty beyond the limits of the plausible. For this law was decidedly unlike anything that had ever been put forth in the past under the title of a bankruptcy law. In the case of *Louisville Bank* v. *Radford*,[28] Brandeis marked off the differences in meticulous detail. In the past, the laws of bankruptcy had sought to relieve the debtor from a burden of indebtedness that engulfed him, and give him the chance to begin anew. At the same time, an attempt was made to honour the obligations to the creditors by distributing the property or assets of the debtor. But against those defining features of the laws on bankruptcy, the Frazier–Lemke Act brought some striking innovations. As Brandeis noted for the Court, no law on bankruptcy, before the Frazier–Lemke Act, had 'sought to compel the holder of a mortgage to surrender to the bankrupt either the possession of the mortgaged property or the title, as long as any part of the debt thereby secured remained unpaid'.[29] No bankruptcy Act had sought to transfer to the debtor a fund of capital with which he could continue his business. Nor had any act sought to encourage or compel the holder of the mortgage to sell the property to the debtor at a reduced price, reflecting the decline in the valuation of the property. In the case at hand, the Radfords had taken out mortgages for $9,000 on 170 acres of land in Kentucky, which had been appraised in the early 1920s at a value of $18,000. The Radfords fell into default in 1931, and by 1933 the market value of the land had fallen, in the Depression, to $4,445. The bank holding the mortgage refused to agree to a sale at that price. But the refusal of the bank to sell at the lower price activated another provision in the Frazier–Lemke Act: the debtors could require the bankruptcy court to stay all proceedings of foreclosure for a period of five years, while the court helped to settle a reasonable rent for the use of the land. In this case, a rental of $325 per month was established for the first year.[30] In other words, the debtor would retain possession of the property, or the control of the assets. In no other instance did a law on bankruptcy compel the holder of a mortgage to relinquish the property to the debtor, free of the lien, unless the debt had been paid in full. In a moment of crisis, then, the Act created a vast asymmetry to the disadvantage of the creditors. Brandeis summed up the curious shift produced by the legislation.

[T]he bankrupt's only monetary obligation is to pay a reasonable rental fixed by the court. There is no provision for the payment of insurance or taxes, save as these may be paid from the rental received. During that period [of five years] the bankrupt has an option to purchase the farm at any time at its appraised, or reappraised, value. The mortgagee [i.e. the bank] is not only compelled to submit to the sale to the bankrupt, but to a sale made at such time as the latter may choose. Thus, the bankrupt may leave it uncertain for years whether he will purchase; and in the end he may decline to buy. Meanwhile the mortgagee may have had (and been obliged to decline) an offer from some other person to take the farm at a price sufficient to satisfy the full amount then due by the debtor. The mortgagee cannot require a reappraisal when, in its judgment, the time comes to sell; it may ask for a reappraisal only if and when the bankrupt requests a sale. Thus the mortgagee is afforded no protection if the request is made when values are depressed to a point lower than the original appraisal.[31]

Even for a judge with Brandeis's liberal reflexes, the legislation filled out, in its details, a design for the depreciation of an asset, or the taking of property, without compensation. The Court suffered no strain—and not a single dissenting vote—as it struck down this legislation under the Fifth Amendment as an unjustified 'taking' of property. And yet the pattern of inequity read so plainly in this bill, was evidently quite as plain to the congressmen who voted for the legislation. In this respect, the telling sign came in the insistence, on the part of senators and congressmen, that they could support this measure only if it were confined to the debts that were in place *before* this legislation was passed. Even the congressmen with farmers among their constituents were determined that this bill should apply only to debts contracted from that point forward. Senator Bankhead registered his own unwillingness to vote for the legislation unless it were amended in that way, and he expressed here the sober sense of the matter: 'When a farmer goes to his advancing merchant, or goes to his banker, or applies to an insurance company for a loan under this bill, I want to know, and I am enquiring with earnest anxiety about it, what effect is it going to have upon those credit facilities for the farmers of this country?' Congressman Peyser put it more directly: 'I believe that . . . you are removing from the farmer the possibility of securing any mortgage assistance in the future. I believe in the enactment of this law and the scaling down of values you are going to take away the possibility of help that may be needed by these farmers in the future.'[32]

These legislators expressed a sober awareness of the world as it was: a world in which the inventiveness of legislation had to find its hard limit in the resistance that men and women could be counted on to offer as they followed their natural reflexes—providing, of course, that they remained free to act upon their interests. The certainty of senators and congressmen on this point was a telling recognition, as I say, of just how reliable and predictable the reaction of the public was bound to be. And even less speculative, in their reckoning, were the consequences that would flow, inescapably, from that holding back of credit. For this bit of conjecture they needed no soothsayer, and no esoteric theory served up by econometricians. The policy was so unsubtle, the partisan shifting of benefits and costs was so emphatic, that it required no particular genius to predict what the consequences would be. And the costs of atrophy, in the 'social body', would be readily seen.

In that vast, compelling project of moral philosophy, the most enduring temptation may be the lure of 'naturalism'. The temptation endures because there has been ample experience to know that a life confirmed in vice can show itself in the wreckage of persons, families, fortunes. But we know also that the connection is, at best, probabilistic. The wicked often, and dramatically, prosper. Beyond that, we know that any theory of morality rooted in 'natural goods' will quickly collapse upon itself, for the reason that any material good will have to be contingent: any item, any good we can name, can be part of a means–end chain leading to a corrupt end. 'Friendship' and 'love' have often been counted among the 'good' things that have a palpable presence in this world. And yet, the bonds of love and friendship can recruit people in support of the gangster Sam Giancana or of Mother Theresa. In accounting for the 'good' of friendship, we are soon compelled to leave the domain of concrete, material goods, and explain the grounds on which certain claims of love and friendship are justified or unjustified. We would be led back quickly to the principles that we use in judging the maxims or the reasons on which our acts are founded; and those principles of judgement cannot have anything contingent about them. As I have tried to show at length elsewhere, those principles of judgement must eventually find their grounding, as Kant understood, in the canons of logic, or 'the laws of reason'.[33] We are immersed in the laws of reason whenever we seek to give a justification, or whenever we are engaged in a conversation about matters of right and wrong. That language and logic of reason is nothing less than the language and logic of natural rights. And that is why natural rights cannot merely be one perspective among many. To ask whether we can set aside the premises of natural rights in favour of some other 'perspective', is rather like asking, 'Do we use syntax when we order coffee?' If we are engaged in a serious conversation about matters of right and wrong, then the laws of reason are as inseparable from that conversation as the patterns of syntax.

Among the writers who linger with these questions, Ralph McInerny and I have been the most explicit in arguing this version of natural rights.[34] But McInerny has extended the argument still further, by suggesting that certain natural goods do come into play, almost as insistently as the canons of logic; and if

that argument can be made, I think it may illuminate the 'naturalism' that provides, finally, the fuller ground of Cicero's moral
understanding.

McInerny has argued, for example, that 'the decision to commit
suicide does not qualify as a moral choice at all, that it is
intrinsically incoherent'. For our own part, we might think that it
is not at all unreasonable for a man such as Adolf Eichmann to
scan his own record and reject his life. And in his case, we may
come to think that suicide may be the administering of a just
punishment. But McInerny would still find the choice of suicide
as incoherent, and he would cast his argument in this way:

> Something or other can be desired, pursued or chosen only insofar as it
> is good for me, and that means, fulfilling of me or a constituent of what is
> fulfilling of me. Anything that could qualify as good in that sense
> presupposes my existence once it is attained. Thus, my ceasing to be
> cannot be chosen as a good. Ceasing to be cannot be my good.[35]

Of course, the ending of Eichmann's life may be a good for
others, in the sense of serving their interests, or in the sense of
vindicating the wrong done to Eichmann's victims. Or perhaps
there was a good in principle that furnished the proper ends of
Eichmann's life—the ends he did not pursue—and he might
choose to destroy his life now as a final act of judging himself,
severely, by the principles he spent his life evading. McInerny
does not quite say enough, then, to settle the issue, but he may in
fact suggest a range of material goods that have to be bound up,
logically, with the choice of our ends. And so, for example, if we
should have such institutions as hospitals, it would be surrealistic
to suppose a life in which some hospitals could be arranged with
an explicit, public policy of euthanasia. Could we imagine a
scene of this kind: that we rush someone to the Emergency Room
of a hospital and discover that the operating philosophy of this
Emergency Room was to admit patients in a crisis for the sake of
relieving their pain and dispatching them to their deaths? If the
end of our act, in calling an ambulance, was to secure the death of
the victim, why should we bother in dashing to the 'hospital'?
And if a hospital saw its mission as facilitating death, why would
it wish to take in patients, rather than blocking them and compelling them to die at the door? Why spend all that money on
equipment and facilities that will mainly go unused? To make

the decision to have a hospital, then, must go hand in hand with a commitment to the good of sustaining life. A hospital that admits the practice of euthanasia is engaged in a cruel incoherence, or worse: a policy of deception that lures patients forward, to be ministered to on the basis of policies that could not be announced.

A notable student of administration once sought to set forth a scheme in the 'science of administration' by marking off the procedures of an organization dedicated to the purpose of making the most 'rational' decisions. The problem, however, was that social science did not recognize any rational ground for moral judgements, and so he did not wish to employ any moral blinders, or personal conceits, which could rule out certain means, plausibly connected to their ends, on the grounds of any 'moral' aversion. He would have enjoined the administrator, then, to consider *every* set of means that was *rationally* connected to the ends of the organization.[36] Herbert Storing subjected this scheme to the most penetrating criticism, and along the way he posed this question: let us suppose that our purpose was to leave this classroom, on the third floor of the building, and get outside for lunch. If we listed every conceivable way of getting from the third floor to the outside, why would we not list the possibility of jumping out of the window?[37]

The natural reflex here is to say, 'But that is clearly unreasonable—so unreasonable that it needn't be discussed.' And yet, it could not be ruled out if it were considered *strictly as a means connected to an end*. It can be ruled out only on the strength of a moral judgement: namely, that the prospect of leaving the building for lunch does not justify the destruction of our lives. But does that not in turn suggest that so many of our engagements in this life must presuppose that we will be alive, that we have an interest in preserving our lives—along with all of those subsidiary goods that may be implicated in our lives? The advantages of leaving the building rapidly do not override the advantages of preserving our lives with our families and friends, or the goods bound up with our careers—perhaps the good of scholarship or knowledge, pursued for its own sake, or with the satisfaction of a good engaged in common with colleagues and friends. Conscious or not, a ranking has been made. But the ranking is grounded in choices so obvious that we may not be aware of them as serious choices. The concrete and enduring goods of life and family, friends and career, have been given a pre-eminent place, over the gains of departing the building without delay.

To recognize the grounds on which we can regard these choices as obvious and reasonable is to recognize the ascendance of certain real goods in our lives. There are occasions on which we may justly override the claims of friendship and family, and even life itself. But the rankings suggested in the leaving of the building are not likely to be altered with contingencies. Certain interests are likely to be regarded, persistently, as ephemeral and trivial, when set against interests that are likely to be regarded as more momentous and enduring. The library books long overdue may elicit the penalty of a fine, but not of capital punishment. Or to take a real case, the man who kills his brother because he ate the last pork chop will not establish the defence of a justifiable homicide. That these cases are rare may merely suggest that, for the bulk of mankind, certain moral judgements are so clear that they rarely need to be posed to us as problems for our practical judgement.

And that may be part of Cicero's point. Our attention is drawn so often to the hard cases, or to the moral problems that strain our wit; and we may fail to see those vast layers of moral judgement that we have settled so surely in our understanding that they no longer seem part of the perplexity of moral life. Still, they mark the many places at which our lives have been given a certain scale or decorum, reflecting the principles of moral understanding. If those understandings are unsettled, then so too would be the ranking of goods that rests on those understandings. And as Cicero anticipated, the result would be a vast derangement of lives, with effects that were instantly evident.

A sceptic might argue that the understanding here may reflect little more than the old notion of 'sunk costs': having entered upon the business of manufacturing Dixie cups, there may be no need to rethink the question of whether we should be better off producing shoes. Having signed a three-year contract to manage the New York Yankees, it would be incoherent for the new manager to wonder, at the same time, if he wished to preserve his life. His signing of the contract must imply that he regards it as a good, at least, to live for three more years. And yet, I do not think that the 'goods' engaged here are contingent even in that degree. The good of continuing our lives, or the lives of others, must be implicated in any decision about the course of our lives and the pattern of our ends. Just how many other goods must be covered in that way, in the hierarchy of goods that gives structure and concreteness to our lives, is a matter that is simply open to our further reflection and the summoning of our imagination. But nothing especially exotic is required. The question should yield, without much strain, to some concentrated reflection about the goods that we can finally see as more or less fundamental, more or less constitutive in our lives.

If I am correct, then, in my reading, this part of Cicero's 'naturalism' was founded on goods that were ranked unambiguously as goods, even though their goodness—or their standing as the objects of moral choice—could be hidden by their own obviousness. This natural ranking of goods rested on understandings that were, we might say, written with a large, unmistakable hand. There was little that was problematic or ambiguous about them. And if we follow Cicero, the same thing would have to be said, I think, for those rules of justice that were bound up with these natural goods. The rules of justice could not rest on fine discriminations and reasonings ever more delicate and ingenious. It was exactly because they were so plainly drawn, so bound up with the commands of equity, so accessible to people of ordinary intellect, that the rules of justice could be counted on to produce their palpable effects as soon as they were violated. Cicero and the American Founders understood in that way the rule that forbade the arbitrary cancelling of debts. And as we have seen, that rule was grasped even by the intemperate congressmen who passed the Frazier–Lemke Act in 1934: they could offer many refined arguments to plead that the problem at hand justified more refined interferences with the relation between debtors and creditors. They could have argued that there was a novel crisis at hand in the Depression. The rules made for more tranquil times might not apply with the same justice during an emergency. And perhaps there were conditions in the economy of the American farms that made contracts with farmers notably different from contracts made with other debtors. Yet, the congressmen knew that none of this would avail. Whatever facile reasoning they offered, the lessons would be understood in a gross way: in a time of crisis a legislature could intervene, even in settled

contracts, and essentially destroy the obligation of the contract.
From that time forward, any man with money to lend would have
to hold back in prudence, rather than hazard his savings in
contracts that were open to political manipulation. The American
Founders sought to foreclose that manipulation by providing in
the Constitution that no state shall pass any law 'impairing
the Obligation of Contracts'. That provision was not made for
tranquil times, to be set aside in times of emergency. The
Founders sought to offer this assurance of justice because they
knew that, in troubled times, there would be a political constituency for the cancelling of debts. It fell to Justice Sutherland
once to state a lesson that would have been obvious to Cicero:
namely, that the bar to the cancelling of debts was meant to be
unambiguous, sweeping, inflexible, unaffected with exceptions
or conditions. As Sutherland summed it up, the provision on
contracts was 'framed and adopted with the specific and studied
purpose of preventing legislation designed to relieve debtors
especially in time of financial distress'.[38] The rule could simply
not retain its quality as a rule of justice if it could be contravened
in a time of depression, when many debtors were likely to default.
Nor could it be made a hostage to the exquisite reasonings
produced by different classes of debtors, to show that there was
something different about contracts made over plastics or pork
bellies, which justified a whole series of 'exceptions' from the rule.

The rule bade political men to stay their hands. It barred
legislators from interfering politically in private contracts. To bar
that interference was to compel the debtor to negotiate again
with the creditor, to seek a settlement with his original partner in
the contract. But to follow the path back in that way was to make
one's way back to the morality of contract that stood antecedent
to the laws on contracts. It was to discover, again, the understanding of the Founders, that the right to engage in contracts was a
'natural' right, which did not depend on the presence of government. As John Marshall once explained, 'contracts possess an
original intrinsic obligation derived from the acts of free agents,
and not given by government'.[39] Even men in the state of nature
might undertake promises to one another. In that condition, they
risk their possessions and safety on the prospect that the promises
will be kept. The man who makes us vulnerable to his promise
faces us with the prospect of a harm if that promise is not

honoured. In that sense we can say, with the force of a moral statement, that he has an *obligation* to keep his promise. We may make our way, then, to a law that enforces contracts, because we can understand, in the first place, that there is an obligation to avert harm for the people who have become dependent on our promises.

I recall these ancient considerations for the sake of bringing out, more explicitly, the layers of understanding that lie behind the rule on the cancelling of debts. That rule drew its moral force from its connection to the original ground of contracts in natural rights. When Cicero and the American Founders condemned the cancelling of debts, their moral conviction was rooted in that understanding of the natural rights and wrongs engaged in a contract. And that same understanding formed the ground of their certainty that the breaking of this rule would bring swift, certain consequences: a rule so bound up with the grounds of equity could not be violated without causing the surest recoil on the part of its victims. Anyone with respect for himself would not put himself at risk of the same injustice; and the result would then be, as Chief Justice Marshall put it, to 'destroy all confidence between man and man'.[40]

A constitution may incorporate some of these deep rules of justice, but the rules would run deeper than the constitution itself. That is another way of saying that a constitution is not an end in itself. As Justice Sutherland reminded us, in a landmark case, the American 'Union existed before the Constitution, which was ordained and established among other things to form "a more perfect Union" '.[41] The Union was not made for the Constitution; the Constitution was made for the Union. The purpose of the Constitution was to preserve, in America, a political community that wished to shape its common life to the character of a republic. We might say that there is a 'good' behind the form and structure of the Constitution; and of course, as the writers of the Declaration of Independence recognized, there are times when a 'Form of Government becomes destructive of [those] ends' for which governments are instituted. At those moments, it becomes necessary to alter or abolish the constitution, as our own first generation displaced the Articles of Confederation in favour of a new constitution. Lincoln once sought to make the same point by drawing on the biblical proverb that 'a word fitly spoken is like apples of gold in pictures of silver' (Proverbs 25: 11): 'The *Union* and the *Constitution*', said Lincoln, 'are the picture of *silver*, subsequently framed around it. The picture was made, not to *conceal* or *destroy* the apple; but to *adorn*, and *preserve* it. The picture was made *for* the apple—*not* the apple for the picture.'[42] This understanding implies a certain detachment from the Constitution, and it seems to have slipped from memory in our own time. But the 'naturalism' in Cicero's natural law would bring that understanding back into view once again—and take us, I think, a critical step beyond.

From the perspective of Cicero's 'naturalism' we might cast the problem in this way: behind the principles of constitutional government, there must be a sense of a real community, with an embodiment in real people; and the purpose of the Constitution is to secure the good, the well-being, and perhaps even the 'flourishing' of that people. And yet, we cannot speak about the well-being or the flourishing of a people detached from those terms of principle that bind them together as a political community. A community may find its happiness and flourishing, for example, in expropriating and dividing the property of a racial minority. When we speak about the project of preserving a nation, or a political community, we must move beyond the sense of biological preservation; we must be speaking about the preservation of a certain 'way of life', or a life lived in accordance with certain principles of right and wrong. As we have seen, Cicero appreciated both sides of this problem: on the one hand, he assumed that a just life will express itself in the visible health of the social body, in the evidence of certain 'natural' goods. On the other hand, he understood that certain people may not wish to purchase their lives, or preserve their common life, on terms that are ignoble. He understood the avowal that 'we would prefer to die as free men than live as slaves'. In the tension between these two sides, we find again the tension between the claims of prudence and the commands of 'categorical' imperatives. Should Lincoln allow the Union to perish because he is reluctant to suspend the Writ of Habeas Corpus? That provision may mark one of the critical differences that separate a constitutional government from a despotism; and yet, as Lincoln asked, should we risk the loss of the whole Constitution for fear of suspending, temporarily, this one part?' '[A]re all the laws, *but one*, to go unexecuted, and the government itself go to pieces, lest that one be violated?'[43]

Would it never be permissible to suspend the Writ of Habeas Corpus, under any circumstances? Or could it be justified to suspend this one standard of constitutional restraint when the very survival of a constitutional government is at stake? If we follow Lincoln, the exercise of prudence here would be governed by a hierarchy of principles: a moratorium on constitutional rules may not be justified by interests that are trivial; the suspension of constitutional government can be justified by nothing less than the interest in preserving constitutional government itself. But there is nothing 'contingent' or problematic about the good of constitutional government. We may say that constitutional government is good in principle; we may even say that it is categorically good. In that sense, we may claim that our exercise of prudence is finally anchored in an understanding of a good that is not at all contingent or shifting. Nor would that good be measured solely in its effects. A free government would not cease to be good even if it failed to make its citizens happy and prosperous. But what if it failed also to secure their safety? Would we be brought back, forcefully, to the awareness of certain natural goods, arranged in a natural hierarchy? If the procedures of constitutional government suddenly presented an impediment to the protection of our lives, would the 'good' of constitutional government have to be put aside for a while in favour of a natural good, even more fundamental?

During the controversy over the Iran–Contra affair, a seasoned scholar and friend set forth again the nearly monarchical powers of the president in foreign affairs. As the Supreme Court had long recognized, the power of the president to deploy troops and protect the nation was not dependent on acts of Congress. And as Justice Sutherland had noted, those powers exercised by the president were older than the Constitution.[44] The Congress bore the responsibility to raise and support armies, to provide the funds that sustained the national defence. But only the commander-in-chief could make decisions about the deployment of those forces. My friend then turned to me and asked: but what would happen if the president made an Executive Agreement that virtually turned over to an adversary the whole American fleet, or the American air force? Congress cannot claim any authority over the structure of command in the military; and yet, he asked, did I think that the Congress would acquiesce in such a move? The answer of course was no. The question was meant to probe the limits of the Constitution, but I'm not sure that my friend realized at the time just how far it reached. It seems almost unthinkable that we should encounter a case of this kind, in which a president showed such a want of loyalty or such a deep corruption of judgement. It is almost as unthinkable as the notion, arising in my earlier case, that we should think of leaving a building by jumping out of the window. That we have not encountered such a case among our presidents may be a mark of the fact that certain judgements would be seen instantly as bizarre, as patently 'unreasonable'. And there may be the lesson: the elaborate design of the Constitution, the intricate assignment of powers, may all rest on assumptions that no one thinks necessary to explain. It is assumed that any of these powers must be exercised without threatening those natural 'goods' that should be evident to any person of reason. If a president of the United States lost his senses one day and delivered American forces to an adversary, the settled provisions of the American Constitution would be treated, at that moment, as so many sentences on paper: they would be swept aside as words without consequence. The danger to the security of the community simply would not be tolerated. Just how Congress could manage to avert this outcome, while working within its constitutional powers, would become a matter for the lawyers to work out, with arguments suitably clever and contrived. The fact is, however, that Congress would find some way to block the move. And behind the case, as I say, lies a Ciceronian point: even the provisions of the most venerated Constitution may be exposed as mere parchment; they will be exposed as mere words on paper if the holders of authority begin to threaten those natural goods that are accessible to any person of natural reason.

Cicero's 'naturalism' would alert us, then, to the reality of certain natural goods that lie beyond the Constitution. But once we have taken this further step, we would seem to license possibilities that are sobering: what if it were possible to preserve a constitutional government only by engaging in acts of genocide? Would those acts cease to be categorically wrong? And what if it turned out that constitutional government, too, was dispensable—that it could be put aside in favour of certain 'goods' that were thought to be even more fundamental yet? Would there be no restraint then on our moral freedom to order up acts of genocide? Would our judgement now be so completely emancipated from the tyranny of rules that they would be untethered to any moral ground?

But to find ourselves left with this question is to find ourselves back with that intractable tension between categorical imperatives and the claims of prudence. And it is to discover again that Cicero never did manage to solve that puzzle. That the problem did not yield to his efforts cannot be attributed to any want of nerve. For there was nothing in him of the wimpish utilitarian: there was no disposition on his part to back away from a commitment in principle as soon as the bills were reckoned and the price of principle seemed to be costly. Nor was there any want of willingness to stake his life on his political ends. But on the other hand, he was not willing to accept the massive destruction of lives, or the laying waste of fortunes, through an obstinate adherence to principle in all cases. And yet, this falling short in resolving the puzzle was not taken as a failure, or a deficit, by Cicero himself. For he made his own, subtle intimations that this central problem of moral judgement was not really soluble in the end. In the close of *De Officiis,* Cicero restated some of his themes, and offered this comparison: 'As I have shown that such expediency as is opposed to moral rectitude is no expediency, so I maintain that any and all sensual pleasure is opposed to moral rectitude':

And therefore Calliphon and Dinomachus, in my judgment, deserve the greater condemnation; they imagined that they should settle the controversy by coupling pleasure with moral rectitude; as well yoke a man with a beast! But moral rectitude does not accept such a union; she abhors it, spurns it. Why, the supreme good, which ought to be simple, cannot be a compound and mixture of absolutely contradictory qualities.[45]

But after expressing himself on this point quite emphatically—more emphatically, one would think, than he needed to express himself in making his point—he ends by offering this work to his son Marcus: he enjoins the young man to study this essay in moral philosophy, and he promises to pursue the subject face to face, in personal conversation, 'when I see that you take delight in this branch of philosophy'.[46] In one paragraph, pleasure and philosophy were not to be mixed; but by the next paragraph, pleasure would be taken as the condition of encouragement, which could beckon the young man into the deeper study of philosophy. As Leo Strauss once taught us, we cannot take it as a gesture without meaning when a seasoned writer offers, quite plainly, a contradiction that would embarrass a schoolboy. He may be directing us, instead, to a teaching he does not care to make explicit. If pleasure can be allied with moral philosophy, then expedience may be reconciled with the life of principle. Or at least, Cicero may be teaching, in the catechism of prudence, that there are no categorical rules: there are no principles that can hold without qualification, without the need to be shaded or compromised or even decorously put aside, under certain exigencies, under the strain of particular cases. This was an understanding best left cloaked in a discreet silence. It would be grasped by anyone who reflected seriously on these questions— and by anyone bright enough to read his lessons in Cicero's primer, with an alertness to Cicero's clues. But if this understanding were elevated into a public doctrine, it could offer the most imprudent licence to those people who would welcome the notion that 'there are no reliable rules, that we must be thrown upon our judgement, from case to case, without any principles that surely command us in the case at hand'. The men who were willing to absorb that notion as a rule of action might not have the patience and the subtlety to understand the qualifications to the qualifications: principles may have to be suspended from one case to another, but there may be deeper principles that tell us when principles are to be suspended.

There are layers, then, beyond layers: behind Cicero's rhetoric of categorical imperatives there is a scepticism about rules unvarying from case to case; but beyond that scepticism is an awareness of hierarchies of goods, which may nevertheless guide the hand of prudence. The man of the world will have to bear the responsibility of his own judgement. He will not have at hand a manual of rules that will free him from the responsibility of judgement, by instructing him, unfailingly, on the course that is bound to be right in the case before him. And yet, if he must face that task of judgement, he is not left unarmed: he is possessed of arts of deliberation, and even principles of judgement, which may still give him an unambiguous sense of the goods, in this world, that are conspicuously, unequivocally, better or worse.

'The first rule of duty', said Cicero, 'requires us—other things being equal—to lend assistance preferably to people in proportion to their individual need. Most people adopt the contrary course: they put themselves most eagerly at the service of the one from whom they hope to receive the greatest favours, even though he has no need of their help.'[47] But if there were a ranking, more generally, of the objects of our duty, Cicero suffered no perplexity: 'country would come first, and parents; for their services have laid us under the heaviest obligation; next come children and the whole family, who look to us alone for support and can have no other protection; finally, our kinsmen, with whom we live on good terms and with whom, for the most part, our lot is one.'[48]

We may dispute the assignments on this list; we may argue over the reasons for making some goods higher or lower than others. But the exercise is so patently open to deliberation precisely because the judgements are directed by reasons. Reason has the ascendance over feelings or intuitions, uninformed by reflection. The discipline of judgement cannot be anything other than hierarchical—it cannot be unaffected by a sense of the things that are higher and lower. For the creature who frames the question has already established a hierarchy, or structure, of the things that are important to know, and the ways of knowing that have a higher claim to his respect. On that decisive question, about the grounds of judgement, there was no perplexity. Cicero would suffer no strains of doubt on this point, any more than those sceptics described by Tom Stoppard, the people who will not concede that the train for Bristol leaves Paddington Station unless they themselves are there to see it leave. And yet even these thoroughgoing sceptics—'these same people will, nevertheless, and without any sense of inconsistency, claim to *know* that life is better than death, that love is better than hate, and that the light shining through the east window of their . . . gymnasium is more beautiful than a rotting corpse'. Those are things that not even the sceptics and the nihilists have failed to know; and they are things that will ever be known through the power of judging that 'nature herself has placed in our ears'.

NOTES

I wish to thank professor Holly Montague who encouraged me to return to Cicero's *De Officiis* after years of writing on other subjects.

1. Cicero, *De Officiis* (Cambridge, Mass.: Harvard University Press, Loeb edn., 1975), 261. All of the succeeding references will be to this volume. Cicero wrote this passage not too long after he saw Caesar's campaign for ascendant power reach its point of maturation. Caesar had spoken of honour, but Cicero saw that campaign for power as based on a string of injustices, which included, most notably, the amassing of an army without public authority, a plan for the 'cancellation of debts and . . . a thousand other wickednesses'. Quoted in David Stockton, *Cicero: A Political Biography* (Oxford: Oxford University Press, 1971; 1986), 257.

2. Dissenting opinion in *Home Bldg. and Loan Assn.* v. *Blaisdell*, 290 U.S. 308, at 455 (1934).

3. In recalling this period, Chief Justice Marshall remarked that the policy of cancelling debts had worked to 'destroy all confidence between man and man. The mischief had become so great, so alarming, as not only to impair commercial intercourse, and threaten the existence of credit, but to sap the morals of the people, and destroy the sanctity of private faith.' See *Ogden* v. *Saunders*, 12 Wheaton 213, at 355 (1827).

4. Cicero, *De Officiis*, 339.

5. Ibid. 341.

6. Ibid. 291.

7. See my book, *First Things* (Princeton, NJ: Princeton University Press, 1986), chs. 2 and 3, pp. 11–50 and 68–70, 85–92.

8. See, on this point, ibid. 68–70.

9. *The Federalist*, no. 31 (New York: Random House, n.d.), 188.

10. Thomas Reid, *Essays on the Intellectual Powers of Man* (Cambridge, Mass.: MIT Press, 1969; 1st pub. 1814–15), 616.

11. See e.g. Aristotle, *Nicomachean Ethics*, 1097^{a}25–36.

12. Cicero, *De Officiis*, 157.

13. Ibid. 160 and 161 (1. 44).

14. Ibid. 163 (sect. 45).

15. Ibid. 317 (3. 11).

16. Ibid. 359, 361 (sects. 21 and 22).

17. See e.g. ibid. 369 (sect. 24) (a reluctance to dance in public, to meet

the terms of an inheritance, should be overridden if the man would bring revenues to the State).

18. Ibid. 299 (sect. 6).
19. Ibid. 289, 291 (sect. 5).
20. Ibid. 303, 305 (sect. 8).
21. Ibid. 289 (sect. 5).
22. Ibid.
23. 'The Orator', in *The Orations of Marcus Tullius Cicero* (London: Henry Bohn, 1852), iv, sect. 57, p. 441.
24. Ibid., sect. 52, p. 440.
25. Ibid., sect. 64, p. 449.
26. Ibid., sect. 51, p. 436.
27. Hersey, *The Lost Meaning of Classical Architecture* (Cambridge, Mass.: MIT Press, 1988), 5.
28. 295 U.S. 555 (1934).
29. Ibid. 581–3.
30. Ibid. 577–8.
31. Ibid. 593.
32. Quoted ibid. 595–6 n. 27.
33. See Arkes, *First Things*, chs. 4–5.
34. See McInerny's paper, 'Life, Medicine and the Natural Law', offered at the Conference on Euthanasia, Clark University, Oct. 1988.
35. Ibid. 12.
36. See Herbert A. Simon, *Administrative Behavior* (New York: Macmillan, 1957), chs. 3 and 4.
37. This is a question that I heard Storing pose as he sought to elaborate on his extended critique of Herbert Simon in 'The Science of Administration: Herbert A. Simon', in Storing, ed., *Essays in the Scientific Study of Politics* (New York: Holt, Rinehart and Winston, 1962), 63–150. This query about jumping out of the window would fit into the argument that is developed in the essay, pp. 69–87.
38. See Sutherland in *Home Bldg. & Loan Assn.* v. *Blaisdell*, at 453.
39. See Marshall in *Ogden* v. *Saunders*, at 354.
40. Marshall ibid., at 355.
41. *U.S.* v. *Curtiss Wright Corp.* 299 U.S. 304, at 317 (1937).
42. Roy P. Basler, ed., *The Works of Abraham Lincoln* (New Brunswick, NJ: Rutgers University Press, 1953), iv. 169; italics in the original.
43. Lincoln, 'Message to Congress' (4 July 1861), ibid. 430.
44. See *U.S.* v. *Curtiss-Wright Corp.* at 317–20.
45. Cicero, *De Officiis*, 401 (3. 33).
46. Ibid. 403 (sect. 33).
47. Ibid. 53 (1. 15).
48. Ibid. 61.

10

Natural Law and Rights

LLOYD L. WEINREB

The philosophy of natural law has on the whole not been much concerned with the matter of rights. Greek sources from which natural law emerged scarcely noticed the subject at all. On the contrary, they sought to locate the individual within a natural order that might strike an individual down without warning or apparent explanation but that was a normative order all the same. The development of this line of thought in Christian theology, which achieved its classic expression in the philosophy of Thomas Aquinas, likewise did not in the first instance uphold rights of the individual; rather, it confirmed his personal responsibility while still within and subject to the Providence of an omnipotent God. Divine Providence contained an assurance of God's benevolent regard for humanity, something that the Greek notion of *moira* (fate) had lacked. And some of the duties that defined one's responsibility were for the benefit of other persons. But any suggestion that, without reference to God, rights are an independent basis of obligations was remote indeed.[1]

Although various theories of rights, or natural rights, appear much earlier,[2] rights are not closely associated with natural law until the seventeenth and eighteenth centuries. Even then, the association is mostly only verbal. The theorists are aware of the natural law tradition and refer to it to support their arguments. But the references are little more than window-dressing. Hobbes, for example, argued that the 'laws of nature' uphold the unlimited rights of all against all in a hypothetical pre-civil society, which give way to the complete absence of rights except those that the sovereign allows in the civil state. One's so-called pre-civil rights, however, are simply the power that one actually has, there being no question of rights or obligations of any kind at all in the state of nature. Locke referred repeatedly to natural law in traditional terms, to shore up the weakest points in his argument. Since he defended Whiggish interests against the Crown, natural law became the source of rights that limited the royal power. So far as his analysis of natural law was concerned, Locke did little more than assert that the Creator's purpose is self-evidently the law of his creation, i.e. nature's law or natural law, and that for rational creatures, also self-evidently, 'Reason . . . is that Law'.[3] What that meant concretely is that natural law is what, so he asserted, is evident to any reasonable person. The reliance on self-evidence is superficially reminiscent of the natural law tradition; but the assertion that ordinary reason is sufficient flouted the issue that was at the heart of natural law and the manner in which it was resolved.

Oddly, Rousseau, who dismissed natural law as nonsense,[4] came closest of the social contract theorists to adopting its analytic framework, although he built on radically different premisses. Freedom and order could be consistent, he reasoned, only if a person participated in the generation of the laws by which he was governed. In place of God's Providence, our participation in which was what Thomas Aquinas had meant by natural law, Rousseau put the General Will; identifying his will with the General Will, a citizen governs himself. For all the structural similarity of the statements of the problem and its solution, substitution of human for divine rule (or inscrutable *moira*) made the two arguments very different, unless one regards Rousseau's theory as wholly unrelated to actual governance by actual human beings (as, indeed, his hapless resort to a super-human Legislator suggests it may be).[5]

In contemporary philosophy, although they are frequently joined for rhetorical effect, there is scarcely any connection, substantive or formal, between natural law and rights.[6] Natural law has not flourished in this century. For the most part, aside from its place in the doctrine of the Catholic Church, it has survived out of the mainstream as a theory about the nature of law or as an ethics with the distinctive, not to say curious, epistemological claim that its fundamental precepts—said to be substantial principles and not merely verbal formula—are necessarily true or self-evident.[7] Natural rights, on the other hand, have flourished, more recently under the ambiguous rubric of 'human rights'. The switch from the 'natural' to the 'human' surely reflects doubt as to whether nature—or any of the equivalent terms for the world as it is—is intelligibly the source of any normative principles at all; 'human' rights can be understood to refer not to the source of the rights in question but to those who possess them, the basis of such universal (human) rights being left comfortably unclear. The important point is that *all* human beings possess the rights, so that the enquiry can cross national boundaries.

There is, I believe, a genuine, strong connection between the philosophy of natural law and rights, which is generally overlooked (partly because of the same misconception about natural law that leads to its association with most theories of natural rights). This connection, properly understood, respects natural law's enduring tradition and, at the same time, reflects contemporary analysis of the concept of rights. It takes seriously the task, essential for a full theory of rights, of establishing the independent reality of rights, rather than deriving them dependently from obligations or posited rules. Also, it allows us to account for the phenomenon that has been most refractory for a theory of rights, the variability of specific rights from one community to another.

The heart of the connection is the relation between rights and human freedom and responsibility. The relation is frequently mentioned in a hortatory way—'No rights without responsibility' and so forth—but not closely examined. And it is asserted as if it were obvious as the basis for conclusions about the kind of being that can possess rights. Such conclusions, however, are strongly contested. I shall argue that rights (other than those that are established and fully explained by enactment as positive law or rules) are in a rather special way constitutive of freedom, and that that indeed is what rights are and all that they are. The duties that are correlative to rights arise because the rights constitute the beings who possess them as autonomous beings—persons rather than things—to whom such duties are owed. Further, the way in which rights constitute freedom is the way of natural law. Rights are a response to the puzzle of human freedom within a determinate natural order. They accomplish for us what was earlier accomplished, albeit very differently, by *moira* and then by natural law itself. The connection with natural law is not, therefore, merely verbal. It is an essential part of what we mean when we refer to human freedom and responsibility.

1. RESPONSIBILITY AND RIGHTS

Not the least of our difficulties when we think about rights is that, despite their ubiquity in our discourse, it is unclear just what a right is.[8] Legal rights can be defined roughly as claims that the law will enforce; 'no right without a remedy', as every first-year law student learns.[9] The law aside, when human rights are at stake, the general issue typically is ignored, and discussion proceeds directly to contested specific rights, it being taken for granted that everyone knows what a right is, well enough at least to be able to affirm or deny the specifics. Yet, abstract discussion of the nature of rights generally indicates a good deal of disagreement. For the most part, whether they are considered from the point of view of the possessor of a right or the point of view of another person, rights are treated as counters in interpersonal relations; as John Finnis has observed, 'modern rights-talk is constructed primarily on the implicit model of a relationship between two individuals'.[10]

That approach to the matter is obvious enough. For the usual pay-off of a right lies in its recognition by someone else in the form of performance of a duty.[11] Many rights are exercised, of course, without the least sense of others that they are performing a duty; although we recognize the right of others to walk on the street, in ordinary circumstances few of us are aware of performing a duty not to assault them. And a conscientious person might want to know his rights in order to decide how to act, even though he is too powerful to be prevented from acting however he should decide. Even so, a right that could (or could not) be exercised regardless of any action that other persons might take would scarcely deserve our notice; for right or no, the possessor's situation would not be different. Most of the time, the practical significance of a right is its prescription of how others should behave.

On the surface, however, at least grammatically, rights are not relational but attributive. Persons are said to 'have' rights, as it were, on their own, as they have brown hair, headaches, or pencils. Reference to a person's right does not require mention of another person or his duty to be complete on its own terms. And far from being the reflexive of another person's duty independently established, it is the other way around. Rights are given as the ground of duties: *because* Smith has a right, Jones has a duty [not] to act in a certain way. It would be extremely odd to say that Smith has a right *because* Jones has a duty; for if Smith did not independently have the right, one would hardly confer it on him simply in order to impose on Jones.[12] Thus, in the first instance, rights appear to tell us something about those who possess them, from which a duty of others arises, not merely by formal implication but substantively.

It has, however, proved powerfully difficult to explicate rights by reference to any such characterization of their possessors. The difficulty has led some philosophers to conclude that there is no such personal characterization to be explained and that rights are, after all, the other face of duties and interpersonal through and through. Rights and duties alike, they say, are different aspects of unitary rules; and possessors of rights are, in effect, incidental beneficiaries of whatever theory of the good gives rise to the rules.[13] Other philosophers have been troubled by the latter conclusion, because it seems to give rights too small a place. Far from rules being the ground of rights, they argue, rights are the ground of rules. Yet, unable to explain the attribution of rights on any basis that implicates individual characteristics of possessors of rights in general or of specific rights, they have been pressed to the position that rights are a primary or fundamental element of normative discourse, which cannot be explained or described in other terms. That leaves them open to the objection that rights are differential, not only among persons but among kinds; and if they are not based on theories of the good and are not otherwise explained, they are arbitrary and indefensible. So the matter tends toward stalemate, and what rights are remains in doubt.

Because we are usually most interested in their interpersonal aspect, we may be inclined to think of a right primarily as normative, directive of behaviour: a person's right is prescriptive or proscriptive of actions of others. From the person's own point of view, however, the significance of a right is just the reverse. Rights do not require that they be exercised. Although if someone has a duty to do x he must have a right to do x, it would be otiose and peculiar, having mentioned the person's duty, to mention the right as well. Rather, one mentions the right when there is no duty; having the right to do x usually signifies that one has also the right not to do *x*. Accordingly, the right itself is not any indication at all that one ought so to act. On the contrary, we may mention a right in just those circumstances when there is doubt whether one ought to do so. The right leaves the question of what its possessor ought to do entirely open.

It is not surprising, therefore, that rights are associated with freedom. Having a right, one is free to do as he chooses. In political debate especially, rights are perceived as the very stuff of freedom, or liberty. But although the freedom is that of the possessor of the right, most of the time, as in the political context, it reflects only the interpersonal aspect of rights and has to do with being free from unjustified constraints imposed by others (including, notably, the government). Accordingly, it is accommodated within the interpersonal account of rights that ties them directly to duties of others rather than to the person of their possessors.

There is another conception of freedom, which may be regarded not as an absence of imposed constraints but as a personal characteristic or state of being, possessing which a person is responsible for his actions and amenable to moral judgement. The two ways of thinking about freedom are obviously related; but they are fundamentally entirely different. Freedom as liberty is ordinarily an element of the other, larger conception, since whatever else may be true about a person, if his behaviour is fully attributable to external constraint, he is not responsible for it. But an absence of constraint is not always necessary for freedom as responsibility; despite the constraint, one may have the capacity to act and be responsible for what he does. In some circumstances, for example, a person may be praised for doing what he had no legal right to do or blamed for not doing it; the basis of the moral judgement is that despite the law's constraint, he retained sufficient freedom to be responsible for what he did (and that he had a moral duty— and right—to act contrary to the law). Nor is an absence of constraint always sufficient. If a child is left unsupervised, a dog let off its leash, or a vine not attached to a trellis, it may be described unobjectionably as 'at liberty'; but child, dog, or vine is not responsible for what it does because, we believe, it lacks that kind of freedom. (Still, the fact that we are more likely to describe it as 'wild' rather than 'free' or 'at liberty' suggests that we do think about the two kinds of freedom together.)

Rights have also been associated with freedom as responsibility. But unlike the commonplace association with liberty, whether there is such a connection between rights and responsibility and if so, what its nature is, are much disputed questions. The two relationships at issue are:

freedom (liberty) $\longleftrightarrow$ rights (interpersonal; absence of constraints)

freedom (responsibility) $\longleftrightarrow$ rights (personal; ?)

There is good reason to suppose that much of the confusion and disagreement concerning the nature of rights arises from the tendency not to keep the two relationships apart. That tendency undoubtedly has its chief source in the uncertain status of the right-hand term in the second of the two relationships. Since it has proved so difficult to explain what it is about rights that confines them to those who are free and responsible or what it is about responsibility that gives rise to rights, those who affirm such a connection generally speak as if the relationships are simply:

freedom (liberty) $\longleftrightarrow$ rights

freedom (responsibility) $\nearrow$

even though the only concrete significance of rights that is given pertains only to freedom as liberty.

Confusion of the two relationships is prominent in the controversy whether only (and all) human beings possess rights or animals and perhaps other kinds as well also possess them. Noting that there are strong duties of concern for the well-being of animals (and other non-human kinds, living and unliving), which duties are widely acknowledged, some philosophers have urged forcefully that it is correct to regard the beneficiaries of such duties as possessors of rights. So, the jargon of public debate now familiarly includes the label 'animal-rights activists'. That view has been opposed by another, probably more numerous group of philosophers, who do not necessarily dispute that there are moral duties having to do with the treatment of animals but argue that it is not correct to correlate such duties with animals' rights because, lacking responsibility, animals do not— cannot—possess rights. Those who take this position need not commit themselves to a particular account of human freedom and responsibility. All that they necessarily assert is that however one understands human responsibility, animals are not responsible in that sense. If rights are associated only with liberty, there does not seem to be much reason to deny that animals have rights; our duties with respect to animals are all that is needed to substantiate the correlative rights. The duty not to inflict pain needlessly, for example, might intelligibly be correlated with animals' right to be free from the needless infliction of pain. If rights require that their possessors be responsible, animals have no rights, whatever duties persons may have regarding their treatment. Those who reject animals' rights assert the latter proposition as if it is obvious. But unless they explain why—how—rights implicate responsibility, their assertion collapses into the connection between rights and liberty.

Some specific rights are not so obviously associated with either conception of freedom. Rights *to do* (to travel, to speak freely, etc.) are easily perceived as aspects of liberty and are those most often mentioned in connection with personal liberty from governmental constraints. Many of the most familiar rights, however, are rights *to have* or *to be* some thing or state of being: food, shelter, education. Such rights are sometimes assimilated into rights to do, on the basis that rights are essentially waivable; it is urged that someone cannot be said to have a right unless he is able to accept or reject it. The ease with which we speak—over vociferous objections, to be sure—of inalienable rights makes it at least not certain that the assimilation is correct. And indeed, why *must* one be able to waive a right? As a practical matter, in circumstances in which a right to things like food and shelter is in question, the likelihood that the right will be waived is next to zero. If the possessor of the right is certain to enjoy, or at any rate to benefit from, whatever it is that he has a right to, what difference does it make whether he might theoretically have waived it?

The requirement of capacity to waive seems in substance to be another way of making the argument that freedom as responsibility is a prerequisite for the possession of rights. Without further explanation, rights to have or to be seem more easily to conform to the theory that rights are not personally attributive but are elements of rules prescribing duties of others. Animals (and human beings) have a right to sustenance and a right not to be tortured, because a world in which starvation and pain are reduced is a better world. If a theory of rights independent of the good is to be sustained, we need a clearer understanding of how such rights attach directly to their possessors not, as it were, as bearers of the good but simply as themselves.

The closely parallel, paired relationships between rights and freedom and the persistent, strongly held, but insufficiently explained belief that rights are properly ascribed only to beings who have freedom in the strong sense that imports moral responsibility are enough to suggest that if rights have a personal, attributive aspect it is to be found there. That there is a connection between rights and responsibilities is, I think, intuitively obvious; but any such intuition fails to disclose its source. Efforts to resolve the issue by analysis of rights are unsuccessful, because the logic and language of rights are ambiguous in the crucial respects. More may be learned if we start on the other side of the connection and, instead of asking what responsibility has to do with rights, ask what, if anything, rights have to do with responsibility.

Responsibility attaches to a person when we identify him as an actor, in the specific sense that he is the originating agent of the conduct in question. Such agency does not preclude entirely discussion of what accounts for the person having been in a position to act or having acted as he did, which may include reference to his prior experiences or personal attributes. We may wonder how the rescuer happened to be on the scene, how he knew what to do, or how he had the courage to do it. But, so long as we consider the rescue as action for which he is responsible personally, at some point we must turn to his motives or reasons for the action as determining factors, which explain it by reference to his decision or choice rather than simply as the consequence of prior occurrences that themselves determined it fully. The action, we say, was determined by the actor; acting as he did, the actor was self-determining. Throughout our lives, we routinely describe conduct in this way, or simply observe it as such. We recognize situations in which persons are responsible agents and distinguish them from others in which they participate only as links in a chain of cause and effect. So ordinary is the distinction that it usually need not be made explicit; it is built into our patterns of speech, as the active and passive voices.

The notion of self-determination that we employ unexception-
ally is, however, deeply problematic, not just in the hard cases
when we are openly in doubt whether the person is actor or acted
upon but in every case. For either way, the person as he is
presently constituted is who he is in virtue of antecedent circumstances that are beyond his control; it makes no difference
whether we describe such circumstances as his past or simply
the past. If some such circumstance was the result of a self-
determined action, then the actor as he was then was who he was
in virtue of antecedent circumstances beyond his cóntrol. So, the
rescuer may have had the necessary knowledge because he
studied industriously some time in the past; but he was industri-
ous at that time because of antecedent circumstances beyond his
control. As with industriousness, so also with courage, and the
rest. At some point, at any rate, that must be true. The argument
is the same whether it refers to the present or retreats into the
remote past.

Some attributes are regarded as excuses that exempt from
responsibility precisely because they establish that the conduct
in question was beyond the person's control. But the range of
excuses is quite limited. And, in principle, all of our present
attributes—not only our physical and mental capacities but our
character as well—are built up out of our past. The child, as we
say, is father to the man. If it were otherwise, if who one is now
were, in any respect, genuinely independent of what one was
before, in what sense would one be responsible for what one is,
inasmuch as *that* person evidently had nothing to do with it?
(Indeed, on what basis would one have a continuous moral
identity at all?) Either way, whether a person's own past determines his present—him as he is at present—or not, it seems
impossible to regard him as self-determining in the way that
responsibility requires.

Much the same puzzle about responsibility arises if, instead of
asking how a person came to be the person that he is, we compare
one person to another. Responsibility attaches to a person as a
fully constituted individual, rather than to any particular attribute
or set of attributes. Despite all the features that we have in
common as members of the same species and other features that
we share to a greater or lesser extent, as fully constituted individuals we are not completely alike. Some are handsomer, more

reasonable, faster, hotter-tempered, wealthier . . . and some are less so. If it is difficult to comprehend self-determination as somehow outside the regular sequence of cause and effect, it is no less difficult to understand how persons differently constituted, in ways not determined by themselves, can be equally responsible for their different actions, attributable to them as thus constituted.

We have many ways of deflecting this question or equivocating about it. Since an individual is a composite of so many attributes, which all who are identifiably members of the species possess in some degree, we generally avoid extreme comparisons.[14] But except by comparing one difference with another, there is no way of saying whether a difference is significant or not. The greater the similarity in other respects, the more significant a particular difference is likely to be. In any case, whether the differences are large or small, the question at bottom is the same: if persons are constituted differently from one another, by circumstances beyond their control, in what sense are they responsible as individuals for what they do?

The currently preferred philosophic way of dealing with this problem is to deny that there is a genuine problem after all. Human beings are constituted differently. Far from being undermined by such difference, personal responsibility, which is insistently individual, depends on it. Were we constituted alike, responsibility would have no purchase; we should all act alike as well. Although some incapacities and, perhaps, some special capacities, like unusual wealth or physical strength, are, or ought to be, subject to amelioration, most differences among persons are not. Even if it be conceded that they are 'arbitrary from a moral point of view',[15] the attributes that differentiate persons from one another are simply the attributes that constitute them as individual persons. There is no vantage from which personal identity can be preserved without such differences.

This argument has force, because no one has been able to explain what would satisfy the apparent demand for non-arbitrary natural differentiation among persons. How can persons be individuals—how can there be individual responsibility—without personal differences? If, however, the abstract statement of the problem can be resisted in this way, its concrete applications continue to perplex us. Some attributes seem so clearly not to sustain responsibility but to defeat it that to find a person responsible none the less would be regarded as plainly incorrect as well as harsh and unsympathetic. But there is no break in principle between those attributes that constitute an excuse and those that that do not. In a concrete case, how can we convincingly demonstrate that a criminal's natural disadvantages and ill nurture do not explain and excuse his conduct as surely as another defendant's insanity explains and excuses his? The issue arises less often, but how can we demonstrate that the hero's heroic conduct is not more apt for explanation than commendation? How, in short, in a concrete case can we ever convincingly dissociate a person's conduct from the not self-determined circumstances that account for his being the person he is? The fact that we allow excuses at all is the visible tip of an iceberg that threatens to sink all attributions of responsibility alike.

A different solution appears in classical Greek philosophy and literature. It was presupposed that the natural order is itself normative and, therefore, that individual circumstances, including our respective individual attributes, are not arbitrary but are 'due', a fulfilment of the normative natural order.[16] In what sense the natural course of events should be regarded as 'due' was not fully disclosed, except by reference to concepts like *moira* that incorporated the normative element without explaining it. Various devices, like a notion of familial guilt, made this aspect of human experience compatible, albeit incompletely, with personal responsibility. Something similar was propounded in Christian theology, in which God's Providence gave assurance of a normative order hidden from human comprehension. There too, the hypothesis of eternal life (as well as the doctrine of the Fall and original sin) made the apparent arbitrariness of our earthly existence not only bearable but also, if not comprehensible, at least manageable philosophically.

Neither of these solutions offers much to the intellect unaided by faith, and they do not figure much in current philosophic discussions. The response to both might be that they do little more than replace a question mark with an exclamation mark. Yet the difference between them and the current view is less than it may seem. Whereas they asserted that the natural order is *not* morally arbitrary and is therefore compatible with individual responsibility, it is asserted now, with no greater plausibility, that *although* the natural order *is* morally arbitrary, it is compatible with individual responsibility. The former assertion threatens the foundations of our understanding of the natural order; the latter assertion threatens the foundations of our understanding of the moral order. The shift perhaps attests that we have now a clearer understanding of the problem; but—some tendencies in modern philosophy notwithstanding—understanding a problem is not the same thing as resolving it.

Although the older conceptions cast the issue in ontological terms and it is now cast as an issue of ethics or moral philosophy, they are alike in presenting it as a reconciliation of the 'natural person', constituted according to regularities that contain no normative element, with the distinctly normative premises of moral accountability. Perforce, the reconciliation is effected by locating the normative within nature or by declaring that the natural, as it is, satisfies the relevant norms. Suppose, however, that the steps in the argument were reversed. Rather than taking individuals 'as they are' and seeking to explain how, so constituted, they can be regarded as personally responsible, one might begin at the other end and ask what are the conditions of self-determination (or freedom or autonomy) that have to be met to validate the idea of personal responsibility and moral reasoning generally. From the answer to that question, we might elaborate a conception of the 'morally constituted' individual, that is, a conception of the person in accordance with the premises of personal responsibility. If we had such a conception, then in so far as a person as actually constituted corresponded with it, he would properly be regarded as responsible. But in addition, in so far as a person's actual situation—attributes, circumstances, the lot—departed from this conception, the two might be brought into correspondence by deliberate interventions having that objective. Thus *re*constituted, the person would properly be regarded as responsible.

To speak of constituting and reconstituting actual persons may smack too much of the mad scientist's secret laboratory, in which he plugs Smith's brain into Jones's head, attaches Green's arms, and adds Brown's personality. We are not in the realm of science fiction, however, but in that of ordinary law and social order. All that is fictional, indeed, is the supposition that there is a 'natural' person unaffected by more or less deliberate societal 'interventions' (or failures to intervene). Each of us as actually constituted is a composite of the effects of nature and nurture; there is no practical possibility of separating the two, nor even a basis for fully separating them theoretically. No more is required to make the notion of reconstituting a person according to normative criteria concrete and familiar than recognition that we are who we are as individuals only within a social context, some aspects of which are 'natural' in the limited sense that they arise without deliberate human effort but many, or most, aspects of which are the product of more or less effective, deliberate, or at any rate alterable, social action.

Approached in this way, rights are specifications of the conception of a morally constituted individual. In place of a person's actual attributes, arbitrary from a moral point of view, are substituted attributes that are his as of right, that is, his from a moral point of view. In so far as his actual attributes are his as of right, they are confirmed; in so far as they are less or more than his due, they are subject to being modified, either enhanced or curtailed. Recognition of rights by deliberate interventions thus carries out the programme of *rectification*, or reconstitution, of persons as personal responsibility requires. Having his rights, a person is responsible for his actions. But also, a person is not (properly regarded as) responsible unless, with respect to the conduct in question, he has his rights. When a person is held responsible, therefore, the judgement about responsibility itself gives content to the conception of a morally constituted individual and the specific rights that it includes. In the all too familiar case of a young person who is convicted of a crime and asks not to be punished harshly because he was not nurtured by his parents, was not taught a trade, was raised in an environment that encouraged crime . . . and the rest, the decision to send him to prison all the same is a determination that in so far as his criminal conduct is concerned he was constituted as was his due, he had his rights and is responsible for what he did. Were that not so, the judgement could not be made.[17]

Personal claims to some benefit or advantage as one's due have the same foundation, although it is not so immediately obvious. Such a claim is based on an attribute or action of the person, which, it is asserted, makes him deserving of the benefit in question. The claim may be contested without questioning that the person indeed possesses the attribute or performed the action, on the basis that he is not responsible for it; the attribute is his or the action is attributable to him not as his due, not as of right, but only circumstantially. So, an applicant for admission to a university may believe that he ought to be admitted because his parent is an alumnus or is eager to make a large contribution to the endowment. But also, much more convincingly, he may assert that he ought to be admitted because he has higher test scores and a record of greater achievement than other applicants. In the latter case as much as the former, if he is denied admission in favour of someone else with weaker credentials, unless the admissions office is prepared to avow that it acted unjustly, the basis for the denial must be that he is not, in the necessary sense, responsible for his achievement. His abilities are his as a matter of fact, but not as a matter of right. Of course, in a certain sense, we know that that is correct. For he no more deserves his high IQ and supportive parents than someone else deserves his low IQ and neglectful parents. The great, great puzzle about affirmative action is how to treat competitive disadvantages—whether due to imposed inferiority in the past or simply as a matter of fact—as not constitutive of the person, not a matter of right, without regarding personal advantages that are the fruits of talent and hard work as similarly circumstantial and not a matter of right either.

Thinking of rights in this way, as the necessary and sufficient ground of responsibility, is consistent with our usual under-standing of rights, so far as it goes.[18] A person who did not have a (moral) right to affect a course of events or who, having the right, was prevented from exercising it would not be held responsible for the outcome. The domain of rights is, however, vastly enlarged to include the full range of human freedom. Rights ordinarily are in issue with respect to capacities that can practically be enhanced (or diminished) by human action. So, for example, although a person would not be regarded as responsible for his failure to leap across a wide river to save a person in danger on the other side, it would be peculiar to observe in explanation that his right to leap long distances had not been respected. Rather, he lacked the power; persons generally lacking the power and there being no ready, practical way to provide it, there is no basis for regarding the power as a right. The notion of personal self-determination and moral responsibility is not a challenge to the entire human condition but is contained within it.[19] Similarly, the ordinary excuses that we allow on the basis of an individual, idiosyncratic incapacity—insanity, youth, preoccupation—are not generally thought of as asserting the denial of a right. It is simply something that happens to be the case—the person as he is. So also, even if we were to aver that a person's unusual capacity in some respect—intelligence, beauty, wealth—were morally arbitrary, we should scarcely describe it as the denial of a right. Having more than one's due is, if anything, a denial of someone else's right. Within the general framework of individual responsibility, however, all such circumstances potentially raise a question about rights, one way or the other. For all of them call for a distinction between those attributes that a person has as his due, with respect to which he is accordingly held responsible and which he may claim as his own and must accept as his own, and those that a person has not as his due but only in fact, with respect to which he is not responsible and which he neither may claim nor must accept. So long as the issue of responsibility is clear and unquestioned—treated, that is to say, as a matter of fact—no question about rights will be raised. It will be recast as an issue about rights if the person's responsibility, or lack of responsibility is challenged: if, for example, someone should be blamed for failing to leap the river or for conduct attributable to an excusing condition like insanity, or if someone were denied the fruits of his intelligence, etc. If the natural attribute itself cannot be rectified directly, for better or worse, it is always possible to rectify it indirectly, by modifying its effects.

If the domain of rights is thus enlarged, the scope of specific rights is reduced. Rather than attaching at large to their possessor, simply as something that he has, rights are action-specific. They bear on the question whether the person is, or is not, responsible for particular conduct. The same significance is ordinarily conveyed by speaking of the right without restriction but confining its relevance so far as responsibility is concerned. From the point of view of the person himself, however, that is its only relevance.

Rights, in short, are inherent to the moral point of view. They enable us to mediate between the perception of human beings merely as beings, 'natural objects' subject to the determinate regularities of cause and effect, and perception of them as persons, self-determining and responsible for their actions. Constituted as possessors of rights, persons have their due. Their actions are determined by their selves; and they are responsible for them.

The paradox of human freedom remains. The antinomic conceptions of human beings as personally responsible and as causally determinate are not dissolved by the idea of rights, but are contained, in suspension as it were, within it. Responsibility does not arise permanently and indefeasibly from a single, unique act at some initial moment of freedom (even if it were possible to identify such a moment); rather, it attaches (intermittently) to specific conduct, in virtue of freedom contemporaneous with the conduct. In order for the conditions of responsibility to be satisfied, not only must persons be constituted according to their due, but also, acting as thus constituted and duly incurring desert, their desert must be fulfilled and they must remain so constituted. Yet, were those conditions satisfied, each person always and invariably acting as he ought duly to act, the notions of freedom and responsibility would have no application. We should be a society not of human beings but of angels. Thus, although responsibility requires that we be morally constituted as possessors of rights, the possibility of morality, which is all that responsibility signifies, requires that we be incompletely so constituted, lest freedom be eliminated. In short, if morally significant freedom requires that one be constituted according to his due, then the exercise of freedom itself has to be determinate, according to desert; but if it is determinate, it is no longer freedom. Unyielding to reason, the antinomy nevertheless is overcome practically in our experience, by the actual recognition of distinct rights.

2. WHAT RIGHTS ARE THERE?

The close connection between rights and responsibility does not provide answers to questions about what rights there are. Among the manifold attributes that constitute the individual human being and differentiate one from another, none is self-evidently due or not due, nor are some 'more' due than others. Nevertheless, perceiving rights as the bridge between self-determination and causal order gives direction to that enquiry and, in particular, accounts for the tension between the appearance of objectivity that characterizes claims of rights and the evident variability of the rights that are acknowledged and asserted in different communities. The lines of argument can only be sketched here.

First, the idea of natural rights or human rights asks whether there are any rights that all human beings have by their nature. Without attention to the constitutive function of rights within moral discourse, the question dissolves into an unstructured assessment of the comparative 'value' of various rights, which typically generates either a barrage of conflicting rights or a comprehensive list too long to be plausible. The question has more content, although it is still not susceptible to proof, if it is understood to ask what, if any, attributes are essential to any responsibility at all. If there are such attributes, then they may be said to attach as rights to any being that is, by nature, self-determining. If it is accepted that all, and only, human beings are self-determining, the categories of natural rights and human rights are equivalent.[20] Although there are extraordinary examples of human heroism in extreme circumstances, rights are to be defined by reference to the normal individual, the human and not the superhuman. A persuasive case can be made that some level of physical, intellectual, and emotional well-being as well as some range of opportunity for significant responsible decisions are essential to one's being as a responsible creature. On that basis, a case for natural or human rights can be made out. The extent of the rights so defined is far less than those now commonly claimed under that heading. They would have, however, a defensible grounding in what is, simply, human.

Second, there are the limitlessly various, differential attributes that are not essential to responsibility as such but on which our identity as individuals depends, among which we have to distinguish those that are a person's by right, constitutive of him as the person that he is, and therefore his due, from those that are his only circumstantially, not himself or his self, and therefore not his due. The distinction is not a familiar one in those terms, but we make it implicitly all the time, not only in assessments of responsibility but also in the most commonplace characterizations of individual conduct. When we describe a person as an actor, we in effect regard the attributes and circumstances that led him to act as he did as constitutive of his self. When we describe him as acted upon, we in effect regard such attributes and circumstances as determinative of the conduct alone, not as constitutive of his self but merely circumstantial. The concept of a person, sometimes self-determining agent and sometimes the locus of effects of other causes, is built up out of myriad indications of this kind, which are part of the fabric of ordinary life and most of the time are recognized and accepted without question. From our own experience, we know and apply without thinking about it the difference between doing something—bending down to tie a shoe—and something happening—stumbling over one's shoelace. Such indications have empirical foundations. Social scientists may convince us that we assign some conduct to the wrong category—what we had thought deliberate action was 'compulsive' behaviour or what we had thought accidental was motivated—but it is not all, all the time, equally subject to revision. The concept of a person is also, however, significantly a social construct. It depends on patterns and perceptions of conduct deeply rooted in and dependent on a society's way of life and not in 'nature' itself. In the classical terms, for which we have no equivalent, it has its source in *nomos* rather than *physis*.[21] Rights so grounded are specific to the community within which they arise; in our own terms, they may significantly be denominated as civil rights.

At any time, most aspects of personhood will, perforce, be settled and non-contentious. Individual responsibility so identified will not be presented as a matter of rights, one way or the other, but simply described as a matter of fact: a person so constituted, engaging in such behaviour, in such circumstances is, or is not, responsible. Some aspects of personhood will be contentious; whether a person so constituted and so behaving ought be regarded as responsible or ought be excused (or, possibly, denied praise), whether he ought be left as he is or be reconstituted, will be regarded as a matter of rights: his right to what he has and responsibility to make do with what he has, or his right to more or less.

The level, extent, and manner of debate about rights within a society is not so much a measure of the quality of life within it as it is an indication of the degree of acceptance and harmony about its fundamental presuppositions: what persons within it properly claim as members of that community. Another society may identify more rights within this spectrum and, nevertheless, experience more acrimony and dissent. Rights so identified have no objective source external to the society within which they are recognized; regarded abstractly, removed from the way of life in which they inhere, they are opposed by other 'rights' that would validate a different conception of the morally constituted individual. There is no perfectly just society, in which all rights are realized and every person has all and only what is his due. Nor is that a coherent, albeit unattainable ideal. Perfect freedom is not within our grasp not only because we are imperfect but because, in a more fundamental sense, we are human. Within our own communities, we can work toward a coherent vision of personal freedom, within the unavoidable constraints of nature but also within the constraints imposed by our own choices of the good.

The approach that I have outlined is strongly Aristotelian. As a practical matter, the approach brings rights into closer relation to issues and questions of responsibility with which we are accustomed to deal and allows us to apply familiar, if seldom explicit, criteria. It is beyond the scope of this essay to indicate more precisely the content of natural rights or to describe concretely how the derivation of rights from a community's *nomos* is carried out. That the specification of rights will often be highly controversial scarcely needs to be said. But it is part of the significance of the connection between rights and responsibility that the derivation of rights is, perforce, carried out. Understanding this connection permits us to adopt a critical stance with respect to rights while at the same time taking account of their socially determined content.

3. NATURAL LAW

What does all of this have to do with natural law? If natural law is thought to affirm the truth of specific, concrete moral principles, which resolve actual moral dilemmas, then the connection between rights and responsibility barely touches it. That kind of claim for natural law indeed resembles claims about specific natural rights, which their proponents insist are obviously or self-evidently true, while at the same time ignoring others' similarly insistent claims for a different set of rights. Belief that natural law gives expression to a kind of revealed moral code unfortunately persists, both among a small and rather special group of defenders of natural law (who are spectacularly unsuccessful in convincing anyone else) and among a much larger group, for whom that view of natural law is sufficient reason not only to reject it but to ignore it.

There is another view of natural law, more consistent with its long historical development and more compatible with current philosophic thought, which justifies the conclusion that rights are peculiarly within its ambit. From its earliest appearances in classical Greek culture, at the very centre of natural law was an affirmation of the reality of our moral experience, not merely as subjective feelings or belief but as objectively real, an aspect of what there is. Confronted by internal and external forces dramatically affecting their lives that they could neither control nor understand, the Greek thinkers affirmed none the less that there was (normative) order and they were responsible.[22] In medieval Christian speculation, natural law retained this juxtaposition of 'natural' and moral order at its core, although it was in other respects transformed. The theology of Christianity being the point of departure, there was never a question of meaning or order. Human moral experience remained a puzzle to be resolved: if God is all provident, how are human beings personally responsible? The question took various forms, referring not only to individual freedom but also to social institutions, like slavery and private property, that challenged belief in individual desert. Thomas Aquinas brought the medieval development of natural law to fruition; but he did not alter its fundamental character. It remained at bottom not a philosophically grounded moral code, or ethics, as we should now think of it, but ontological, an affirmation of moral reality.

So understood, natural law is a philosophy of rights. It affirms the reality of individual responsibility within—despite—the determinate natural order. Human beings, constituted as they are by circumstances not within their control, nevertheless are self-determining. Projecting the puzzle of human freedom onto the external world, the older versions of natural law contained an assurance that—somehow, in the fullness of time—persons are actually constituted according to their due. As a philosophy of rights, natural law locates the puzzle of freedom within ourselves and resolves it normatively. It does not guarantee that a person's rights will be recognized; only that it is intelligible and correct to regard a person as endowed with rights. It is not the case that 'chance is all in all'.[23] Men and women are moral beings.

The philosophy against which natural law speaks may be described as ethical positivism: the view that moral perception and judgement depend ultimately on the positing—affirmation or acceptance or enforcement—of the moral principles that they implicate; in the terms of the scholastic controversy, it is a dependence on will rather than reason.[24] The positivist may, as much as anyone, affirm moral principles and, in particular, individual rights. It has, indeed, been among the main tenets of legal positivism that positive law is subject to moral criticism and that it may be morally obligatory not to obey an iniquitous law. Whatever one's moral obligation may be, however, the positivist insists that the validity of a law, and hence one's legal obligation under it, is coextensive with its extent as posited. Therefore, the posited law within an effective legal order is not merely a threat backed by the force of the state but is the source of an actual legal obligation. Whether it establishes also a moral obligation of compliance is another, different question, to be answered by reference not to law but to principles of morality.

The unstated implication of the positivist's assertion that positive law is a source of genuine (legal) obligation is that all obligation, moral as well as legal, depends ultimately on the positing, or acceptance of the validity, of the underlying principle. For, since it is possible to posit any obligation at all, if it were otherwise and some obligation had another foundation independent of its being posited, the fact that a conflicting obligation was posited would not establish it as a genuine obligation; the fact could be regarded only as a datum bearing on what, all things considered, the former obligation required. A positive law in conflict with a moral principle that was independently established as correct would of itself create no valid obligation whatever, although the fact that it was the law might have a bearing on one's obligation. So, Lon Fuller was able to characterize the positivist's notion of a legal obligation that conflicted with one's moral obligation as a choice 'between giving food to a starving man and being mimsy with the borogoves'.[25] Understood in this light, the assertion of natural law that a law contrary to moral principles is 'no law at all' is intelligible and meaningful. The legal positivist's ridicule of that proposition is misplaced. (But so also, alas, have been many of the attempts to support it.)

Beyond the range of law, then, the positivist concludes that the validity of moral obligations arises finally from acceptance of the underlying moral principle. That is not to say, of course, that acceptance and validity mean the same thing. Rather, an obligation is valid, it really obligates, only from the point of view of one who accepts it as valid. For anyone else, the positivist asserts, the obligation does not exist, even though he may be obliged to comply. Although many facts and arguments may be brought to bear in an effort to induce someone to accept a moral principle, there is, he says, no objective standpoint from which it simply is true or not. The positivist is not, I think, committed except methodologically to the denial of such an objective reality; only, if there is such, he argues, it is altogether, irremediably, opaque to our understanding. The question cannot be asked.

If the positivist alternative is clearly set forth, there is special reason to regard natural law as a philosophy of rights. Although positivists can and do defend individual rights and condemn legal regimes in which persons' rights are disregarded, they are, strictly speaking, committed to rejecting an affirmation of rights as a matter of fact. From the positivist point of view, a statement that 'Smith has a right to ——' is at best a loose way of speaking. For the statement omits reference to a particular point of view; and, according to the positivist, a statement about rights cannot be made without such a reference, because it does not express a matter of fact. (Nor, of course, can the positivist assert that 'Smith ought to have a right to ——', without reference to some posited system of rules or normative principle. To whom would such an unqualified prescription be addressed?) Statements about rights, accurately rendered according to the positivist, have the form, 'Smith ought to be treated as if he has a right to ——'. That rendering is indeed consistent with the view that a moral order implicating individual responsibility congruent with a determinate natural order can only be posited or not; one cannot ask whether it is real. Yet, if the latter question is left aside, one may wonder how any moral argument even begins. In the absence of moral order, why *ought* anything at all?

Does it matter? The question whether morality is real has an unfamiliar, if not distinctly peculiar, ring. As motivation, attitude, concern, psychological and social force, morality is obviously 'real' in the only sense in which we are likely to use the term. Furthermore, although we may ponder the justice or fairness of it all and wonder why fortune so favours one person and neglects another, we do in fact perceive persons as morally responsible. The hard cases that trouble us are not taken to be an indication that morality as such is problematic, but only that responsibility sometimes is difficult to assess. Perforce, that is our universe, in which we dwell more or less comfortably, even though we do not fully understand.

Natural law does not furnish an additional argument for moral responsibility. Having argued as well as one can for a course of conduct on the ground that it is morally obligatory, one does not amplify the argument by adding, 'And you really are obligated'. Natural law may not matter a great deal 'functionally'; it is not likely to affect how one's obligations are established, the weight one gives them, or the consequences of meeting or failing to meet them. The full existential dilemma, to which natural law responds, is more potent in literature than in actual lives. And for a reason: the ordinary agency of human beings is not at bottom a hypothesis that we entertain and accept or reject. It is given directly in the structure of our experience, as the difference between persons and things. From a human perspective, the true opposition is not between freedom and determinism. It is between experience and reason, what we know to be true but are unable to account for or even to express coherently.

Ought we therefore to conclude that we describe the same universe—the same human condition—whether we affirm that it is, simply *is*, a moral universe or we conclude, to the contrary, that we act as if it is, perforce but without warrant? Or, if it is not the same, that it makes no difference which it is? It seems to me that we ought not. One may conclude that, even as an intellectual matter, natural law is, after all, very close to faith. In any case, so long as we regard the issue as worth our attention, the philosophy of rights belongs to natural law—a reason, perhaps, for regarding it as worth our attention.

NOTES

1. For a general account of the Greek material, see L. Weinreb, *Natural Law and Justice* (Cambridge, Mass.: Harvard University Press, 1987), 15–42, and of the Christian development, see ibid. 43–66.
2. See R. Tuck, *Natural Rights Theories* (Cambridge: Cambridge University Press, 1979).
3. J. Locke, *Two Treatises of Government*, bk. 2, sect. 6, ed. P. Laslett (Cambridge: Cambridge University Press, 1960), 311.
4. In the first draft of 'The Social Contract', the so-called Geneva manuscript, Rousseau made a withering attack on natural law. *Du Contrat Social* (première version), in J.-J. Rousseau, *Œuvres complètes* (Paris: Gallimard, Pléiade edn., 1964), iii. 284. Natural law is not mentioned in the final version.
5. See 'Du Legislateur', Rousseau, *Du Contrat Social*, bk. 2, ch. 7, *Œuvres complètes*, iii. 381.
6. Various theories of rights are sometimes derided as 'natural law theories'. Justice Black famously criticized Justice Frankfurter's view of due process as such a theory, a characterization that Frankfurter accepted. See e.g. *Adamson* v. *California*, 332 U.S. 46 (1947); *Rochin* v. *California*, 342 U.S. 165 (1952). In fact, a good case could be made that Black, rather than Frankfurter, was closer to the spirit if not the letter of the natural law position, as it is commonly understood. See also John Ely's criticism of natural law as a basis for constitutional interpretation: 'It has . . . become increasingly evident that the only propositions with a prayer of passing themselves off as "natural law" are those so uselessly vague that no one will notice—something along the "No one should needlessly inflict suffering" line.' J. Ely, *Democracy and Distrust* (Cambridge, Mass.: Harvard University Press, 1980), 51 (footnote omitted). Such criticism perhaps suggests that there is more connection between natural law and rights than I suppose. But the criticism consists mostly of attaching a negative label, without much awareness of or attention to the label's proper reference. Frequent references to 'natural rights' and the mistaken but common assumption that any argument, of any form, for natural rights is *ipso facto* within the camp of natural law no doubt make the connection look stronger and broader than it is. Some supporters of natural law have sought to uphold the connection more substantially. John Finnis in particular has urged that the essential elements of

natural law can be expressed in the vocabulary of rights. J. Finnis, *Natural Law and Natural Rights* (Oxford: Clarendon Press, 1980), 198–230.

7. See e.g. Finnis, *Natural Law*, 81–133, esp. 85–6, 125–7. I have criticized that position in Weinreb, *Natural Law and Justice*, 108–15. For a defence, see R. George, 'Recent Criticism of Natural Law Theory', *University of Chicago Law Review*, 55 (1988), 1371–429.

8. There is a large body of recent literature about rights. For a good start, see J. Feinberg, *Rights, Justice, and the Bounds of Liberty* (Princeton, NJ: Princeton University Press, 1980), 130–251; R. Flathman, *The Practice of Rights* (Cambridge: Cambridge University Press, 1976); A. Melden, *Rights and Persons* (London: Blackwell, 1977); L. Sumner, *The Moral Foundation of Rights* (Oxford: Clarendon Press, 1987); J. Thomson, *The Realm of Rights* (Cambridge, Mass.: Harvard University Press, 1990); J. Waldron, ed., *Theories of Rights* (Oxford: Oxford University Press, 1984) (bibliography).

9. And, it must be admitted, later unlearns or substantially qualifies. Still, as a broad generalization, the proposition is acceptable.

10. Finnis, *Natural Law*, 216. Rights against the government are an important subset of this model.

11. Joel Feinberg has emphasized the importance of the *non*-exercise of rights, as an aspect of personal relations. 'A Postscript to the Nature and Value of Rights', in Feinberg, *Rights, Justice, and the Bounds of Liberty*, 156. It is an important point, too easily overlooked, that many personal relationships, typically including those that are closest, are not constructed on the basis of rights. Still, the non-exercise of a right assumes importance because it might have been exercised.

12. That is not to say that every duty implies a correlative right. It would not be odd to say that Smith has a right *inasmuch as* Jones has a duty, the right being an implication of the duty. But the duty can hardly be the reason for the right.

13. e.g. S. Benn and R. Peters, *The Principles of Political Thought* (New York: Free Press, 1965), 101: 'To say that X has a right to £5 is to imply that there is a rule which, when applied to the case of X and some other person Y, imposes on Y a duty to pay X £5 if X so chooses.'

14. Whether a difference is regarded as a difference of degree or as the presence or absence of a distinct attribute depends on how the attribute is defined. We might describe one person as strong and the other as weak or describe one as stronger than the other.

15. R. Nozick, *Anarchy, State, and Utopia* (New York: Basic Books, 1974), 226.

16. To say that the natural order was conceived as 'normative' passes by

a number of complex conceptual hurdles. The Greek presupposition was that the natural order is purposive; but since it is *the* natural order, it is a necessary order. Its purposiveness was contrasted with blind chance—*tyche*—which, being non-purposive, also is necessary, but in an entirely different way. Fate and Providence are our nearest equivalents to the Greek conception of normative natural order.

17. If a person is found not to be responsible—e.g. someone who is found to be criminally insane—that judgement also gives content to the conception of a morally constituted individual. The judgement is based on a conclusion that in his case, generally or with respect to the particular conduct in question, the conditions of self-determination are not met. Unless the failure of those conditions is attributable to the conduct of others, whether action or inaction, we do not ordinarily describe it as a denial of the person's right(s) but simply as a matter of fact. It follows from what I have said that a being that is not in any circumstance responsible does not have rights in the sense that I have described. That includes some categories of human beings, such as infants, the senile, and the insane, as well as animals (and trees and non-living kinds). They may, however, have *legal* rights, meaning that their interests are to be taken into account in certain ways. The law may prescribe measures presumed to be in their interest or it may empower some person(s) to act in their behalf. Such legal rights may have an entirely utilitarian grounding—a world in which beings of that kind are protected in the prescribed way is a better world—or, in the case of non-responsible human beings, their grounding may be a shadow or reflection of rights possessed by responsible human beings, who are of the same natural kind. 'To the extent . . . that we ascribe rights to entities other than [moral] persons we use the term in an extended or secondary sense which will require a grasp of the relevant institutional norms, such as norms of law or etiquette, to understand.' S. Benn, *A Theory of Freedom* (New York: Cambridge University Press, 1988), 9.

18. In the case of legal rights, considered only as such, the applicable rule of law, with its problematic validity, replaces the conception of a morally constituted individual.

19. Albert Camus's play *Caligula* explores the theme of self-determination as a challenge to the human condition itself. The emperor's last, unsatisfied demand is to have the moon.

20. Some conceptual issues as well as concrete practical issues are swept aside by the broad generalization that all and only human beings are self-determining. On one hand, all human beings during some

portion of their lives and some human beings throughout much or most of their lives are not self-determining. On the other hand, some animals display behaviour that might plausibly be regarded as, at least minimally, self-determining and responsible. Although such instances make the category of persons (as distinguished from things) problematic around the edges, it remains generally true as a practical matter that, so far as terrestrial creatures are concerned, human beings and persons are coextensive categories.

21. *Nomos* is commonly translated misleadingly as 'convention', and *physis* as 'nature'. *Nomos* conveyed a sense of something much weightier and more stable than what we think of as convention. It took its meaning to a large extent from the contrast with *physis*, which signified what was necessary and unalterable.

22. The puzzlement was not confined to chance fortune or misfortune. It included aspects of character and 'internal' determination that also seemed to be fortuitous from a moral point of view. A wrong decision that led to catastrophe might be explained as the work of a god, or of *ate*, a madness not one's own or oneself, which took over and overwhelmed one's reason. See generally E. Dodds, *The Greeks and the Irrational* (Berkeley, Calif.: University of California Press, 1951).

23. Sophocles, *Oedipus the King*, trans. D. Grene, line 977, in D. Grene and R. Lattimore, eds., *The Complete Greek Tragedies* (Chicago: University of Chicago Press, 1959–60), ii, *Sophocles* (1959), 52.

24. The term 'positivism' has historical associations with e.g. Saint-Simon and Comte, which I do not intend here. 'Legal positivism' has significance for legal philosophy parallel to what I intend by 'ethical positivism'. Although it is related to relativism, it is not quite the same; the emphasis here, as in legal positivism, is not on the variability of moral principles but on the validity of the principles as posited. Another term that might be used, also with slightly different emphasis, is ethical voluntarism.

25. L. Fuller, 'Positivism and Fidelity to Law—A Reply to Professor Hart', *Harvard Law Review*, 71 (1958), 656.

PART IV
LEGAL FORMALISM AND LEGAL RATIONALITY

11

Formalism and the Rule of Law

JOSEPH RAZ

1. COMMON THREADS

Except at the hands of its detractors the ideal of the rule of law is today a minority preoccupation among legal and political thinkers. Its theoretical marginality can, however, be misleading. The ideal is deeply entrenched in the common 'official' culture of liberal democracies. It is a potent political ideal, whose validity is accepted and implementation assumed and taken for granted. Occasional violations of the rule of law are admitted and condemned by all the main political groupings as a matter of great concern and urgency, which can mobilize political action across party lines. Though not uncommonly it will be disputed whether a violation occurred, hardly anyone will actually argue that it was justified if it took place.

It might be thought that it is this general non-controversiality of the ideal which accounts for its relative theoretical neglect. Those who think so will be surprised at the range and variety of accounts of the rule of law offered by its defenders. These go beyond differing justifications of the same ideal. They amount to completely different understandings of what the ideal is.

And yet beyond these differences certain common images persist. The rule of law is generally claimed to protect people's liberties, and to curtail arbitrary power. The rule of law is an ideal which transcends politics, it is non-political, and, at least to a degree, it protects people from the consequences of the political contest. Finally the rule of law is an ideal rooted in the very essence of law. In conforming to it the law does nothing more than be faithful to its own nature.

In this chapter I will discuss one account of the rule of law, developed by E. Weinrib, which takes the last point as its cue. It regards the rule of law as nothing but an articulation of the essence of law.

2. WEINRIB: AN ESSENTIALIST[1] THEORY OF LAW

2.1. *The Essentialist Merger*

The Rule of Law claims that law can be its own end, and that certain content can be rejected as incompatible with law's inner nature. (RL 68)

Law is not subservient to external ideals because it constitutes, as it were, its own ideal, intelligible from within and capable of serving as a constraint upon radical idealisms which postulate its depreciation. (RL 63)

What does Weinrib mean by his repeated assertions that law is its own end? First, and unwaveringly, Weinrib regards this as entailing 'the internal intelligibility of law' (LF 953). The law should be understood in its own terms, without recourse to external factors. It should be understood through its own form, and the form of anything is the totality of its distinctive and essential properties.[2] Second, though this is less clear, Weinrib understands the law being its own end as meaning that it provides its own justification, that it does not rely on external factors to establish its moral force. The law is, to use Unger's term which Weinrib borrows, 'an immanent moral rationality'.[3]

By suggesting that the rationality of law lies in a moral order immanent to legal material, formalism postulates that juridical content can somehow sustain itself from within. (LF 955)

The function of law for the formalist is to express this immanent rationality in the doctrines, institutions, and decisions of the positive law. (LF 957)[4]

The justification of law is in its letting its content be determined by its form, i.e. by its nature, by its distinctive and essential properties.

All this is extremely obscure, and we will have to spend some time trying to unravel Weinrib's meaning. One lesson is, however, clear. For Weinrib, the rule of law is not one political ideal among many. It does not compete with liberty, equality, fairness, justice, efficiency, and other ideals, nor is it to be understood as standing alongside them. It is the one and only virtue of the law. To understand it we should do no more than understand the nature of law, and to respect it we should do no less than let the essential nature of law unravel itself unhindered in its institutions and doctrines. The theory of the rule of law is simply the theory of law.

2.2. *Form and Content*

What could Weinrib mean when he says that the law is intrinsically intelligible because it can and should be understood through its essential properties? How else can the law be understood? Is there a way of understanding what chairs are which does not involve understanding that they are items of furniture made to sit on (both essential characteristics of chairs)? Can one get to know what chairs are by learning that some are owned by me and that some are green (both accidental properties of chairs)? If that is what the intrinsic intelligibility of law means it is such a truistic idea that one wonders why Weinrib feels that he is a lonely voice in putting it forward.[5]

The answer is that Weinrib's uniqueness is in how much he thinks can be learnt from the essential features of law. Contrast Weinrib with other legal philosophers who had a view about the nature of law, for example H. Kelsen or H.L.A. Hart. They tried to understand the essential properties of law in terms of concepts such as the basic norm, or the unity of primary and secondary rules, but they did not believe that such an understanding helps to answer questions about the content of tort law, or of the doctrines which should figure in it. Weinrib, as we saw, has much higher hopes of the distinctive and essential properties of law. For him the essence of law dictates (all or much of) its content.

[L]aw has a content that is not imported from without but elaborated from within. . . . The paradigmatic legal function is not the manufacturing of legal norms but the understanding of what is intimated by juridical arrangements and relationships. (LF 956)

Weinrib thinks that this conclusion follows from the fact that an essentialist approach is inconsistent with an instrumentalist view of the law.

The central issue in the modern debate is whether law is to be understood in instrumental or non-instrumental terms. Only in so far as law is conceived as non-instrumental can law be insulated from the purposes which might be projected on it by political and economic interest. (RL 61)

The rejection of instrumentalism leads to the distinction between law and politics (see LF 950) and to the conclusion that the content of law is to be determined by its distinctive and essential nature.

This was the mistake of Kelsen and Hart, and of Unger and Posner, and of all other legal theorists:

The dominant tendency today is to look upon the content of law from the standpoint of some external ideal that the law is to enforce or make authoritative. Implicit in contemporary scholarship is the idea that the law embodies or should embody some goal (e.g., wealth maximisation, market deterrence, liberty, utility, solidarity) that can be specified apart from the law and can serve as the standard by which law is to be assessed. Thus law is regarded as an instrument for forwarding some independently desirable purpose given to it from outside.

The external relation which these scholars believe exists between law and the content it comes to have reflects their positivist understanding of law. In the positivist conception, a legal reality is brought into existence by an act of will that transforms into law that which is otherwise not law. The content of law as such is only the product of some law-creating act. (LF 955)

All legal norms, even those elaborated by judges, depend on the meta-morphosis into law of material that is originally non-legal. (LF 956)

As against this Weinrib explains that

law is constituted by thought: . . . Law is identical to the ideas of which it is comprised, and the intelligibility of law lies in grasping the order and connectedness of these ideas. (LF 962)

Law, for Weinrib, is not to be confused with 'positive law':

The positive law may provide only a defective rendering of the juridical significance of what happened. Similarly, a juridical relationship is not defined historically or sociologically in terms of the development of this positive law or of the societal considerations that sustain it. The juridical nature of a relationship refers . . . to a paradigmatically legal mode of intelligibility that goes beyond the physical, the positive, the historical, or the sociological. (LF 957–8)[6]

We have then a body of allegedly interlocking propositions.

(1) The distinctive and essential properties of law determine its content.

(2) Its content is not, nor should it be, determined by an attempt to implement political ideals such as welfare, liberty, equality, or solidarity.

(3) Its content is not determined by law-making activities of political or judicial bodies.

(4) The law is not to be identified with positive law. While sophisticated positive law attempts to work out what the law is and to give it effect (see LF 957) it may go wrong, and be at odds with the law.

We can see in these propositions the shadow of several of the ideas commonly associated with the rule of law. It is an ideal which the law of this state or that can flout. It derives from the essential properties of law, and conformity to it assures that people are governed by law and not by man. Moreover, the ideal protects people from being ruled by politics. Instead they are, to the extent that the ideal is observed, ruled by law alone.

2.3. *The Argument against Instrumentalism*

So much for an initial presentation of Weinrib's position. What arguments support it? As we saw, Weinrib believes that propositions 1–4 follow from the fact that the law is to be understood through its distinctive and essential properties. Since this assumption is itself a logical truth[7] we can accept it and look for the argument based on it. It is presented by Weinrib as a two-stage argument:

The second consequence of the connection between law and the immanent intelligibility of form is that legal form is inherently non-instrumental. [The first stage:] An instrument can be understood only by reference to the purpose it serves. The instrument's intelligibility lies outside itself in the end toward which the instrument is a means. Therefore, to the extent that juridical relationships can be seen in the light of their underlying forms and thus by reference to themselves, there is no need to grasp them instrumentally. . . .

[The second stage:] The mere possibility of a non-instrumental understanding renders instrumental understandings of the same legal material superfluous, but not vice versa. This follows from the paradigmatic quality of immanent intelligibility. Instrumental understandings are by their nature imperfect. They first transfer the burden of intelligibility from the subject of the inquiry to the external end this subject serves and then, in turn, require that end to be grasped somehow, presumably by reference to some further external end. Unless this endless shifting of ends can be arrested at a point of non-instrumental stability, the understanding is caught in a game of musical chairs, in which it seems to know everything only because it knows nothing. (LF 964–5)

To start with the second stage, the point embedded in it is cogent, but it does not at all support the conclusion it is adduced to support. It is true that while we have instruments to make, maintain, or protect, other instruments, the point of having any instrument is that it is hoped that it will serve ends which are, at least in part, valued intrinsically. This does not show, however, that the possibility of a non-instrumental understanding of the law makes it unnecessary to understand it instrumentally, or is a reason against so understanding it. The point is simple. If it is possible to understand something instrumentally this is because such an understanding is true and contributes to the understanding of its nature. Since there are things, and institutions, which are both intrinsically and instrumentally desirable we will not understand them unless we realize their dual nature.

The more serious flaw in the argument is in its first stage. It rests on nothing more than a metaphor gone wild. Throughout his discussion Weinrib uses metaphors invoking images of internality/externality. Their insistent repetition makes them the dominant theme of Weinrib's writings. Yet these are, at root, spatial metaphors, with no fixed non-spatial reference. They are used to invoke a contrast depending on context (for example, the deed is external to the thought, but the end is external to the deed). Weinrib provides an account of what the form of a thing is. It is its distinctive essential properties (see above). Immanent rationality and related expressions are then to be understood as referring to understanding what something is through understanding its form, i.e. its distinctive essential properties. If so then it is simply false that an 'instrument's intelligibility lies outside itself'. Moreover this is logically false. The intelligibility of anything lies in its essential properties and they are, for so Weinrib chose to employ the metaphor, internal to it. The form of a chair is (in part) that it is used to sit on. You may say, if you like, that it is immanent (internal) to instruments that their form includes an external end. In the previous sentence the metaphor is used in two ways in one sentence. To say as Weinrib does that because of this instruments cannot be immanently understood, is to confuse these two uses of the metaphor. He concludes that instruments do not have essential properties, because their essential properties include their being meant to be used for some end. This is worse than a *non sequitur*. It is incoherent.

Since instruments have forms it does not follow from the fact that the law has a form that it is not an instrument. If it may be no more than an instrument it may be that it ought so to be understood (that that is its immanent rationality) for things are to be understood as they are.

2.4. *The Argument from Justice*

The demise of the anti-instrumentalist argument does not show that the anti-instrumentalist thesis is mistaken. We need an independent argument to establish what is the form of the law, and it may establish Weinrib's conclusions. The most general feature of law is that 'juridical relationships are paradigmatically those that obtain between parties regarded as external to each other, each with separate interests of mine and thine'. (LF 977)[8] Two forms govern the possibility of understanding external relations between people. They are the forms of corrective and distributive justice:

Corrective and distributive justice are the forms that are immanent to the understanding of transactions and distributions. As patterns of interpersonal ordering they exhibit the nature of rationality in their respective types of arrangement and do not refer to some external purpose towards which these arrangements ought to be oriented. Each pattern represents a different mode of coherence for external relationships. Corrective justice treats the transaction between the doer and sufferer as a unity that can find juridical expression in the sum that the defendant must transfer to the successful plaintiff. Distributive justice treats the distribution as a unity that integrates the benefit or burden to be distributed, the persons who might be subject to it, and the criterion according to which the distribution takes place. Since the law, as an ordering of external relationships, is directive of transactions and distributions in accordance with their immanent intelligibility, the content of law is required to be an adequate realization of these forms of justice. (LF 982)

Adjudication of private disputes can be understood as the actualisation of corrective justice, and the legislative and administrative direction of the community as the pursuit of distributive justice. (Ibid.)

The forms of justice are the most abstract and inclusive representations of the kinds of unity that can be expressed in juridical relationships. (LF 985)

Thus all aspects of the law are covered by one or other of the forms of justice, which are therefore the forms of the law.[9] It may be disappointing that the search for the form of law ends up with two forms of different aspects of the law.[10] But this need not matter. The important thing is that each form determines the content of some aspects of the law, and that neither of them serves an external purpose.

They exhibit the nature of rationality in their respective types of arrangement and do not refer to some external purpose towards which these arrangements ought to be oriented. (LF 985)

Or do they? When we turn to Weinrib's discussion of distributive justice we discover that politics has a major role to play.

In distributive justice, by contrast, the relation between persons is mediated by the criterion that assigns things to them in accordance with a proportional equality. The whole complex of persons, things, and criterion is an expression of a particular mediating purpose. Because it mediates, this purpose is not immediate to the relationship of person to person but is brought to bear upon them from outside. The intelligibility of this purpose is thus extrinsic to the relationship of person to person as such. (LF 988)

A particular distribution is the product of political institutions that have the capacity and authority to evaluate the full range of possible distributions, and that are accountable for their choices from among those possibilities. . . . The authorisation of some distributions and the rejection of others involve decisions about the interests of all members of the community. Those responsible for these decisions should correspondingly be answerable to all. (LF 989)

Distributive justice implies that a political authority must define and particularize the scope or criterion of any scheme of distribution. This selection cannot be completely insulated from the interplay of power, persuasion, sympathy, and interest that characterises the political process. The purpose of a specific distribution is not elaborated from within distributive justice, but must be authoritatively incorporated into the schedule of collective aims. (LF 989–90)

Distributions have a two-fold intelligibility, facing outward to the extrinsic purposes that they serve and inward to the form they embody. (LF 992)

These statements appear to contradict all four theses which set the foundations for Weinrib's philosophy of law, and for his understanding of the rule of law. The content of law, inasmuch as it displays the form of distributive justice, is determined not by its form, but by politics, by political action whose function is to do precisely what Weinrib in other parts of the article denied it should do, i.e. make the law serve an extrinsic purpose, subject it to the rough and tumble of political debate, to the clash of interests in the society. 'The dominant tendency today' which looks 'upon the content of law from the standpoint of some external ideal that the law is to enforce or make authoritative. . . . that the law . . . should embody some goal (e.g. wealth maximisation, market deterrence, liberty, utility, solidarity) that can be specified apart from the law . . . [so that] law is regarded as an instrument for forwarding some independently desirable purpose', turns out to be right after all. Finally, the observations quoted about lawmakers and administrators being accountable to the electorate suggest that the forms of justice do not govern those aspects of public law that regulate the distribution of power in society. The ideals of democratic accountability that Weinrib gives voice to are not derived by him from either form of justice. They appear at this point as *dei ex machina*. Is there any way of reconciling the subservience of law to politics and its independence of it, both proclaimed by Weinrib?

3. THE FORMAL MORALITY OF LAW

3.1. *Form as Constraint*

Weinrib's doctrine as presented above identifies the rule of law with the rule of the form of law. The rule of law is observed when the form of law is allowed to dictate its content, which is thus internally determined, has nothing to do with any external purpose, and is therefore insulated from any political influences. The common understanding of the ideal of the rule of law is radically different. It regards the rule of law as a constraint on its content. On the common understanding the law should serve many external purposes. But it should also conform to the rule of law. Often that requirement is regarded as a constraint on the legitimacy of the law pursuing any other purpose. No purpose may be pursued by law in a way which violates the rule of law.

There is a good deal of textual support for attributing this view to Weinrib. At times he says not that the law has only an internal end, and that it is a mistake to think that it should serve an external one, but that

[f]ormalism abstracts from any substantive goal to the coherent ensemble of features into which that goal might fit. . . . Without disputing the legitimacy of politics the formalist insists that the product of politics live up to the conception of justificatory coherence that is immanent to it. (LF 973–4)

Here the form of justice does not supplant politics. It merely constrains it. Law has to comply with the form of justice first, and only within the bounds allowed by such compliance may it serve external, political goals. This reading is supported by various other texts which can be read as saying no more than that the form of law constrains its content. For example, in the sentence quoted at the beginning of section 2 above the resounding declaration 'The Rule of Law claims that law can be its own end' is followed by the more qualified 'and that certain content can be rejected as incompatible with law's inner nature'. Conformity to the rule of law is therefore a necessary condition for a law to be acceptable. It does not determine its content, i.e. the form of law does not determine the content of law.

How much of Weinrib's text has to be withdrawn in order to make all his statements compatible with this understanding? Remarkably little. (Almost) all we have to do is to understand that when Weinrib talks of the law he does not refer to the law, but to the concept of law. So, for example, when he says 'law has a content that is not imported from without but elaborated from within' (LF 956, see above) he means that the concept of law has a content which is not elaborated from without. Similarly, his repeated reference to the internal intelligibility of law means nothing more than the internal intelligibility of the concept of law.[11]

Not all of Weinrib's remarks can be reread in this way to make his theory consistent on the point under discussion. For example, his observations about legal positivism (LF 955, quoted above) can be so reread only at the cost of suggesting that Kelsen, Hart, Posner, and others think not that the law should be used to implement moral ideals, but that the concept of law should so be used. As this is obvious nonsense Weinrib's criticism of 'the dominant tendency today' cannot be salvaged and has to be abandoned.

Still, one may think that this reinterpretation has much to recommend it. Not only does it leave most of Weinrib's text intact, and consistent, it also brings it closer to the conventional understanding of the rule of law as a moral constraint on its content. But things are not that simple. It was noted above that merely saying that understanding the concept of law is a matter of understanding its essential properties is a truth not disputed by much of the philosophy that Weinrib identifies with 'the dominant tendency today'. It seems an affirmation of a logical point too thin to sustain any substantive conclusions. Why does Weinrib think that it is the crucial, much neglected, key to the understanding of law? When the question was posed at the beginning of this chapter the reply was that the special feature of Weinrib's view is that the concept of law determines its content. Now this reply has been withdrawn as inconsistent with his discussion of distributive justice. What, of substance, does Weinrib tell us? The temptation is to revise the first answer by toning it down: Weinrib claims, the revision suggests, that the concept of law partially determines its content, that is, the content of law must conform to the concept of law.

But the revised interpretation does not seem to save Weinrib from the charge of triviality. Think, for example, of a play that Jane has written last year. In what sense is the content of her book determined by having to exhibit the essential properties of a play? One may want to say this does not determine the content of the book. After all there are lots of books that are not plays. Books do not have to be plays. That a book exhibits the essential properties of a play makes it into a play. Otherwise it would be something else, an autobiography, or a novel, or a legal textbook, etc. All we can say is that if the book is a play then it has the properties of a play. It is only in this sense that its content is determined by being a play. If it is a play then it is a play. It is very misleading to describe this by saying that the form of a play determines in part the content of the book that Jane has written. Instead we should say that we can tell something about the content of the book if we know that it is a play. It is true that if Jane desires to write a play she succeeds only if she writes one, i.e. writes a book which has the necessary properties of a play. But here it is her desire which determines the content of the book, not the form of the play.

Applied to law these remarks mean that it is misleading to say that the form of the law partially determines its content. But if all we can say is that a system of social control (e.g. international law, or canon law) which does not have the form of law is not law, then how can the form of law pose an ideal, the ideal of the rule of law, that all law should conform to? If it is part of the form of the law then law conforms to it, or it would not be law. Nothing that is not law need conform to it since it is not its form, but the form of the law.

To recap: there is nothing much to be learnt from the obvious point that everything has the essential properties which make it a thing of the kind it is (or the thing it is). The special feature of Weinrib's view is not in his claim that to understand the nature of law one has to understand its essential qualities. It is in the fact that he regards those essential qualities as setting an ideal for the law. They are not properties every legal system has; rather, they are properties that every legal system should have. This cannot be part of the very notion of an essence or a form. If the form of the law determines the content of law in any non-misleading sense this can only mean that it sets an ideal for the law to live up to, and this must be a result of the particular content of that form. That is, the special feature of Weinrib's view is his belief that the form of the law is essentially moral. Its form is the immanent morality of the law. To examine that possibility we should explore the sense in which the form of law can be normative.

3.2. *The Normativity of Form*

In what way could the fact that a normative characteristic is part of the essence of law partly determine its content? Assume that it is of the essence of human beings that they are bipeds and that they ought to be truthful. As argued above, the straightforward sense in which these properties determine what humans are is that if we know that an animal is human we can infer that it is a biped. There is nothing wrong or defective in an animal not being a biped. This does not show that it does not conform to the essence of humanity, except in the trivial sense that it shows that it is not human. It may be a dog, or a swallow. Similarly, on the above assumption, if it is false that a certain animal ought to be truthful it follows that it is not a human animal, and there is nothing wrong or deficient about it just because it need not be truthful. If an animal is a human animal then it follows, on our assumption that it ought to be truthful. There is therefore something wrong if such an animal is not truthful. Similarly it may be of the essence of the state that it ought to be just. If so then the essence of the state sets an ideal for all states to live up to.

Is Weinrib saying something similar about the law? One reason to think that he is is that if he is not then, by the previous arguments, his theory does not seem to make any sense.[12] Other reasons concern his embrace of Unger's term 'the immanent morality of the law', his claim that the form of law is (identical with) the form of justice, clearly a moral notion, and his clear statement that the form of law is 'a single justificatory structure' (LF 970) that the law (positive law, to use Weinrib's term) should, but may fail, to conform to. He protests that

the objection that an account in terms of form is inherently apologetic . . . misses the radically critical lever that an internal understanding makes available. (LF 975)

He illustrates this critical lever by using his understanding of tort law to criticize the loss-spreading and the deterrence and compensation rationales of tort law, and their applications, where they deviate from the ones consistent with tort law's true form. He rejects as inconsistent with the form of tort law doctrines of strict liability.[13]

All this makes it amply clear that the form of law for Weinrib is a normative property, it is that the law ought to conform to justice. But is it a moral ought? Again the talk of the morality of law and of justice suggest that it is. In his explicit discussion of the moral nature of the legal form Weinrib is anxious to claim that the moral ideals he has argued for are not political.[14] But he clearly asserts their moral character:

What . . . is the moral force of these forms? For clearly they must have a moral dimension if the law is required to conform to their structure. (LF 995)

It is not obvious what question Weinrib can have in mind. We can ask what makes a particular legal system just, but can we also ask what makes justice just? Can we ask what makes justice moral? Or why one should be just if one ought to be just? There is of course the question whether it is the case that the law ought to be just. For Weinrib this is the question of whether it is the form of law that it ought to be just. But that is not the issue he is raising in the quotation above. His concern is yet again to show how the metaphors of immanence and internality apply to the form of law understood as a moral idea. One might have thought that the answer is obvious. Justice is the form of law, and justice is internally desirable for it is not desirable as a means for some other end. Justice itself is a virtue, an intrinsic good. But that is not Weinrib's answer.

[T]heir moral force must come from the very integration of immanence and intelligibility in a juridical relationship. (LF 996)

This sentence is very obscure. In Weinrib's text it refers not to justice, i.e. to the form of law, as I suggested. Rather the moral force here explained is said to be that of 'juridical relationships'. If a juridical relationship is something like that I hit you over the head, i.e. performed a tortious act, then it does not seem to have any moral force. If it is that I have a legal right of way over your land then it too may lack moral force, for if the law fails to be just as it ought to be, my having such a legal right may be itself immoral. So I think that the moral force here explained should be understood to be that of the form of the law. It was the form of the law that Weinrib discussed in the preceding paragraphs. But how could the 'integration of immanence and intelligibility' (whatever that may mean) explain the moral force of the form of law, i.e. of justice? How can anything explain the moral force of justice?[15] Later on Weinrib says

For the formalist, corrective and distributive justice are normative not because something else makes them normative, but because they constitute the essential nature of normativity with respect to the external relationships of persons. (LF 996)

This virtually amounts to saying that justice is normative because this is its nature, which is the right answer, uninformative though it is. The reference to the 'very integration of immanence and intelligibility' may mean nothing more. But I suspect that it does, or at least that it connects through verbal association with one of the most elusive of Weinrib's thoughts.

While Weinrib thinks that justice is the form of law and therefore that it is a necessary truth that the law ought to be just, he never expresses the thought in anything like this way. When actually applying, in the abstract or through examples, his basic idea to the analysis of law he repeatedly refers to unjust laws not as such but as deviations from the intelligible form of the law, and condemns them not for being immoral but for lack of intelligibility, for confusion or incoherence. I will give only a couple out of many possible examples:

[Talking of the cost-spreading rationale for tort law:] For the formalist these defenses are unsatisfactory because of their *incoherent* joinder of the doctrinal and the institutional. (LF 971)

Holding the legal content to its immanent form allows an assessment, in its own terms, of the legal system's congratulatory self-understanding. The determinations of the legal system can be adjudged *confused or mistaken* to the extent that they are inadequate expressions of the underlying form. Thus arises a form of criticism that is decisive precisely because it is internal. (LF 975)

These examples provide two of the three rational explanations of Weinrib's reluctance to invoke moral terms in his discussion of law. The first, and most important one, does not find explicit expression anywhere, but seems to me to be implied by much that is said by Weinrib. The emphasis on coherence and intelligibility suggests a normativity deeper than the moral, the normativity of the rational. We ought to be rational. This ought is fundamental, but not in any obvious sense moral. This point contradicts Weinrib's identification of the normativity of his legal form as moral. His association of the normativity of the form of law with the normativity of rationality is none the less real enough, and it helps explain his unease about the moral force of his legal form.[16] The second reason, expressed in the second quotation above, is that Weinrib connects the fact that failure to conform to the form of law is a case of imperfect intelligibility, of confusion or incoherence, with the explanation of why conformity to the form of law is a value or a requirement which takes precedence over all other values. The third reason, intimated in the first quotation above, is that the emphasis on coherence shows that the law has the form it has because it has the institutions it has, and because it employs the basic concepts that it does. Let us consider these points in turn.

3.3. *Intelligibility and Conflict*

The thought that there could be something more (or other) than a moral defect in a legal system which is less than completely just is suggested by the claim that any such system does not conform to the form of law. Does not this make it incoherent, less than completely intelligible? Does it not signify a failure of rationality on the part of such a legal system?

I want to put on one side any doubt as to whether legal systems, rather than people or other animals, can be rational or irrational. Somebody may argue that to say that a legal system is irrational (rather than to say that a judge or a legislator, or perhaps a commentator, makes irrational remarks about it or irrationally enacts certain laws) is like saying that sun spots are irrational rather than that someone said something irrational about them. Putting this difficulty, which may well be solvable, on one side, we can turn to the main difficulty. It is not clear that a less than just law (or even an unjust one) is less than completely intelligible, nor that it is incoherent. Intelligibility relates to the ability to be understood. Unintelligible speech is speech which cannot be understood. But unjust laws are, often, perfectly well understood. This is reflected in comments on them by their supporters and by their critics alike. It may be reflected in the actions of those who implement them and those who suffer by them. Whatever test of understanding one employs there is no reason to think that unjust laws are as such unintelligible. Nor is there any reason to think that they are incoherent. There can be coherent injustice. To be effectively unjust a law must be both coherent and intelligible to a high degree.

Weinrib may protest that the incoherence he has in mind is between a statute or a judicial decision and the form of law. But remember what that means. The form of law is that it ought to be just; there is nothing in the offending statute or judicial decision which is at odds with that. There is nothing in them which denies, conflicts with, or contradicts that the law ought to be just. All that was established is that an unjust statute or an unjust decision exists. That makes them, and the law, morally imperfect, or worse. But it does not make them incoherent, nor does it make them unintelligible or confused, though they may be all that on other grounds.

Compare the case of the law with the case of an unjust person. Imagine that Robin is unjust. This makes neither him nor his unjust actions confused, incoherent, or unintelligible. But, one may say, is not the difference that it is not the form of Robin, nor that of human beings generally, to be just. This invites two responses. Is it true and does it matter? Take the second question first. Assume that it is an essential property of human beings that they ought to be just. It is, let us assume, only an accidental property of Robin that he ought to be a devoted chairman of the company he is chairman of. It is a contingent property of his because it is only contingent that he is chairman of that company, and that it deserves to be conscientiously managed (it would not deserve that, for example, if it is grossly immoral, and its immorality infects its shareholders and employees). Does it follow that Robin is incoherent when he acts unjustly but (merely) immoral when he fails in his duty to his company? There is nothing to suggest that. The fact that the duty of justice is essential to him as a human being, whereas his duty as a company manager is not tells us that under no circumstances will he be free from his duty of justice, whereas he can be free from his duty as company manager, for example by losing that position. It has no bearing on the coherence or intelligibility of Robin's failings.

Turn now to the other question. Is it essential to human beings that they ought to be just? Perhaps not, after all it is not true that babies ought to be just (though it may be essential that the human being who is this baby be a just human being). Possibly it is not true that the severely insane, or the comatose, or people suffering from advanced dementia, ought to be just. If so then perhaps we should say that persons essentially ought to be just, or that moral agents have the essential property that they ought to be just. The point I am trying to bring out is that there is nothing remarkable in the claim that justice is an essential property of beings of a certain kind. One may venture the following generalization: everyone who ought to be just belongs to at least one class which has the essential property of having to be just. This does not mean that it is a trivial thing to say that the law ought to be just. But it may be trivial to say that not only is it the case that the law ought to be just but it is necessary that it ought to.

Weinrib's thought that it is otherwise is tied up with the second reason for the emphasis on coherence and intelligibility mentioned above. Because the requirement to be just is of the essence of law it overrides any other value with which it may conflict (e.g. solidarity, fraternity, liberty, equality, welfare). The form of law issues an implicit demand 'to the positive law . . . that overrides any extrinsic political purpose' (LF 996) and any other moral value.[17] But this view is without foundation. Whether a moral requirement arises essentially or not tells us of the considerations which give rise to it. It implies nothing about its stringency or importance. It may be of the essence of corporations that they ought to maximize profits, and it may be only contingently true of corporations that they ought not to sell weapons to the IRA.[18] It does not follow that a corporation should sell weapons to the IRA if doing so maximizes its profits.

Some people maintain that a legal system that does not adequately promote the welfare of its subjects, does not adequately enhance and protect their liberty, etc., cannot be just. They regard justice as applied to the law not as one virtue it may possess among many, but as its resultant virtue. The just law is like the morally good person. It is the law which possesses to the right degree all the virtues which the law should possess. On this view too justice is never overridden by any other values. But on this view it never conflicts with them either. If one regards justice as one virtue among many that the law should possess, as Weinrib obviously does, then the fact that it is the essential virtue of the law does not show that it is an overriding virtue.

Is there any insight to be gained from the claim that it is of the essence of law that it ought to be just? I pointed out above that the third reason that Weinrib refers to failures of justice in the law as failures of coherence is that he believes that there is an institutional foundation for the identification of the form of the law. The starting-point is the isolation of features found in positive law, which are 'Archimedean points in legal consciousness' (LF 967). These are points such as that private law deals with transactions in which people causally interact, or that public law deals with the distribution of things to persons. On various occasions he has taken pains to emphasize that he does not recommend the perpetuation of tort law with its form of corrective justice. He is merely holding that so long as we have courts judging transactions between two persons corrective justice is the form of tort law, because the courts are no good at giving effect to distributive schemes, etc.[19]

Again, Weinrib's position warrants less than he thinks. The fact that the form of law is a requirement to be just does not depend, by his own argument, on any fact other than that the law regulates external behaviour. Justice is the essential virtue of any such regulation, according to Weinrib.[20] Of course, while it is virtually impossible to think of human society existing without there being a need to regulate external behaviour, it may be possible for that regulation not to involve the existence of law. Short of that, however, there is little specific institutional support in any fundamental concepts that we have for the claim that justice is the form of law. Weinrib is thinking primarily of the possibility of replacing tort law as relating to accidents with a scheme of national insurance against accidents. Doing this will be a major change in the law. But it will not make corrective justice inapplicable or redundant. It will merely redefine its sphere of application to the relations between individuals and the insurance agency. I do not think that these comments contain anything that Weinrib would disagree with. I am merely emphasizing that the Archimedean points that Weinrib talks about concern the application of the doctrine of justice, which on any theory of justice depends on empirically contingent factors. They do nothing to support the essential claim that the law ought to be just, and to conform to both corrective and distributive justice.

3.4. *More on Coherence and Intelligibility*

The remarks in the preceding section were critical of the role of coherence in Weinrib's work. They are not meant to deny that he lays much store by this idea. His very notion of a form is not just that of the distinctive and essential properties of the thing whose form it is. The form of a thing is its distinctive essential properties as they form a coherent whole. He emphasizes again and again the tendency to generalize, to subsume forms of parts of the law under the general form of the law, and the tendency to integrate, to find the whole which apparently discrete properties may be elements of.[21]

If there is a genuine difference between a hybrid and a single whole, then the claim that the form of the law is not an assembly of essential properties but a coherent whole is far from a logical truth. In fact there is no reason to think that it is true at all. The virtues that it is of the essence of the law that it should possess, like the virtues of people, may form an irreducible plurality. The morally good person is just the person who possesses the moral virtues to a sufficient degree.[22] Since the moral virtues are irreducibly many moral goodness is not a distinctive virtue. It is merely a resultant judgement that the person concerned does not lack any of them. The fact that being morally good is not having any distinctive virtue to be put alongside the others is manifest in the fact that the morally good may vary in their virtues. There is no one right proportion of generosity, truthfulness, integrity, sensitivity, courage, etc. which makes one a good person. There are good people who are good by excelling in some virtues at the expense of others. Others excel in a different set of virtues. Is the same true of the virtues possession of which is required of the law, by its very nature? There is no a priori reason to think otherwise. Could one argue that the law is like an artefact, like a knife or a chair, and artefacts have one coherent virtue? In many ways the law is unlike an artefact (as Weinrib will be the first to insist), and artefacts may have several essential purposes (e.g. to adorn and to keep one warm).

Weinrib's own discussion gives one no reason to be confident about the coherence of justice. It seems to be a resultant virtue, just like moral goodness, even if it is not a comprehensive resultant virtue, i.e. even if it does not encompass all the virtues the law should possess. He emphasizes that

because the forms of justice represent mutually irreducible conceptions of coherence for juridical relationships, no single juridical relationship can coherently combine the two forms. If a corrective element is mixed with a distributive one, each necessarily undermines the justificatory force of the other, and the relationship cannot manifest either unifying structure. (LF 984, see also 996)

Of course the law is not a single juridical relationship. But there is nothing which blends the combination of the different forms of justice into one virtue of justice except that they are two different ways of being just.[23] I conclude that the rejection of irreducible pluralism is neither a condition of intelligibility nor a moral desideratum, and that there is no reason to think that an explanation can be given of the law which is not pluralistic in nature.[24]

4. THE INNER COLLAPSE OF FORMALISM

4.1. *The Role of the Courts*

The argument up to this point has been sufficiently long and complex to justify pausing to take stock. I offered two readings of Weinrib. On the first and most natural reading of his most general theoretical statements the essential properties of law determine its content. The rule of law, according to this reading, consists in positive law manifesting to the highest degree the nature of the ideal of law. That is, the rule of law triumphs when the content of positive law is determined by the form of law. This reading is flatly contradicted by Weinrib's analysis of the role of distributive justice in the law.[25]

A second reading of Weinrib was then found, according to which the essential properties of law only partly determine its content. We saw that what Weinrib means is that the essential properties of the law are moral properties. They determine the content of law in the sense that it ought to be moral in the way appropriate to the law. Once understood in this way Weinrib's theory is seen to contain little that was ever disputed by any serious theory of law.[26] Weinrib's uniqueness is in claiming (1) that essential moral requirements take priority over any other moral requirements; (2) that failure to meet them is a failure of coherence and intelligibility; and (3) that the only moral quality the law should possess in virtue of its nature is justice. It was argued that the first two propositions are false and the third is either a tautology which undermines Weinrib's own position (if justice is the resultant virtue of all the virtues which apply to the law) or unsubstantiated by Weinrib. This undermines the second interpretation of Weinrib's views on the rule of law according to which they are a constraint on the law, i.e. that whatever other value it should pursue it should do so only inasmuch as this is consistent with the requirement of its form to be just.

It is true that much that he writes is entirely untouched by anything said so far. But most of it concerns his moral theory, his understanding of justice, and not his theory of law. Still, one may well feel that the account of Weinrib's views given so far leaves out an important element. It does not take account of Weinrib's doctrine concerning the role of the courts. Weinrib has a good deal to say about the role of the courts. When taken as part of the second interpretation (the form of law as a constraint on its content) it makes it a much more substantial and challenging doctrine, even after the second interpretation is cleansed of the confusions criticized in the previous section.

Weinrib's view of adjudication is encapsulated in an important thesis:

> Thesis of Judicial Duty: Judges should always decide in a way which is consistent with the forms of justice.[27]

This thesis is derived from another:

> Thesis of Judicial Special Role: The special role of the courts is to articulate the juridical, to bring out the intelligible form in any transaction or distribution.

These theses give legal teeth to the claim that justice is the form of law. They apply both to corrective and to distributive justice:

The forms' [of justice] immanence to the understanding of the interactions they govern means that officials charged with explicating the juridical—in our legal culture, pre-eminently judges—can treat the ordering of an interaction as an interpretive function in which they draw out the juridical significance of the features that unify the interaction from within. Adjudication involves holding the particular transaction or distribution to its coherence as a transaction or a distribution. . . . The judge's role is to apply, in the context of a particular episode of adjudication, the form of justice appropriate to it. (LF 987)

In the case of corrective justice this means that the courts should derive their conclusion from the nature of the transaction between the parties before it:

Corrective justice does not, therefore, refer merely to an official act of dispute settlement; rather, the court's intervention is intelligible as specifying what is implicit in the relationship that already exists between the parties. (LF 980)

In the case of distributive justice the courts should enforce the scheme of distribution adopted through the legislative process to the extent that doing so is compatible with observing the form of distributive justice. Distributive justice requires that things be distributed among persons in accordance with a consistent scheme.

As expositors of the juridical, judges have a legitimate role in developing the notions of personhood and equality. Although judicial review does not allow the substitution of the court's preferred distribution for the one laid down by the authoritative political organ, a court can insist that, in setting up and executing a scheme of distributive justice, political authority not treat persons as things or violate the equality of persons under the distributional criterion. Juridical activity of this sort does not encroach on the prerogatives of the political organ; it only insists that the favoured distributions conform to their own intelligible form. (LF 991–2)

This is a very far-reaching claim. Of course, Weinrib does not say that that is what the courts always do or that they always try to do so. Positive law may deviate from the form of the law. But he is here making a much more radical claim than the one we examined in the previous section. His thesis here is not merely that the law ought to be just, nor only that the courts ought to see to it that it is just. He is putting forward the proposition that in all legal systems the courts have a *legal duty* to enforce the form of justice. This is a universal legal duty which courts have in all legal systems, regardless of the content of their positive law. Here he is claiming not merely that positive law may be out of step with the form of law. Here he is arguing that when it is it should be disregarded by the courts, that the courts have a legal duty to disregard the positive law when it fails to conform to the form of the law.

Two examples will illustrate the radical nature of this claim. Imagine that Parliament passes legislation which adopts the loss-spreading rationale and makes it the principle which governs all cases of litigation arising out of accident. It purports to impose a legal duty on the courts to follow the cost-spreading rationale. However, according to Weinrib appearances are misleading. In

fact the statute is not legally binding, and the courts remain
under the unalterable legal duty to disregard cost-spreading
considerations and follow the corrective justice doctrine which is
implicit in the form of law. Imagine further that Parliament
passes legislation which legalizes and regulates surrogacy. It
makes, let us imagine, both contracts for adoption concluded
prior to conception and the remuneration they specify enforcible
in law. According to Weinrib, the courts have authority to
examine the legislation in light of the form of distributive justice,
and if they come to the correct conclusion that it violates it by
treating persons (babies) as things they have a legal duty to
disobey the statute. Moreover, they have such legal duty not only
in countries such as the USA in which courts possess powers of
constitutional review, but also in countries such as Britain in
which one of the most fundamental constitutional principles
asserts the supremacy of Parliamentary legislation.[28]

Weinrib criticizes various writers who,

[p]ointing to the courts' relative lack of institutional competence and
democratic accountability . . . have demarcated legitimate court activity
by reference to two considerations. First, the courts' role is anchored by
the preexisting body of rules, standards, policies and principles . . .
second, the courts are expected to distance themselves from the realm of
'current political controversy'. (LF 986)

Their 'considerations are insufficiently grounded'. The features
which determine the role of the courts are

conceptual rather than contingent. They refer not to what may come
within the purview of judicial or legislative treatment in a given
jurisdiction, but to the elements of structure that mark the intelligibility
of external interaction among persons generally. (LF 986)

This aspect of Weinrib's views may lead one to reconsider the
second interpretation of this theory which was adopted above. It
may be thought to support the view that when he talks of 'the
law' he really refers to the law rather than to the concept of the
law. But this interpretation cannot be supported. There is only
one form of the law, and since Weinrib says that the content of
the law is determined by its form, if by 'the law' he refers to the
law it follows that all legal systems are identical in content. This
is not only implausible, it is also inconsistent with his statements

about the role of politics in determining the content of the law (see LF 991, 1011). It has to be admitted that Weinrib's use of 'the law' is confusing. But the best interpretation is that 'the law' refers to the concept of law. Weinrib's thesis is, therefore, that the form of law is (1) that the law ought to be just, and (2) that the courts have a legal duty to follow the form of justice, regardless of what the rest of the law is.

The difficulty with Weinrib's claim about the legal duty of the courts is that it is entirely unsupported by his own arguments. Weinrib's reason for this claim is encapsulated in the previous quotations, which articulate what I called the thesis of the special responsibility of the courts. The law is internally intelligible only if it conforms to the form of law, i.e. only to the extent that it is just as it ought to be, and it is the job of the courts to make it intelligible. But this argument will not do. It has been pointed out above that Weinrib's discussion of the intelligibility of the law is confused.[29] Weinrib's claim that the courts have special responsibility for seeing to it that the law be just is not supported by his arguments. They contain nothing to suggest that the duty of legislators to be just is less than the parallel duty of the courts. It may be said that while all legal institutions ought to act justly, the special feature of the courts is that that is their sole duty. But first, one needs an argument to support this conclusion. Second, even if this is the case it does not follow that the courts have the right and the duty to override other laws in the name of justice.

Weinrib's theory lacks any consideration of institutional responsibility. He condemns theorists whom he dubs as legal positivists for concentrating precisely on this issue. He seems to think that the role of legal institutions follows automatically once the form of the law is established. His own discussion belies this belief. We saw above that he feels compelled to refer to the desirability of democratic institutions, with little argument and without reference to the form of law. A claim that the courts have a legal duty to override unjust democratic decisions cannot be justified without a reasoned theory of legal authority which sets the reasons for the legitimacy of the authority of democratic institutions, and the limits to their authority. Not only does Weinrib lack such a theory, he denies the need for it. Instead he seems to be saying that when courts are not ready to override unjust democratic decisions their actions lack intelligibility, and that shows that they have a legal duty to override unjust decisions. This claim feeds on the confusions nourishing his use of 'intelligibility'.

4.2. *The Formality of the Forms*

The absence of a doctrine of legal authority, and the claim that the implementation of justice is the special responsibility of the courts, undermine Weinrib's doctrine of justice as well. Since the courts have to reject any legislation which is unjust it follows that whatever the legislature decides within its proper authority is just. According to Weinrib the form of distributive justice requires that things be distributed among persons by some consistent criterion of distribution. Any scheme of distribution observing these conditions is just:

Distributive justice goes to the inner coherence of a distribution, not to the choice of one distribution over another. (LF 989)

This selection [of the scheme of distribution] cannot be completely insulated from the interplay of power, persuasion, sympathy, and interest that characterises the political process. The purpose of a specific distribution is not elaborated from within distributive justice, but must be authoritatively incorporated into the schedule of collective aims. (LF 989–90)

Any scheme which does not violate the conditions specified by Weinrib (a consistent and faithful application of a criterion for the distribution of things among people) is just or at least it is just once adopted by the relevant political authorities. Two consequences of this approach stand out. First, the role of the political is thus demoted into the choice between schemes which are either indifferent or at least governed by only secondary considerations. Second, justice, it turns out, is an easy ideal to meet. The most extreme versions of the free market, the most extreme versions of a command economy, a system distributing goods and benefits by need or one which distributes them by degrees of faithfulness to some religious ideal, or by the nobility of one's blood, are all equally just.[30]

We can see now how Weinrib's formalism collapses under its own weight. The idea that the essential properties of law determine its content leaves no room for politics. To make it plausible

Weinrib reads it to mean merely that it sets a limit to what the law may be. It only sets a necessary condition to the content the law may possess. But given that the necessary form of law is that it ought to be just this claim borders on the trivial. Of course the law ought to be just. This sets no limit to the law as even a legal system which ought to be just may be as unjust as anything can be. Weinrib salvages his theory from triviality by advancing the claim that it is also part of the form of the law that the courts have a legal duty not to apply positive law which is unjust. But this thesis veers back to the other extreme, suggesting that political decisions are thoroughly reviewable by the courts, thus again demoting politics to be the handmaiden of the courts. This conclusion Weinrib seeks to avoid by holding that justice is greatly underdetermined in the sense that many schemes of distribution are just as are many alternative solutions to claims based on grounds of corrective justice. This restores the practical importance of politics, but by making justice an easy principle to satisfy it regards politics primarily as a process of choice among a multiplicity of equally just social schemes. This leads to an impoverished notion of justice, whereby various forms of gross injustice count as justice.

Even this distortion does not save the theory from the final charge, namely that its claim that the courts have a legal duty to enforce the form of justice regardless of what institutional arrangements are made by the law of the country concerned is not only unsupported by any of his arguments, but cannot be supported by the kind of arguments he advances. It is a claim about the authority and responsibility, moral and legal, of an institution. It can only be supported by a doctrine of institutionalized authority. Weinrib not only lacks such a doctrine, the whole thrust of his theory is to prove that such a doctrine has no central role to play in a theory of law.

NOTES

1. Throughout this chapter, references to E. Weinrib, 'Legal Formalism: On the Immanent Rationality of Law', *Yale Law Journal*, 97 (1989),

949, appear in the shortened form LF. References to E. Weinrib, 'The Intelligibility of the Rule of Law', in Patrick Monahan and Allan C. Hutchinson, eds., *The Rule of Law: Ideal or Ideology?* (Toronto: Carswell, 1987) appear as RL.

Weinrib calls his theory 'formalist', but as the form of anything consists of its distinctive essential properties (LF 958–9) I will keep to the more familiar label 'essentialist'. In calling himself a formalist Weinrib has the pleasure of casting himself in the devil's role, identifying his position with the straw man castigated by generations of bad legal philosophers. He may indeed have become the sole upholder of an impossible position. But the term 'formalism', used so often in so many obscure senses, triggers involuntary responses, which cloud the argument, and is best avoided. While Weinrib believes in necessities *de re*, my own remarks about the essential properties of things in the sequel are neutral as to whether they are *de re* necessities or merely necessities *de dicto*.

2. 'Form is the ensemble of characteristics that constitute the matter in question as a unity identical to that of other matters of the same kind and distinguishable from matters of a different kind' (LF 958). It is 'the attributes so decisive of the thing's character that they can truly be said to characterise it, and this entails a differentiation between the attributes that are definitive of the thing and those that are merely incidental' (LF 959). In brief the form of the law consists of its properties without which it will not be law. Weinrib adds a coherence requirement, which will be discussed below.

3. R.M. Unger, 'The Critical Legal Studies Movement', *Harvard Law Review*, 96 (1983), 571.

4. In a footnote to the quoted sentence Weinrib remarks: 'The positive law is immanently rational to the extent that it captures and reflects the contours of rationality that are internal to the relationships that law governs.'

5. 'In current academic discussion, the avowed formalist is the missing interlocutor' (LF 950).

6. Later on Weinrib remarks of the legal forms, as analysed by Aristotle, 'Not only are these forms immanent in any sophisticated legal system, but the adequacy of the law's content to these immanent forms is the measure of that system's sophistication' (LF 977). This remark opens the possibility that the law of a particular country may, at the cost of being 'unsophisticated', deviate a good deal from the form of law. This is a puzzling thought. What is one to say of a country which finds that it has good (moral) reasons to pay the price of lack of sophistication? Is there anything wrong (morally or otherwise) in being 'unsophisticated'? Not knowing what could

count as satisfactory answers to such questions, within the general framework of Weinrib's theory, I will disregard that passage, and others suggesting sophistication as the main normative force of the forms of law, as an aberration.

7. That is, it is a logical truth that the nature of law is understood once its essential characteristics are understood. *Pace* Weinrib, understanding the nature of law may require more than understanding only its distinctive characteristics.

8. Here as in many of his other remarks Weinrib is both putting forward his own view and providing an explanation of Aristotle, for his own view is identical with his understanding of Aristotle. I will consistently avoid any issue relating to the accuracy of Weinrib's interpretation of Aristotle. Weinrib explains that 'external' refers to a relationship where 'the separateness of their interests is conceived as the defining feature of their relationship'. (LF 977 n.) As he explains, the relations between lovers are not external. The existence of large tracts of family law seems to contradict the idea that the externality of a relationship is crucial to its being subject to legal regulation. Furthermore, large tracts of public law, in reasonably just legal systems, in defining the proper relations between a citizen and the state are not dealing with areas of conflict of interest but with areas in which the interest of the citizen is in the prosperity of the state. What Weinrib overlooks is that one may need legal regulation in order to define the commonality of interest which makes the relationship non-external. But this criticism is immaterial to my argument in the text.

9. Weinrib adds a special proviso to explain how the criminal law belongs to corrective justice. I will discuss his view of constitutional and administrative litigation in Sect. 4 below. He does not address the functions of courts in probate, adoption, uncontested divorce, child-care proceedings between social services and parents, guardianship proceedings regarding the mentally retarded, or absentees, and similar aspects of the courts' jurisdiction. Nor does his discussion make clear where in his scheme belong issues such as the prohibition against using pornography, or the right to do so, the right to use contraceptives, the right to naturalize, etc. My argument in the text does not depend on these omissions.

10. Weinrib seems to have promised one form for law: 'Coherence is inherently expansive: It resists compartmentalisation and seeks to encompass as much as possible. . . . Formalism seeks to confirm the possibility that tort law, for example, is not only coherent on its own, but that the underlying contours of this coherence can be found throughout private law (and perhaps beyond). In this way, private

law as a whole might be understood as a massive expression of legal form' (LF 972). Nor can the form of law be justice, or else every thing which ought to be just will be law. It would thus follow that banks or universities or nations ought not to be just since they are not law. It follows that Weinrib never gave us more than one (or a few) of the law's essential properties.

11. Similarly when he says that 'a juridical relationship is not defined historically or sociologically in terms of the development of this positive law' (LF 957, see above) he merely means that the nature of the juridical relation as law, the aspect of it which makes it law, is not a matter of positive law but of the concept of law: 'The juridical can be defined as that which is contained within the intelligibility of external interaction' (LF 987).

12. I will argue later that he is saying more than just this. The current point is simply that this claim is part of his meaning.

13. See e.g. LF 970–3, 993. The rejection of strict liability is derived from the Kantian premisses set out in Weinrib's 'Towards a Moral Theory of Negligence', *Journal of Law and Philosophy*, 2 (1983), 37, though in that article he suggests, contrary to the later claim in 'Legal Formalism', that the Kantian conclusions do not follow from the form of justice itself. It seems that the discrepancy is accounted for by the fact that in the earlier article he used the term 'forms of justice' with a different meaning.

14. I do not wish to discuss here Weinrib's use of 'political', except to say that it is much narrower than that of those who regard law as political. There is therefore no genuine joining of issues here.

15. We can, of course, ask the general question what explains the fact that any moral quality, e.g. justice, is reason giving. But this is not Weinrib's meaning, nor is his answer an answer to this question.

16. In the passage quoted above from LF 995 he expresses himself as someone driven to concede moral force to the form of law. If it is normative, he says, doesn't it follow that it is moral as well? The implied answer is that it does. But the correct answer is that it does not. The suggestion that the normativity is the normativity of the rational is one alternative.

17. His usual fondness for the internal/external imagery leads Weinrib to attribute the overriding standing of justice to the fact that it is immanent or internal. As we saw the only meaning this has is that of being essential.

18. Once the IRA gives up terrorism the prohibition may be removed.

19. See on considerations relating to the competence of the courts LF 986, 989, 1006.

20. One may notice here that it is therefore not the form of the law at all,

according to his own definition of the term. It is not a distinctive legal virtue. The requirements of justice apply to others as well.

21. I suspect that a preference for coherence understood in something like this way, i.e. as a requirement that the law be understood as exemplifying one distinct virtue, which is not a mere amalgam of various irreducible virtues (a little liberty and a little welfare, etc.) is one of the intuitions behind Weinrib's claim that the form of the law overrides all other virtues it may display. To mix them is not merely a betrayal of essence in favour of a non-essential virtue. It is also a betrayal of coherence in favour of a hybrid. In the absence of an argument for the moral superiority of single virtue institutions over pluralistic ones Weinrib's implied invocation of such considerations is unfounded.

22. Which is not to say that he cannot become better still.

23. Weinrib also claims that they are the only two ways of being just. He never establishes this point. But in any case it does not bear on the disjointedness of the two forms of justice.

24. In one respect my account of Weinrib's position is unjust to a valuable point it includes. He claims that the fact that the law ought to be just is relevant to the way the law, even when it is less than just, is understood. Though he provides no argument in support of this point it seems to me to be right. It has been most thoroughly argued for by J. Finnis in ch. 1 of *Natural Law and Natural Rights* (Oxford: Clarendon Press, 1980), and has been endorsed by such diverse writers as Bentham and Dworkin, as well as by me.

25. Though I did not rely on this point, it is also contradicted by his analysis of the role of corrective justice.

26. Though various writers who hold the sort of view which Weinrib regards as positivist have not considered whether the fact that the law ought to be just, etc. marks an essential property of it. I have argued that it does in various publications since my book *Practical Reason and Norms* (London: Hutchinson, 1975; 2nd edn., Princeton, NJ: Princeton University Press, 1990).

27. When cautious Weinrib expresses the thesis in a more restricted way. He merely claims that given our institutional arrangements this role, which essentially exists in all legal systems, falls to the courts. Since he relies on no special features of our institutional arrangements in supporting this claim I will disregard it in the sequel. In any case he clearly regards the courts as having this role in all common law legal systems, and all the critical comments below hold good even if restricted to such systems only.

28. Correspondingly in countries with an entrenched constitution the courts have a legal duty to violate the constitution when it is unjust.

29. A further difficulty with the argument is that once it is recognized that the essential virtues the law should display by its nature do not necessarily override other virtues that it should possess then the requirement that the courts do justice at all costs seems arbitrary. Once it has been shown that justice is only one of the virtues the law should possess, there is no reason to think that it should always prevail over other virtues of the law when it conflicts with them. To claim that the courts ought always to prefer justice over other virtues the law should possess means that it is sometimes the courts' legal duty to act immorally. This conclusion is of course accepted by most of the writers whom Weinrib dubs positivist, as well as by many natural lawyers. But it is usually associated with the view that no law exists in all legal systems regardless of their positive law. If the law requires courts to act justly, regardless of the positive law, is there any reason to think that it requires them to act morally, even if this demands compromising justice on occasion?

30. See also LF 1005. His discussion of indeterminacy in the law suggests that a similar argument may be directed against his view of corrective justice. (See LF 1009–11.) But he says too little about the degree of indeterminacy that he believes to exist in cases of corrective justice to be sure that it does allow, as his account of distributive justice clearly does, for gross injustice to count as justice.

12

Why Legal Formalism

ERNEST J. WEINRIB

INTRODUCTION

Legal formalism postulates the coherence of juridical relation-ships.[1] Drawing on the connection discerned in antiquity between form and intelligibility, the formalist seeks to elucidate the forms, i.e. the coherent structures of justification, immanent in a sophisticated legal system. For the formalist, these forms go to the intelligibility of legal concepts and institutions, and they are therefore crucial to understanding the law's content. Because the forms are justificatory structures, they provide normative frame-works for legal argument. And inasmuch as they are immanent to the juridical relationships they inform, they shed light on the traditional claim of natural law theory that law is an ordering of reason.

This essay illustrates and supports these wide-ranging asser-tions by describing formalism's response to the deficiencies of contemporary legal scholarship. My exposition focuses on tort law—not on specific doctrines, but on the way in which under-standing a body of law can illuminate fundamental questions. Tort law is particularly appropriate, because it has stimulated the production of a rich and diverse theoretical literature. This essay contrasts legal formalism with the methodological presupposi-tions of much of that literature.

My discussion proceeds as follows. The first section outlines two strikingly different positions in contemporary tort theory. My argument is that these positions none the less share important methodological premises. The second section criticizes these premises and presents formalism as the cure for their defects. The third section outlines the various constituents of formalism. As we shall see at that point, formalism puts forward a certain conception of intelligibility, proposes justificatory structures that embody that conception, grounds those structures in a stringent notion of normativeness, and connects them with the concepts and institutions that characterize a sophisticated legal system. Crucial to formalism is the idea of form, which integrates the contraries of the rejected premises into a single approach to legal understanding. Formalism thus conceived synthesizes aspects of the tradition of natural law and natural right. To the extent that contemporary legal scholars ignore this tradition, their efforts to understand law inevitably fail.

1. THE STANDARD FRAMEWORK OF LEGAL SCHOLARSHIP

Let us start with two well-known treatments of tort law: the currently dominant economic analysis[2] and George Fletcher's theory of fairness.[3] These approaches differ in substance, orientation, and vocabulary. Economic analysis sees liability rules as a means of promoting efficiency, while Fletcher elucidates the role of excuses in the fair treatment of accident losses. Economic analysis focuses instrumentally on tort law's contribution to economic well-being; Fletcher, in contrast, considers tort law to be a repository of non-instrumental norms of individual fairness. Economic analysis employs the discourse of social science, Fletcher the language and concepts of moral theory.

None the less, Fletcher and the economic analysts share a set of methodological assumptions. For behind their contrasting accounts of tort law lies the same conception of what constitutes an account. This conception has three features. First, neither Fletcher nor the economic analysts treat the tortfeasor and the victim as participants in a unified juridical relationship. Second, both approaches blur the distinction between tort law and other modes of legal ordering. Third, they are indifferent to pervasive elements—not the same ones in each case, to be sure—in the conceptual structure of tort law.

Consider economic analysis. Economic analysis takes the promotion of economic efficiency to be the aim of law. From the economic standpoint, liability rules provide incentives for cost-justified precautions. The basic claim of economic analysis is that a defendant should be liable for failing to guard against an accident only when the cost of precautions is less than the probable cost of the accident. The various practitioners of the economic approach flesh out this claim in different ways. Common to all of them, however, are the following features.

First, economic analysis treats the parties as subject to separate incentives, without linking the plaintiff and the defendant in a unified juridical relationship. The inducing of cost-justified precautions supports taking money from the defendant but does not necessitate its transfer to the plaintiff.[4] Similarly, economic analysis ties the plaintiff's receipt of the damage award to separate incentives (such as the need to induce enforcement of the norm and to prevent prospective victims from pre-empting the precautions incumbent on actors)[5] that do not require taking the money from the actual defendant. Both parties are thereby involved in the damage award but for separate reasons. Efficiency might as easily be served by two different funds, one that receives tort fines from inefficient actors, the other that disburses the indicated inducements to victims. Instead of linking each party to the other, economic analysis construes the presence of both as a consequence of combining incentives that are independently applicable to each.

Second, economic analysis ignores the distinctiveness of tort law as a mode of legal ordering. From the economic standpoint, tort law is not a form of private law that vindicates the entitlements of a wrongly injured person. Rather, tort law is a judicially created and enforced regime for the taxation and regulation of inefficient activity. Courts act as administrative tribunals that set norms for efficient behaviour and exact fines when those norms are breached. The plaintiff's function in initiating a lawsuit is not to secure redress for wrongful injury but to claim a bounty for prosecuting inefficient economic activity. Economic analysis thus submerges the private nature of tort law in a public law of economic regulation.

Third, the economic analysis of tort law operates independently of the characteristic doctrines, concepts, and institutions of tort law. While economists applaud legal results that coincide with efficiency, their framework does not respect on their own terms the concepts that characterize tort law. The economic analysis, for instance, is in theory indifferent to the element of causation. Because both parties might have taken precautions, the task is to determine who could have avoided the accident more cheaply. That the plaintiff was the victim of an injury caused by the defendant is in itself of no relevance.[6] Whereas tort law makes causation essential to liability, the economic approach regards causation as extraneous to its concerns.[7]

One might suppose that these three features—the decomposition of the juridical relationship between plaintiff and defendant, the running together of different kinds of legal ordering, and the effacement of the law's characteristic concepts and doctrines—are peculiar to the instrumentalism of the economic analysis of tort law. Instrumentalist approaches, to be sure, are particularly prone to such tendencies. Because the instrumentalist proposes an independently justifiable goal, lack of congruence with the law's characteristic doctrines and concepts is hardly surprising. Moreover, the goal's overarching nature leads the instrumentalist to construe the plaintiff–defendant nexus not as a relationship with its own integrity but as a conglomerate of elements justifiable to the extent that they contribute to the goal's realization. Finally, because the achievement of an instrumentalist goal requires a collective political effort, private law naturally coalesces with the policy-oriented mechanisms of public law.

These three features also appear, however, in George Fletcher's non-instrumental interpretation of tort law.[8] Unlike the economic analysts, Fletcher makes individual fairness paramount. In his view, fairness to individuals requires that excuses, such as compulsion and unavoidable ignorance, be available to tort defendants. Excuses exonerate the wrongdoer without denying the commission of a wrong. Fletcher regards excuses as expressions of compassion for human failings in times of stress. Moreover, because everyone would have acted the same way in the circumstances, he argues that excusing conditions precludes singling out the defendant for tort liability.

Although Fletcher's emphasis on individual fairness differentiates his views from those of the economic analysts, his account none the less shares the same three premises. First, the operation of an excuse segments the relationship between the parties. An excuse deals entirely with the actor's personal blamelessness. It thus focuses on the defendant in isolation from the plaintiff, allowing wrongful injurers the benefit of a normative space unencumbered by the claims of the victims. Fletcher accordingly suggests that excusability be considered a separate issue having to do with whether the defendant ought to pay—and distinct from the question of whether the plaintiff ought to recover.[9] Thus, the one-sided moral relevance of excuse bifurcates the tort enquiry, so that a court that accepted Fletcher's theory would confront the defendant's excuse independently of the plaintiff's right to compensation. Instead of integrating the plaintiff's entitlement with the defendant's liability, Fletcher envisages the former's subsisting without the latter.

Second, excuses blur the distinctiveness of tort law as a mode of ordering. One can see this on the side of both the plaintiff and the defendant. Since excuses bifurcate the tort enquiry, the plaintiff's entitlement cannot signal—as one would expect in tort law—a correlative obligation in the defendant. Accordingly, Fletcher suggests that the plaintiff's free-floating entitlement might generate a claim of priority under a social insurance scheme.[10] Fletcher thereby elides the plaintiff's right as a matter of private law with possible indemnification within a collective insurance arrangement.[11] On the defendant's side, the operation of an excuse assimilates tort law to criminal law (from which Fletcher transposes his account of excuses)[12] by allowing the defendant's blameworthiness to be considered in isolation. Thus, Fletcher's notion of excuse transforms tort law from a mode of redress for the victims of civil wrongs to a vehicle for manifesting compassion for wrongdoers who act in exigent circumstances.

Third, Fletcher's approach cuts across the characteristic doctrines and concepts of tort law. In particular, he repudiates the central idea of negligence law, that the defendant bears no liability for harms resulting from reasonable risks, on the ground that reasonableness involves the instrumentalist validation of risks whose benefits exceed their costs.[13] To avoid orienting tort law to the community's welfare, he proposes that excusability, which looks to individual fairness, should fulfil the exonerating function now performed by reasonableness. He thus substitutes his preferred category for the one that is pivotal to tort law as presently understood.

Although economic analysis and Fletcher's theory of excuses are substantively quite different, they share an explanatory structure. Both approaches deny the unity of the plaintiff–defendant relationship: economic analysis by positing different incentives that operate independently on plaintiff and defendant, Fletcher through the idea that excuses focus one-sidedly on defendants.

Both assimilate the tort mode of ordering to other kinds of legal arrangements: economic analysis construes tort law as a scheme of privately enforced regulation or taxation, and Fletcher sees tort law as mixing the excuses of criminal law with potential claims against an insurance fund. And both efface characteristic aspects of tort law, causation in the case of economic analysis, reasonableness in the case of Fletcher's excuses.[14]

It is no accident that Fletcher and the economic analysts, for all their substantive disagreements, work within the same explanatory framework. This framework is, in fact, standard to current scholarship on the theory of private law.[15] Underneath the rich diversity of academic attitudes and conclusions lie the three premisses common to Fletcher and the economic analysts. Thus, accounts of private law that differ significantly from one another none the less flower from the soil of a uniform methodology.

2. THE CONTRAST WITH FORMALISM

Formalism rejects that methodology. The formalist not only offers a different substantive account of private law, but also proposes a different conception of what constitutes an account. Formalism features a more stringent idea of the possible coherence of juridical relationships, as well as a greater respect for the character and distinctiveness of different modes of legal ordering. Thus, the formalist position extends along a broad front that includes both the content and the structure of explanation. From the formalist standpoint, the flaccidity of the standard framework's three premisses preordains the failure of contemporary legal scholarship.

Both formalist and non-formalist scholarship elucidate law in terms of certain justificatory considerations. The standard framework, however, faces two troubling questions. First, in view of its distancing of scholarly explanation from the law's characteristic concepts and distinctive orderings, does the standard framework actually take the law as the subject-matter for elucidation? Secondly, given the segmentation of the juridical relationship, can the various considerations adduced within the standard framework be truly justificatory? Let us examine each of these in turn.

First, by effacing the law's characteristic concepts and by

eliding different kinds of legal ordering, the standard framework undermines the connection between legal scholarship and its supposed subject-matter. If, for instance, the economic analysis of tort law is indifferent both to tort law's characteristic conceptual structure and to the distinction between tort law and other modes of legal ordering, how does economics help us to understand *tort* law? Since the economists' apparatus is doing all the work, their analysis proceeds independently of what it is analysing. The connection to tort law is merely a matter of possibly coincidental convergences and divergences of result. Although economists who perceive extensive convergences proclaim that 'the structure of the common law of torts is economic in character',[16] the structure of tort law is precisely what they ignore. Similarly, the claim that economics provides the implicit logic of the common law[17] is mere puff without the demonstration of a systemic connection between economics and the law's structure.[18] In a fundamental sense, tort law is superfluous to this way of theorizing about it. When applied across the board, this framework paradoxically makes law irrelevant to legal scholarship.

The second difficulty concerns the normative significance of legal arrangements. In fracturing the nexus between plaintiff and defendant, the framework treats each party as the bearer of unrelated justificatory considerations, for example the economist's separate incentives and Fletcher's defendant-centred excuses. How can these unilateral considerations maintain their justificatory character when brought together in a bilateral adjudicative procedure?

The nature of justification makes this difficulty particularly pressing. The point of justification is to shape whatever falls within its scope. Justification defies artificial restriction. To treat a justification seriously, we must allow it to govern whatever it applies to. The standard framework does not treat its justifications in this way. In countenancing justifications that pertain separately to one or the other of the litigants, it makes a legal relationship the locus of mutually frustrating considerations, each of which is limited not by the boundaries to which its justificatory force entitles it, but by the competing presence of an independent consideration. In this mixing of unrelated justifications, no single one of them occupies the entire area to which it applies. Thus, none of them actually functions as a justification.

Fletcher's theory of excuses illustrates the difficulty. Fletcher posits two stages to the analysis of tort liability. The first establishes the plaintiff's entitlement to redress for the wrongful injury suffered at the defendant's hands; the second deals with the excuses that go to the defendant's lack of personal blameworthiness. The justifications underlying these stages cut against each other. For if the first stage establishes the plaintiff's entitlement against the wrongdoer, the cause of action is complete and there is no reason for depriving the plaintiff of that entitlement on the basis of a consideration personal to the defendant. To do so would sacrifice fairness to the innocent victim by saving the wrongful injurer from liability. If, on the other hand personal blameworthiness is important, why does it not prevent the plaintiff's entitlement from arising in the first place? The plaintiff's entitlement, if we take its justificatory basis seriously, leaves no room for the defeat of the plaintiff's suit through Fletcher's conception of excuse. Conversely, the defendant's lack of personal blameworthiness, again if we take its justificatory force seriously, precludes the assignment to the plaintiff of even an initial entitlement to redress. The separate justifications underlying the two stages do not harmoniously coexist in a single juridical relationship. The mutual limits that they impose on each other preclude either of them from playing a properly justificatory role.

Instead of illuminating tort law, the standard framework of legal scholarship renders it unintelligible. Once one assumes that tort law's characteristic conceptual structure does not matter, that independent and mutually limiting justificatory considerations apply to the two parties to the litigation, and that tort law is not distinguishable from other modes of legal ordering, tort law becomes an arbitrary hodgepodge of competing normative factors and of different ways of treating injury. Many tort scholars, indeed, notice the senselessness of tort law. But rather than reconsidering the methodological assumptions that have produced this senselessness, they suggest replacing tort law with administrative or compensatory regimes that more adequately reflect the various modes of ordering that it already supposedly contains.[19]

The scholarship on tort law illustrates a more general point, that there is a connection between the standard framework and the apparent unintelligibility of law. This connection at least in part explains the appeal of Critical Legal Studies. Many exponents of Critical Legal Studies are profoundly sceptical about the coherence of law. They allege that law is shot through with contradictions and competing principles.[20] These scholars present themselves as radicals because of the particular beliefs that they hold. But, as our discussion of Fletcher and the economic analysts shows, divergences about substantive views do not necessarily indicate deep methodological disagreements. From the stand-point of scholarly method, exponents of Critical Legal Studies build on the mainstream scholarship that they criticize; but whereas mainstream scholars seem unaware of or unperturbed by the fact that their method renders law unintelligible, Critical Legal Studies scholars make that lack of intelligibility the grounds for reproach, and then generalize to the entire phenomenon of modern legalism. Seen in this light, they do not so much uproot the standard framework of legal scholarship as accentuate and extend the incoherences already present in it.

The barrenness of the standard framework influences scholar-ship in another way. Many legal scholars working within the standard framework focus their energies away from the law. Lack of interest in the conceptual structure of distinctive modes of legal ordering precludes them from deriving much intellectual sustenance from within the law. They therefore locate the key to the law's intelligibility in other disciplines. Economic analysis is a conspicuous example of an approach that takes over and applies to law the techniques and terminology of an external perspective. Economics, however, is only one of the many extrinsic sources of inspiration. History, sociology, political theory, moral philo-sophy, and literary studies also have their champions. The world of academic law presents a rich interdisciplinary menu of 'Law and ——'. The vital element in this pairing, however, is invariably the non-legal one. For it fills the vacuum left by the effacement of the law's conceptual structures and by the elision of different modes of legal ordering.

The formalist, in contrast, rejects the three assumptions of the mainstream framework and offers a different approach to legal understanding. The principal question for the formalist is how legal arrangements can be understood as coherent and rational in their own terms. To the formalist, the standard framework neither construes law as a coherent normative enterprise nor takes law seriously as an object of study. The formalist elucidates the coherence of juridical relationships through an explication of their interior structure. Because sophisticated legal systems value and tend toward their own coherence, the formalist looks upon the characteristic concepts of such systems not as encrustations to be shaped to an extrinsic ideal but as gateways to a specifically legal kind of intelligibility. Similarly, the lawyer's awareness of differences between modes of ordering becomes itself the object of theoretical examination and refinement.

In rejecting the three assumptions of the standard framework, the formalist does not merely register disagreement with each seriatim. The premises of the standard framework are interconnected in a single matrix of explanation. The formalist replaces that matrix not with three different individual premises but with an alternative single approach to legal understanding.

The interconnection between the three assumptions of the standard framework can be formulated in general terms as follows. The denial of the unity of a juridical relationship in the first assumption implies a conception of how the various components of the relationship coexist. This conception bears on the second assumption, about the distinctiveness of different modes of ordering, because the way in which the law joins the components of a juridical relationship defines the kind of relationship it is. The third assumption follows because, in a sophisticated legal system, the characterizing quality of legal concepts reflects their role in the kind of relationship in which they figure. Thus, the running together of modes of ordering determines and is determined by the status of the legal concepts. And both these features of the standard framework reflect its disassembling of the juridical relationship.

Our examples of tort scholarship illustrate this interconnection. Under its first assumption, the standard framework decomposes the plaintiff's claim against the defendant into normative considerations that apply independently to one or the other of the litigants. Tort law is, on this view, an amalgam of intrinsically unconnected elements that positive law happens to bring together. This leads to the blurring of different modes of ordering in accordance with the second assumption. Since the conjunction of elements in tort law has no inner integrity, tort law does not rank as a mode of ordering that scholarly analysis ought to respect on its own terms. Accordingly, the independent components of the tort relationship are intelligible only in the light of the other modes of ordering in which they figure.[21] This, in turn, implicates the third premiss of the standard framework. Not recognizing that tort law is a distinct and coherent mode of ordering, scholarship under the standard framework ignores at least some of the concepts that express that distinctiveness and coherence.[22]

The formalist construal of tort law is quite different. Formalism is committed to the attempt to make sense of tort law's conceptual and institutional structure. Essential to the intelligibility of tort law is the coherence of the nexus between plaintiff and defendant. Formalism denies the first assumption by postulating an intrinsic connection between the action of the injurer and the claim of the victim. This connection excludes segmenting the plaintiff–defendant relationship into justificatory considerations that pertain separately to the two parties. The consequence is a rejection of the second assumption as well: because the doing and suffering of the tort constitute a single and indivisible normative unit, tort law is a mode of ordering that is categorically different from other legal treatments of injury. Finally, a sophisticated legal system such as the common law tends toward its own coherence and, therefore, articulates the relationship between the parties through concepts and institutions that express that coherence. Because these concepts and institutions are signposts to the intelligibility of tort law, the formalist takes them seriously on their own terms.

Accordingly, legal formalism avoids the difficulties that beset the standard framework. Formalism makes law the object of its enquiry. Whereas the standard framework brings extraneous techniques and insights to bear in a way that is indifferent to the most characteristic features of legal arrangements, legal formalism aims to elucidate the inner rationality of the law's conceptual and institutional structure. Under formalism, there is no danger that law might become irrelevant to legal scholarship.

Moreover, formalism views justification seriously. The operation of mutually limiting justificatory considerations is incompatible with the formalist's postulate of coherence. Accordingly, formalism does not tolerate the artificial truncation within a single juridical relationship of one justificatory consideration by another. When a justificatory consideration applies, it applies entirely and exclusively.

3. THE CONSTITUENTS OF FORMALISM

So far I have criticized the assumptions animating contemporary legal scholarship and outlined the advantages to which formalism lays claim. Formalism, however, constitutes not merely a critical standpoint but a comprehensive theoretical position. This section sets out the elements of that position and sketches their inter-connection. In so doing it exhibits the range of formalism, as well as its wellsprings within the tradition of natural law and natural right.

The seemingly narrow question of how to understand tort law opens on to broad philosophical vistas. Implicit in the rejection of the standard framework is a conception of the intelligibility of legal relationships. For the formalist, intelligibility is formal in the sense that it depends on the elucidation of the forms or justificatory structures immanent in a sophisticated legal system. Thus, formalism has several interrelated constituents. It proposes a conception of intelligibility, specifies structures of intelligibility, and elucidates the normative grounding for those structures. It also presents, both generally and in connection with specific areas of law, an account of how these theoretical considerations are immanent to the positive law of a sophisticated legal system.

3.1. *The Conception of Intelligibility*

Central to the formalist conception of intelligibility is the idea of form, which was first articulated in ancient Greece and thereafter remained a staple of the rationalist tradition of European philosophy. Form is the ensemble of characteristics that constitutes a given entity as a unity classifiable with the entities of the same kind and different from entities of a different kind. Form embraces three aspects: (i) the character of something as revealed by the ensemble of attributes that are so essential to it that they can be said to characterize it; (ii) the connection between those characteristics such that they form a single unified entity; and (iii) what we may call the 'genericity' of the entity, i.e. what distinguishes this entity and others of the same kind from entities of a different kind.[23]

When applied to law, form refers to the structure of justification immanent in a juridical relationship. Formalism focuses on the ensemble of concepts and institutions that gives a specific juridical relationship its character. The coherence of the juridical relationship consists in the participation by these concepts and institutions in a single justificatory structure. Generic differences between juridical relationships reflect differences in their underlying justificatory structures. Formalism accordingly elucidates the possibilities for justificatory coherence latent within specific juridical relationships.

These aspects of form go to the character, unity, and genericity of a juridical relationship. They are the counterparts of the three premises that underlie the standard framework of contemporary legal scholarship. From the formalist standpoint, the standard framework of scholarship ignores the character, disintegrates the unity, and misapprehends the genericity of juridical relationships. The aspirations of formalism are entirely different: to make sense of the interior conceptual structure characterizing a sophisticated legal system, to maintain the justificatory coherence of juridical relationships, and to differentiate between distinctive modes of legal ordering.

Form is an integrative notion. The three aspects of form—character, unity, and genericity—constitute a single conception. Just as the three assumptions that formalism rejects are interconnected, so these three aspects of form come together in a single framework. Character refers to the features of a unified entity, unity to the connection between those features, and genericity to the differentiation between entities that share these unifying features and other entities. Accordingly, the formalist opposition to the standard framework does not reflect a miscellany of categorically different objections. Form is the master idea that marshals its own constitutive aspects into a coherent conception of intelligibility.

3.2. *The Structures of Juridical Intelligibility*

Juridical relationships are characteristically those in which the interacting parties are conceived as having separate interests.

There are two patterns for the coherent organization of such relationships. The forms on which legal formalism draws are these patterns represented in the most abstract and comprehensive way. Following Aristotle, we can call these forms corrective justice and distributive justice.[24] Justice in this usage does not refer to particular substantive principles. Rather, a form of justice is a justificatory structure to which a substantive principle must conform if it is to be coherent within its legal context.

Corrective justice is the form that underlies the bipolar relationships of private law. In corrective justice the plaintiff and the defendant stand to each other as the doer and sufferer of the same harm. Because the doing and the suffering of the same harm are correlatives one to the other, the justificatory considerations of corrective justice simultaneously implicate both parties. Corrective justice is the justificatory structure applicable when the sequence from the defendant's action to the plaintiff's injury is considered as a single normative unit.

Distributive justice, on the other hand, filters the interaction through some distributive criterion. In distributive justice the parties are eligible for a common benefit or subject to a common burden. Distributive justice postulates the existence of a thing to be distributed, persons among whom it is to be distributed, and a criterion that divides out the former among the latter. The coherence of the distributive relationship is a matter of the mutual suitability of the criterion, the subject-matter, and the participants in the distribution.

Aristotle's singular contribution was to demonstrate that these two forms of justice are categorically different structures. In corrective justice, the interaction directly connects doer and sufferer; in distributive justice, a distributive criterion mediates the interaction. Corrective justice allows for no more than two parties; distributive justice allows for any number of parties, with the size of each person's share varying inversely with the number of the parties.

The two forms of justice are alternative structures of coherent legal ordering. Aristotle's scheme does not postulate the superiority of either corrective or distributive justice. Nor does a particular form attach automatically to a given event. Rather, the forms are the structures of coherence that can intelligibly be brought to bear on the legal treatment of an event. The fact that I have injured you, for instance, does not in itself bring the incident under one form or the other. The legal system may treat this injury correctively through tort law or distributively through a publicly regulated insurance or compensation programme. Formalism insists only that the law coherently elaborate and apply whatever arrangement is in place.

3.3. *The Normative Grounding*

For the two forms of justice to serve as *justificatory* structures, they must have a valid normative dimension. Formalism explicates this dimension in Kantian terms. As the most comprehensive representations of coherence in interaction, corrective and distributive justice presuppose a normatively significant conception of the interacting parties and their holdings. Kantian legal philosophy supplies that conception.

Through his elucidation of the concept of right, Kant[25] (and Hegel after him)[26] sets out the most abstract, and yet most stringent, conception of the juridically normative. Right is the totality of norms governing the interaction of free-purpose agents. Essential to the agency of such beings is the capacity to resile from anything given, so that reason becomes the determining ground for action. Obligation, the imperative necessitated by reason, is implicit in free and purposive agency. Just as the forms of justice provide the abstract structure of interaction and then insist that particular interactions conform to one or the other of those structures, so Kant's moral philosophy elucidates the abstract structure of agency and then insists that particular actions conform to that structure. On the Kantian view, obligation is the system of constraints incumbent on self-determining agents by the very nature of their agency.

Each of the forms of justice presupposes the Kantian notion of agency. Corrective justice links the parties as the doer and sufferer of harm. As Aristotle himself notes, corrective justice abstracts from all moral considerations except those that pertain to the correlativity of doing and suffering as such.[27] Kant's legal philosophy explicates the normative basis of the thin notion of action engaged by corrective justice. The normative dimension of corrective justice surfaces in Kant's legal philosophy as the principle of right, under which the action of one freely willing person is conjoined to the freedom of another in accordance with a universal law.[28]

Distributive justice also has Kantian underpinnings. Under distributive justice, a distributive criterion determines the allocation of things to persons. For distributive justice to have normative significance, however, the distinction between persons and things must itself be morally grounded. The Kantian conception of personality fulfils this desideratum. In Kantian legal philosophy, persons are loci of self-determining agency and, therefore, ends in themselves. They are categorically different from things, which, being devoid of freedom, are usable as means. In this way, the conceptual components of Kantian legality are presupposed in distributive justice as a condition of its having normative force.

3.4. *The Immanence of Form in Positive Law*

The forms of justice are not extrinsic impositions on the positive law of sophisticated legal systems. Inasmuch as such systems tend toward their own coherence, the two justificatory structures are latent within them. A legal system is coherent to the extent that the juridical relationships between parties with separate interests actualize one or the other of these forms.

At the most general level, one can discern the immanence of form by a two-step procedure.[29] One first identifies the features of an area of law that, in the lawyer's experience, constitute its essential characteristics. These are the features so central that any understanding of the legal phenomenon in question must encompass them. In tort law, for example, the causation of injury is such a feature. Its centrality is certified by the recognition among lawyers that an account of tort law that does not explain (or at least explain away) causation is seriously defective.

At the second stage one examines all the features thus identified in any area of law with an eye to their mutual coherence. In addition to causation, for instance, other characteristic features of tort law include the nonfeasance–misfeasance distinction and the requirement that the losing defendant pay damages to the victorious plaintiff. There are also certain characteristic institutional arrangements, such as adjudication in response to a claim by the plaintiff against the defendant. The issue at the second stage is whether such characteristic features constitute a coherent ensemble. If they do, these characteristics can be understood as the specifications in positive law of one of the forms of justice. If they do not, the promise of coherence held out by the categories of the legal system turns out to be deceptive. Formalism then serves to locate and criticize the feature(s) disruptive of the law's coherence.

The two steps are internal to the juridical phenomena to which they apply. The first highlights the salient features of inarticulate legal experience. The second reflects on that experience, taking coherence as the dynamic principle that governs a sophisticated legal system from within. Formalism thus treats the features characterizing an area of law as indicators and products of the justificatory structure implicit in the area's organization.

From this emerges a formalist account of particular areas of law. Consider the treatment of negligence in the law of torts.[30] The concepts of negligence law instantiate corrective justice by tracing different aspects of the progression from the doing to the suffering of harm. Throughout, negligence law treats the plaintiff and the defendant as correlative to one another: the significance of doing for tort law lies in the possibility of causing someone to suffer, and the significance of suffering lies in its being the consequence of someone else's doing. Central to the linkage of plaintiff and defendant is the idea of risk, for 'risk imports relation'.[31] The sequence starts with the potential for harm inherent in the defendant's act (hence the absence of liability for nonfeasance), and concludes with the realization of that potential in the plaintiff's injury (hence the necessity for causation). The further requirements of reasonable care and remoteness link the defendant's action to the plaintiff's suffering through judgements about the substantiality of the risk and the generality of the description of its potential consequences. Each category traces an actual or potential connection between doing and suffering, and together they translate into juridical terms the movement of effects from the doer to the sufferer. Thus, negligence law presents an integrated ensemble of concepts that bracket and articulate a single normative sequence.

Formalism elucidates the coherence of juridical relationships through a set of mutually supporting ideas. Form provides a notion of intelligibility that unites characteristic features into a coherent whole. The forms underlying juridical relationships are the justificatory structures of corrective and distributive justice. These forms are grounded in the correspondingly formal conception of agency that Kant and Hegel elucidated. Inasmuch as sophisticated legal systems tend toward an internal coherence, the elements of formalism are latent in them. As the example of tort law shows, specific areas of law are intelligible to the extent that they actualize one or the other of these justificatory structures.

CONCLUSION

Formalism is not presently in fashion among legal scholars. Instead they adopt a framework of premises—that juridical relations lack coherence, that different modes of ordering are not distinct, and that there is a disjunction between legal theory and the law's characteristic concepts—which deny that law can embody justifiable norms or be the object of serious intellectual enquiry. The dominance of instrumentalism and scepticism about law within this framework is hardly surprising.

The dead ends to which the standard framework leads ought to alert scholars to the enduring significance of legal formalism. By elucidating the justificatory structures latent in different kinds of legal ordering, formalism remedies the defects of the standard framework and shows how juridical relations can be intelligible and coherent in their own terms.

Formalism, however, does not merely react to current academic inadequacies. It mines the rich tradition of philosophical reflection that starts with antiquity's attention to form and continues through the modern expositions of the concept of right. Only this tradition offers the possibility of vindicating law, in Aquinas' striking phrase, as 'a certain ordering of reason'.[32]

COMMENT: RAZ ON FORMALISM

Elsewhere in this volume, Professor Joseph Raz offers a spirited critique of my conception of formalism. I wish here briefly to indicate why his critique fails.

Raz begins by misstating my idea of form. 'The form of anything', he writes, 'consists of its distinctive essential properties.' His adjectives 'distinctive' and 'essential' perhaps cover the aspects I term genericity and character. Missing, however, is reference to form as a principle of unity. Formalism is, above all, a theory of the coherence internal to juridical relationships. What matters, therefore, is the interconnection and not the mere coexistence of distinctive and essential features.

Raz's omission is crucial. Having skipped over the aspect of unity, he not surprisingly cannot make sense of the claims that follow from it, that immanent intelligibility is paradigmatic of understanding and that law is immanently—and therefore non-instrumentally—intelligible. For him immanence is 'nothing more than a metaphor gone wild', because 'images of internality/ externality . . . are, at root, spatial metaphors with no fixed non-spatial reference'. This comment about internality is simply mistaken. The statement, for instance, that the Pythagorean theorem is a proposition internal to Euclidean geometry, does not make a spatial reference (e.g. to a page in a book entitled *Euclidian Geometry*) but rather indicates a conceptual connection between mathematical ideas of a distinct kind.[33] Coherence in a legal relationship is similarly a matter of conceptual connection.[34]

Only two-thirds through his essay, after repeatedly saying that form involves nothing more than distinctive and essential properties, does Raz reveal that '[Weinrib's] very notion of form is not just that of distinctive and essential properties' but only 'its distinctive essential properties as they form a coherent whole'. Raz does not, however, rethink the criticisms that this acknowledgement undermines. Instead, he takes my point about coherence to be an assertion that a single substantive value ought to pervade law. At this juncture, too, his objections make no contact with my position, which is that coherence goes to the justificatory structure of a juridical relationship, not to the substantive values inscribed in law as a whole.

At the root of Raz's misapprehensions is his tendency to criticize formalism without confronting its formalist nature. For the formalist, structure is paramount, not substance.[35] The formalist judges substance by first asking whether the reasons supporting particular legal doctrines are adequate to a coherent justificatory structure. Thus, what Aristotle calls the forms of justice are structural not substantive ideas. By unthinkingly translating the formalist's structural considerations into his own substantive ones, Raz misses the argument.

The confusion of structure and substance accounts for Raz's mystification at my enquiry into the normative grounding of the forms of justice. To him the question of what makes justice moral does not make sense, because what is substantively just cannot lack normative significance. What he does not notice is that the structural orientation of formalism necessitates establishing the normativeness of the forms of justice. Since these forms are structures latent in a sophisticated legal system, they may be nothing more than amoral heuristic devices, like Weber's ideal types.[36] The fact that I have followed Aristotle's terminology in calling them forms of justice does not of itself prove anything about their normativeness. Hence the importance of connecting the forms of justice to the postulates of Kantian legal theory.

Once he mistakenly decides that the Kantian underpinning is superfluous, Raz ignores it even where it bears on his criticisms. He asserts, for example, that my emphasis on such notions as coherence and intelligibility 'suggests a normativity of the rational' that 'contradicts Weinrib's identification of the normativity of his legal form as moral'. He here forgets that a Kantian does not share his premiss that a claim about rationality cannot simultaneously be a claim about morality.

Hegel once wrote: 'The genuine refutation must penetrate the opponent's stronghold and refute him on his own ground; no advantage is gained by attacking him somewhere else and defeating him where he is not.'[37] By this standard, Raz's critique is disappointing. Raz proliferates quotations and subtleties and complexities without ever coming to grips with the position he means to discredit.[38] In his polemic against formalism, Raz struggles only with his own hallucinations.

NOTES

© Ernest J. Weinrib 1992.

1. Weinrib, 'Legal Formalism: On the Immanent Rationality of Law', *Yale Law Journal*, 97 (1989), 949.

2. See esp. G. Calabresi, *The Costs of Accidents: A Legal and Economic Analysis* (New Haven, Conn.: Yale University Press, 1970); R. Posner, *Economic Analysis of Law*, 3rd edn. (Boston: Little, Brown & Co., 1986); W.M. Landes and R. Posner, *The Economic Structure of Tort Law* (Cambridge, Mass.: Harvard University Press, 1987); S. Shavell, *Economic Analysis of Accident Law* (Cambridge, Mass.: Harvard University Press, 1987).

3. G.P. Fletcher, 'Fairness and Utility in Tort Theory', *Harvard Law Review*, 85 (1972), 537.

4. Posner, *Economic Analysis of Law*, 2nd edn. (Boston: Little, Brown & Co., 1977), 143 ('It is essential that the defendant be made to pay damages . . . But that the damages are paid to the *plaintiff* is, from the economic standpoint, a detail').

5. Posner, *Economic Analysis of Law*, 3rd edn. (1986), 176.

6. Indeed, economic analysis postulates no difference in theory between a negligence regime, under which the plaintiff bears the injury costs except where the defendant could have taken cost-justified precautions, and a regime of strict liability with a contributory negligence defence, in which the defendant is liable except where the plaintiff could have taken cost-justified precautions.

7. Landes and Posner, *The Economic Structure of Tort Law*, 229 ('the idea of causation can largely be dispensed with in an economic analysis of torts'); G. Calabresi, 'Concerning Cause and the Law of Torts: An Essay for Harry Kalven, Jr.', *University of Chicago Law Review*, 43 (1975), 69, 105 ('the alien language of causation'). For detailed criticisms of the economists' treatment of causation, see R. Wright, 'Actual Causation vs. Probabilistic Linkage, The Bane of Economic Analysis', *Journal of Legal Studies*, 14 (1985), 435.

8. Fletcher, 'Fairness and Utility'.

9. Ibid. 542.

10. Ibid. 554.

11. The claim of priority that Fletcher suggests on behalf of 'those who have been deprived of their equal share of security from risk' (ibid.) reflects his appeal to distributive justice regarding a branch of law that he none the less wants us to conceptualize in corrective justice terms (ibid. 547 n. 40). For a discussion of this confusion, see J. Coleman, 'Moral Theories of Torts: Their Scope and Limits: Part I', *Journal of Law and Philosophy*, 1 (1982), 389.

12. G.P. Fletcher, *Rethinking Criminal Law* (Cambridge, Mass.: Harvard University Press, 1978), 798–854.

13. 'Fairness and Utility', 556–64.

14. There is this important difference between Fletcher and the economic analysts. Fletcher affirms—as the economists do not—the

importance of distinguishing between different modes of ordering and of maintaining contact with the law's conceptual structure; see Fletcher, 'Fairness and Utility', 547 n. 40 ('What is at stake is keeping the institution of taxation different from the institution of tort litigation'); Fletcher, 'Punishment and Compensation', *Creighton Law Review*, 14 (1981), 703 ('economic jurisprudence cannot possibly offer a faithful account of the concepts that we actually employ on discussing legal problems'). My comments about Fletcher's methodology are aimed, however, not at what he intends and professes, but at what is actually implicit in his work.

15. For discussion of the work on tort law of Judith Jarvis Thomson, Richard Epstein, and Jules Coleman, see Weinrib, 'Causation and Wrongdoing', *Chicago-Kent Law Review*, 63 (1987), 407. For discussion of the contract theories of Charles Fried and Anthony Kronman, see Benson, 'Abstract Right and the Possibility of a Nondistributive Concept of Contract: Hegel and Contemporary Contract Theory', *Cardozo Law Review*, 10 (1989), 1077, 1095–147.

16. Landes and Posner, *The Economic Structure of Tort Law*, 302.

17. Posner, *Economic Analysis of Law*, 3rd edn., 229–33.

18. One of the marvels of the American economic analysis of law is that its champions (to my knowledge, at any rate) never refer to the pioneering work that might support their pretensions. See E.B. Pashukanis, *Law and Marxism: A General Theory* (London: Ink Links, 1978).

19. e.g. Franklin, 'Replacing the Negligence Lottery: Compensation and Selective Reimbursement', *Virginia Law Review*, 53 (1967), 774; Sugarman, 'Doing Away with Tort Law', *California Law Review*, 73 (1985), 555. The arguments supporting this suggestion are exemplary of the standard framework. The analysis first breaks the requirement that the losing defendant pay the successful plaintiff into two independent goals: the compensation of plaintiffs and the deterrence of defendants. It then correctly shows the arbitrariness both of restricting compensation to circumstances requiring someone else's deterrence, and, conversely, of gearing deterrence to the occurrence and extent of another's injury. The mutual interference of the goals that separately pertain to the two parties makes it senseless to pursue these goals through tort law.

20. For a discussion of the positions taken by Critical Legal Studies Scholars, see A. Altman, *Critical Legal Scholars: A Liberal Critique* (Princeton, NJ: Princeton University Press, 1990), 104–48.

21. In economic analysis, for instance, the court's imposition of liability regulates defendants in the same way that administrative tribunals do, so that tort law is merely an ungainly form of administrative law.

22. Thus, the economic analysis of tort law regards the concept of causation as alien, despite its essential role in linking the defendant to the plaintiff.

23. The ancient Greeks, who introduced the idea of form, applied it to a wide range of entities, including natural and artefactual ones; see, for instance, Plato, *Republic* 596b (on the form of beds and tables). The legal formalist follows the classical tradition in holding that intelligibility is paradigmatically formal. However, the legal formalist's attitude to natural and artefactual entities is different. For the legal formalist, form is a way of representing the immanent intelligibility consequent upon pushing unity to its extreme. The most stringent kind of unity is a conceptual one, where thought reveals the intrinsic interconnections that render the whole of something a distinct entity greater than the sum of its parts. Entities that have this sort of unity are immanently intelligible, because the activity of thinking can comprehend them in their own terms. The formalist maintains that the interlocking concepts that characterize juridical relationships render law immanently intelligible. Natural objects and instruments, in contrast, do not satisfy the demands of this stringent unity. The various properties of a natural object are jointly present in the same thing without manifesting a principle of unity; see G.W.F. Hegel, *The Phenomenology of Spirit*, ch. 2. The properties of an instrument are united not by something internal to them but by their contribution to an external purpose.

24. Aristotle, *Nicomachean Ethics*, 5. 2–4; Aquinas, *Summa Theologiae*, IIa IIae, q. 58. For discussion of this text, see Weinrib, 'Aristotle's Forms of Justice', *Ratio Juris*, 2 (1989), 211.

25. See Weinrib, 'Law as a Kantian Idea of Reason', *Columbia Law Review*, 87 (1987), 472 (Symposium on Kantian Legal Theory).

26. Weinrib, 'Right and Advantage in Private Law', *Cardoza Law Review*, 10 (1989), 1283 (Symposium on Hegel and Legal Theory).

27. Aristotle, *Nichomachean Ethics*, 1132^{a}2–7.

28. Kant, *The Metaphysical Elements of Justice*, trans. Ladd (Indianapolis: Bobbs-Merrill, 1965), 34–5.

29. Weinrib, 'Legal Formalism', 966–70.

30. For more complete treatment of the ideas summarized here, see Weinrib, 'Understanding Tort Law', *Valparaiso University Law Review*, 23 (1989), 485 (the 1988 Monsanto Lecture on Tort Law Reform and Jurisprudence); Weinrib, 'Causation and Wrongdoing'; Weinrib, 'The Special Morality of Tort Law', *McGill Law Journal*, 34 (1989), 403; Weinrib, 'Liberty, Community, and Corrective Justice', *Canadian Journal of Law and Jurisprudence*, 1 (1988), 3; Weinrib, 'The Insurance Justification and Private Law', *Journal of Legal Studies*, 14 (1985), 681.

31. *Palsgraf* v. *Long Island R.R.*, 248 N.Y. 339, at 344 (1928) (Cardozo J.).
32. Aquinas, *S.Th.* Ia IIae, q. 90, a. 4.
33. Raz's stigmatization of words like 'inner' as 'metaphors gone wild' does not prevent him from using them both elsewhere (see Raz, 'The Inner Logic of the Law', *Rechtstheorie*, 10 (1986) 101) and here (see sect. 4 of his polemic, entitled 'The Inner Collapse of Formalism').
34. I have criticized the view that the constituent elements of a legal relationship can be regarded as merely sharing a common space; see 'Law as a Kantian Idea of Reason', 474–7.
35. It was to drive this point home and to anticipate misinterpretations such as Raz's that I inserted the section on 'The Formalism of the Forms' in 'Legal Formalism', 981–5.
36. Some scholars who argue in the natural law tradition make Weber's ideal types central to their understanding of law. See e.g. J. Finnis, *Natural Law and Natural Rights* (Oxford: Clarendon Press, 1980), 9; Fletcher, 'Two Modes of Legal Thought', *Yale Law Journal*, 90 (1981), 970, 997–1003. Given Weber's notorious positivism (reflected in the professed amorality of analysis by ideal type), this seems to me an unpromising strategy for exponents of natural law.
37. Hegel, *Science of Logic*, trans. Miller (London: Allen, 1969), 581.
38. Apart from the comments noted above, Raz frequently makes observations that might astonish readers of the work he criticizes. Early in his essay he speculates whether and to what extent form determines content, but does not consider my treatment of determinacy in 'Legal Formalism', 1008–11. Later he fabricates something he grandly calls Weinrib's Thesis of Judicial Duty, and then notes as a 'difficulty' that this thesis of his own concoction is entirely unsupported by my arguments. Toward the end there appears this remarkable sentence, not a single clause of which reflects my position: 'There is only one form of law, and since Weinrib says that the content of the law is determined by its form . . . it follows that all legal systems are identical in content.' *Et multa alia*.

INDEX